The Official History of

DERBYSHIRE
COUNTY
CRICKET CLUB

THE CHRISTOPHER HELM
COUNTY CRICKET SERIES

Series Editors:
Peter Arnold and Peter Wynne-Thomas

GLAMORGAN
Andrew Hignell, with a personal view by Tony Lewis

HAMPSHIRE
Peter Wynne-Thomas, with a personal view by John Arlott

KENT
Dudley Moore, with a personal view by Derek Underwood

LANCASHIRE
Peter Wynne-Thomas, with a personal view by Brian Statham

MIDDLESEX
David Lemmon, with a personal view by Denis Compton

SURREY
David Lemmon, with a personal view by Peter May

WORCESTERSHIRE
David Lemmon, with a personal view by Basil D'Oliveira

The Official History of

DERBYSHIRE
COUNTY
CRICKET CLUB

John Shawcroft

With a personal view by
BOB TAYLOR

CHRISTOPHER HELM

London

© 1989 John Shawcroft and Bob Taylor
Christopher Helm (Publishers) Ltd, Imperial House,
21–25 North Street, Bromley, Kent BR1 1SD

ISBN 0-7470-3022-7

A CIP catalogue record for this book is available from the British Library

Typeset by Cotswold Typesetting Ltd, Gloucester
Printed and bound by Biddles Ltd, Guildford, Surrey

CONTENTS

DERBYSHIRE COUNTY CRICKET CLUB
1988

PRESIDENT:
His Grace The Duke of Devonshire, P.C., M.C.

VICE PRESIDENTS:
Rear Admiral Sir David Haslam, K.B.E., C.B., F.R.I.C.S.
Sir Edward Thompson, M.B.E., T.D., D.L.

F. Burton
D. B. Carr, O.B.E.
Major J. W. Chandos-Pole
Dr. G. M. Cochrane
The Rev. V. T. Ducker
C. S. Elliott, M.B.E.
R. Green
J. A. C. Lilley

L. G. Litchfield
H. W. Lund
J. W. Moss
F. G. Peach
F. A. Perks
K. C. Turner, C. B. E.
D. G. Young

COMMITTEE:

Chairman: C. N. Middleton
Vice Chairman: D. C. Robinson
Hon. Treasurer: R. Gratton
Hon. Secretary: A. T. Blount
Chief Executive: R. J. Lark

C. S. Elliott, M.B.E.
J. R. Cater
K. S. Roe
I. P. Samways
G. L. Willatt

R. W. Taylor, M.B.E.
B. Holling
F. E. Marsh
C. J. Tunnicliffe

Secretary: I. Edwards
Captain: K. J. Barnett
Scorer: S. W. Tacey
Coach: P. E. Russell
2nd XI Captain: A. Hill
Head Groundsman: B. Marsh

FOREWORD

His Grace, The Duke of Devonshire, P.C., M.C.

TO MANY LOVERS OF DERBYSHIRE CRICKET it may not seem very long since John Shawcroft produced his memorable *History of Derbyshire County Cricket Club*, which is now a collectors item, to celebrate the Club's Centenary in 1970. So much has happened in the years since, including the winning of the Nat. West. Trophy in 1981, that another History is now necessary to bring the story of the Club up to date.

The author has not merely added to his text but has substantially re-written it and the Club is greatly indebted to John, and to Frank Peach the Club Historian.

The appearance of the Derby Head-quarters has radically changed during those years with the building of the office block, the Lund Pavilion, the open stands, the Sports Club and the Scoreboard, and it is hoped that the Benefit Year, to which this History is a contribution, will provide funds for further development and for the fostering of youth cricket in the County. Both are worthy objectives and I trust that followers of cricket will enjoy reading this book and supporting the Benefit Year.

Devonshire

INTRODUCTION

Christopher Middleton, Chairman of Derbyshire County Cricket Club

MUCH WATER HAS FLOWED down the Trent since John Shawcroft first undertook to write *The History of Derbyshire County Cricket Club* for the Club's Centenary in 1970. Many new facts about the history of the Club have come to light and a great deal of hard work and painstaking research has been carried out by John Shawcroft on the text, and by Frank Peach, the Club's Historian, and David Baggett on the statistics.

Preparing the history of a cricket club is in many ways a thankless task, since no other game raises the keeping of precise records and statistics to the status of Holy Writ and no other body of men takes greater delight in discovering and highlighting a factual error than the followers of cricket. They will, however, have to rise very early in the morning to catch John Shawcroft, Frank Peach and David Baggett napping!

Cricket is not merely a game of records and figures; it is a game of artistic subtlety and physical endeavour, and of tactics and strategy worthy of great generals, but above all it is a game of personalities and characters. Derbyshire has often been short of money and members, and the trophy cabinet is far from overflowing, but the rich human pageant unveiled in the following pages is one to rival that of any other County. I hope that our members and supporters, and those who have an interest in the game of cricket in general will enjoy this book and the story that it tells.

We owe a great debt of gratitude to John Shawcroft for whom this book has been very much a labour of love and who has devoted many months if not years to its preparation. In addition we are most grateful to Frank Peach who for decades has been the guardian of the statistical records of Derbyshire, and to David Baggett who has assisted him in preparing the statistical section for this book. Lastly our thanks mut go to the publishers, Christopher Helm Limited and particularly to Alison Starling, who have been endlessly patient during the production of the book and without whose help it could not have been produced.

The royalties from this book go to the Derbyshire Club Benefit Year whose ultimate donation to the County Club will be used for the improvement of members' and spectators' facilities and for the promotion of youth cricket within the County. We are grateful to all who have contributed to the success of the Benefit Fund.

Chris Middleton
Rotherham, February 1989

A PERSONAL VIEW
Bob Taylor

MY INVOLVEMENT WITH DERBYSHIRE CRICKET began on a dull, wet afternoon at the Goodyear Sports Ground, Wolverhampton, during the summer of 1960.

I was keeping wicket for Staffordshire in a Minor Counties Championship game against Durham. Rain had halted play and I was sitting in the dressing room, glancing at a magazine or just watching other people play cards while it was pouring down outside. Then Lawrence Hancock, the Staffordshire secretary, came in and said 'Bob, there are two people from Derbyshire wanting to speak to you.'

The club chairman, Mr Robin Buckston, and the former secretary, Mr Will Taylor, had arrived and asked to have a chat with me. I was thrilled to bits. I remember going outside and seeing Mr Buckston's big, old Rover car, with the windows steamed up in the rain. They asked me if I had ever considered a career in county cricket and I think the sum of £350 a year was mentioned. But the money didn't matter – it was a dream come true.

Unknown to me, the door to Derbyshire had been opened by Cliff Gladwin, who had just finished his first-class career. He joined Longton in the North Staffordshire League and after he had played against my club, Bignall End, he tipped off his old county about my wicket-keeping.

The first contact Derbyshire made was when Denis Smith, the coach, came over to see me play. I was told he was watching me but he did not say anything to me that day. Later, the official approach was made by Mr Buckston and Mr Taylor. That year, 1960, was a watershed for me. I made my first-class debut in June, keeping wicket for the Minor Counties against the South Africans at Stoke, and then played in two second eleven matches for Derbyshire against Lancashire at St Helens and Northamptonshire at Derby.

I had received a letter from Donald Carr, who was then Derbyshire's secretary, arranging for me to meet Denis Smith in Leek, from where I would travel with him to St Helens. I was to look out for a black Morris Minor – registration number 695 DTO – they were impressionable years and I can still recall that number plate nearly 30 years later – and this meant that I had to get a bus from Hanley, one of the Five Towns of the Potteries, at around 7.30 am. I waited for a long time but no black Morris arrived. I had arrived ridiculously early but after about an hour and still no sign of Mr Smith I was ready to return home. I decided to give it another five minutes before catching the bus back to Hanley, convinced that Derbyshire had found somebody else to keep wicket and did not want me. Then suddenly, around the corner came this black car. Denis Smith leaned out and said 'Where the bloody hell have you been?'

Such was my introduction to Derbyshire cricket. I have often wondered what would have happened if Mr Smith had been five minutes later and I had returned home. I don't think there would have been a second chance.

In the second team I found myself playing alongside cricketers who had been just names to me from the sports pages. Edwin Smith had been out of the first team with an

I

arm injury, Arnold Hamer and John Kelly were approaching the end of their careers, Peter Eyre and Billy Oates were on the fringe of the senior side.

Six months later, in February 1961, I travelled over from Stoke-on-Trent to formalise the signing of my three-year contract with Derbyshire. At that time I had only travelled past the County Ground along Nottingham Road with my parents on the bus to visit friends in Nottingham. I had been impressed by the Grandstand with its dome and seating, which was visible from the road, and I used to think the County had a top-class ground at Derby. When I came to Derby to sign the forms I walked from the Midland Railway Station to the ground and went straight to the Grandstand, thinking that the offices were situated there. I was disappointed when I found that the Ministry of Agriculture used that building and that Derbyshire's administration was carried out in a poky little office in the corner of the ground. But I was too starry-eyed at the prospect of playing county cricket to worry too much about that.

Paint peeling off the dressing room walls, bird droppings falling through the ceiling of the indoor nets and the state of the showers and toilets did not matter overmuch. Years later, after several England tours, I became embarrassed by the set-up at Derby, and the splendid modernisations which were carried out in the 1980s were not before time.

The Spartan and inadequate facilities at the County Ground, Derby, were a direct contrast to the professionalism I found at the Club. Admittedly pre-season training in those days – as with most counties of that time – was a joke in comparison with that endured by the modern county pro. A couple of laps of running and a spell in the indoor nets have been replaced by sessions that resemble a commando course. As a part-time professional soccer player with Port Vale I found that I was one of the fittest players on the staff in those days and I have always emphasised that fitness is a key factor in that high degree of concentration which is so vital a component in the make-up of a professional cricketer, particularly a wicket-keeper who is involved in a game more than most.

In terms of cricketing know-how I discovered a hard school of sheer professionalism at Derby. Senior players were addressed as 'Mr' and the juniors had to knock on the dressing room door before entering. Discipline was severe. After fielding practice with the second eleven one day, I donned cavalry twill trousers, a yellow waistcoat and a collar and tie and settled down to watch Colin Cowdrey batting for Kent against the senior side. It was a hot day. I had never seen Cowdrey bat before so I left my sports jacket in the changing rooms and prepared to enjoy the experience. Denis Smith promptly bawled me out for not wearing a jacket!

We were expected to listen and learn, to absorb the wealth of cricketing knowledge that the pros had accumulated over season after season in the game. For the first three years of my county career I was fortunate enough to travel around the circuit with Les Jackson, Derek Morgan and Laurie Johnson. All possessed a wide range of technical knowledge. At the start of the season these three, Charlie Lee and one or two others would forecast the results of the coming season with uncanny accuracy. Today, with the general levelling up of the counties' strength, I don't suppose it can be done to the same degree but there they were, predicting victories over the likes of Nottinghamshire (twice), Leicestershire and Glamorgan and so on while I listened in astonishment. They knew their profession inside-out and as a course in the mastery of cricket's myriad variety of tactics it was beyond price.

In later years I was able to put the fruits of all of this into practice both with Derbyshire and with England. The Derbyshire pitches at the County Ground and in that lovely setting of Queen's Park, Chesterfield, traditionally favoured pace and when I got into the first team I was keeping to bowlers of the calibre of Les Jackson, Harold Rhodes, Brian Jackson, Ian Buxton and Derek Morgan and the off-breaks of Edwin Smith, usually the solitary spinner in the side.

At first Morgan and Buxton wanted me to stand back to them but I was confident I could stand up to Buxton's big in-swing and Morgan's off-cutters. I remember Mike Smith, the Middlesex opening batsman, being either bowled by Buxton or stumped off his bowling on several occasions. When conditions suited him Ian could cause no end of problems for batsmen and his bowling gave Mike Smith a lot of trouble. Mike Selvey had a good laugh after Buxton retired from the game. He found a newspaper cutting with the headline 'Buxton back for Derby'. It was about a junior footballer but the Middlesex lads showed it to Mike Smith and pulled his leg unmercifully.

As the years passed I discovered that a wicket-keeper is ideally placed for an important role in the county grapevine, that unofficial system by which a batsman's strengths and weaknesses are analysed and assessed. We found that David Gower, for instance, did not quite get over his forcing shot in the gully area and Mike Hendrick always fancied getting him out there. So we would place a man at backward point and gully, keep David quiet for a time with short-of-a-length bowling and then give him one outside the off-stump in the hope that he would slash at it. Hendrick and Alan Ward would always slip themselves against Geoff Boycott and try and get him out before he settled into that unhurried, methodical groove.

It was knowledge that was not acquired overnight and I like to think that it had something to do with Derbyshire's great traditions for producing fast and fast-medium bowlers and wicket-keepers. I was always conscious that I was part of a line of keepers which stretched back through George Dawkes, Harry Elliott, Joe Humphries and William Storer to people like Jimmy Disney, Tom Mycroft and Alfort Smith and the dawn of the Club's history.

On the county staff, the young keeper relies on the senior one for advice and help in practice. Although batting is important I am convinced that a side should always play its best wicket-keeper and generally that is what Derbyshire have done.

There was a variation in this policy at my expense in 1964 after I had twisted my ankle playing football but had told the Club I did it when I slipped on an escalator while shopping with my wife, Cathy. Looking back, I ought to have told them the truth but I thought they might not be too pleased if they knew the real circumstances. I missed the early matches that summer, and Laurie Johnson, who had kept wicket occasionally, deputised for me and did quite well, standing back to everybody except Edwin Smith.

Derbyshire were usually short of runs and with Johnson doubling up as wicket-keeper it left a spare place in the side for another batsman. The Club seemed perfectly happy with the situation and it might have continued but for some pointed comments in the Press by cricket writers such as Mike Carey, which helped in my reinstatement.

On the other occasion I was out of the side, it followed a serious eye injury when I suffered a detached retina after getting a top-edge to a sweep shot against Jack Birkenshaw's bowling at Leicester. Bob Stephenson came in. I missed the last month of the 1967 season and I was competing for a place against a genuinely good keeper in Bob the following year. It went my way. I played in every Championship match and Bob moved to a rewarding career with Hampshire.

I learned a lot from George Dawkes and I like to think I passed on some good advice to my eventual successor, Bernie Maher. At one point he lost his place to Chris Marples and for a time they both suffered from lack of concentration, which led to inconsistency. But Bernie eventually fought back and has now become a very valuable member of the side as a wicket-keeper and batsman. I have told him that I fully expect him still to be keeping for Derbyshire in the year 2000, which would mean an 80-year period with just four regular keepers – Elliott, Dawkes, Taylor and Maher.

The tradition of Derbyshire bowlers extends as far back in time as the wicket-keepers, a tradition of pace and fast-medium bowling of immaculate length which has produced an impressive sequence of names – Mycroft, Davidson, Hulme, Bestwick, Warren, Copson, the Popes, Jackson and Gladwin, Rhodes and Brian Jackson, Ward and Hendrick and now Holding and Mortensen. It was a rich heritage and being a part of that line meant that a young bowler such as Harold Rhodes, for instance, had the example set by Jackson and Gladwin to try and emulate.

I don't think that time distorts the mind in my memories of the great Les Jackson. He was approaching the end of his career when I was starting mine and although he was still quite sharp he was losing a bit of his old pace. Les was never an out-and-out fast bowler in the manner of Tyson or Trueman at their quickest but in the right conditions he could be equally as hostile.

I remember the ball coming through to me every time a batsman got a nick off Les. You could see the seam, straight up, vertical all of the time. None of the turning over and whirring which is associated with deliveries from some bowlers. The ball used to come straight through, seam up. If they got a nick there was no dipping or swerving, the ball just came straight into the gloves. You could see a little patch on the wicket the size of a handkerchief where he kept hitting the pitch. Even in the twilight of his career he was still a beautiful bowler.

Les's new-ball partner in my early days was Harold Rhodes, who bowled better the older he got. His career was overshadowed by the great throwing controversy which dominated cricket in that period and for a long time there was a question mark over Harold's action.

It is always very difficult to say whether a bowler throws or not without breaking down his action on film. Harold, of course, had that unusual hyper-extension, in which his arm bent the opposite way, and eventually his basic action was declared fair. But it took eight years before he was cleared and the controversy ruined his Test career. I find it difficult to see how anybody bowling with an action like Harold's could throw. Basically, his left foot was down the pitch and he bowled sideways on. You can see photographs of people who were correctly no-balled for throwing with their left toe pointing towards third man and their action chest-on. Harold was very unlucky.

Later on came Mike Hendrick and Geoff Miller, colleagues with me on many occasions in the England side. Both were high-class cricketers, Hendrick with a lovely bowling action and uncanny accuracy at fast-medium, Miller as an all-rounder whose ability should have made him a permanent fixture in the Test team in his best years. Success in the context of five or six wickets in an innings always eluded Hendrick at Test level. In my opinion he tended to bowl a yard too short and he seemed unable to get a batsman playing half-back or half-forward to the ball which was starting to deviate. He had a lot of bad luck with injuries and although he never took five in an innings in a Test match he was capable of destroying the best of county sides when conditions suited him.

It always struck me as ridiculous that Geoff Miller, a fine middle-order batsman and off-spin bowler, was unable to break the barrier of his maiden century until he had been playing first-class cricket for more than a decade. We used to try all sorts of tricks in the dressing room to get him over the psychological problems of getting out in the 90s but nothing seemed to work.

Geoff almost left the County in 1981, when he resigned the Derbyshire captaincy; like me he found it difficult to captain players he had grown up with over the years. He was a fine sportsman, a decent man and great to play cricket with. On the day I finished my county career he shook my hand as we walked off the field and said: 'Bob, thanks very much for everything – it's been a privilege to play with you.'

Talk of the captaincy and Geoff Miller brings me to my own period as captain of Derbyshire. Donald Carr was my first skipper and he could be severe on people who were sloppy; I remember being told off in no uncertain terms when my lobs back to the bowler fell short. To this day I always address him as skipper whenever I see him. In 1986, after I had retired from the first-class game, I was on duty for Cornhill at Lord's where England were playing New Zealand. England's wicket-keeper, Bruce French, was injured and I kept wicket as substitute for 73 overs. On the Monday morning I was back on duty with Cornhill when I spotted Donald behind the pavilion.

He said: 'Robert, are you an amateur or a professional now?'

I replied: 'Are you referring to the way I kept wicket on Friday?'

He said that he was referring to the fee, and I told him: 'Once a professional, always a professional, skipper.' Needless to say, I did not receive a fee!

Donald was succeeded as captain by Charlie Lee for a couple of seasons and then Derek Morgan took over. Derek was a fine, dedicated professional who always tried to get the best out of his team and I thoroughly enjoyed playing with him. Ian Buxton was at the helm for a few years and then came Brian Bolus. He did well with a struggling side for a couple of seasons until the start of the 1975 season when things went wrong. We were eliminated from the Benson and Hedges Cup, and Brian had business worries and his form suffered. When he stood down as captain the committee asked me to take over and I agreed to do so until the end of the season providing the cares of captaincy did not affect my form behind the stumps.

We did quite well in 1975. After being bottom of the Championship table three times in the previous four years we won five games and reached the semi-finals of the Gillette Cup. My own form did not suffer but soon after the start of the 1976 season – I had been re-appointed captain – I began to feel I was getting bogged down with petty problems, some of which had little to do with the actual cricket.

Off-the-field activities were taking up more of my time. The team bus, which our then chairman George Hughes had introduced in a laudable attempt to save money, was an example. Unfortunately its reclining seats did not recline, the television fell off its raised area and we couldn't hear the stereo because of the noise of the engine. And it only travelled at about 40 mph, which meant long, tiring journeys to and from away games, with another drive home from Derby at the end of it all.

I think we all grew sick of the sight of one another, cooped up as we were for long periods in coach, dressing room and hotel. Then Carlin Beardmore, our scorer, revealed that the savings on travelling expenses were nowhere near as much as had been anticipated. It was not worth damaging team spirit for such a sum and we reverted to travelling by car.

It was around this time that, for the first time in my career, I found I was not looking forward to going to the ground. I seemed to be giving players a rocket over discipline in the daytime and then going home at night and ticking off my 13-year-old son Mark for the sort of things youngsters get up to at that age.

Eddie Barlow had joined us a year earlier and I talked to him about the possibility of his taking over the captaincy. He suggested that I should give it a bit longer but the crunch came one day when I realised that the responsibility was having an adverse effect on my performances as wicket-keeper. Phil Sharpe was standing in his usual position at first-slip and I was a yard in front of him. Just as the bowler was coming in, Phil suggested moving a man close in. He didn't mean to distract me and it was a genuine tactical suggestion made a moment too late. But I wasn't quite ready for the next ball, which took an outside edge and I dropped a straightforward chance because my concentration had been broken and my mind distracted. I had missed chances before, of course, but I don't think that one would have gone down had I not been captain.

So I resigned and recommended that Eddie Barlow should take over. He did a tremendous job for Derbyshire, both on and off the field. His period as captain is given due recognition elsewhere in this book; suffice it to say here that he brought about an amazing transformation, with the emphasis on fitness and positive cricket. He was a marvellous motivator and his three seasons as captain coincided with my happiest spell at the Club.

Eddie, in my opinion, ranks as the best of our overseas signings. We were a bit slow off the mark in getting into the overseas market and I don't think we always bought wisely. This is no reflection on the quality of some of our overseas players but we never seemed to do the obvious thing and go for a fast bowler or a top-class all-rounder. We started with Chris Wilkins, an attractive batsman and a good fieldsman who was also a useful medium-paced bowler. Then came the Indian off-spinner Venkataraghavan at a time when we had people like Geoff Miller and Bob Swindell coming through and we really needed a strike bowler or an all-rounder. The West Indian batsman, Lawrence Rowe, was a nice man and a magnificent batsman but he never came to terms with the county game and his top score for us was only 94. He was a man for the big occasion and did not seem to relish the grind of domestic cricket. Peter Kirsten and John Wright were tremendous players and they produced probably the most magnificent batting in Derbyshire's history. Peter was another who never quite came to terms with the county game and he returned home but John continued to give Derbyshire marvellous service, although his final seasons were frustrating because he had to share the one overseas place with Michael Holding. Not until Michael arrived in 1983 did we get the permutation right and we could really have done with somebody of his class and Wright or Kirsten over the previous five years.

Eddie's influence remained long after he left Derbyshire. His legacy came to fruition when we won the NatWest trophy in 1981, Derbyshire's first major success since the Championship in 1936. We had reached two Lord's finals, being beaten in the 1969 Gillette Cup by Yorkshire and losing to Kent in the Benson and Hedges Cup in 1978 under Barlow's captaincy. I have contrasting memories about those competitions. In 1969 we gained a remarkable victory over Sussex in the semi-final at Queen's Park after we had been dismissed for 136. Sussex had a very strong batting side but they got themselves into all sorts of trouble by going very slowly against our pace bowlers. Alan Ward – who was very fast in those days (I used to stand about 25 yards back to his bowling) – and Harold Rhodes restricted them to 10 for two from their first 14 overs and they never recovered. Peter Eyre, who took six for 18, and Fred Rumsey finished them off and they were all out for 49. We were in the final, but Yorkshire shattered our dreams a few weeks later.

Nine years after this Kent proved too powerful for us in the Benson and Hedges final. That was the game in which Eddie Barlow and I dropped Bob Woolmer off consecutive balls from Mike Hendrick. I remember being disappointed when Eddie missed the chance at slip and then failing to get fully across to the next ball which took the shoulder of Woolmer's bat – another example of the need to concentrate.

But it all came right in 1981 when we won a thrilling semi-final against Essex at Derby, Paul Newman and I scampering a single to level the scores off the last ball, Derbyshire winning because they had lost fewer wickets. My six victims in that game was a record for a 60-overs competition so I had a special reason for remembering it.

So to that memorable final at Lord's in which we defeated Northamptonshire, again levelling the scores off the last ball and conceding fewer wickets. Memories flooded back to me as I took it all in that Saturday evening, of past players and events spanning two decades with Derbyshire.

That team, captained by Barry Wood and including John Wright, Alan Hill, Peter Kirsten, Kim Barnett, David Steele, Geoff Miller, Colin Tunnicliffe, Paul Newman, Mike Hendrick and myself was the strongest Derbyshire side of my time. Eight of us, including Kirsten who has played for South African representative teams, were current or future internationals and in reserve was Steve Oldham, a very useful fast-medium bowler.

It was a memorable year. A chapter in my autobiography, *Standing Up, Standing Back*, is headed 'Life begins at 40' and I suppose my attainment of that grand old age (it doesn't seem so old now!) is a perfect illustration. In that summer I scored my maiden first-class hundred, I was recalled to the England side and took part in two of the greatest finishes of recent years, I established a world record number of catches, established a new career-record of Derbyshire dismissals, was awarded the MBE for services to cricket and received a testimonial of £54,000.

My career with Derbyshire ended in 1984, by which time I had shared in the dismissal of 1,304 batsmen for the County, 1,157 of them caught and stumped. The first one was

Ken Suttle, caught off Ian Buxton at Derby on 7 June 1961, and the last for Derbyshire was Hampshire's captain Mark Nicholas, stumped off Geoff Miller on 10 September 1984. My world record now stands at 1,649 and I established that with a stumping off Geoff Miller at Brisbane on 24 October 1982 so it was all the more pleasant that the Derbyshire connection was maintained when I broke John Murray's record.

But for all the memories of world and County wicket-keeping records and the heady emotions of the NatWest final in 1981 I think one of my most enjoyable experiences with Derbyshire occurred at Abbeydale Park in June 1983 when we beat Yorkshire by 22 runs. I had scored my only first-class hundred on the same ground two years earlier and our success in 1983 saw us gain our first victory over Yorkshire since 1957. In other words it was the first time I had played in a Derbyshire team that had beaten our old enemy and I remember it for some marvellous batting by Kim Barnett and Geoff Boycott and outstanding bowling performances from Phil Carrick, Ole Mortensen and Dallas Moir. I didn't have a bad match myself, 33 not out being the second best score in our 148 in the second innings, while I held six catches in their first innings. Yorkshire were not the force of old but it was still nice to beat them.

That was the season Kim Barnett became captain of Derbyshire and brought some stability to a job which had become a bit of a merry-go-round in the preceding seasons with David Steele, Geoff Miller and Barry Wood having followed Barlow over a four-year period.

Kim, of course, is an outstanding talent and as a fellow-Staffordshire lad I like to think I had something to do with bringing him to Derbyshire. It was obvious at an early age that he had ability. He had been for trials with Warwickshire and Northamptonshire and clearly it would not be too long before somebody snapped him up. I used to bring him over to Derby and I was trying to convince him that he should come to us. I used to tell him that he might be able to join a more fashionable county but he might not be happy in the same way that he would with Derbyshire. There is more to life for a cricketer than cricket and as a young player he might spend a lot of time in digs, when at Derby he would be only a cock stride away from home. I know he lives in Derby now but I think I helped to convince him that he would find job-satisfaction with us.

The advice I gave to Kim Barnett reflects my own philosophy about Derbyshire cricket. The old, sub-standard facilities are long departed at the County Ground. Now we have nice changing rooms, a sponsors' room, a banqueting room which is usually booked almost every night during the winter, in short, a club which should have a bright future.

I always felt very fortunate to be a professional cricketer, to be paid for doing something I loved and which was a hobby.

If I had to do it all again I would not change a thing – and I have no regrets at all about playing for Derbyshire. I enjoyed my career with them and I am still very much involved as a committee member, serving on the cricket committee with Guy Willatt and Charlie Elliott. Our coach Philip Russell is bringing along some good young players and I see no reason why the present side should not continue to improve in the years ahead.

Cricket has been good to me and I am delighted that I am able to maintain my links with the game as Product Manager – Cricket with Mitre Sports at Huddersfield.

I suppose my only regret is that it is not possible to do it all over again. I had no idea that rainy afternoon in Wolverhampton nearly 30 years ago, when Mr Buckston and Mr Taylor drove over to see me, that I was on the threshold of a career that would bring me a world record, 57 Test caps and a dozen overseas tours.

I shall always be grateful to Derbyshire for giving me that opportunity and I am proud to have played an active part in their history.

BEGINNINGS

THE STORY OF CRICKET IN DERBYSHIRE has its origin in a year which marks perhaps the most significant national event ever to occur in the county. On 4 December 1745 the army of Prince Charles Edward Stuart – Bonnie Prince Charlie, the Young Pretender – arrived in Derby, having invaded England in an attempt to regain the Crown for the House of Stuart. A detachment occupied Swarkestone Bridge on the Trent but this was the limit of the advance of the Young Pretender's army. Two days later it began its retreat northwards to its fate at Culloden.

Those momentous days were recorded in the *Derby Mercury*, itself only 13 years of age at the time of the uprising. There, too, in August 1745, is the *Mercury's* first reference to cricket, a reproduction of a report of a women's match at Gosden Common in Surrey.

Arguably the first Derbyshire cricketer to make any sort of name for himself was, fittingly in view of his family's later patronage of the game in the county, William Cavendish, the Third Duke of Devonshire, who on 21 April 1730 played cricket in Hyde Park with the Duke of Richmond, the Earl of Albemarle, Lord James Cavendish and about twelve more. He was scheduled to play a match a week later for 100 guineas. The first reference to the game being played in Derbyshire comes in September 1757 when the *Mercury* reported on a match at Brampton Moor near Chesterfield between elevens from Wirksworth and Sheffield for £50 a side. The game ended in a dispute over the circumstances of a Sheffield player's dismissal but was later given in favour of Wirksworth and the money paid.

Thus was established an early rivalry between Derbyshire and Yorkshire, apparent again in 1783 when Sheffield defeated Chester-field in what appear to have been two keenly contested games. Indeed some of these early cricket matches in Derbyshire were too keenly contested for the participants' own good. William Waterfall appeared at Derby Assizes in August 1775 charged with unlawfully killing George Twigg in a cricket match at Bakewell Common in May that year. He found guilty of manslaughter and sentenced to be burnt in the hand and imprisoned for nine months. Ten years later, on 4 August 1785, Thomas Hadley and Edward Smedley, two noted Derby cricketers, played a match on Nun's Green, the common land in the town, for five guineas a man. After the game had been 'well contested' for nearly three hours it was won by Smedley by eight notches. A dispute then arose and the men fought for half an hour, Hadley again being defeated and paying his money.

The Nun's Green incident is the first reference to cricket being played in the town of Derby. In 1792 the standard of the game in the town was indicated by the outcome of a match in Derby against Castle Donington, won by the home side by an innings and 12 rus. But when they met Sheffield on Monday 9 September 1793 at South Wingfield, Derby were beaten by nine wickets.

By 1823 the Chesterfield-based North Derbyshire Cricket Club had more than 40 members, its annual ball and supper being a noted county social event, while in Derby the Old Club, the Independent and Derby Town Club led the way. On 30 August 1824 the Old Club beat Chesterfield by an innings; eleven years later the South Derbyshire Cricket Club came into being with a ground at Chaddesden provided by Sir Henry Wilmot. It was the start of the beginning as far as a county club was concerned. Enrolled as members by May 1836 were the Duke of Devonshire, the Earl of Chesterfield and about 70 noblemen and gentlemen, and the club employed a professional, Sam Dakin, a Leicestershire man who was a lace weaver by trade.

For all the significance of the founding of the South Derbyshire CC there were important matches elsewhere, notably between Chesterfield and Sheffield Wednesday, and cricket was by this time firmly established in what were to become the major centres of first-class matches in the county – Derby, Chesterfield, Ilkeston, Buxton and across the Staffordshire border in Burton-on-Trent.

In 1848 the South Derbyshire Club moved from Chaddesden to share the Holmes Ground, situated near to the present site of Derby's central bus station, with Derby Town CC. Their new headquarters almost immediately staged the most important cricket match in the county to that date when the famed All England Eleven visited Derby. The AEE met Twenty of Derbyshire in August of that year in a match played for Sam Dakin's benefit but the occasion was ruined by rain, no play being possible on the first day and little on the second. There was time, however, for George Parr and Alfred Mynn to show their talents and for Derbyshire's bowlers to deliver no fewer than 25 wides.

A year later the AEE returned to face Twenty of Derbyshire and Burton, the local team including three of the most renowned cricketers in the East Midlands, Tom Hunt, John Paxton and Robert Crispin Tinley. Hunt was an all-rounder of the highest quality, a stylish opening batsman, fast round-arm bowler and a wicket-keeper of note. As a youngster he played for Chesterfield and he was the first Derbyshire cricketer to make a real impact on the national game. Known as the Star of the North, he made 102 for North against South at Manchester in 1856 off an attack including Wisden, Martingell, Dean and Caffyn. Tom Hunt met his death in tragic circumstances, being run over by a train at Rochdale in September 1858 when he was 39. Both legs were severed and he died a few hours after the accident.

John Paxton was a lacemaker, *Scores and Biographies* giving his height as 5 ft 9½ in and his weight as ten stone. He was described as 'a very fast round-arm bowler, in the field generally short slip'. Paxton, who took 59 wickets in eight games against AEE between 1849 and 1858, played for a very strong Ilkeston Rutland side. A Sutton-in-Ashfield player who batted against him received a blow on the body 'from the effects of which he died a few weeks afterwards'.

Cris Tinley was a Nottinghamshire man who began his career as a round-arm fast bowler but later turned to lobs which he bowled with great success. He was to play for the AEE and Nottinghamshire, eventually winning further renown as Derbyshire's umpire in an era when each county provided its own official, Tinley first standing in 1872.

Against the bowling of Paxton and the 18-year-old Tinley the AEE could make only 104 and 74 in the 1849 match, Paxton taking five for 22 and six for 25. The Twenty of the Derbyshire and Burton Clubs made 185, Hunt scoring 61, and won by an innings and seven runs.

It was a victory which aroused great interest and excitement, not least because the AEE had by far the better of the exchanges with sides in Derbyshire. They lost only twice, the 1849 game at Derby and that at Chesterfield in 1858 when Twenty-two of Derbyshire won by 13 wickets on the drill field of the Chatsworth Rifles, with Hunt, Tinley and Paxton again being prominent.

In 1863 the South Derbyshire CC changed its headquarters again. In 1861 a large part of the Holmes was used for the building of the cattle market. A move to a ground at Chaddesden Park was considered unsatisfactory so eventually South Derbyshire made its home at the Racecourse Ground on Nottingham Road – the present County Ground at Derby. The area on which the new ground was situated was once crossed by a Roman road from Derventio (Little Chester) to the Trent at Sawley. The land was later in monastic hands and was given to the town by Queen Mary Tudor in 1554, the probable use of agricultural or grazing continuing. The first race meeting was held in 1848 and the new four-acre cricket ground was situated to the south of the racecourse, a turf in front of the grandstand being prepared and levelled. The playing area was probably similar to today with the wickets believed to have been pitched in an east–west direction. The first match played on the new ground was between South Derbyshire and the Rugby School 2nd XI on 24 and 25 June 1863. The South Derbyshire team included John Smith who became Official Receiver for Derby, Unwin Sowter and Walter and Henry Boden (the Bodens having been educated at Rugby), all founder members of the county club and who all, except Henry Boden, played for Derbyshire. Walter Boden, a Derby lace mill owner and a useful cricketer, was to become one of the great founding fathers of the county club, serving as Hon Secretary in 1870–81 and as President in 1895–98.

There was another example of the broadening interest in the game when the Australian Aborigines met South Derbyshire at the Racecourse Ground on 2 and 3 September 1868. South Derbyshire won by 139 runs largely as a result of John Smith's bowling which brought him four wickets with consecutive deliveries in the first innings and a hat-trick in the second.

Several influential people now began to sound out opinion about the possibility of forming a county club. The prime movers were businessmen such as Walter Boden and E. M. Wass of Wirksworth, and John Cartwright, who was born at Eastwood and moved to Ilkeston where he served his apprenticeship to an ironmonger. Cartwright came to Derby in 1853, working as a clerk for George Wheeldon & Co, whose malting business was situated near the Racecourse Ground. Cartwright wrote for the local press and played cricket for a number of teams in Derby. In 1865 he suggested that Derbyshire cricket lovers should aim at the formation of a county club. A year later he wrote to the *London Sporting Life* saying the time was ripe for the formation of a county club, commenting that 'we have a nice little ground of some four acres situated in the centre of the racecourse opposite the Grandstand and it is in good condition'. He included a list of 17 cricketers from which a satisfactory eleven could

South Derbyshire v the Australian Aborigines at Derby in September 1868. John Smith is the bowler-hatted player at the extreme left, Unwin Sowter is sixth from the left, Samuel Richardson is the wicket-keeper and the umpire, in dark trousers, is Dove Gregory.

SOUTH DERBYSHIRE
v AUSTRALIAN ABORIGINES

Played at Derby, 2 and 3 September 1868

SOUTH DERBYSHIRE WON BY 139 RUNS

S. DERBYSHIRE	FIRST INNINGS		SECOND INNINGS	
W. Boden	b Mullagh	29	not out	4
U. Sowter	b Lawrence	11	c Bullocky b Cuzens	14
J. Smith	lbw b Lawrence	4	c Cuzens b Mullagh	57
W. G. Curgenven	c Peter b Mullagh	7	c and b Lawrence	14
S. Richardson	b Lawrence	1	b Twopenny	0
G. C. Moor	b Lawrence	1	c Twopenny b Mullagh	9
F. Davenport	not out	32	c Dick-a-Dick b Cuzens	8
W. S. Sutton	run out	0	b Mullagh	1
J. Tompkins	c Cuzens b Mullagh	4	c Peter b Cuzens	0
H. Bass	b Lawrence	4	c Redcap b Mullagh	0
A. Powys	b Mullagh	20	c Bullocky b Twopenny	14
Extras	b 2, lb 5, w 1	8	b 3, lb 1	4
Total		121		125

1st inns: 1-43, 2-45, 3-53, 4-57, 5-59, 6-59, 7-59, 8-69, 9-76, 10-121
2nd inns: 1-0, 2-9, 3-9, 4-15, 5-60, 6-93, 7-106, 8-119, 9-121, 10-125

BOWLING	B	M	R	W		B	M	R	W
Lawrence	120	9	67	5		96	6	37	1
Mullagh	113	9	46	4		124	14	40	4
Twopenny						60	6	11	2
Cuzens						116	15	33	3

AUST. ABORIGINES	FIRST INNINGS		SECOND INNINGS	
Lawrence	c Curgenven b Smith	2	c Sowter b Smith	1
Mullagh	b Davenport	8	c Bass b Smith	0
Bullocky	c Bass b Davenport	13	b Smith	0
Tiger	c Richardson b Davenport	4	c Davenport b Smith	1
Cuzens	b Smith	7	c Curgenven b Smith	4
Red Cap	c Sowter b Smith	0	c Smith b Davenport	15
Twopenny	c Boden b Bass	33	c Richardson b Davenport	0
Mosquito	b Smith	0	not out	2
Peter	b Smith	0	b Davenport	8
Dick-a-Dick	st Richardson b Smith	0	c Sowter b Davenport	0
C. Dumas	not out	8	c Sowter b Smith	0
Extras	b 1	1		
Total		76		31

1st inns: 1-6, 2-13, 3-27, 4-34, 5-34, 6-34, 7-34, 8-34, 9-34, 10-121
2nd inns: 1-1, 2-1, 3-1, 4-1, 5-1, 6-16, 7-28, 8-28, 9-28, 10-31

BOWLING	B	M	R	W		B	M	R	W
Smith	84	9	28	6		52	7	16	6
Davenport	80	9	31	3		55	9	15	4
Bass	21	2	7	1					
Tompkins	16	0	9	0					

Umpires: D. Gregory and W. Shepherd

A COUNTY CRICKET CLUB FOR DERBYSHIRE.

On Friday afternoon a public meeting was held in the Grand Jury Room, Town Hall, Derby, to consider the best mode of establishing a cricket club in Derbyshire which should represent the strength of the whole county. Amongst the gentlemen present were the Rev. E. W. Northey, the Rev. Mr. Anson, Captain Pountain, Captain Levett, Captain Blane, and Messrs. R. Smith, M.P., W. T. Cox, E. M. Wass, W. G. Curgenven, J. Huish, Walter Boden, W. T. Cox, J. Smith, P. Wallis, Kingdon, Sowter, Billyeald, Edwin I-Dalby, Whitehouse, Booth, J. Cartwright, F. Richardson, &c.

On the motion of Mr. BODEN, Mr. W. T. Cox was voted to the chair.

The CHAIRMAN said he had been a cricketer in his younger days, and this game had always appeared to him to be a mainly game and one which was conductive to health, and which tended to bring about pleasant reunions. He believed there was a great want of a county cricket club in Derbyshire, and he hoped one would be formed.

Mr. WALTER BODEN then stated that at a preliminary meeting he had been requested by several gentlemen as being the oldest playing member in the county club to call that county meeting. He had received several letters from gentlemen who were unable to be present. One of them was from the Duke of Rutland, and another from Lord Vernon, who was in London, and who promised that if the club should be supported by the many, he should be very glad to give it his support (Hear, hear). Letters had also been received from Dr. German, Mr. Offley Shore, and Mr. A. R. Goldie, and verbal promises of support had been made by several gentlemen, amongst whom were the Hon. W. M. Jervis and Colonel Wilmot, M.P., the latter having also expressed deep regret at not being able to be present at the meeting, as he was detained in Yorkshire. He believed it was in 1867 that the strength of the county was tried by a match between the cricketers of the north and those of the south portions of the county. Financially that match was not a success, but it brought together many cricketers who would not otherwise have met. This year, as they would be aware, had been played, one between the strength of the county and Marylebone club, and the other between the gentlemen of Derbyshire and the gentlemen of Kent, in both of which Derbyshire was victorious. He now proposed "That a cricket club for Derbyshire be formed which shall represent the strength of the whole county, and that it be called the Derbyshire County Club" (Hear, hear).

Mr. E. M. WASS, in seconding the motion, said that in the district in which he resided, for a long time it had been felt that if they in Derbyshire were to aspire to any rank amongst the cricketing counties in England a county club was not only desirable but necessary (Hear, hear). He had not been aware until the subject had been mentioned by Mr. Boden that so far back as 1867 an attempt was made to establish a county club. That attempt had evidently failed, and he hoped this attempt would be more successful (Hear, hear). He had no doubt that there was excellent talent in the county, and he thought the *physique* of Derbyshire men would bear comparison with that of men in any other county: in fact, they were proverbially strong in the arm (laughter); he would not mention the other characteristic which often accompanied that particular kind of strength (Laughter). If the club were formed he believed it would receive a considerable amount of pecuniary support, as well as the support of the best playing talent in the county. The names of the president and vice-president were those of gentlemen

who, they would all say, were well fitted for the posts, and success was almost certain to attend the establishment of the club with such gentlemen at its head.

After the motion had been carried,

The Rev. Mr. ANSON moved, and Mr. HUISH seconded, "That the Earl of Chesterfield be requested to accept the office of president of the club, and G. H. Strutt, Esquire, the office of vice-president," which was also carried.

The Rev. E. W. NORTHEY then moved "That a donation of not less than 10l., or an annual subscription of not less than one guinea shall entitle to membership of the club." He said it was very important that there should be two ways of becoming members of the club as suggested in the resolution. A great patron of cricket who happened to be in the neighbourhood might wish immediately to become a member of the club. If he left the county after paying the 10l. ot was obvious that the benefit to the club would be greater than if his membership had been obtained by the annual subscription of a guinea.

Mr. KINGDON, in seconding the motion, thought so large a meeting augured well for the success of the club that was to be formed. As one of the members of the southern division he hoped they would not be wanting in the "sinews of war."

Mr. J. SMITH was sure the playing talent would be forthcoming if the club were formed.

Mr. BILLYEALD remarked that the subscription to the County Cricket Club of Nottingham only commenced with 10s., and the club had many members. He thought a guinea was too high a subscription.

Mr. DALBY expressed himself of the same opinion.

Mr. HUISH believed the subscription would be found to amount to a greater sum if 10s. were the sum instead of a guinea.

Mr. DALBY then suggested that the subscription should be 10s. 6d.

The Rev. E. W. NORTHEY and Mr. KINGDON consented to have the resolution altered accordingly, the latter remarking that the lower subscription did not preclude persons from paying the 10l. donation to become members.

Mr. WASS stated that many clubs had collapsed owing to their having been of too exclusive a character.

The resolution was then carrried unanimously.

Mr. BODEN remarked that he had already had two promises of donations towards the expense of starting the club—5l. each from the Hon. W. M. Jervis and Colonel Wilmot, both of whom had also promised to give the same subscription as other members (Hear, Hear, and applause).

Captain BLANE moved, and Captain LEVETT seconded, "That a committee be formed to select a secretary, solicit subscriptions, and make other necessary arrangements for establishing the club, and to report to a future meeting, such committee to be formed of the following gentlemen:— The President, Vice-President, and Secretary for the time being, the Hon. W. M. Jervis, Mr. G. H. Strutt, Mr. C. Childers Radford, Mr. M. E. Wass, Mr. Walter Boden, Mr. W. G. Curgenven, Mr. J. Smith, Mr. W. J. Lyon, Mr. Godfrey Meynell, and the Secretaries of the South Derbyshire, Ashborne, Chesterfield, Glossop, Ilkeston, Riddings, Staveley, and Wirksworth Cricket Clubs, with power to add to their number."

On the motion of Mr. Smith, seconded by Mr. BODEN, the name of the Secretary of the Ilkeston Club was added to the resolution, which was carried.

The meeting then terminated with a vote of thanks to the Chairman.

The Derby Mercury reports the inaugural meeting of Derbyshire County Cricket Club in November 1870.

be chosen. Thirteen of these players later appeared in first-class matches for the county.

In June 1870 a trial game was played at Wirksworth between a Derbyshire County XI and Fourteen Colts of the County. It was followed by the Gentlemen of Derbyshire defeating their Kent counterparts at the Angel Ground, Tonbridge, by an innings and 14 runs, John Smith making 29 and taking twelve wickets in the game. On the following two days, 21 and 22 July, an eleven known as 'Derbyshire' defeated MCC and Ground at Lord's by five wickets. MCC were dismissed for 67 and 86, Dove Gregory having a match analysis of eleven for 69. Derbyshire made 107, John Platts getting 19 and Smith 18, and, needing 47 to win, reached 49 for five in their second innings, Attenborough being undefeated with 29.

These victories provided the catalyst for the formation of the county club. With interest mounting the scheme was again put forward and Walter Boden, Henry Boden, Colonel Sir Henry Wilmot, MP, E. M. Wass, John Smith, John Cartwright, Rev E. W. Northey, Vicar of Chaddesden, and Rev T. A. Anson, Vicar of Longford, were all in favour of the launch of a county club.

Walter Boden arranged a meeting on Friday, 4 November 1870 in the Grand Jury Room in the Guildhall, Derby, 'to consider the best mode of establishing a Cricket Club for the Shire that should represent the cricketing strength of the whole county'. In the absence of Sir Henry Wilmot, who was away in Yorkshire, the chair was taken by Mr W. T. Cox.

Mr Boden said he had received letters promising support from the Duke of Rutland and Lord Vernon and verbal pledges from Hon William Monk Jervis and Colonel Wilmot. He proposed: 'That a cricket club for Derbyshire be formed which shall represent the strength of the whole county, and that it shall be called the Derbyshire County Club.'

Mr E. M. Wass seconded the motion, which was carried, and subscriptions were set at 10s 6d. The Earl of Chesterfield, who was elected president, died a few months later and was succeeded by the Hon W. M. Jervis, a descendant of Sir John Jervis, whose great naval victory at Cape St Vincent had created the earldom. William Monk Jervis, who lived at Quarndon Hall, was to hold the post from 1871 to 1876, and Walter Boden took over as secretary.

Everything, then, promised well. The County Club was formed, with the promise of rich and influential backing. The South Derbyshire Club (which continued to play matches until around 1884) allowed Derbyshire to play matches at the Racecourse and two games against Lancashire were arranged for the 1871 season. It was a time for optimism.

CHAPTER TWO

A BALL FROM PLATTS

IN THE SUMMER BEFORE THE COUNTY CLUB was formed a Derbyshire
player was at the centre of a controversy which still echoes down the
years. John Platts, playing for the MCC against Nottinghamshire at
Lord's on 13, 14 and 15 June 1870 delivered a ball on the final day
which struck George Summers on the head, the batsman dying four
days later.

Platts, then 21, became one of Derbyshire's finest all-round
cricketers, a hard-hitting middle-order left-hand batsman and right-
arm fast bowler. In 1869 he had been engaged by Dudley Town and
that season took 15 wickets for Twenty-two of Worcester and District
against the United South of England, twice dismissing W. G. Grace.
Subscriptions for Platts amounted to ten guineas and he was presented
with the cash by Lord Coventry who had much to do with his
engagement by MCC in 1870. Consequently, he made his first-class
debut in the game against Nottinghamshire nearly five months before
the formation of the County Club.

Pitches during this period were often bad and the bowlers were
generally dominant. Lord's did not have a good reputation, although
1870 was the first season in which the heavy roller was used on the
pitch, a practice which along with the perfection of the mowing
machine was to lead to much better conditions.

Platts ranked among the fastest bowlers of his day. Young and
strong, eager to impress, he could, despite his small stature, generate
tremendous pace and swing the ball, a point which added to his
hostility. On the first day Nottinghamshire were all out for 267,
Richard Daft making 117 and Summers 41 before he was bowled by a
shooter from Platts who took three for 74 in 48 overs. MCC were
dismissed for 183, W. G. Grace carrying his bat for 117, and following
on, 240, leaving Nottinghamshire 157 to make to win the match.

They began their quest on the final morning. It was not long before
Summers started his fateful innings. The first ball he faced from Platts
rose sharply, possibly having struck a small pebble which had worked
its way up to the surface, and hit him on the head. There were several
witnesses who left behind their recollections of the incident.
W. G. Grace wrote in *Cricket*:

The injury to Summers occurred early in the second innings. The
first ball bowled to him by Platts was a little bit short, and it bumped
and hit him on the head, and concussion of the brain followed. Platts
was in no way to blame, for the ball did not bump higher than many
I had to play in the same match: but unfortunately Summers treated

the blow too lightly, appearing on the ground next day in a hot sun, and afterwards travelling by rail to Nottingham, which shook him terribly, and developed symptoms which subsequently proved fatal.

Wisden described the pitch as 'excellent' and the MCC wicket-keeper William Yardley recalled in *Talks with Old English Cricketers*:

> If Summers had been able to duck and avoid the ball, I must inevitably have got it between the eyes. I have often felt sorry since that it was not I who was struck, for I don't suppose the result would have been more than a pair of lovely black eyes to me, whereas Summers was struck in a vital part – i.e. on the thinnest part of the temple which was fractured by the blow, it appeared, at the post-mortem examination. In all my career I never saw a ball get up with such lightning rapidity. The pitch of the ball and the blow on Summers' head appeared to be simultaneous.

Yardley added that the blow was the 'purest accident' and that when he was struck Summers 'reeled like a teetotum, and fell'. With the help of C. I. Thornton, Yardley carried Summers to the parlour of the Tavern. The long-stop, C. E. Green, was the first to reach Summers and he felt that from the way Summers' fists were clenched it was obvious that he was seriously injured. W.G. was the first to give medical assistance, feeling Summers' pulse and saying: 'He is not dead.' Thornton described the accident as 'a fearful crack on the temple, and when struck he jumped up in the air, and then fell all of a heap'.

The next man in was Richard Daft, who walked out to bat with a towel around his head covered with a scarf tied under his chin. Thornton said:

> The first ball he had pitched about halfway, and went clean over his head. He did let Platts have it and no mistake, and the bowler was taken off after that over.

Alfred Shaw was given the job of looking after Summers, and after being given brandy the young batsman insisted on sitting in the hot sun to watch the remainder of the match (this is probably what W.G. meant in his comment about Summers appearing at the ground next day in a hot sun), which Nottinghamshire won by two wickets. Platts took three for 56 in 27.2 overs.

The match ended on Wednesday afternoon and Summers, who said he wanted to go home and see his parents, now decided to travel back to Nottingham against the advice of a London doctor. He received herbal treatment in his home town but this proved unsatisfactory and he died of brain concussion on the Sunday following the game – 19 June 1870, two days before what would have been his 26th birthday. A tombstone was purchased by MCC for his grave in Nottingham General Cemetery 'to mark their sense of his qualities as a cricketer and to testify their regret at the untimely accident at Lord's ground which cut short a career so full of promise'.

The incident had a profound effect on Platts – W.G. saying he would never forget the Derbyshire man's mental distraction – and although he was not blamed he was deeply upset and is said to have resolved never to bowl fast again. Whether he did is open to conjecture, for match reports in later years refer to his fast bowling, notably a match in 1877 when he took five for 18 in Lancashire's second innings, *Wisden* saying it proved his fast bowling was still dangerous. In 1878 Platts took three Nottinghamshire wickets with lobs in a game at Derby, *Scores and Biographies* saying: 'In the first innings he got his wickets by lobs, his usual style being fast round-armed.' This was the final match of the 1878 season and might have marked the beginning of Platts' period as a slow bowler. In an article on his career the *Derbyshire Cricket Annual* (1885) says of the 1879 season: 'It was this year that he commenced bowling slows, and the new style adopted by him answered well . . .'

F. G. Forman, who like Platts was born at Chellaston, suggested that Platts moderated his pace after the death of Summers. He first remembered Platts 'bowling slow stuff and not liking being taken off' in village cricket after his county career ended in 1884. Mr Forman's father, who was Platts' cousin and knew him well, was captain of the village club and he told Mr Forman that Summers was given brandy and sat in the hot sun before returning home although Alfred Shaw said every care was taken and Summers did not leave his hotel until just before starting the journey. 'This is what I was told by my father, with the addition that the treatment which Summers received afterwards at home was not suited to his injury.'

The death of Summers did not seem to have any particular effect on Platts' form in 1870, whatever his state of mind after the incident. The *Derbyshire Cricket Annual* said that after the Lord's match he 'played but seldom during the remainder of the season'. It does refer to his bowling for Grimsby against Brigg when he took seven wickets with ten balls, five with consecutive deliveries, without conceding a run. And in July he appeared again at Lord's for a Derbyshire team against the MCC when he took four second innings wickets and scored 19 in the first innings of a two-day game.

It was said that after the Summers incident Platts never enjoyed playing at Lord's. Outside of Derbyshire matches he was to appear in half-a-dozen representative games at various grounds, although not for MCC in a first-class match. But he did play for Derbyshire against the MCC at Lord's in later years.

Another story concerning Platts was told by a Chellaston resident who said that after Summers' death he always walked on to the field wearing a black glove on his right hand and the belief persisted down the years that he never bowled fast again after the tragedy.

What may have happened is that Platts possibly gave up bowling fast after the accident but gradually increased his pace as the pitches improved. Certainly the 1879 season appears to have seen a formal change of style, though probably not as a result of the death of Summers. Platts left county cricket when he was nearly 36 when, of course, he would have lost a great deal of his pace whatever his intent, and he was bowling slow in village cricket.

Allowing for *Wisden's* description of the pitch as 'excellent' (but by 1870 standards) it emphasised what could happen when a fast bowler such as Platts operated on the pitches of those days. Incidentally there were conflicting versions of just where Summers was struck, some reports saying on the temple, others on the side of the head or cheekbone.

Platts was given the Yorkshire match at Derby in 1885 – a year after he finished playing county cricket – for his benefit. He became an umpire and also organised football medal competitions after his retirement, later taking over as landlord of the Rose and Crown at Chellaston.

Money problems and failing health brought about his death at his home in Derby, where he had recently moved, in August 1898, three months before what would have been his 50th birthday.

THE 1874 CHAMPIONSHIP

WITHIN A YEAR OF SUMMERS' DEATH JACK PLATTS was preparing to take the field as a member of the Derbyshire team which faced Lancashire in the County's initial first-class match at Old Trafford on 25, 26 and 27 May 1871.

Captaining the side was Sam Richardson, a wicket-keeper and batsman who had played for the South Derbyshire club. Richardson, who was born at Derby, was a small, dapper man, the proprietor of a gents' outfitters in the town. He was to captain the County in 1871–75, and finished playing in 1878. He was assistant-secretary in 1880–89 when he absconded with around £1,000 of the Club's money and went to Spain, where he lived under an assumed name. Here he became court tailor to King Alfonso and lived to be 93 before his death in Madrid in 1938.

Two other members of the South Derbyshire club, John Smith and Unwin Sowter also played at Old Trafford. Sowter was a useful middle-order batsman and a good fieldsman at point. For several years he served on Derbyshire's committee.

Robert Posnett Smith (no relation to John) was one of the most promising batsmen in the County. He was a gentleman farmer at Sawley and a fine all-round sportsman. A sound middle-order batsman, he relied chiefly on back play but a repertoire of off-side strokes meant that he could be attractive to watch. A fine fieldsman at point, he was captain in 1876–83.

Richardson, the two Smiths and Sowter were amateurs but the remaining seven members of the team were professionals. Tommy Attenborough, from Ilkeston, a useful batsman and slow left-arm bowler, had played for his home town against the AEE and at 37 was now in the veteran stage of a career which, in the main, preceded first-class cricket in the County.

Spearheading the attack was Dove Gregory, a fast bowler who had been employed as professional by South Derbyshire CC. Gregory was not to enjoy a long career in county cricket for he died in May 1873, aged only 33, after a spectacular start to his belated entry into the first-class game.

His opening partner at Manchester was William Hickton who, in those days before the 1873 rules of qualification, actually played against Lancashire and also appeared for them in 1871. He was a fast bowler and, like Gregory, a good slip fieldsman. At Old Trafford in 1870 he took all ten tickets in an innings for Lancashire against Hampshire.

Joe Davidson was the father of Frank and George, who both later played for the County. A medium-pace off-break bowler, he himself played in only four games, in 1871–74. Similarly John William Burnham made only a few appearances after a promising start as an opening or middle-order batsman. John Tilson, a batsman and medium-pace bowler, was another who flitted briefly across the first-class cricket scene and, like Burnham, earned a measure of fame only because he played in the first match.

There was rain about, no play being possible on the first day. The second day's play was sensational, Lancashire having no answer to the bowling of Gregory and Hickton and being all out in an hour for 25. Only wicket-keeper Alfort Smith (born at Bury, he later moved to Glossop and played for Derbyshire) made double figures.

Gregory's association with Hickton can be regarded as the forerunner of the great pairings of Derbyshire fast bowlers, although this was an era when sometimes slow bowlers would open the attack and there was no particular tradition of opening with pace. A mixture of pace and spin was also generally used, but in Derbyshire's case, perhaps because there was never any depth of spin, the fast bowlers tended to operate in pairs at an earlier period than in some other counties.

In reply to Lancashire's 25 Derbyshire made 147, and although Lancashire did better in their second innings they were beaten by an innings and eleven runs, Platts finishing the game before heavy rain fell for the rest of the day. *Wisden* commented that Burnham 'long stopped well' and described Derbyshire's victory as 'an encouraging and deserved success'.

In the return game at Derby in August 1871 – Derbyshire's only other first-class game that season – Lancashire won easily, not a single boundary being struck in the match. Lancashire also won both games in 1872 and again in 1873 and they were the only county to meet Derbyshire in these initial three years of their history. By now, though, the Derbyshire team was gradually being strengthened by the arrival of such players as Dr W. G. Curgenven, a forcing batsman who had a flourishing medical practice in The Friary, George Frost, a batsman from Wirksworth, and another Wirksworth man, Joe Flint, a slow round-arm bowler.

Although they were dismissed for less than a hundred for the tenth consecutive innings, 1873 was a turning point in the Club's fortunes. It marked the first appearance of William Mycroft (fast left-arm), one of the greatest bowlers in the history of the Club, and there was also a remarkable match at Wirksworth on 4 and 5 September 1873 when Sixteen of the County defeated Nottinghamshire by an innings and eight runs after dismissing them for 14 in the first innings, Flint taking

LANCASHIRE *v* DERBYSHIRE

Played at Old Trafford, Manchester, 26 and 27 May 1871

DERBYSHIRE WON BY AN INNINGS AND 11 RUNS

LANCASHIRE	FIRST INNINGS		SECOND INNINGS	
Mr A. N. Hornby	c Gregory b Hickton	1	run out	0
J. Ricketts	b Hickton	2	b Gregory	7
C. Coward	c Burnham b Hickton	1	c and b Hickton	36
Mr J. R. Hillkirk	c Sowter b Hickton	1	b Gregory	17
W. Burrows	b Gregory	0	c Sowter b Hickton	3
Mr A. B. Rowley	b Gregory	0	b Platts	1
T. Whatmough	b Gregory	5	not out	28
A. Smith	not out	11	b Gregory	7
E. Wadsworth	b Gregory	2	b Hickton	8
Mr W. G. Mills	b Gregory	2	b Platts	1
*F. R. Reynolds	c Davidson b Gregory	0	c Attenborough b Platts	0
Extras		0	b 1, lb 2	3
Total		25		111

BOWLING	O	M	R	W		O	M	R	W
Gregory	12.3	7	9	6		32	11	46	3
Hickton	12	5	16	4		37	15	58	3
Platts						5.3	5	4	3

DERBYSHIRE	FIRST INNINGS	
Mr R. P. Smith	b Mills	17
Mr J. Smith	c Reynolds b Whatmough	1
Mr T. Attenborough	c Smith b Whatmough	8
J. W. Burnham	b Reynolds	31
Mr U. Sowter	not out	47
J. Tilson	run out	8
J. T. B. D. Platts	c Whatmough b Reynolds	2
J. Davidson	b Reynolds	8
W. Hickton	c Smith b Mills	7
*Mr S. Richardson	st Smith b Reynolds	5
Dove Gregory	st Smith b Reynolds	5
Extras	b 2, lb 4, w 2	8
Total		147

BOWLING	O	M	R	W	
Reynolds	35	10	54	5	
Whatmough	25	5	52	2	
Mills	23	12	22	2	(1w)
Rowley	13	8	11	0	(1w)

In another account Sowter makes 57 and in another 37, also Platts scores 13, wides are 3 and the total 147, 148 or 157.

Derbyshire's first first-class match.

23

six for 7 and Mycroft four for 6. Nottinghamshire were regarded as joint champions that year and the result astonished the cricket world.

There was a story that a local wine and spirit merchant 'topped up' the visitors before they began their first innings but even this charming tale should not detract from Derbyshire's success. Although it was not a first-class match owing to its against-odds nature it provided a great deal of encouragement for everybody connected with the Club.

Consequently for the 1874 season eight games, four of them first-class, were arranged in the most ambitious programme the Club had undertaken. Of the first-class counties Kent, in addition to Lancashire, agreed to meet them, probably because the Hon W. M. Jervis, Derbyshire's president, was an uncle of Lord Harris, who became a member of Kent's committee at the age of 19.

By now Tommy Foster, of Glossop, a middle-order batsman and wicket-keeper who was also a good field and a useful fast-medium bowler, had appeared on the scene. Another newcomer was Abraham Shuker, who for many years was a master at Trent College. A steady batsman, Shuker made 41 on his debut against Lancashire at Old Trafford, Derbyshire making 190. Lancashire were then all out in an hour for 38, Mycroft taking six for 23 and Flint four for 14. Following on Lancashire were dismissed for 181, Derbyshire making 30 for one to win by nine wickets.

More good fortune was to follow in the Kent match at Wirksworth, Derbyshire winning a low-scoring game by 33 runs, the first time they had won a first-class match in the County.

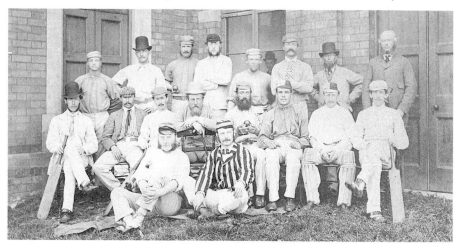

The Derbyshire XVI of 1874, who met the United South of England XI at Derby. Standing: T. Foster, J. H. Frost, W. Hickton, R. P. Smith, J. Tye, W. Mycroft. Umpires: R. C. Tinley, H. Killick. Seated centre: G. Frost, J. Platts, S. Richardson, W. Boden (President), J. Flint, W. Rigley, A. Smith, R. Allsop; Front: U. Sowter, W. J. Humble. Absent: Dr. W. G. Curgenven.

SIXTEEN OF DERBYSHIRE
v ELEVEN OF NOTTINGHAMSHIRE

Played at Wirksworth, Derbyshire, 4 and 5 September 1873

SIXTEEN OF DERBYSHIRE WON BY AN INNINGS AND EIGHT RUNS

THE SIXTEEN OF DERBYSHIRE
FIRST INNINGS

J. Smith (Derby)	c Selby b J. C. Shaw	5
W. Rigley	c Oscroft b Daft	15
S. Richardson Esq	run out	21
G. Frost	b Oscroft	15
Rev. R. C. Moncrieff	b Oscroft	0
R. P. Smith Esq	b Oscroft	2
T. Foster	c McIntyre b J. C. Shaw	0
J. Frost	b Morley	2
J. Howarth	b Morley	7
R. Allsop Esq	c Martin b Daft	22
J. Flint	b J. C. Shaw	12
J. Platts	b J. C. Shaw	1
W. Hickton	run out	3
W. Allen	c and b J. C. Shaw	2
W. Mycroft	b J. C. Shaw	2
E. Tatlow	not out	0
Extras	b 2, lb 3	5
Total		114

BOWLING	O	M	R	W
J. C. Shaw	48.1	23	40	6
Morley	40	28	20	2
Daft	14	2	33	2
McIntyre	9	5	7	0
Oscroft	7	3	9	3

THE ELEVEN OF NOTTINGHAMSHIRE

	FIRST INNINGS		SECOND INNINGS	
Bignall	b Flint	0	b Mycroft	3
F. Wyld	b Mycroft	1	hit wkt b Flint	11
Mr C. Clifton	c and b Flint	0	st Richardson b Flint	0
William Oscroft	c Flint b Mycroft	4	c Flint b Mycroft	12
Richard Daft	c Platts b Mycroft	5	st Richardson b Flint	0
R. Tolley Esq	c and b Flint	0	c and b Flint	0
J. Selby	lbw b Mycroft	0	not out	14
Martin McIntyre	c J. Smith b Flint	1	b Hickton	23
G. Martin	c and b Flint	0	run out	23
Morley	not out	0	b Hickton	0
J. C. Shaw	b Flint	2	b Platts	3
Extras		b 1	b	3
Total		14		92

BOWLING	O	M	R	W	O	M	R	W
Flint	16	10	7	6	26	9	44	4
Mycroft	16	12	6	4	28	9	34	2
Platts					6	4	5	1
Hickton					5	3	6	2

Umpires: E. Horrobin and W. H. Luck.

Derbyshire's surprising defeat of joint champions Nottinghamshire.

DERBYSHIRE *v* KENT

Played at Wirksworth, 13, 14 July 1874

DERBYSHIRE WON BY 33 RUNS

DERBYSHIRE	FIRST INNINGS		SECOND INNINGS	
R. P. Smith Esq	lbw b Remnant	5	b Willsher	3
G. Frost	c and b Draper	37	c Henty b Willsher	17
J. Frost	c G. McCanlis b Willsher	18	b Willsher	1
W. G. Curgenven Esq	b Willsher	5	b Draper	0
J. Platts	c Remnant b Draper	16	b Willsher	0
W. J. Humble Esq	b Draper	7	b Willsher	0
J. Tye	b Willsher	3	b Draper	7
W. Boden Esq	not out	2	c Byas b Willsher	0
J. Flint	b Willsher	4	c Draper b Willsher	2
W. Mycroft	c Hodgson b Willsher	0	not out	0
J. Cooke	b Willsher	0	b Draper	6
Total		97		36

BOWLING	O	M	R	W	O	M	R	W
Willsher	35	18	36	6	16	7	22	7
Draper	18	9	22	3	17	11	14	3
Remnant	16	2	39	1				

KENT	FIRST INNINGS		SECOND INNINGS	
William McCanlis	c Platts b Flint	6	c Smith b Platts	28
Capt Swinford	b Mycroft	6	b Mycroft	1
Remnant	run out	1	c Humble b Flint	11
Rev G. H. Hodgson	c J. Frost b Mycroft	0	b Mycroft	4
Geo McCanlis	b Mycroft	0	b Flint	2
Draper	b Mycroft	0	b Mycroft	3
Croxford	lbw b Flint	3	b Platts	0
J. E. Byas Esq	b Mycroft	0	run out	2
Willsher	c G. Frost b Flint	7	c Platts b Flint	9
Henty	c J. Frost b Flint	0	not out	7
R. Palmer	not out	0	b Flint	5
Extras			b 1, lb 2	3
Total		25		75

BOWLING	O	M	R	W	O	M	R	W
Flint	12	6	17	4	27	9	35	4
Mycroft	11	8	8	5	39	30	15	3
Platts					12	5	22	2

Umpires: R. C. Tinley and Fryer

Derbyshire's first first-class win at home.

Ten days later in the return at Tunbridge Wells Derbyshire gained their third victory of the season with a notable win. Hickton was in devastating form, taking six for 15 and five for 68 as Kent were dismissed for 88 and 198 and Derbyshire made 92 in their first innings. Needing 195 to win – a stiff task in those days – Derbyshire began well with R. P. Smith and John Smith sharing an opening partnership of 50, John Smith hitting six fours in making 27. R. P. Smith went on to make 47, Platts hit six boundaries in his 26 and Richardson made 24. Then Foster and Rev W. J. Humble shared an unbroken stand of 41 which took the score from 155 for seven to 196, Derbyshire winning by three wickets.

In the following match against Lancashire at the Recreation Ground, Saltergate, now the home of Chesterfield Football Club, Derbyshire drew a rain-ruined game in which Hickton took six for 61 in his old colleagues' total of 161, Derbyshire replying with 104.

Outside of the county games, Derbyshire drew two matches against Yorkshire United CC, a breakaway organisation from the County Club which had been formed earlier in the year but was not to last for very long.

But it was Derbyshire's against-odds matches which probably caused most excitement in 1874. Sixteen of Derbyshire defeated Nottinghamshire at Trent Bridge at Whitsun after more good bowling by Mycroft and Flint, and then in the final match of the season at Derby Sixteen of Derbyshire defeated the United South of England XI, including W. G. Grace, who was making his first appearance against Derbyshire. Grace's late arrival delayed the start, but a then record crowd of 3,000 saw him make 51 before being bowled off his pads by Platts. It was in this game that Derbyshire's wicket-keeping problems, arising out of an injury to Sam Richardson, were solved by Alfort Smith, who was destined to become the county's regular 'keeper until succeeded by Jimmy Disney in 1881.

It is one of those anomalies of cricket history that for more than 50 years Derbyshire were recognised as the 1874 County Champions although the Club never laid claim to the title and some members must have gone to their graves unaware that such an honour had been bestowed.

In that period various periodicals printed tables based on inter-county results and some of them pronounced a Champion County each season, but no recognised method of deciding the order of the counties existed. Indeed, some cricket annuals simply printed tables of results in alphabetical order and no official system was devised until 1890, when the county secretaries adopted a method of deducting losses from wins and ignoring drawn games.

Then in 1895 a book written by Alfred Gibson entitled *County*

Cricket Championship was published. Gibson used a system of 'least lost' matches to decide the order and worked backwards into history to produce a list of previous 'winners'. The Rev R. S. Holmes, the Yorkshire historian, brought it up to date in a book with a similar title to Gibson's which was published in 1896, having published similar articles in *Cricket* in 1894. The *Derbyshire Cricket Guide* for 1896 listed Derbyshire as the 1874 Champions, no doubt copying Holmes and Gibson, who had made similar claims on the basis of Derbyshire not having lost a match in 1874. Previous editions of the *Guide* – first published in 1885 – had made no such claim. For 51 years *Wisden*, from 1911 to 1962, recorded that Derbyshire won the County Championship in 1874 before substituting Gloucestershire in the 1963 edition. Regrettable though it might seem that Derbyshire should be 'deprived' of the honour, it must be stated that the Club never claimed to be Champions in 1874 and neither did the local press.

Under the 'least lost' system the Championship table for that year is as follows:

	P	W	D	L
Derbyshire	4	3	1	0
Gloucestershire	6	4	1	1
Kent	4	1	1	2
Lancashire	6	1	2	3
Nottinghamshire	8	5	0	3
Yorkshire	12	8	1	3
Middlesex	6	1	1	4
Sussex	8	1	2	5
Surrey	10	3	1	6

In his book *County Cricket Championship*, published in 1957, historian Roy Webber wrote:

It has been decided officially for many years that Derbyshire were Champions in 1874, and as they went through the season without defeat ended top of the table, but various books of the time give Gloucestershire the honour, while W. G. Grace gives Yorkshire as the leading county. Derbyshire played four matches, winning three and drawing one, but it seems hard that counties who undertook a more strenuous programme should lose the title. Yorkshire, who lost three matches, played all the other first-class counties with the exception of Derbyshire and Kent. However, if the results in 1874 are related to the points-scoring method in use today, Derbyshire are still at the top of the table and this appears to prove that however hard the position might be on some of the other counties, the assessment of Derbyshire as Champions does carry some justification.

Cricket historian Rowland Bowen cast serious doubts on Derbyshire's acceptance as Champions when he thoroughly examined the situation of 1864–89 in an article in the 1959 edition of *Wisden*. Bowen researched contemporary publications such as *John and James Lillywhite's Companion*, *James Lillywhite's Annual*, *Wisden* itself and various other publications.

None of the annuals published a formal table in those days. *Wisden* did not always designate a Champion and did not publish a table until 1888, although it published an order of merit for the two previous seasons. The *Companion* never published a table but usually listed the counties in order of merit, like *Wisden* conventionally placing Surrey first. The *Annual* first published a table for 1872 (which included all games) but did not do so for 1874. Bowen wrote of 1874:

> Both Annual and Companion were in no doubt that Gloucestershire were champions, and Wisden listed them second to the conventionally placed Surrey (listing Derbyshire last!). The History of Gloucestershire County Cricket Club made the definite claim that Gloucestershire were champions in 1874; Derbyshire County Cricket by Piper, published 1897, made no claim for Derbyshire to have been champions in 1874, though it said they were the only unbeaten county, but it is fair to say that the unofficial Derbyshire Cricket Guide for 1896 did make the claim (prompted no doubt by A. Gibson). On the other hand 'Feats and Facts of Derbyshire Cricket' in the Derbyshire Cricket Annual for 1887 did not mention Derbyshire as champions in 1874 – surely it would have if anyone in or out of the county had made the claim? In the face of contemporary unanimity on the subject, there can be no doubt that the present list is wrong, both in supposing that the champions were designated with reference to fewest matches lost, and in designating Derbyshire as champions. At the time, Gloucestershire were accepted as champions, and claimed to be champions; Derbyshire were not, and did not, and the modern list should therefore be corrected. As a matter of interest, Gloucestershire – playing Yorkshire, Surrey and Sussex – won four, drew one and lost one; Derbyshire – playing only Kent and Lancashire, both very weak teams at that time, won three and drew one.

After the writings by Holmes and Gibson, *Wisden* eventually published the list in 1901 but omitted 1873 and 1874. It was reproduced again in 1907 and then in 1911 *Wisden* added 1873 and 1874. Bowen's amended list was finally given *Wisden's* seal of approval in 1963.

The *Derby Mercury*, which surely would have lodged a claim to the Championship had it felt it was justified – made no mention of the title until the eve of the 1875 season when on 7 April it looked back on the previous season with the comment: 'The brilliant success achieved last year by Gloucestershire entitled that County to the enviable title of "Champion".'

Conclusive proof, indeed, and yet there may have been one influential follower of Derbyshire cricket who was unconvinced. This was John Cartwright, who had worked so hard to help bring the County Club into being. Thirteen years later, in August 1887, he wrote to the *Sporting Life* in an attempt to help retain the Club's first-class status. Cartwright referred to a sketch he had previously written in *Sporting Life* about Derbyshire's performances 'from the formation of the DCCC in 1870 to end of the season of 1875 . . . the latter being the season when Derbyshire stood No. 1 amongst the counties on account of not losing a match'.

Cartwright presumably meant 1874 since in 1875 Derbyshire lost three of their six matches against the other counties. It suggests that in 1887 at least, there was possibly one man who had felt Derbyshire had been Champions, although by that time *Lillywhite's Annual*, which had referred to 'least lost' as a yardstick, had not consistently applied it. It may have been that the 'least lost' custom dated further back than Bowen implied. Further research by Peter Wynne-Thomas (*The Cricketer*, May 1981) found that there was contemporary evidence of the use of the 'least lost' method. The earliest reference he discovered was 1879, but he cited several instances which suggested that the custom existed before that date.

Wynne-Thomas's assessment of the situation in the 1870s and 1880s was that 'least lost' was in general use for most of the period before it was gradually superseded by a points system in the early 1880s, the 'official' Championship starting in 1890.

In 1874 Gloucestershire defeated Yorkshire (twice), Surrey and Sussex, lost to Surrey and drew with Sussex. They did not meet Nottinghamshire, who were twice beaten by Yorkshire that summer. In the light of such a record the Gloucestershire claim to the Championship is justified, although at the time Derbyshire's unbeaten record was acknowledged and just might, in Cartwright's mind, have constituted a claim to be the 'No. 1' county.

By 1911, then, Derbyshire's deeds in the fine, dry summer of 1874 had led to them being accepted as Champions, although from time to time some doubt was expressed. When they won the Championship in 1936 *Wisden* (1937) commented on the doubts but added: 'The fact remains that no claim has been made to the Championship title of 1874 by any other county.'

In *Derbyshire County Cricket* (1924), F. S. Ashley-Cooper proclaimed Derbyshire as champions. In the 1953 edition of *Wisden*,

Mr W. T. Taylor, Derbyshire's secretary, repeated this in an article on the Club's history, observing of the 'least lost' method: 'What an inducement to play for draws!' At length, after initially declining to alter the accepted list, the editor of *Wisden* replaced Derbyshire with Gloucestershire as the 1874 champions. Nobody connected with the Club in 1874 could possibly have had any idea of the furore that season would arouse among future historians!

THE MYCROFT ERA

DERBYSHIRE NOW ENTERED A PERIOD of relative prosperity which was due almost entirely to the bowling of William Mycroft. With only a handful of first-class matches behind him Mycroft, at 34, became one of the most feared bowlers in England. It is an accolade which can be supported by an array of mind-boggling statistics.

Mycroft's late start in county cricket – he was 32 when he made his debut – is only partially explained by Derbyshire not playing first-class matches until 1871. At 15 he was showing great promise as a left-arm bowler, most of his early cricket being played with Brimington, Chesterfield and Staveley. Mycroft worked as an ironstone miner, thus launching the great tradition of Derbyshire miners (albeit usually colliers) who became fast bowlers.

It was another time-honoured tradition – that of a young player winning his spurs against the All England Eleven – that launched Mycroft on his spectacular career in county cricket, although in his case he could hardly be described as young. At 31 he played for Twenty-two of Chesterfield and District against George Parr's AEE, his analysis reading 75-52-50-8. Impressed, Parr secured his services for the remainder of the 1872 season and Mycroft continued his links with the touring eleven until it broke up. He was also engaged as a professional with the Birkenhead Park Cricket Club in 1872.

Early in 1873 Derbyshire, at last, invited Mycroft for a trial, having apparently turned a deaf ear to repeated earlier recommendations. He was asked to play for the Colts against the County XI and his reply was in keeping with another tradition inherent among the County's fast bowlers, in that it was typically blunt and forthright. He refused, saying that if he was good enough to play for England then he was fully qualified to play for the county side. Eventually the committee relented and Mycroft took six for 35 against Lancashire at Derby on the first occasion he bowled in a county match.

In all first-class cricket (1873–86) he took 863 wickets in 138 matches at 12.09. His best performance was nine for 25 against Hampshire at Southampton in 1876, a match in which he took 17 of 19 wickets which fell for 103 (Hampshire won by one wicket). Thirteen were bowled and four caught. In the first innings he had a hand in the fall of every wicket, holding a catch in the slips off George Hay. When Hampshire began the final innings of the game they needed 144 for victory – the highest total of the match – and the ninth wicket fell at 135, nine runs being needed with one wicket to fall. R.-G. Hargreaves (who married Alice Liddell, the inspiration for Lewis Carroll's *Alice in*

Wonderland) was well set and when only three runs were needed Mycroft changed ends. The first ball he delivered was hit for four by Hargreaves and Hampshire had scraped home in the face of some remarkable bowling by the Derbyshire man.

Mycroft also took nine wickets in an innings against Lancashire at Derby in 1875 and his record is spattered with similar spectacular analyses. He did well on his first appearance at Lord's for Derbyshire against MCC and he was quickly snapped up by MCC, remaining on the ground staff for 17 years, with the exception of 1880, when he was engaged by Lord Sheffield to coach the young Sussex players at

William Mycroft. His powerful left-arm dominated Derbyshire cricket for a decade. For several seasons he ranked with Alfred Shaw as the best bowler in England. His clashes with W. G. Grace were a feature of the 1870s and he clean-bowled him on four occasions.

HAMPSHIRE *v* DERBYSHIRE

Played at Southampton, 24 and 25 July 1876

HAMPSHIRE WON BY ONE WICKET

DERBYSHIRE	FIRST INNINGS		SECOND INNINGS	
W. Rigley	b Ridley	8	b Ridley	22
J. Smith, Esq	c and b Galpin	17	b Galpin	1
R. P. Smith Esq	c Tate b Galpin	1	c Tate b Ridley	6
S. Richardson Esq	b Galpin	0	c Hargreaves b Ridley	0
J. Platts	st Hyslop b Ridley	28	c Tate b Galpin	36
Amos Hind	b Ridley	13	st Hyslop b Ridley	3
T. Foster	b Galpin	15	c Foster b Ridley	11
W. G. Curgenven Esq	b Galpin	10	b Galpin	3
A. Smith	b Ridley	0	not out	0
G. Hay	not out	9	st Hyslop b Ridley	3
W. Mycroft	c Tate b Ridley	11	b Galpin	4
Extras	lb 3	3	lb 2	2
Total		115		91

BOWLING	O	M	R	W	O	M	R	W
Galpin	34	16	42	5	23	7	40	4
Mr Ridley	33.2	10	70	5	26.1	11	37	6
Holmes					3	1	12	0

HAMPSHIRE	FIRST INNINGS		SECOND INNINGS	
G. Carter Esq	b W. Mycroft	0	b W. Mycroft	30
Hyslop	b W. Mycroft	0	c Hind b Platts	8
G. H. Longman Esq	c A. Smith, b W. Mycroft	0	b W. Mycroft	19
A. W. Ridley Esq	b W. Mycroft	24	b W. Mycroft	13
C. Booth Esq	b W. Mycroft	14	b W. Mycroft	12
R. Hargreaves Esq	b W. Mycroft	4	not out	35
A. F. Jeffreys Esq	b W. Mycroft	4	b W. Mycroft	3
H. Holmes	b W. Mycroft	3	c Richardson b W. Mycroft	8
H. Tate	c W. Mycroft b Hay	0	c Richardson b W. Mycroft	1
F. Foster Esq	b W. Mycroft	10	c sub. b W. Mycroft	2
Galpin	not out	4	not out	1
Extras			b 5, lb 8	13
Total		63		145

BOWLING	O	M	R	W	O	M	R	W
W. Mycroft	21.3	13	25	9	42.1	11	78	8
Hay	14	6	19	1				
Platts	7	3	19	0	11	4	22	1
Hind					26	9	32	0

William Mycroft's career best bowling performance.

Sheffield Park. Twice he took more than a hundred wickets in a season, 157 at 12.27 each in 1877 and 116 at 10.31 in 1878, when his 101 at 9.45 each made him the first Derbyshire bowler to take a hundred wickets in a season for the County. But perhaps his most remarkable season was 1875 when 90 wickets at 7.38 placed him at the top of the national averages. His best days were behind him when the era of Test cricket began in England so his representative matches were limited to Gentlemen *v* Players, North *v* South and for the MCC and the All England Eleven, his clashes with W. G. Grace being a feature of this period.

What manner of man, then, was this bowler who put fear into batsmen everywhere, be they Derbyshire Colts facing him in the annual trials or the cream of England and Australia? He stood 5 ft 9 in and weighed 12 stone, his powerful physique making him the ideal build for a fast bowler – not too tall, and broad where it mattered! Contemporary publications described his bowling as fast left-hand, or rather above medium-pace, saying that he could spin the ball and was very fond of the yorker. It was this deadly yorker which brought him many wickets but some regarded his action as doubtful, particularly when he delivered this ball. During the 1880s there was to be an outcry against bowlers with suspect actions, although during this period Mycroft was reaching the end of his career. An article in the *Sportsman* in 1878 contains probably the most telling description of his methods of delivery:

> Mycroft's delivery is not the most easily to be seen, and batsmen need some nerve to play him with confidence when the ball bites or the wicket is at all rough. At times his action very closely resembles a throw, as he gets his arm very high up over his shoulder, and in a manner occasionally suggestive of a 'shy'. He is possessed of great power, is as strong as a lion, and as he pounds the ball down puts such a lot of powder into it that if it is at all short pitched, and the ground not of the smoothest, it operates in an unmerciful manner about the knuckles and ribs of a batsman.

His bowling brought out the best in Derbyshire's fieldsmen, R. P. Smith, his county captain for most of his career, excelling at point and Alfort Smith dispensing with the services of Frost at long-stop and standing up to take the deliveries of Mycroft, Hickton and Hay on those difficult pitches. George Hay first appeared in 1875 as a fast-medium bowler who served the county well for a decade. He was a member of the MCC ground staff for 30 years and in addition to his bowling he was a good fieldsman in the covers.

In 1883 Mycroft had a severe attack of rheumatism from which he never fully recovered. Towards the end of that season an England XI defeated Lancashire and Yorkshire in a match at Derby played for his benefit but the expenses were heavy and Mycroft did not make much from it. He played his final first-class match for MCC in 1886, a year after his retirement from county cricket, although he continued to play against minor opposition for MCC after this, turning out against Derby School only a year or two before he died. He also umpired first-class matches.

Derbyshire's bowlers had established a national reputation for accuracy: not a single wide ball had been delivered by Mycroft, Hickton, Platts, Flint and the rest from the club's formation to the end of the 1874 season. John Lillywhite's *Companion* was commenting in 1875 that: 'Derbyshire has so fine a bowler in Mycroft that we should never be surprised to hear of a victory over any opponent.' Victories there were, two by an innings over Kent at Derby and at Catford Bridge in 1875, and three in 1876 over Hampshire and Kent at Derby, and MCC at Lord's.

The bowlers were feared by all Derbyshire's opponents. Henry Perkins, the MCC secretary, described the side as 'ten bowlers and a wicket-keeper' which was a little unkind, as in 1875 they had made 307 against Kent at Derby, with W. G. Curgenven hitting 71 and Platts 60.

At the age of 28 Platts in 1877 now enjoyed his golden summer. He made history at Derby when he became the first Derbyshire batsman to make a century for the County in the match against Hampshire. The game started in what the *Derby Mercury* described as 'squally and unfavourable weather', Hampshire being dismissed on a lively pitch for 120. Platts, batting at number four, started steadily after two batsmen had received painful knocks. He opened his score with an off-driven four before rain stopped play for the day. The next day – Tuesday, 24 July 1877 – became historic in Derbyshire cricket. In fine weather they made 319, then their highest-ever total, and Platts hit three sixes and eight fours in his 115.

Derbyshire won easily and in the next match Platts nearly emulated his feat. Going in during Derbyshire's second innings against Yorkshire at Derby with his side 205 behind, Platts made 90 not out in a total of 220, a hard-hitting innings which helped Derbyshire to save the game. Platts, who was also to become the first Derbyshire bowler to perform a hat-trick for the County against Yorkshire at Derby in 1880, finished the season in 15th place in the national batting averages and at the head of the professionals with 478 runs in ten games, average 26.55.

Season 1877 was memorable too for the County, with five wins – a record number of victories – and two defeats in eight county matches, leaving them runners-up to Gloucestershire among the ten first-class

Derbyshire v Yorkshire at Sheffield in 1877. This is the oldest known photograph of a Derbyshire XI. Standing: R. P. Smith (capt.), J. Smith, W. Mycroft, A. Hind, W. Hickton, J. Horsley (umpire). Seated: L. Jackson, T. Foster, W. Rigley, A. Smith, J. Platts, G. Frost.

counties if the 'least lost' yardstick is adopted. Indeed, *Lillywhite's Companion* acknowledged that although even its 'staunchest supporters' would not claim for it the title of the second strongest county in England, 'even the enemy cannot deny that, statistically, it claims the second place'. Lillywhite could not acknowledge Derbyshire as the second-best eleven though, 'in the matter of matches won in proportion to matches played, the county claims second honours'. Interesting that three years after 1874 Lillywhite was hinting at the proportion of games won to matches played as a statistical yardstick and not 'least lost'.

Ironically the opening game of the season belied Derbyshire's reliance on Mycroft for Lancashire were beaten by 34 runs at Derby while he was playing for North against South. Hampshire were beaten both at Southampton and Derby and there was a one-wicket victory over Kent at Derby after a splendid game, an unbeaten 54 (twelve fours) from Tom Foster proving the decisive innings when Derbyshire had to make 189 to win. In the return at Tunbridge Wells Kent were beaten by three wickets.

It was a false dawn. In 1878 Lancashire were beaten by an innings at Derby and Hampshire by a similar margin at Southampton. Yorkshire were beaten for the first time by Derbyshire by seven runs after a thrilling encounter which was watched by a large August Bank Holiday crowd at Derby, Mycroft's bowling tilting the balance in a low-scoring game. But there were six defeats in ten county games and further reverses at the hands of the MCC and the All England XI. This was followed by almost total humiliation in the wet summer of 1879 when only six games were arranged, Nottinghamshire, Lancashire and Yorkshire being the opponents. Both the Yorkshire matches were won, Mycroft's bowling being the decisive factor, but there was a complete breakdown at Trent Bridge when Derbyshire were dismissed for 16, their lowest-ever first-class total. Going in after Nottinghamshire had made 159 they lost their last four wickets without adding to the total and, following on, two more wickets without scoring – six wickets falling without a single run being scored.

Shaw and Morley bowled unchanged throughout the match, Morley having a match analysis of 33.2-18-35-12. The two victories over Yorkshire followed but in the return against Nottinghamshire at Derby Shaw and Morley again bowled unchanged in totals of 59 and 36, Morley's match analysis being 61-39-53-14. In two games he had captured 26 Derbyshire wickets at three and a third runs apiece, Shaw having 13 with one run out. After these disasters the Nottinghamshire games were dropped from Derbyshire's fixtures between 1880 and 1885.

In 1880 the county met the Australians for the first time, the game being played at Derby in perfect Whitsun weather and watched by large crowds. The pitch was in poor condition, Spofforth taking 13 wickets in the match which the tourists won by eight wickets. Hay took five for 49 in the Australian first innings, but of eight county matches that summer five were lost and two won, Kent being beaten at Derby and Sussex at Brighton. The captain, R. P. Smith, Foster, Rigley, Platts, Mycroft, Hay, Alfort Smith (in his final season) and G. B. Barrington played in every county match so the nucleus of a reasonable side was there.

Barrington, a gifted amateur batsman from Kirk Langley, was never able to bridge the gap between club and county cricket. In 1881 he made 190 for The Friars against the Gentlemen of Nottinghamshire at Derby, sharing a first-wicket partnership of 287 with Captain D. A. Johnston (216), The Friars total reaching 742. Barrington scored prolifically in this class of cricket but did not really enjoy the first-class game and had little success.

The Club had long since recognised the need to foster young talent by staging such trials as the county eleven meeting the Colts in against-odds games or North v South Colts matches. One young player to develop through this system was wicket-keeper Jimmy Disney, who quickly impressed and made his County debut against Sussex at Derby in May 1881. That summer he held seven catches out of 13 wickets that fell in the match against Yorkshire at Derby, finishing the season with 24 dismissals in eight games.

Disney's emergence was not the only bright feature of the 1881 season for at long last an amateur batsman of quality and class, Ludford Charles Docker, established a regular place in the side. L. C. Docker was born at Smethwick in Staffordshire and educated in Birmingham. In his debut summer the 20-year-old Docker produced such good form that he finished sixth in the national batting averages in 1881 with 447 runs in eight first-class games and an average of 31.92. A powerfully built man, six feet in height, he had a penchant for driving and was an elegant and stylish player. Docker's biggest innings was 107 at Maidstone and he made 52 and 80 at Brighton, sharing in the County's first century opening partnership of 113 with Shuker (40). Two of his brothers also appeared for the county and L.C. was to captain the side in 1884 before moving to Warwickshire in 1887.

Docker was not the only amateur to strike form on that southern tour in August 1881. Fast-medium bowler Henry Evans had made his debut in 1878 and played three matches in 1881. He took six for 60, including a hat-trick at Brighton, and seven for 47 against Kent during the same week. In his last game for the County he took three for 63 against the 1882 Australians at Derby. Thus in his third match he performed a hat-trick and in only five games during his career he took 19 wickets in the seven innings in which he bowled at 13.26 each. It is a perfect illustration of the difficulties which faced Derbyshire. Evans and his brother Thomas, who played twice in 1883, both rose to occupy high positions with the Midland Railway, which restricted their appearances in county cricket. In a county with such limited resources as Derbyshire such losses could be ill-afforded.

Evans' bowling and Docker's hundred earned Derbyshire a three-wicket victory at Maidstone but the only other win in eight matches in 1881 was by five wickets over Sussex at Derby. The 1882 campaign proved a dismal one, five out of six county matches being lost and only one being won. This was an innings victory over Sussex at Derby in which Mycroft produced what was to be his last great match-winning performance in a county match for Derbyshire. He and Platts were the leading wicket-takers although John Richardson, a fast bowler from Duckmanton, had a good season; like James Stubbings, another pace bowler who had done well in 1880, he made only a few appearances for the County. Docker and Foster, who made 101 against Yorkshire at Derby and 52 out of an innings total of 77 against Lancashire, also at Derby, were the best batsmen.

These were changing times, however, and in 1882 Arthur Wilson succeeded Walter Boden as hon secretary, a position he was to hold with a one-year break until 1889. He was born at Mitcham and educated at Rugby and Oxford, although he did not gain a place in either eleven. While at Rugby he helped establish the famous amateur team the Butterflies and for more than a quarter of a century he directed the operations of The Friars in Derby.

The 1882 season was notable for the first appearances of two all-round cricketers of immense promise, William Cropper and William Chatterton, the one destined for tragedy, the other to become one of the finest cricketers produced by the County. Cropper, a middle-order right-hand batsman and left-arm medium-pace bowler, was to prove a most useful all-rounder and, with a peculiar jump in his run-up to the wicket, he became known as the bowler with the kangaroo hop. Sadly, his career was only short-lived. On Sunday, 13 January 1889 he died in the dressing room of Grimsby Town FC on the morning following the match against Staveley after being accidentally kicked in the stomach by a Grimsby player. He was too ill to be moved to hospital and his death at 26 was a severe blow to the County.

Chatterton was born at Thornsett. At the age of 13 he moved with his parents to Hyde in Cheshire, learning his cricket with the Flowery Field Club. In 1880 he accepted his first professional engagement at Christ's College, Finchley, and coached students there for the next three years, being spotted by the Derbyshire executive. Chatterton, a sound, middle-order right-hand batsman and right-arm slow bowler, was also an excellent fieldsman and it soon became obvious that a rare talent had been unearthed. After three moderate seasons he broke through in 1885, after which he was offered an engagement by the MCC at Lord's. He was to become a batsman who played with great ease and confidence and a fielder who was equally good whether in the deep or close in. He was also a fine rugby player, one of the fastest three-quarters of his day with Burton-on-Trent and other clubs, and a good soccer forward with Derby County.

Chatterton and Cropper soon established themselves in the team but others who would later play a significant role in Derbyshire cricket took longer before they became regulars in the side. Sydney Herbert Evershed, for example, who made his debut in 1880, was on the threshold of a long and distinguished career which was to span 20 years and lead to the captaincy of the County. Evershed, only 19 when he played his first county match, had enjoyed some successful seasons at Clifton and although it would be another nine years before he made a real impact he was already rich in promise. Of medium height and strongly built, he crouched as he awaited the ball which he often met with all his weight behind his strong arms. He excelled with off-side hitting but often pulled his drive and got himself out in an endeavour to score quickly. An excellent rugger half, he played for Midland Counties and was reserve for England. Later he was knighted and his was a name famed in association with Burton-on-Trent and brewing. Evershed was one of four brothers who played for the County, S.H., Edward and Wallis playing in first-class games and Frank second-class. S. H. Evershed was to captain the County in 1891–98.

Another future great name to emerge in this period was Levi George Wright, who was to become one of the County's most successful batsmen. L. G. Wright, who was born in Oxford in 1862, came to Derby as an assistant schoolmaster in 1881 and after impressing in Colts matches first appeared in 1883 but with little success. It was a long time before 'L.G.' bridged the gap between playing for Derby Midland and the County Club but he gained valuable experience. An attacking opening batsman Wright was predominantly a forward player who had a strong defence, and like many of his era scored chiefly on the off-side. He was to become a brilliant fieldsman at old-fashioned point, where his first county skipper, R. P. Smith, had excelled, and was occasionally to keep wicket. Also he left a valuable literary contribution in his autobiography *Scraps from a Cricketer's Memory* which was eventually published by the Derbyshire County Cricket Supporters Club in 1980. Wright puts flesh on the bones of Derbyshire cricket of his time in this fascinating book, with recollections of his early days when he played alongside R. P. Smith, Mycroft, Platts and Hay, and a more detailed look at the main part of his career, which was to last until 1909.

Another young amateur to show promise was E. A. J. Maynard, a batsman from Chesterfield who, like S. H. Evershed, L. G. Wright and Chatterton was a future captain. Maynard first appeared in 1880 but he was never able to produce his best form in county cricket with any degree of consistency. Educated at Harrow and Cambridge University he captained the side in 1885 and 1886 and part of 1887. George Glossop Walker was another product of this period. He was a left-hand batsman and left-arm bowler who began his career as a slow bowler and graduated to fast. Walker, an amateur, began his career in 1881 and L. G. Wright recalls that he was one of the happiest cricketers who ever played for the County. Always ready for a joke or a story he used to say he only played to please his father.

Walker was destined to become a stalwart member of the attack and so, too, was George Porter, a fast-medium bowler who made the most of his height (6 ft 2 in) and his weight (200 lb) and who delivered the ball at a good pace. Porter, who was born at Kilburn, was always associated with Spondon and was known as the 'Spondon Giant'. His career was to be ended by a back injury in 1896 and he later became an umpire before his death from sunstroke at the age of 46.

Derbyshire won two of their eight county games in 1883, with a good win over Surrey at Derby in the first meeting between the counties in which some fine bowling by James Brelsford saw them home. Brelsford, a medium-pace bowler, had a remarkable debut season in which he took 24 wickets in seven matches at 19.20 each. Curiously he was not persevered with, for apart from a solitary match in 1886 he never played again.

The other victory of 1883 was at Brighton where Sussex were defeated by 29 runs after Derbyshire had trailed by 113 and been forced to follow on. In their second innings Sussex were dismissed for 74, Joe Marlow, a medium-pace bowler who had first appeared in 1879, taking six for 27.

It was a reasonably successful season, particularly as Mycroft was no longer able to salvage the lost causes. This was the year in which he was struck down by rheumatism – his benefit year – and there was a dramatic decline in his performances. His day was over and with it, despite the arrival of new players, there came a startling collapse of Derbyshire cricket. Mycroft's bowling had played a significant role in 70 per cent of Derbyshire's victories between 1874 and 1882; now there was no match-winner and the County's results suffered.

It was a period of transition. Shuker and Rigley finished in 1882, R. P. Smith, Platts and Foster (who in 1883 held six catches in an innings when keeping wicket at the Oval) finished in 1884, Mycroft in 1885 and Hay a year later. A ground staff was formed, largely as a result of the efforts of the club president, Hon W. M. Jervis, and Chatterton, was appointed ground bowler. But the experiment was short-lived and faded through lack of funds.

Smith, who had led the side for eight seasons, suffered a broken bone in his hand in 1883 and relinquished the captaincy, L. C. Docker taking over in 1884. With Mycroft in decline and the team undergoing change Derbyshire embarked on one of the worst seasons in their history. Home and away matches with Lancashire, Surrey, Kent, Yorkshire and Sussex were arranged but all ten games were lost. There was an innings defeat by the Australians at Derby, with only a seven-run victory over MCC at Lord's to lighten the gloom, apart from the arrival of newcomers such as the brothers Frank and Walter Sugg and the fast bowler Frank Shacklock.

The Suggs were born at Ilkeston, Walter in 1860 and Frank two years later, and each appeared for Yorkshire before joining their native county. Frank, at 22, made an immediate impact with Derbyshire by making 73 in his first innings in the season's opening game at Old Trafford. A tall, quick-sighted batsman Sugg was a fine, aggressive

Derbyshire, 1884. Standing: W. Wood-Sims, W. Cropper, F. H. Sugg, W. Chatterton. Seated: S. H. Evershed, G. B. Barrington, L. C. Docker, G. G. Walker, W. Evershed. On ground: Foster and Marlow.

player who excelled in leg-side hitting and powerful driving. He stood 6 ft and his attacking style meant that he could be a poor starter but he could turn the course of a match, particularly on a bad wicket. Sugg was also a brilliant outfielder who could cover a lot of ground very quickly and he had a safe pair of hands in the deep. Unfortunately this fine cricketer stayed with Derbyshire only until 1886, joining Lancashire the following year and playing in two Test matches in 1888, remaining with the red rose county until his career ended in 1899.

His brother Walter was not quite in the same class but he was a good, free-hitting batsman, a useful medium-pace bowler and a fine cover fieldsman. Although he was not to prove as successful as Frank he had a good eye and flexible wrists and sometimes looked the better batsman. More importantly for Derbyshire he spent his career with them, playing his final match in 1902.

Frank Shacklock stood nearly 6 ft and bowled fast, sometimes around the wicket, with a slinging action which made the ball swing

away. He was considered especially difficult because of this pronounced swerve from leg, varied with an off-break that came very
quickly off the turf. Shacklock began his first-class career with
Nottinghamshire in 1883, a year before joining Derbyshire only to
return to Notts in 1886. Sir Arthur Conan Doyle is said to have based
the name of his famous detective Sherlock Holmes on Shacklock after
batting against him but it was more probably derived from a
combination of Shacklock and the Nottinghamshire wicket-keeper
Sherwin. Mycroft became the Christian name of Holmes' brother,
thus maintaining the Derbyshire connection.

Following the disasters of 1884 things could hardly get worse and
there was an upward trend in 1885, Derbyshire pulling off a
magnificent victory over Lancashire at Old Trafford. They were all
out for 54 in their first innings and trailed by 161, but some fine batting
by Frank Sugg, Cropper and Eadie helped them to a total of 318 and,
ultimately, a 73-run victory.

There was also a fine win over Hampshire at Southampton
following a record-breaking performance by Frank Sugg, whose 187
not out led to Derbyshire's highest total to that date, 427. Sugg hit a
six, a five and 17 fours. Shacklock took five wickets in Hampshire's
first innings and Cropper wrecked the second with seven for 25
including a hat-trick, Derbyshire winning by an innings and 243 runs.
The return at Derby was won by seven wickets and Shacklock was
again in splendid form in Platts' benefit match against Yorkshire at
Derby, taking eight for 45 and five for 97, match figures of 13 for 142,
the game being drawn.

Sugg made 462 runs in ten first-class matches, averaging 27.17,
Cropper being the leading bowler with 35 wickets at 14.68 each, but
apart from Chatterton the remaining batting was weak. Nevertheless
there was now a more settled appearance about the side and they were
by no means the worst of the first-class counties in 1885. Maynard had
succeeded Docker as captain; the batsmen, led by Docker, Frank
Sugg, Chatterton and Cropper, were capable of making respectable
scores; the bowlers, with Shacklock, Cropper, Walker and Marlow,
aided by Disney behind the wicket (Tom, half-brother of William,
had kept in 1884 when Foster was ill), were a match for all but the best.

Seldom can optimism have been so misplaced. At the end of the
season Shacklock rejoined Nottinghamshire and of nine inter-county
games in 1886 eight were lost and one drawn. There was a good fight
against the Australians, who won by six wickets after Giffen had taken
16 wickets in the match, and Yorkshire earned victory the hard way at
Leeds and Derby. Gloucestershire were met for the first time in 1886,
George Davidson taking nine for 42 in an innings against them at
Derby.

Indeed, the 20-year-old Davidson was the find of the season. He was born at Brimington, the son of Joe and brother of Frank, who also played for the County, and he was to become one of the finest all-rounders Derbyshire ever produced. Davidson developed into a stylish batsman but it was as a bowler that he made his initial breakthrough. A man of barely medium height he had an appearance that suggested great strength of muscle and constitution. He started his run-up from near mid-off and bowled at a good pace with great accuracy, making the ball move appreciably off the pitch. In common with many of the great fast-medium bowlers he had the ability to keep going for long spells without losing accuracy and, apparently, pace.

The rot, however, had set in. In the wake of Shacklock's decision at the end of the 1885 season to rejoin Nottinghamshire, Frank Sugg went to Lancashire after the 1886 season and Docker to Warwickshire. These were severe losses. In players like Cropper, Davidson, Disney and Chatterton Derbyshire had the basis of a good side, but few counties could have withstood the loss of three of their most talented players. Funds were low and the 1887 fixture list was depleted, for only three first-class counties – Yorkshire, Surrey and Lancashire – played against Derbyshire. Sussex declined a fixture, and the Kent match was omitted because of lack of cash.

All six first-class county games were lost and the batting averages made sorry reading, Davidson topping the list with 302 runs (average 25.2), Cropper having 208 (17.4), while Walker, Davidson and Cropper led the bowlers. Maynard resigned the captaincy owing to lack of form, Chatterton taking over, and the publication of the averages in the national press was accompanied by a concerted cry for Derbyshire to be deprived of their first-class status. The *Morning Post* commented that for years Derbyshire had been in 'very depressed condition'. It went on:

> Funds have been scanty, the wickets on the county ground at Derby have been bad, their best batsmen have deserted them, their captains have scarcely ever been able to win the toss, and defeat has followed upon defeat with such frequency that of the 33 first-class county matches played during the past four years there is only one victory to place against 29 lost games . . .
>
> Even in the face of this accumulation of disasters Derbyshire might still have been regarded as a first-class county. But the reduction of the programme to six matches is fatal, and for the future Derbyshire must be looked upon as second-class.

In its look at the 1887 season the *Derby Mercury* pointed out that Derbyshire had met the strongest counties with a young and inexperienced team and that, in a batsman's season, they were stronger in bowling. Derbyshire's record of one win and 29 defeats in 33 games between 1884 and 1887 is not quite as dismal when the two victories over Hampshire in 1885 are included (three wins in 35 games) as they are today. At the time they were not considered first-class by the leading publications assessing Derbyshire's right to remain among the premier counties. Even so the evidence against Derbyshire was overwhelming. In 1887 there were two victories over Essex and one over Leicestershire, both not then first-class, but the 'championship' table leaves no room for doubt;

	P	W	D	L	Points
Surrey	16	12	2	2	13
Lancashire	14	10	1	3	$10\frac{1}{2}$
Nottinghamshire	14	8	3	3	$9\frac{1}{2}$
Yorkshire	16	6	7	3	$9\frac{1}{2}$
Middlesex	10	4	4	2	6
Kent	14	1	5	8	$3\frac{1}{2}$
Gloucestershire	14	1	4	9	3
Sussex	12	2	2	8	3
Derbyshire	6	0	0	6	0

The unofficial points system allowed one point for a win and half a point for a draw.

In an atmosphere bent on classification and the proper organisation of a County Championship, a mood which had changed since the comparatively carefree outlook of the 1870s, Derbyshire's position seemed untenable. Arthur Wilson made an impassioned plea for mercy but perhaps the most poignant moment came in August when John Cartwright wrote to the *Sporting Life* in an attempt to retain the first-class status of the club he had helped to create:

Will you kindly allow me, as a cricketer of over forty years experience, and as a native of Notts, to say a few words in favour of Derbyshire, respecting whose claims to rank as a cricketing county I wrote in the *Sporting Life* as far back as 1866, and of whose performances, from the formation of the DCCC in 1870 to the end of the season of 1875 I wrote you a sketch, the latter being the season when Derbyshire stood No. 1 amongst the counties on account of not losing a match? Now, after years of struggling against numerous and trying difficulties, some of them caused by stronger clubs seducing some of the best men from their native shire, and just when there is a likelihood of the club being assisted out of its financial troubles, the public is informed that Derbyshire must stand out from the first-class shires. Why is this, and who has the settling of such matters? Had Derbyshire allowed the second-class counties to defeat her then there would have been some reason in the suggestion. Essex and Leicestershire are excellent elevens, but the Peakites have shown themselves superior, and until they show themselves only equal to such they ought to be encouraged in their efforts to retrieve their position. County cricket is the best of all cricket, and those in authority ought to do all in their power to promote the best form of England's most manly and health-giving sport.

It was all to no avail. The short-lived County Cricket Council was formed in 1887 with a view to legislating on county qualification and classification but its scheme in 1890 for a division of the counties into three classes with automatic promotion and relegation was to founder and lead to its dissolution. The second-class counties had opposed that proposal and there was, too, the meeting of representatives of eight first-class counties on 10 December 1889 which agreed on a method of deciding the County Championship by ignoring drawn matches and subtracting losses from wins, an 'official' Championship decided by the counties thus starting in 1890. By then Derbyshire's fate had long been sealed in arbitrary fashion by the London sporting press with Charles Pardon, editor of *Wisden*, one of the chief protagonists. The newly formed Cricket Reporting Agency was clearly anxious to draw a definitive line between first- and second-class counties and Derbyshire were doomed. Pardon, from 1887 onwards, used a points system in *Wisden* to decide the order but this produced a triple tie in 1889, in turn leading to the meeting of the counties in December that year. Pardon set out the position in *Wisden* in 1888 when he wrote of Shacklock and Docker leaving Derbyshire, commented on the 29 defeats in 33 matches over the past four seasons and said that through lack of funds the Kent fixture had been abandoned. Kent were the only county of first-class rank in which the result was to some extent not a foregone conclusion against Derbyshire.

'For these various reasons Derbyshire can no longer be regarded as a first-class county. We think the team still good enough to do themselves credit in less powerful company and we hope after a time to be able to welcome them back among the leading shires,' Pardon added. *Wisden* and other leading publications ceased to regard Derbyshire as first-class after 1887 although *Cricket* was not to follow this line until a year later. In 1888 Derbyshire arranged seven games against first-class counties, one more than 1887, and *Cricket* regularly included them in its weekly tables for 1888 until early in August, although the others had dropped them before the start of the season.

In retrospect the later cases of Northamptonshire and Somerset, both of whom had long spells at the bottom of the Championship table without paying the penalty, can be cited but all things considered Derbyshire's relegation was justified.

No pleas of ill-fortune, of players deserting the Club, of lack of funds or promises of better things to come, could erase the sorry record of few first-class fixtures and 29 defeats in 33 or 35 games, whichever way you look at it, during the past four seasons.

SKELETON IN THE CUPBOARD

THINGS WENT FROM BAD TO WORSE with Derbyshire in 1888 seemingly betwixt and between first and second class. Not surprisingly the County's executive was reluctant to lose any opportunity of meeting first-class opposition yet this was precisely what *Wisden* advocated at the time of Derbyshire's reduced status.

In 1888 the club played seven matches against first-class counties, losing six games and defeating Yorkshire. Of the ten counties making up a Second Class Championship they won and lost against Essex and were beaten by Leicestershire. Three matches hardly qualified them for any sort of standing among the second-class counties and they duly finished ninth or next to the bottom in a competition in which some teams played ten games.

Clearly it irritated *Wisden*, Pardon, in his quest for order and conformity, making the point that they had not played enough matches against either first or second-class counties strictly to entitle them to come into competition with either. Advocating a second-class competition in which the counties played a similar number of games *Wisden* suggested that Derbyshire should drop their match against Yorkshire in favour of one against, say, Northamptonshire. That would have been unfortunate since the brightest aspect of the summer was a victory over an admittedly weak Yorkshire side at Derby in August.

The match was a triumph for Joe Hulme, who had a match analysis of 15 for 70, eight for 30 in 26 overs in the first innings and seven for 40 in the second. Needing 83 to win Derbyshire got the runs for the loss of three wickets, L. G. Wright making an undefeated 35.

Hulme, a left-arm fast-medium bowler, who stood 5 ft 8 in and weighed eleven stone, gave a fine display of accurate and hostile bowling.

Appearing in the match against Yorkshire was W. H. Hodges, a Cheltenham schoolboy who played a couple of games in 1888 and who, at 16 years 10 months, became the youngest player to represent the County. Fred Swarbrook, four months younger when he played against Cambridge University in 1967, eventually deprived him of this record. The second-class era had got away to a good start with victories over MCC at Lord's and Essex at Leyton but this success against Yorkshire was the only other bright spot in another dismal summer which brought nine defeats in 12 games. At Old Trafford Derbyshire were dismissed for 17; in the return at Derby spectators, angry with Frank Sugg who was now playing for Lancashire, barracked the visitors, Hornby leading his men off the field for 15 minutes.

In many ways the lack of playing success was indicative of a general malaise throughout the club, although off-the-field efforts were being made to right the ship. In 1884 there had been major changes at the County Ground. The Derby Recreation Company, the lessees of the racecourse who sub-let the ground to the cricket club, decided to widen the racecourse. They took over a strip of land 20 yards in width in front of the Grandstand. The pitch had to be moved further to the west as a result and, as it was already a considerable distance from the

Derbyshire's 'grand old man of cricket', L. G. Wright, who shared in an opening partnership of 191 with Charlie Ollivierre in the famous match against Essex. He was 47 when he finished his career in 1909, his 14,800 runs and 20 hundreds then being club records. Almost to the end of his life – he died in his 91st year – 'L.G.' could be seen at the County Ground, and his 90th birthday in January 1952 was marked by a celebration at the Bell Hotel, Derby.

Grandstand this could no longer be used as a pavilion. Members and others subscribed to a fund for a new pavilion and in 1884 this was erected on the west side of the ground, both ground and pavilion coming into use at the same time. Derby County Football Club played on a pitch to the north of the ground, the whole area now occupying some 17 acres. Two years later Mr James Ragg moved the pavilion to the north side of the wicket, renovated it and added a second front towards the football enclosure. Soccer fans were able to watch Derby County from the verandah of the pavilion until the Rams moved in 1895.

The soccer club was formed in 1884 as an off-shoot of the cricket club, their first colours being those of the cricket club – chocolate, amber and pale blue. The association was so strong that the football club wanted to call itself Derbyshire County FC. The local FA objected to this but for some time the club was known as the Derbyshire County. Derby County's first home game was played on 27 September 1884 and in 1888–89 they became one of the 12 founder members of the Football League. They moved to the Baseball Ground in 1895. Steve Bloomer's recollections of life during the winters at the County Ground make interesting reading to cricket lovers and players who have endured the biting summer winds: 'We had no high falutin' gadgets, but we did have plenty of fresh air and cold water.'

The Nottingham Road ground was the venue of an FA Cup final in 1886 when Blackburn Rovers defeated West Bromwich Albion 2-0 in a replay watched by more than 15,000 people. Several FA Cup semi-finals were played there and in March 1895 England defeated Ireland 9-0, Bloomer scoring twice on his international debut.

County cricket matches were to be played on the new site until 1954, the following year the playing area being moved back towards the Grandstand, in all probability to a point near to that on which the first county match was played in 1871. The old racecourse grandstand was demolished in 1911 but racing continued until August 1939, Gordon Richards riding in the last meeting, Steve Donoghue also having ridden on the course. The ground was used by the army during the Second World War and afterwards the Derby Town Council decided that racing brought too many undesirables to the town and it did not recommence. The Recreation Company's lease lapsed during the war and the council's Parks Department laid out soccer pitches around the area of the cricket ground, the present grandstand being used as a vantage point after the next set of changes occurred on the ground in 1955.

Despite the work carried out during the 1880s the state of the ground matched that of the Cricket Club's playing fortunes but the appointment of Albert Widdowson as groundsman brought about a dramatic improvement. Widdowson was born at Bingham in Nottinghamshire and became groundsman at Lower Broughton, Manchester. He was recommended to Derbyshire by George Porter, who was then professional at the Club. Anxious to return nearer to his home at Bingham Widdowson accepted an offer of a weekly wage of 22 shillings and he was appointed groundsman at Derby on 8 September 1889.

Later he said that when he first sighted the ground he nearly caught the train back to Manchester. Great clumps of long grass surrounded the playing area and the cricket net, which had been missing for some time, was discovered rotting beneath piles of cut grass. Widdowson applied himself to his task of scything, digging, rolling, patching and top dressing, tramping mile after mile over the eight-acre ground with his horse-drawn roller and mowing machine. Eventually the County Ground, Derby, was to enjoy a reputation of being one of the finest pitches in the country and the perfection of Widdowson's work is perhaps best reflected by some of the massive scores which were to be compiled at Derby in the 1890s. He was to remain as groundsman at Derby until September 1930, completing a span of 41 years.

A £1,000 debt in 1887 was cleared largely as a result of the efforts of the president, Mr G. H. Strutt, and the hon secretary, the Hon W. M. Jervis, although all too soon this was followed by yet another financial crisis. Then in 1889 there was a real shot in the arm for Derbyshire cricket with the arrival of Frederick Robert Spofforth, the famous Australian 'demon' bowler. Hostile and fast, Spofforth's great talent lay in the clever concealment of his variations of pace and a perfectly controlled off-break which he delivered with deadly effect. He was, without question, one of the greatest bowlers of all time.

Spofforth had already made his mark against Derbyshire, taking 13 for 85 against the county in 1880, ten for 57 in 1882 and 12 for 83 in 1884. He was back again in 1886 and it was then that he courted Phillis Marsh Cadman, daughter of a tea merchant, Joseph Cadman, of The Cedars, a grey mansion on a hill above the village of Breadsall. Joseph Cadman, who was born at Quarndon, had prospered as a grocer and tea dealer in Lancashire, founding the Star Tea Company which had shops, warehouses, cafes and hotels in London and other cities, including Derby. On 23 September 1886 Spofforth, now 33, married Phillis at Breadsall Parish Church. Among the guests was Sam Richardson, Derbyshire's assistant secretary and former captain.

Spofforth and his bride returned to Australia but his wife could not settle there and in July 1888 they came back to England, renting a house in Kedleston Road, Derby. Spofforth became Midland representative for the Star Tea Company but although he was now concentrating on business he let it be known that he would like to play

Frederick Robert Spofforth, the famous Australian 'demon' bowler.

in an occasional match for Derbyshire, who naturally welcomed the opportunity.

It was hoped that Spofforth would be available to play in 1889 and that the authorities would relax the two-year qualification rule which meant he would have to live in the county for that period before playing. The Derbyshire Committee, meeting in November 1888, proposed an amendment to the rule and, because Derbyshire were second-class, it was thought there would be little reason why he should not play. But the amendment was rejected by 12 votes to two by the County Cricket Council on 10 December 1888 so at the annual general meeting in February 1889 it was decided to ask each of Derbyshire's opponents if they would consent to the appearance of Spofforth. This was done, Nottinghamshire and Yorkshire agreeing to his playing, but Surrey objecting.

In the event Spofforth played only against Yorkshire in 1889, Surrey and Nottinghamshire having both agreed to play against 'Derbyshire plus Mr Spofforth', only Yorkshire giving unconditional assent to his appearance. He attended the annual meeting of the

County Club on 27 February 1889 and became a member of the new committee. It was reported that the amount owing to the bank had increased from £227 to £808.

When Spofforth turned out for the County against Yorkshire he was applauded by 'the largest crowd seen at the County Ground for some time' and took seven for 45 in the Yorkshire first innings and eight for 36, six of them bowled, in the second – match figures of 53-19-81-15 – but Yorkshire won the game by 54 runs.

The return game at Sheffield was ruined by rain and Spofforth did not bowl. This was to be the only away match he played for Derbyshire, suggesting that his business interests – he was then in his 36th year and would be looking to further his career with the Star Tea Company – had priority over his cricket.

The 1889 season saw two major changes in the laws of cricket, the over being increased from four balls to five and the batting side for the first time being allowed to declare its innings closed. Derbyshire played four matches against the second-class counties, two being drawn and Essex and Leicestershire defeated. They thus finished runners-up to Warwickshire. However they lost five games against first-class opposition, a one-wicket victory over MCC at Lord's being the only victory. In the match against Essex at Leyton Chatterton made 168 and Davidson 129 in a total of 384 for five, Derbyshire declaring for the first time in their history.

Spofforth's arrival and the appointment of Widdowson as groundsman were positive steps but still all was not well with Derbyshire cricket. At the annual meeting on 25 February 1890 the committee report referred to the 'great evils' of indiscipline among the players, with reports of some of them staying up late and drinking to excess during the period of a match. One of them 'could neither bowl nor field' on the last day of the Essex match because he had been drinking and smoking until four o'clock that morning. But the most serious aspect concerned the former captain Sam Richardson, who had been assistant secretary since 1880.

In his spare time Spofforth had thoroughly examined the Club's account books and had discovered serious discrepancies. It appeared that Richardson had embezzled around £1,000 from the funds of both the cricket and football sections of the Club and had departed for Spain.

Richardson had, on his own admission, systematically robbed the Club for the past nine or ten years, possibly even longer. Not only had he secretly issued, and received payment for, a large number of tickets both for football and cricket for which he had not accounted, he had also 'from time to time appropriated considerable portions of the receipts from matches'.

54

The accounts showed £1,018 due to Crompton and Evans' bank and the estimated adverse balance was £861, besides £148 due from Richardson on the ticket account. But £400 had been promised, including £100 each from Mr W. H. Worthington, president in 1890, and Mr G. H. Strutt, and £50 from the Duke of Devonshire.

At the annual meeting in the Bell Hotel, Derby, some blame was attached to the committee 'whose duty it was to control Mr Richardson and to investigate the accounts'. The hon secretary, Arthur Wilson, who was elected a vice-president of the Club, said he accepted some blame, feeling he should have 'looked after Richardson a great deal sharper' even though he lived some distance away. But the meeting agreed that Mr Wilson was not to blame for what had occurred. There were reports about professionals failing to receive their money during the progress of a match and Mr Wilson commented on the 'extraordinary, almost imperial power' which Richardson had had over the destinies of the professional cricketers of Derbyshire. When he asked one player why he had not told the committee he had not been properly paid he was told: 'I didn't like to say anything. I thought Mr Richardson had more to do with putting me in the team than anybody else.'

The meeting heard of the committee's implicit trust in Richardson and there was a suggestion from Mr Ley that if he had been watched more closely he would not have robbed the Club and would now have been an honest tradesman in the town. It was agreed that in future the committee would be instructed to receive receipts for any payments over ten shillings.

But in a leader the *Derby Mercury* of 5 March 1890 felt that much of the condemnation of the committee was unnecessary. It accepted that the confidence was too freely given but pointed out that the committee members would have other business to attend to besides the Cricket Club and that in any case no complaints had been received.

The Richardson incident marked one more chapter in Derbyshire's tale of woe but at least there was one bright feature in the AGM in that Spofforth was appointed captain for the 1890 season, his first task being to restore morale and self-respect. The Australian and J. H. Richardson were also appointed auditors.

Spofforth led by example, although he did not play until the visit of the Australian tourists in July. A low-scoring game was spoiled by rain, the tourists making 108 and 75 for nine, with Spofforth taking three for 34 and six for 42, and Derbyshire 54. In the next game he led the County to a splendid innings victory over Yorkshire. Derbyshire made 312, L. G. Wright scoring 80, Chatterton 66 and Davidson 58. Yorkshire were all out for 177, Davidson taking five for 69 and Spofforth two for 84 in 34 overs. In the second innings they made only

110, Spofforth having four for 20 and Davidson three for 15. Spofforth's best performance of the season was against Leicestershire at Derby in August when he took nine for 56 in the first innings and five for 58 in the second to return a match analysis of 54-19-114-14. He also took seven for 26 in the innings victory over Norfolk at Derby. Of Derbyshire's 14 games he played in six, taking 42 wickets at 11.80 each, Davidson and Walker being the leading wicket-takers, with Hulme absent playing league cricket with Nelson in Lancashire.

Spofforth's influence could be seen at all levels. In the second-class competition Derbyshire finished second with victories over Leicestershire (twice) and Essex in four games. Yorkshire were beaten at Sheffield and two innings wins were registered over Norfolk. Surrey, the first-class Champions , were dismissed for 79 at Derby, Davidson taking six for 36, but won the game by 28 runs.

Heading the batting averages in 1890 was Harry Bagshaw, a left-hand batsman who first played for the County in 1887. Bagshaw was also a useful right-arm medium-pace bowler and he was to become one of the stalwarts of the side in the 1890s as a free-hitting opening batsman who was to forge a successful association with L. G. Wright. He later became an umpire and was buried wearing an umpire's white coat and with a cricket ball in his hand.

The Spofforth era was almost over, however. He played for several local clubs, such as Littleover Free Lances and Belper Meadows but at the end of the season there were suggestions that he might be moving to the London area to expand the Star Tea Company and these reports proved to be correct. Star Tea became a limited liability company in 1892 and when Joseph Cadman died in 1897 Spofforth, who had moved to Hampstead in 1891, succeeded him as managing director. He played only once more for Derbyshire after the 1890 season, turning out against Leicestershire in May 1891.

Thus ended Spofforth's association with Derbyshire. S. H. Evershed, who in his early days had preferred rowing to cricket, was appointed captain. W. Barclay Delacombe had become the first paid secretary in 1889, the executive side of the club at least having achieved stability mainly as a result of Spofforth's influence.

There was a good win over Yorkshire at Headingley but the most noteworthy achievement of 1891 and perhaps Derbyshire's entire spell in the second-class wilderness was a ten-wicket victory over Surrey at The Oval. Surrey, Champions in three consecutive years, 1890–92, were immensely strong but some magnificent bowling by Davidson (six for 41) and Porter (four for 60) dismissed them for 104, the pair bowling unchanged and each delivering 32 overs. Derbyshire replied with 187, Bagshaw making 80 and Chatterton 59, and then Porter (six for 61) and Davidson (three for 41) – again unchanged save for two overs from Walter Hall, a medium-pace bowler from Whitwell – wrecked Surrey's second innings for 111, Derbyshire making 31 without loss to win in two days.

Nottinghamshire won both matches against Derbyshire comfortably in 1891 but the County's overall record of six wins and four losses in 12 games was respectable. In the second-class competition they won three and lost two of six matches to finish third in the table.

During the winter of 1891–92 Chatterton toured South Africa with W. W. Read's English team. He headed the batting averages with 956 runs, average 41.13, and opened the England innings in the only Test at Cape Town in March when he scored 48.

Within a month of Chatterton's return he was carrying his bat for 109 not out for MCC against Lancashire at Lord's but he did not produce his best form for Derbyshire in 1892. Davidson had an excellent year with the ball, and in the second-class competition Hampshire and Cheshire were each beaten twice and Leicestershire once, five wins in eight games leaving them runners-up to Warwickshire. Overall 13 matches were played, with five wins – the second-class games -- and seven defeats.

In 1893 there was an even better performance when seven of the eight second-class matches were won and Derbyshire were joint champions with Warwickshire, the two clubs not meeting that season. But none of the eight games against first-class opposition were won.

In the spring of 1894 Derbyshire followers got their wish when it was decided by the captains of the leading counties that matches played by Derbyshire, Warwickshire, Leicestershire and Essex would be regarded as first-class. Later in the year MCC, to whom the matter had been referred, issued a scheme for the future regulation of the County Championship. The four new first-class counties did not compete in the 1894 championship because the fixtures had already been arranged but in 1895 they were to join the other nine teams. In October 1894 it was decided to add Hampshire to the list although their 1894 matches were considered second-class.

INTO THE GOLDEN AGE

TO BE ABLE TO COMPETE ON EQUAL TERMS with the best of his contemporaries is perhaps the finest accolade that can be paid to any cricketer. In that magnificent golden age of cricket which Derbyshire entered in 1894 William Storer's batting, for a time, was on a par with the best. He was also England's wicket-keeper before losing his place to Dick Lilley, one of the finest 'keepers of all time.

Storer was a member of a Derbyshire side which, on paper, seemed to differ only a little from that which had had such a miserable time in 1887. But whereas then it was young, inexperienced and lacking in self-confidence, seven years on it was hard, professional and of age.

Along with L. G. Wright, Harry Bagshaw, William Chatterton, Walter Sugg and the captain S. H. Evershed, Storer was a member of one of the strongest batting sides in the County's history. George Davidson was an all-rounder of quality, Evershed now a captain with three years' experience of leadership and Hulme, Porter and

Derbyshire in 1894. Standing: W. Chatterton, S. Malthouse, G. Porter, C. Evans, J. H. Hulme. Seated: G. A. Marsden, G. G. Walker, S. H. Evershed (capt.), L. G. Wright, W. Sugg. In front: G. Davidson and W. Storer.

G. G. Walker completed, with Davidson, a fine quartet of bowlers. It was a good, solid team and Storer provided it with that extra spark of talent which touched on greatness.

Like his nephew Harry of later soccer and cricket fame, Billy Storer was a man of his area, having been born in the mining district of Ripley about ten miles north of Derby. He was an outspoken individual, a man who was no respecter of persons, nor one who suffered fools gladly. His early career was handicapped by the club's relegation and his batting showed little progress until 1891. His wicket-keeping, however, earned him a reputation far beyond Derby and in 1893 he was chosen to play for MCC against the Australians at Lord's, a match in which he earned wide praise for the manner in which he took the express bowling of Kortright, standing up to a man who was considered the world's fastest bowler and not allowing a single bye in the second innings.

His career was now set to blossom. There was a splendid opportunity for a young wicket-keeper, Pilling having died, Sherwin being near the end of his career and Lilley not yet ready for big cricket. In 1895 Storer made over a thousand runs, including a memorable 93 for the Players at Lord's.

For Derbyshire in 1896 he had a magnificent season, heading the batting averages with 1,125 runs, average 51.13, and making two separate hundreds in the match against Yorkshire at Derby, 100 and 100 not out. He followed this with an unbeaten 142 at Leicester to complete three consecutive centuries, and in the next game, the return with Yorkshire at Sheffield, scored 16 and 122 to extend the run to four hundreds in five innings, a total of 480 runs in three completed innings. In all first-class matches he scored 1,313 runs, average 42.35, finishing seventh in the national averages.

Storer's batting was described as resourceful rather than stylish. He was strong in defence and adept at pulling. He would frequently cut or drive a good length ball for four off the middle stump, a somewhat risky venture but one which often brought him rich rewards on the fast Victorian pitches. Sir Pelham Warner described him as 'a somewhat ugly bat, but he was a rare cutter and hooker, and full of courage and determination'. As a batsman, incidentally, Storer was orthodox early in his career but adopted a crouching stance later on. Keeping wicket, he bent rather than squatted and was upright when taking the ball. He was also a useful leg-spin bowler.

After another good year in 1897 he was chosen to tour Australia as wicket-keeper/batsman with A. E. Stoddart's 1897–98 party – the first Derbyshire player to be chosen for a tour 'down under' while with the County. He appeared in all five Tests, making 208 runs, average 23.11, and holding eleven catches. Ranji described him as a batsman who, though lacking in style, knew no fear and had no nerve. Ranji said that he demoralised bowlers by pulling good length balls from the off almost to square leg but also cut, leg-glanced and cover-drove to effect. It was a costly tour, though, for Storer injured a thumb in the first Test and fractured his right forefinger in the fourth game. This injury was to prove troublesome in later years and was one of the reasons why Storer gave up keeping wicket at a relatively early age.

There was to be one more Test, the Trent Bridge game against Australia in 1899 when W. G. Grace made his final appearance for England and Wilfred Rhodes, J. T. Tyldesley and Victor Trumper played in their first Tests. Storer also appeared in 13 matches for the Players against the Gentlemen between 1893 and 1901 in addition to his six Tests. Seven of these were in the 'showpiece' game at Lord's – a record number for a Derbyshire player, Chatterton appearing in four Lord's games, D. B. Carr and Les Jackson in three, Copson, Mitchell and Leslie Townsend in two, and Cochrane, Willatt, Bestwick, Davidson, Gladwin, William Mycroft, George Pope and Denis Smith in one each.

In 1898 Storer averaged 50 in the Championship and was selected for the Players at Lord's as a batsman, making 59 and 73 off an attack which included Kortright, while Lilley kept wicket. In all games he scored 1,548 runs, average 41, and was one of *Wisden's* Five Cricketers of the Year in the 1899 edition. In the Oval game of 1898 he made 86 for the Players, sharing a last-wicket partnership of 96 with Lockwood. His career-best score of 216 not out came against Leicestershire at Chesterfield in 1899 but 1900 was to be the last of his great seasons, his career going into decline, illness playing a part in this. He did well out of his benefit game against Yorkshire in 1902 but after a dismal time three years later he finished with first-class cricket.

There are many tales of Storer's outspokenness and unhappily he was part of a dressing room in which the atmosphere must have been fraught, to say the least, at times. During a game at Southampton in 1894, there was an incident which seems typical of the festering nature of Derbyshire's team spirit in those days. The players visited the Isle of Wight and during dinner Davidson made an unkind remark about George Porter's feet. Porter, upset, left the room, and Chatterton, who as senior pro was at the head of the table, remonstrated with Davidson. The pair of them did not speak for the rest of the season unless it was absolutely necessary. L. G. Wright tells of the feuds between 'the three leading professionals' (who were Chatterton, Storer and Davidson) and their unhelpful attitude towards young players, particularly those on trial. Walter Hall 'turned it up in disgust' because he felt he could not get fair treatment owing to the attitude of these players and a committee which could see no wrong in what they did. Joe Hancock, a left-arm medium-pace bowler, was another who had an unpleasant time when he first joined the team. Wright felt that jealousy of each other, as well as anyone else, was the chief cause of the trouble.

Consequently Derbyshire were not always welcome visitors in the 1890s although paradoxically all three 'star' players appeared in the big games at Lord's. There undoubtably was ability, for in the first home match of 1894 Lancashire were dismissed for 35, Hulme taking seven for 15, Derbyshire winning by five wickets. Perhaps the most creditable display was at Sheffield where Yorkshire were beaten by nine wickets. Davidson (eight for 33 and one for 21) and Hulme (one for 43 and nine for 27) bowled unchanged throughout the match in which Yorkshire were dismissed for 81 and 50. Leicestershire (twice), Warwickshire and MCC were Derbyshire's other victims in 1894, six of the 14 first-class games being won. It was an excellent year for Davidson, who took 97 first-class wickets at 13 each, 90 of them for the County.

Derbyshire competed in the reshaped County Championship for the first time in 1895 and had a highly successful summer, five victories (over Warwickshire, Yorkshire, Hampshire, Lancashire and Leicestershire) leaving them in fifth place.

Acrimony apart, Derbyshire's three leading professionals enjoyed a season of almost unbroken success. George Davidson may well have played for England in 1895 had there been a Test series. His 1,296 runs and 138 wickets made him only the third man in history to achieve the 'double' and the first professional to do so. For Derbyshire in the Championship he took 89 wickets, he and Porter virtually carrying the attack, Hulme being absent in league cricket.

There was 'a most sensational victory' (to quote W. J. Piper, the County's early historian) over Lancashire at Derby. Davidson took eight for 25, including a hat-trick in the first innings, and Storer made 108 (his maiden first-class century) to set a target of 303. Lancashire were cruising comfortably to victory when, with 73 needed, Porter took the last five wickets in six overs, Derbyshire winning by 63 runs.

By now Widdowson's pitches were among the best in the country and 1896 brought a summer of sunshine and towering scores, particularly at Derby. Four victories over Hampshire (twice), Leicestershire and Warwickshire (MCC also were beaten at Lord's by one wicket) in 16 games enabled Derbyshire to finish seventh in the Championship table.

Their best performance was reserved for the match against Lancashire at Old Trafford in August. There had been showers but the pitch seemed to be in fairly good condition when Derbyshire began their innings five minutes after noon on Monday. They were captained by W. Barclay Delacombe, Evershed being absent, and began badly, Wright, whose 81 against the Australians at Derby that summer was an individual record which lasted until 1948, and Bagshaw being out with the score at 26, but Chatterton and Davidson took the total to 123 for two at lunch.

In the afternoon Davidson was badly missed off Briggs at long-off when he was 78. Chatterton made a chanceless 104 in 195 minutes, the pair adding 208 for the third wicket in less than three hours, Davidson reaching his century after batting for a similar period of time. He and Storer continued to pile on the agony for the Lancashire bowlers, 300 going up in 260 minutes. By the close Derbyshire were 381 for three, Davidson having made 185 and Storer 56.

Rain delayed the start until after one o'clock on Tuesday and the 400 went up after 350 minutes. Davidson reached his double century with a boundary which also took him past 1,000 runs for the season but at 211 he survived an easy stumping chance. By lunch the score was 450 for three and when play resumed at ten to three Storer reached his century after three and a half hours. The total reached 500 after 430 minutes, Frank Sugg almost bowling Davidson with a lob. After the fourth-wicket stand had reached 308 Davidson was caught at long off for 274, an innings which lasted seven and a quarter hours. It was the first double century recorded by a Derbyshire batsman and it remains an individual record for the County.

Davidson was out with the score on 542 and the innings eventually closed for 577 after 495 minutes, Storer making 116, his fifth century of the summer.

For all the warring factions in the Derbyshire side the batting at Old Trafford was of high quality, L. G. Wright describing the form of Davidson, Chatterton and Storer, who completed his thousand runs for the season in this game and became the first batsman to exceed a four-figure aggregate for the County, as superb. All three exceeded 1,000 runs in all first-class games that season although only Storer did so for the County. Bagshaw, Wright, Evershed and Walter Sugg also did well and it was a far cry from the hapless surrenders to Shaw and Morley a few years earlier. The attack, however, left much to be desired. Davidson and Hulme led the bowlers but Porter struggled, Bennett fell away and Walker made only a few appearances. Indeed, Porter's career was ended by a back injury and before the 1897 season began Hulme entered hospital for a kidney operation. Of an already inadequate attack only Davidson remained and Derbyshire had a lean time. Nine of 16 championship games were lost, not a single victory recorded and they finished bottom of the table.

The batting was still formidable and at Trent Bridge Derbyshire ran up a total of 570, Wright (133), Davidson (121) and Evershed (90)

LANCASHIRE *v* DERBYSHIRE

Played at Manchester, 10, 11 and 12 August 1896

MATCH DRAWN

DERBYSHIRE	FIRST INNINGS	
Mr L. G. Wright	c Sugg b Hallam	3
H. Bagshaw	b Briggs	13
W. Chatterton	b Hallam	104
G. Davidson	c Sugg b Briggs	274
W. Storer	c Paul b Briggs	116
W. Sugg	c Paul b Briggs	11
J. Hulme	c Tyldesley b Hallam	5
Mr G. A. Marsden	st Smith b Briggs	4
Mr H. G. Curgenven	c Sugg b Hallam	13
Mr W. B. Delacombe	not out	2
G. Porter	b Briggs	0
Extras	b 22, lb 6, w 4	32
Total		577

BOWLING	O	M	R	W
Briggs	90	32	185	6
Hallam	73	31	127	4
Baker	20	8	45	0
Lancaster	46	18	97	0
F. Ward	20	9	39	0
Paul	11	2	28	0
A. Ward	4	1	11	0
Tyldesley	3	1	6	0
Sugg	4	2	7	0

LANCASHIRE	FIRST INNINGS		SECOND INNINGS	
Mr E. Rowley	b Davidson	50	c Curgenven b Chatterton	14
A. Ward	b Davidson	8		
A. Paul	b Porter	50	c Curgenven b Chatterton	0
J. H. Tyldesley	c and b Hulme	1	not out	20
F. H. Sugg	st Wright b Storer	96	not out	26
F. Ward	b Davidson	10		
G. R. Baker	c and b Hulme	30		
J. Briggs	lbw b Hulme	18		
A. Lancaster	c Curgenven b Hulme	7		
C. Smith	not out	1	c Wright b Curgenven	3
A. Hallam	b Hulme	4		
Extras	b 1, lb 1, w 1	3		
Total		278		63

BOWLING	O	M	R	W	O	M	R	W
Davidson	57	34	75	3				
Hulme	48.3	19	94	5				
Porter	29	10	57	1				
Curgenven	7	1	16	0	15	4	31	1
Storer	15	3	33	1				
Chatterton					12	4	16	2
Bagshaw					4	0	16	0

Umpires: W. A. Woof and A. Chester

Davidson made a record score for the County.

George Davidson, the leading Derbyshire all-rounder of the 1890s, whose 274 against Lancashire is the highest score for the County.

getting amongst the runs and the 21-year-old Maynard Ashcroft giving a glimpse of his potential with 99.

Ashcroft was born at Chorlton, Manchester, and played for the County on a residential qualification for he made his home for a short time at Mellor, a small village near New Mills. His studies were to prevent him from making regular appearances before he qualified as a doctor in 1902 and his career was regrettably brief for he retired after the 1906 season to begin a practice at Levenshulme, Manchester. Ashcroft, who jointly captained the side in 1904–05, was a free-scoring right-hand batsman who strengthened the amateur element in the side and was also a useful off-break bowler.

Davidson toiled away in the attack in 1897, his 56 championship wickets costing 22 each. There was no Porter or Joe Hulme this year and the main support for Davidson was provided by Joe Hancock, with Storer and Chatterton chipping in with useful wickets. Arnold

Warren, later a great name in Derbyshire cricket, appeared in eight Championship games but his five wickets cost 63 runs each.

A sequence of 22 Championship games without a win was ended by a ten-wicket victory over Hampshire at Southampton in 1898 and this was followed by an innings victory over MCC at Lord's. Davidson took 12 wickets in this match and followed it with 15 for 116 against Essex at Leyton only to finish on the losing side. His remarkable run of success continued against Leicestershire at Derby, a match Derbyshire won by an innings, when his nine wickets completed a haul of 24 wickets in two games, his brother Frank taking six for 36 with his medium-pace bowling in the first innings. Frank's bowling looked full of promise but he was not to enjoy a lengthy career. In 1898 umpires began a campaign to stamp out throwing and Frank Davidson's action was regarded as suspect. Wright thought his problem was caused by a stiff arm and he said that even Chatterton was not above suspicion because of the amount of wrist action he developed. Fred Bracey, a slow left-arm bowler who played for the County in 1906–14, also came under suspicion, L.G. saying that no objection was raised until he started to take wickets. Another bowler in trouble was Noah Buxton, of Codnor, who appeared in seven matches between 1902 and 1911. His career was to end abruptly after the only match in which he played in 1911 when he delivered three overs at The Oval and was then taken off following a complaint by Tom Hayward, for 'cobbing' them – a common term for throwing. None of these bowlers was no-balled during the throwing controversy around the turn of the century but the suspicion left a cloud over their careers.

After the victory over Leicestershire not another match was won and of 15 Championship matches two victories left Derbyshire in ninth position. The bowling was the main problem and of several colossal scores registered against Derbyshire the most spectacular was at the new venue of Queen's Park, Chesterfield. The park had been opened in honour of Queen Victoria's Golden Jubilee in September 1887 with a lake, a cricket ground, a gymnasium and football pitch and a cycling track. Bands played twice weekly during the summer, there were flower shows and boating on the lake, the first cricket match taking place there in 1894.

It was clear that Chesterfield had a first-class leisure area and in 1898 a new cricket pavilion was opened. Derbyshire had played a match at Saltergate Recreation Ground, home of Chesterfield FC in 1874 but since their reinstatement to first-class in 1894 all home games had been staged at Derby. This continued until 30 June, 1 and 2 July 1898 when a match was played against Surrey at Queen's Park, the visitors winning by an innings. D. L. A. Jephson's lobs caused problems for Derby-shire's batsmen, much to the disgust of the home crowd who deemed his bowling unfair. A feature of cricket at Chesterfield has been the predominantly mining community which has so frequently subjected the players to ribald comments of varying knowledge and humour, this being one of the earliest examples.

Financially the experiment of playing at Queen's Park had been successful and this was not lost on the Derbyshire veteran Walter Sugg, who had been allocated the match against Yorkshire at Derby for his benefit. He persuaded the committee to transfer the game to Chesterfield and the move was successful, the proceeds amounting to £340. But this was the only bright feature of the game from Derbyshire's point of view. Two major factors were highlighted – the paucity of Derbyshire's attack and the ability of high-class batsmen to score freely on the new ground.

With Hulme in poor health for much of the season, Frank Davidson had earned a place in the side but another young bowler, Bill Bestwick, who played in eight games with little success, was twelfth man against Yorkshire. When George Davidson, who was not fully fit and should not have played, broke down after bowling only one over the scene was set for a run feast.

Virtually the whole responsibility for the attack devolved on Frank Davidson and the 38-year-old G. G. Walker, and the Yorkshire openers, J. T. Brown and John Tunnicliffe, took complete command. By the close of play on Thursday Yorkshire were 503 without loss, Brown being on 270 and Tunnicliffe 214. With no declaration permissible until the last day Yorkshire batted on, the opening partnership reaching 554 in 305 minutes before Tunnicliffe was out for 243. Five minutes later Brown, who gave four chances, was dismissed for 300, each batsman having hit 48 fours. Derbyshire, forced to follow on 544 behind, lost the match by an innings and 387 runs and the record was to endure for 34 years until Holmes and Sutcliffe made 555 at Leyton in 1932.

However, Derbyshire were not always on the receiving end. About a fortnight before the Yorkshire match their batsmen had enjoyed remarkable success in the game against Hampshire at Derby where they took full advantage of the perfect pitch which Widdowson had prepared and amassed a total of 645 which has remained a County record. It was the August Bank Holiday fixture and was graced by glorious weather which attracted 2,300 people to the ground by one o'clock. Evershed won the toss and had no hesitation about batting first, opening the innings himself with L. G. Wright. Both batted with the utmost confidence, 50 going up after half-an-hour, Wright reaching his half-century after 55 minutes and the hundred partnership and Evershed's fifty coming after an hour. Incidentally, with the score at 80 Quinton had troubled Wright with lobs – interesting that an underarm bowler should go on during the first hour of the first day's play!

Evershed (67) played on with the score at 134 in 75 minutes, having struck six boundaries, and Bagshaw then helped push the score along until he was caught at slip for 19 at 174. Wright and Storer carried the total to 186 for two at lunch, Wright having batted with 'admirable correctness'.

The crowd had almost doubled when play resumed, Wright reaching his century with a snick to leg and a straight drive for four after 150 minutes. Soon after 3.30 pm the 250 went up but at 296 Wright was caught for 134 in just over three and a quarter hours, hitting 14 fours. Storer, who passed his thousand runs for the season during the innings, and Chatterton took the score to 350 by 4.40 pm but Storer survived a difficult chance in the slips. Shortly before five he reached his century after two and a quarter hours, the score being 372 for three. There was a short break then for refreshments but with only three added Storer was well taken at the wicket for 100. His innings included ten fours. Chatterton reached his 50 with a four to leg at 5.40 pm and 450 was passed at 6.20 pm, Chatterton having made 90. He reached his hundred with a four through the slips from the last ball of the day, the close of play score being 477 for four with Chatterton and Davidson together on 103 and 34 respectively.

Next morning, before another large crowd of 2,500, runs came quickly, the 500 being passed after 330 minutes. Davidson reached his 50 after 110 minutes but after more rapid scoring from Chatterton Quinton went on with lobs at the Nottingham Road end. He caught and bowled Chatterton with his second delivery for 142 (one five, 15 fours) in just under three hours, surviving a chance in the long-field at 74. He and Davidson had added 176 for the fifth wicket, the total now being 552 for five.

At a quarter to one the score reached 600 in six and a half hours, a very rapid rate of scoring even by 'Golden Age' standards. Davidson, who reached his hundred, and Sugg put on 68 in half an hour before Sugg was out and then Davidson left at 634 after making 108 in 165 minutes (eleven fours). Quinton's lobs now met with some success against batsmen trying to force the pace and the innings closed at a quarter past one for 645. It was Derbyshire's highest ever total and also the biggest ever recorded in a first-class match on the ground, exceeding the Australians' 625 in 1896.

L. G. Wright recalled how Davidson's innings had not gone 'according to plan'. Evershed had asked him to get out as soon as possible because they already had sufficient runs on the board. But

DERBYSHIRE *v* HAMPSHIRE

Played at Derby, 1, 2, 3 August 1898

MATCH DRAWN

DERBYSHIRE	**FIRST INNINGS**	
Mr L. G. Wright	c Barrett b Webb	134
Mr S. H. Evershed	b Steele	67
H. Bagshaw	c Barton b Steele	19
W. Storer	c Bennett b Martin	100
W. Chatterton	c and b Quinton	142
G. Davidson	c Steele b Quinton	108
W. Sugg	c Martin b Quinton	33
Mr E. M. Ashcroft	c Webb b Quinton	10
Mr A. Charlesworth	c Poore b Lee	4
F. Davidson	not out	0
J. Hancock	c Bennett b Quinton	0
Extras	b 11, lb 11, w 1, nb 5	28
Total		645

BOWLING	**O**	**M**	**R**	**W**
Tate	39	7	118	0
Martin	33	6	109	1
Steele	37	8	109	2
Lee	21	4	58	1
Quinton	21	0	93	5
Webb	30	4	91	1
English	4	1	16	0
Barton	6	0	23	0

HAMPSHIRE	**FIRST INNINGS**		**SECOND INNINGS**	
V. Barton	b G. Davidson	5	c Storer b F. Davidson	2
Mr E. I. M. Barrett	c Storer b G. Davidson	18		
A. Webb	c Chatterton b G. Davidson	5	lbw b F. Davidson	51
Capt F. W. D. Quinton	c Evershed b G. Davidson	0	not out	101
Major R. M. Poore	not out	121	b F. Davidson	15
Mr E. A. English	c Chatterton b G. Davidson	0	not out	14
Mr E. C. Lee	b F. Davidson	44		
Mr D. A. Steele	b Chatterton	17		
Mr R. A. Bennett	b Chatterton	4	b G. Davidson	16
E. Tate	c Evershed b Storer	15		
Martin	c F. Davidson b G. Davidson	3		
Extras	b 6, lb 2	8	b 26, lb 3, w 1, nb 3	33
Total		240	(for 4 wkts)	232

BOWLING	**O**	**M**	**R**	**W**	**O**	**M**	**R**	**W**
G. Davidson	31.4	14	42	6	42	19	73	1
F. Davidson	31	12	68	1	36	20	42	3
Storer	19	0	77	1	5	0	16	0
Hancock	6	0	23	0	14	1	36	0
Chatterton	7	2	22	2				
Sugg					10	1	26	0
Bagshaw					4	1	6	0

Umpires: A. F. Smith and A. A. White

Derbyshire's highest innings total.

Derbyshire line up for the camera after making their highest-ever score – 645 – against Hampshire at Derby in 1898. Standing: (unknown), W. Chatterton, W. B. Delacombe (sec.), H. Bagshaw, J. W. Annable, A. Wilson, W. Sugg, W. J. Piper (scorer). Seated: A. Charlesworth, E. M. Ashcroft, L. G. Wright, W. Boden (president), S. H. Evershed (capt.), J. Hancock, F. Davidson. On the ground: G. Davidson, W. Storer. Note the old Derby grandstand in the background.

instead of hitting out and risking his wicket in the pursuit of quick runs Davidson preferred to play his own game and gradually reached his century.

Although by 1898 Arnold Warren and Bill Bestwick had taken their first tentative steps into county cricket new talent was badly needed. Derbyshire had quite a respectable record in the 1890s but most of the regular members of the side were now the wrong side of 30. Then on 8 February 1899 there came a grievous blow when George Davidson died at the age of 32. A bout of influenza developed into pneumonia and Davidson's death was sadly typical of many professional cricketers of his day in that he left a widow, six children under the age of seven, and, despite a benefit in 1897, little money. He had his faults but he had been a key figure in the team since pre-relegation days and had rejected an approach from Warwickshire to continue his Derbyshire career.

His death left followers of the Club wondering how Derbyshire would be able to get sides out. Although Joe Hulme returned to the side in 1899 it was obvious that at least one young bowler had to be found, for the ageing Hulme, changing to bowling slows, could no longer be expected to shoulder the responsibility. Fortunately the burly figure of Bill Bestwick emerged from the pits near his native Heanor. He was to become one of the greatest fast-medium bowlers ever to play for the County and certainly the most remarkable character.

At the age of eleven Bestwick was working at Coppice Colliery near to his home and later played soccer for a team known as Heanor Salmon Tin Rovers. In a challenge cricket match between this outfit and Heanor Town the young Bestwick took eight wickets and scored 60 runs, thus becoming an overnight sensation. He had never played cricket seriously before but his magnificent physique and great strength tempted him to try his luck as a fast-medium bowler and the results were astonishing. His performances at Heanor attracted the attention of Arthur Millward, an old Worcestershire player, and he arranged for Bestwick to have a trial with Warwickshire. Bestwick and that county failed to agree terms and consequently the player went to Leicestershire for whom he appeared in several club and ground games. Here L. G. Wright, who was playing for Derby Midland at Leicester, noticed Bestwick playing in another match on an adjacent pitch. He was soon booked for his long career with Derbyshire.

Sir Samuel Hill-Wood, that great patron of cricket in Glossop, who was then plain S. H. Wood and was County captain in 1899–1901, also took an interest in his career. He was largely instrumental in Bestwick getting an opportunity in county cricket after a spell with Nelson in the Lancashire League.

Davidson's death resulted in Bestwick's selection for all 18 Championship matches in 1899 and he took 48 wickets at 29.52 each. He provided useful support for Hulme, who dismissed 93 batsmen at 22.86 apiece, a magnificent achievement after his illnesses and injuries. Evershed resigned the captaincy owing to business pressures, S. H. Wood taking over, but Wood could not play very often and T. A. Higson, later a Test selector in 1931–34, led the side frequently in his first season with the Club. Not surprisingly, in view of their misfortunes Derbyshire finished last with only two victories, over Hampshire at Southampton and Essex at Leyton.

In 1900 there was another desperate fight to avoid bottom place. Victories over Hampshire at Southampton and Worcestershire at Chesterfield enabled the County to finish third from the bottom. Storer, Wright and Bagshaw each exceeded a thousand runs and Ashcroft and A. E. Lawton also did well. Lawton, always known as Bertie, was a very tall man who became a prodigious hitter and a magnificent fieldsman. He was born in Cheshire into a wealthy family and was involved in the cotton industry. He was to play for Derbyshire in 1900–10, and he became friendly with W. G. Grace, who often included him in his London County teams and sometimes stayed at Lawton's Cromford home when he visited Derbyshire. Years later Bertie Lawton became a BBC commentator.

Bill Storer was now beginning to give way to Joe Humphries behind the stumps and concentrate on batting. Humphries, who was born at Stonebroom, played in a few games in 1899 and made eleven appearances in 1900, showing exceptional promise, although he was only a moderate batsman. By 1902 he had emerged as Storer's natural successor and was to enjoy a long and rewarding career.

Hulme and Bestwick still shouldered the burden of the attack but new players were now appearing. Sam Cadman was to enjoy a career as player and coach with the County which was to span nearly 40 years. Cadman was born in Lancashire but soon came to live in Glossop, where he showed promise as an all-rounder, a steady opening or middle-order batsman and a medium-pace bowler. In 1900 he joined the staff, impressing in Colts matches and playing in a couple of Championship games.

The link with Glossop was apt, for Derbyshire played two games at the Peakland venue in 1900, their first match having been played in 1899 when Lancashire were the visitors. Samuel Wood guaranteed the financial success of cricket there and he regularly brought first-class cricketers to turn out for his Glossop team in the Central Lancashire League. One of these was the West Indian Charles Ollivierre, who played for St Vincent, the island of his birth. He was a member of the first West Indian team to tour England in 1900 and stayed in England to qualify for Derbyshire, playing for Glossop during this period. Ollivierre's first appearance for the County was in 1901 against London County and his qualification was complete in July 1902. He was an attractive, if rather inconsistent opening batsmen who on his day could destroy an attack but who found difficulty coming to terms with English pitches.

Although L. G. Wright, Storer, Chatterton and Lawton each made over a thousand runs in 1901 – Lawton captaining the team in the frequent absence of S. H. Wood – Derbyshire had a disastrous summer, losing 13 of 20 Championship matches and failing to win any of them. Again they finished in bottom place as the old stars began to fade. There were more newcomers: Gilbert Curgenven, younger son of Dr W. G., an aggressive batsman who had headed Repton's averages and who was to enjoy a colourful if erratic career, and Ernest 'Nudger' Needham, a solid, dependable left-hand batsman who did not play county cricket until he was 28. His greatest fame was achieved on the soccer field where, as a wing-half, he won 16 international caps and appeared in three FA Cup finals for Sheffield United. Needham ought to have been tried earlier, for he scored 57 on his debut against the South Africans. This at a time when gloom surrounded Derbyshire's batting and the bowlers were often on the receiving end, the final averages reflecting the misery. Bestwick's 71 championship wickets cost more than 27 each, Hulme had 53 at 42 apiece and Storer 28 at 51.

Possibly Arnold Warren had the most cause for despondency in 1901. The fast bowler dismissed seven batsmen in the Championship and conceded 592 runs in 149 overs. It seemed impossible to imagine that within three years he would become one of the leading fast bowlers in the country and one of the finest cricketers to play for the County. The speed was evident but it was to take a spell in the leagues to iron out the creases. Mr W. T. Taylor, the former Derbyshire secretary who saw all of the County's fast bowlers from Warren and Bestwick to Ward and Hendrick, had the impression that he was probably the fastest of them all, at least on his day:

> He was hostile and very fast with a devastating off-break off the seam. He possessed a long, bounding run-up to the wicket, a quite lovely action and he was one of the finest opening bowlers in the country. He was also a first-rate slip fielder and a useful batsman, indeed, a very fine all-round cricketer.

Mr Taylor was also an admirer of Bestwick. The burly miner already looked every inch a bowler. He had a lovely run-up to the wicket and a beautiful action but perhaps his most outstanding ability was his phenomenal stamina. He could maintain a good pace at around fast-medium for long spells and had the rare knack of being able to strike back after heavy punishment, an outstanding attribute for a fast bowler in any era but particularly in the high-scoring Golden Age.

Warren's bowling showed a distinct improvement in 1902, when four matches were won and Derbyshire rose to tenth in the table. A win over Hampshire at Southampton ended a sequence of 33 Championship games since July 1900 without a win, and victories over Warwickshire at Derby (by an innings and 250 runs, after Derbyshire had made 561, Ollivierre scoring 167 and Lawton 126), Essex at Leyton and Leicestershire followed. Lawton's appointment as captain brought about an all-round improvement in form and team spirit and with the captain hitting three centuries, Ashcroft two and Wright and Ollivierre one apiece, it meant that four amateurs had recorded a century during the summer, a rarity for Derbyshire in a period when most counties were rich in amateur batting but when they themselves had not enjoyed similar prosperity.

It was as well the amateurs rose to the occasion for Storer's form declined, Chatterton was dropped and retired at the end of the season and Walter Sugg and Harry Bagshaw were also at the end of their careers. Tom Forester, who had previously played for Warwickshire, also made his first appearance in 1902. A right-arm medium-pace bowler, he did not find the time to play regularly until 1911 but his accurate length and skilful variation of flight and spin made him a valued member of the attack when he was available.

In 1902 a Derbyshire gentleman who was on a visit from Australia, Mr C. Arnold, presented the Club with £525, which cleared a debt and left a useful balance in hand. But a wet summer in 1903 caused more problems. Four of the Championship games were won, leaving Derbyshire twelfth in the table, but the rain had an effect on gate receipts.

There was a win over Surrey at Chesterfield, Bestwick taking seven for 20 in their first innings of 68 and a victory over Leicestershire at Derby. Then came an historic match against Nottinghamshire at Derby in which Derbyshire recorded their first-ever victory over their neighbours on even terms. Some good batting by Wright (52) and Ollivierre (71) enabled Derbyshire to make 234 and then Cadman and Warren bowled their side to a first innings lead of 117. A steady display by Needham (51 not out) helped to set Nottinghamshire a target of 316 and with Warren taking six for 93 Derbyshire won by 114 runs. More good bowling by Warren and Bestwick and a maiden century from Needham brought about the other win that year, over Hampshire at Derby.

Warren and Bestwick were now well established as the spearhead of the attack and the 41-year-old Joe Hulme gave them excellent support in his final season, beginning in remarkable form but dropping out of the side later on.

Inside two years Chatterton, Bagshaw, Sugg and Hulme had gone and Storer and Wright entered the veteran stages of their careers. It was a time of change but optimism was high.

73

THE GREATEST MATCH

BY 1904 THE TRANSITIONAL PERIOD through which Derbyshire was passing had almost ended. The team was beginning to achieve a settled look. L. G. Wright and C. A. Ollivierre had developed into a successful opening pair with Storer, E. M. Ashcroft, A. E. Lawton and Needham all capable runmakers. Joe Humphries was establishing a reputation as one of the country's best wicket-keepers, Warren and Bestwick emerged as opening bowlers with their best years ahead of them and Sam Cadman was set to take over Hulme's role as the chief supporting bowler. Youngsters such as Gilbert Curgenven and Arthur Morton were on the threshold of the side, a fairly youthful one by the standards of those days with only Wright (42) and Storer (37) coming into the veteran category.

The season began on a high note with a 122-run victory over Surrey, their first at The Oval since 1891. Bestwick took eight for 103 in the first innings, Wright and Ollivierre shared a new record opening partnership of 173 and Warren (six for 96) and Bestwick destroyed the home team's second innings. Storer made a hundred at Lord's in an eight-wicket victory over MCC and then, after an indifferent run in the Championship, Derbyshire won a remarkable game against Essex at Leyton. On the first day the match was heavily tilted in favour of Essex, Derbyshire having been dismissed for 125 and Essex being 244 for eight at the close. They had a first innings lead of 122 after Warren had taken five for 71 and Bestwick four for 33 and with seven second innings wickets down Derbyshire's lead was only 87. Then Cadman, hitting freely all around the wicket, and Humphries changed the whole complexion of the game by adding 134 for the eighth wicket. Cadman made 126, Humphries 44, and Derbyshire, all out for 349, set Essex 228 to win. They were rocked by superb bowling by Arnold Warren on the second evening. He bowled Fane, had the in-form Perrin caught for two (thus dismissing him for a total of three runs in the match) and then held a return catch to send back Carpenter. At the close Essex were 37 for three still needing 191 to win. On the final morning they were all out for 188, Warren having a match analysis of 49.4-4-137-11, Derbyshire winning by 39 runs.

There was an innings victory over Warwickshire at Glossop but ignominious defeat by Nottinghamshire at Chesterfield when they were all out for 32 in the second innings after being 15 for seven. But the in and out form continued with a 306-run win at Leicester, where Wright and Ashcroft made centuries and Bestwick took 11 wickets in the game.

Derbyshire's season had brought them four victories and six defeats in 12 Championship games, with four defeats in the previous five games. They were eighth in the table, three places higher than Essex who were to be their next opponents at Queen's Park, Chesterfield, a match which was to be played on Monday, Tuesday and Wednesday, 18, 19 and 20 July 1904.

Essex had a powerful batting side, Fane, Carpenter, Percy Perrin, McGahey, Rev F. H. Gillingham, Sewell, Keigwin and the youthful J. W. H. T. Douglas, with Perrin, tall and elegant and a magnificent player of fast bowling, at his peak at the age of 28. Ashcroft, captaining Derbyshire in Lawton's absence through business commitments, lost the toss and Fane had no hesitation about batting on a beautiful pitch in weather which contemporary reports described as 'simply scorching'.

Derbyshire got away to a splendid start, Bestwick bowling Carpenter with a ball which 'came across a lot' at 12. A similar delivery, pitched on the off-stump, caused problems for Perrin, passing behind the batsman, but afterwards Essex took complete command. They reached 89 for one after 24 overs, Perrin next passing 50 in an hour, with eleven fours. At 132 Fane was lbw to Curgenven for 63, he and Perrin having added 120 for the second wicket in 70 minutes. Bestwick bowled McGahey almost on the stroke of lunch when the score was 179 for three, Perrin being 74.

There were around 2,000 people on the ground to see Perrin reach his hundred in two hours (21 fours), the score then being 211 for three. In brilliant sunshine he and Gillingham took complete control, the score racing towards 300, at which point Warren returned for a new spell at the lake end.

Under that hot July sun he had sent down 13 overs for 58 runs and failed to take a wicket, having been slightly handicapped by an injury to his right knee, and severely punished by Perrin. But in his 14th over he caught and bowled Gillingham for 43 to end a fourth wicket partnership of 121 in 70 minutes. In his 16th over Perrin (152) was missed by Bestwick at mid-on, an incident that changed the course not only of the game but of a part of cricket history. Warren's reaction typified the spirit of the top-class fast bowler. With his fifth ball he bowled Sewell and the next bowled Reeves to make Essex 314 for six. Perrin quickly regained control, taking two boundaries from each of five consecutive overs from Warren. By the close Essex were 524 for eight, Perrin being 295 not out, an innings which included 58 boundaries, only eight short of a new record of boundaries in an individual innings, Archie Maclaren having struck 65 in his 424 for Lancashire against Somerset at Taunton in 1895. Next morning Essex took their score to 597, Perrin making 343 not out (with a new record of 68 fours) in $5\frac{1}{4}$ hours.

It was a massive target for Derbyshire. They faced enormous odds, 448 needed to avoid the follow-on; two innings totals of 300 each would leave Essex with only a single boundary hit to win the game. There was, too, speculation surrounding the pitch and whether it would last, for the fast bowlers had raised plenty of dust in the closing stages of the Essex innings that morning.

Yet according to the 1905 *Derbyshire Cricket Guide*: 'Derbyshire knew the weakness of the Essex attack and were not dismayed.' And although Wright gave a difficult half-chance to Gillingham at mid-on, the openers soon settled, 50 being passed in half-an-hour and the century partnership after 55 minutes. At lunch Derbyshire were 144 without loss, Ollivierre, who batted brilliantly, being 91 and Wright 44.

After lunch, with 3,000 spectators ringing the ground, Ollivierre reached his hundred (a five and 19 fours) in 95 minutes and the pair soon passed their previous record of 173. The partnership had produced 191 runs when Wright was caught off Reeves for 68 and then Storer, after a shaky start, joined Ollivierre in another big stand.

They added 128 in 75 minutes before Storer, hitting out, was bowled for 44, the score being 319 and Ollivierre 191. The West Indian reached his 200 (a five and 33 fours) after 190 minutes, becoming only the third Derbyshire batsman (Davidson and Storer being the others) to achieve a feat which Ashcroft celebrated by having a drink brought out to him.

Ollivierre went on to make 229 before Reeves bowled him at 378. He returned to the pavilion to what must have been one of the greatest ovations ever given to a Derbyshire batsman. He had hit a five (four overthrows) and 37 fours in an innings of brilliant aggression, full of daring and unorthodox strokes and surely one of the finest ever played in the County's history. He hit well all around the wicket and frequently pulled the ball from the line of the off-stump to the leg boundary – a risky stroke but one which brought him runs and excited the spectators. Thrilling late cuts delighted the crowd and neither was he afraid to hit over the top. Several of his strokes would have qualified for sixes instead of fours had modern rules been in vogue (as would Perrin's). Ashcroft made 34 and by the close Derbyshire were 446 for four, 151 behind with six wickets in hand.

Play began, by mutual consent, 15 minutes earlier on the Wednesday in fine, dry but cooler weather. At ten to one Derbyshire's innings closed at 548, 49 behind, and a draw appeared likely, as indeed it had throughout most of the game.

But in a remarkable pre-lunch session Essex broke down against the pace of Warren and Bestwick. Carpenter was caught by Warren in the slips off a rising ball from Bestwick and a fast yorker from Warren shattered Fane's stumps. Perrin took two leg-side boundaries off Warren and then drove the third delivery of the fast bowler's fourth over back with tremendous power, Warren hanging on to a difficult return catch. Essex had lost three wickets for 17 and with Gillingham in bed with lumbago, Derbyshire's bowlers, after only 45 balls of the innings, found themselves attacking the middle order batsmen. By lunch the score was 27 for six, Bestwick having taken three for 13 and Warren three for 14, each having delivered eight overs.

News of Derbyshire's success spread quickly and 2,000 people were on the ground as Sewell and Douglas set about the task of restoring the innings in positive fashion. Soon Essex had reached 80 for six, but a double change which brought Cadman on at the pavilion end and Curgenven at the lake end paid dividends, Curgenven having Sewell well caught by Cadman at mid-off for 41.

It was another example of the consistent Derbyshire fielding in this innings for Needham had earlier held a fine catch to dismiss Keigwin, racing for the ball which was travelling fast and high, stopping it with his left hand and catching it with a flying leap to his right. Cadman had also held a fine one-handed catch at mid-off to send back McGahey.

At ten to four Essex were all out for 97, Gillingham, hurriedly summoned from his Nottingham hotel, failing to arrive in time. Warren took four for 42, Bestwick three for 34 and Curgenven two for seven. An editorial on Warren in a national newspaper said: 'Tall and wiry he can maintain a remarkable pace and even on the best wickets the speed is so remarkable that the best of players are demoralised.'

Derbyshire needed 147 for victory in 125 minutes, play going on until 6.15 pm. Ollivierre again began brightly but at 11 Wright was caught and Essex must have felt at this point that if they could get rid of Ollivierre quickly they might have a chance to bowl Derbyshire out. But again the West Indian threatened to take the attack apart and in the 13th over of the innings he sent up the 50 after 35 minutes batting with a four to leg off Buckenham to make his own score 33.

He raced to his 50 in even time (eight fours) and the 100 came up in an hour. With more than an hour left to play Derbyshire, 108 for one, Ollivierre 74, needed only 39 for victory.

Both Ollivierre and Storer were now in pursuit of individual hundreds and half-centuries, Storer trying to 'bag' the bowling in a late burst of scoring which brought him within sight of his 50 and the bonus money to which, as a professional, he would have been entitled. Eventually neither of them attained their goals, Ollivierre finishing on 92, with 15 fours, and Storer 48 as Derbyshire reached 149 for one to win an amazing match by nine wickets. The runs came in 80 minutes, and 45 minutes remained to play.

Charles Ollivierre, who was a member of the first West Indies side to tour England in 1900, and later qualified for Derbyshire. His 229, made with great panache and aggression against Essex at Queen's Park in 1904, was one of the finest innings ever played for the county. Yet he had mixed feelings about Chesterfield. After a night spent celebrating, he dropped several catches on his first appearance at the ground next morning, dashed to the pavilion and doused his head in a bucket of water. Returning to the field, he told his captain, 'It's no use, please find a substitute. I am ill and no wonder I drop catches. Even the church steeple seems to be falling on me!' It was his first sight of Chesterfield's famous crooked spire.

There has been no real parallel since in English cricket. Hampshire, all out for 15 in their first innings, defeated Warwickshire by 155 runs at Edgbaston in 1922 in what was perhaps the most remarkable recovery in county cricket. Lancashire defeated Warwickshire at Southport in 1982 after facing a first innings total of 523 for four but this was a match helped along by declarations, while Derbyshire and Essex played theirs out to a finish, maintaining an over rate of some 23 an hour and a run rate of 4.06 per over.

Exceptionally hot weather, particularly on the first two days, a fine pitch, moderate supporting bowling and brilliant batting which took full advantage of the fast outfield and relatively short boundaries, were the main ingredients which made such a result possible.

Derbyshire could, said the *Daily Telegraph*, 'fairly claim to have gained the most astonishing victory in the history of cricket'.

The match was to become part of the folklore of Derbyshire cricket, not least because of the personal duel between Warren and Perrin. Each was at his peak in 1904, Warren in 22 matches taking 124 wickets at 20.94 each, 101 of them in the Championship. Had there been a Test series that summer it is likely both players would have been selected for England.

Perrin returns to the pavilion after his 343 not out against Derbyshire at Chesterfield. In later years he evoked the awe and respect among Derbyshire followers which was to be accorded also to Tom Dollery and John Langridge, who always seemed to make runs against the county. On seven occasions he passed three figures against Derbyshire, the first at Derby in 1898, the last and unbeaten hundred on the same ground in 1922 when he was 46. His 68 boundaries – some of which would have counted six in later years – are still a world record.

DERBYSHIRE *v* ESSEX

Played at Queen's Park, Chesterfield, 18, 19 and 20 July 1904

DERBYSHIRE WON BY NINE WICKETS

ESSEX	FIRST INNINGS		SECOND INNINGS	
*Mr F. L. Fane	lbw b Curgenven	63	b Warren	2
H. Carpenter	b Bestwick	5	c Warren b Bestwick	2
Mr P. A. Perrin	not out	343	c and b Warren	8
Mr C. P. McGahey	b Bestwick	32	c Cadman b Bestwick	5
Rev F. H. Gillingham	c and b Warren	43	absent ill	—
E. H. D. Sewell	b Warren	10	c Cadman b Curgenven	41
W. Reeves	b Warren	0	b Bestwick	0
Mr R. P. Keigwin	lbw b Ashcroft	14	c Needham b Warren	0
Mr J. W. H. T. Douglas	b Ollivierre	47	not out	27
†A. E. Russell	c Humphries b Cadman	23	b Curgenven	0
C. P. Buckenham	lbw b Bestwick	3	b Warren	8
Extras		14		4
Total		597		97

BOWLING	O	M	R	W		O	M	R	W
Warren	29	3	143	3		16.1	5	42	4
Bestwick	42.1	8	160	3		16	4	34	3
Cadman	22	3	65	1		2	0	10	0
Storer	7	0	41	0					
Curgenven	16	1	67	1		5	2	7	2
Ashcroft	7	1	38	1					
Morton	8	1	39	0					
Wright	4	0	15	0					
Ollivierre	3	0	15	1					

DERBYSHIRE	FIRST INNINGS		SECOND INNINGS	
Mr L. G. Wright	c Fane b Reeves	68	c Carpenter b Buckenham	1
Mr C. A. Ollivierre	b Reeves	229	not out	92
W. Storer	b Buckenham	44	not out	48
*Mr E. M. Ashcroft	b Sewell	34		
E. Needham	b Reeves	47		
Mr G. Curgenven	b Buckenham	31		
A. Morton	b Reeves	16		
A. Warren	b Douglas	18		
S. Cadman	c Douglas b Reeves	34		
†J. Humphries	not out	2		
W. Bestwick	lbw b Douglas	0		
Extras		25		8
Total		548	(for 1 wkt)	149

BOWLING	O	M	R	W		O	M	R	W
Buckenham	43	5	176	2		13	0	78	1
Keigwin	7	1	36	0					
Reeves	51	7	192	5		13	1	43	0
Douglas	15.3	1	54	2		2	0	14	0
McGahey	11	2	34	0		2	1	6	0
Sewell	7	0	31	1					

Umpires: W. Wright and S. Brown

Derbyshire's amazing victory in 1904.

Perrin's mighty innings, extended to 343 not out because declarations were not then allowed before lunch on the second day, is the highest individual score made in a first-class match in the county and also the highest by a batsman from the losing side.

There was a suggestion that Essex had celebrated Perrin's feat a little too enthusiastically on the second evening and that this contributed to their poor batting display. The teams certainly met socially on the first evening when they visited the Stephenson Memorial Hall for a performance of 'His Excellency the Governor' by the Midland Dramatic Club as part of a fund-raising effort by Derbyshire CCC. But although their batting lacked application it was probably due to complacency given the 'certain draw' aspect of the game at that stage rather than any collective hangover.

The bowling of Warren and Bestwick must also be given its due. They were now approaching the peaks of their careers and not only were they magnificent fast bowlers but they could also have taught Essex a thing or two about the art of celebration. It was an age when many men, certainly coal miners and not least fast bowlers, drank liberally, and Warren and Bestwick were no exceptions.

In 1904 Bestwick took 92 wickets and with Wright and Ollivierre each exceeding a thousand runs Derbyshire ended the season in tenth place. Warren, in particular, had emerged as a fine fast bowler, regarded in some quarters as the natural successor to Tom Richardson. Against Nottinghamshire at Welbeck in 1904 he took 15 of the 18 wickets that fell for 112 – eight for 69 and seven for 43. His bowling against Yorkshire at Derby in 1905 – seven for 57 and five for 69 – which helped his side to a nine-wicket victory over that season's Champions, impressed the England captain, Hon F. S. Jackson, and he was included in the England team for the third Test against Australia at Leeds.

In 19.2 overs at Leeds Warren took five for 57 in the Australian first innings, including the wicket of Victor Trumper, who cut the ball into his stumps. Noble, Joe Darling, the Australian captain, and Warwick Armstrong were among his other victims. 'Warren takes a fairly long run and bowls very fast, coming quick off the pitch, but the great merit of his bowling is that so many of his balls get up and three of his wickets were got by catches in the slips and two of them off rising balls,' reported *The Times*.

This is an interesting point and brings the question of sheer pace and Derbyshire's long line of fast and fast-medium bowlers into perspective. Express speed of the type generated by Kortright, Larwood and Tyson has been rare in English cricket in comparison with the West Indies abundance of pace bowlers in recent times. The structure of the game in England and the conditions under which it is played have been among the reasons why the majority of the great home-produced bowlers have been fast-medium or medium-paced. In Derbyshire's case Warren, Ward and Rhodes, Copson in his opening overs, and Holding have been the quickest with Mycroft, Shacklock and Platts also classed as fast, although comparison with those distant days is difficult. Devon Malcolm can also be classed in the category of high pace. Many people would rank Les Jackson only as fast-medium but his bowling could be decidedly unpleasant in helpful conditions. His bowling was very hostile and facing him with the new ball on a green pitch was a more dangerous proposition than batting against some bowlers of higher pace.

Warren clearly had that priceless ability to obtain lift off a good length or just short of a length and he struck quickly in the Australian second innings on the final day, Trumper cutting his second ball straight to Hirst at third slip before he had scored. But his bowling lacked its first-innings fire and his solitary wicket cost 56 runs, although Hill was badly missed by Hayward in the slips in his second over. Herein lies a classic tale of Warren's inconsistency. When he died in 1951 his obituary in *Wisden* described him as 'one of the fastest right-arm bowlers of his time'. It was perfectly accurate, but perhaps David Frith came closest to the truth in his book *The Fast Men* in which he wrote that Warren's problem was inconsistency: 'one day he bowled like a world-beater, the next merely a work-a-day bowler. This may have had something to do with his fondness for a glass of beer.' Headingley provided a perfect example and Mr W. T. Taylor told a story of Warren's epic celebrations of his first-innings feat, when he was joined by friends and relatives, and the effects this had on his bowling in the second innings. No doubt F. S. Jackson was not amused and this and other circumstances combined to prevent him from playing for his country again. A strain suffered in the Test kept him out of Derbyshire's match against the Australians and the Gentlemen *v* Players match at Lord's, although he played in The Oval fixture. He took eight wickets in that game but generally his form declined in the remainder of the season and this, the general strength of English cricket at the time, plus his apparent lethargy in the second innings at Leeds put him out of the running for the last two Tests, his place going to Walter Brearley.

There is no doubt that Warren and Bestwick were fit, strong men who were capable of giving Derbyshire a hundred per cent. They had to be to achieve such excellent figures during the 'golden age' when they frequently had to bowl on good pitches against high-class batsmen with little support in the field or from the County's change bowlers. Drink may have had only a negligible effect on them at this stage but as time passed it took its toll. Warren was beset by other

The ball with which Arnold Warren took five for 57 in Australia's first innings at Leeds in 1905 was mounted and presented to him by friends and admirers in Derbyshire. It was his only Test match.

problems at various stages of his career: a brush with the law following a brawl, a spell of destitution and family tragedy when his marriage was ended by his wife's early death which left him with a five-year-old son. There seems little doubt his loss of a settled married life influenced his career in a negative fashion.

Bestwick, too, met similar problems. He and Warren enjoyed much success, each taking a hundred wickets for the County in 1908, Warren also achieving the feat in 1904, in all first-class matches in 1906 and 99 in 1909. Bestwick's bowling brought him 100 wickets in 1905, 1906, 1908, and, spectacularly, in 1921.

Bestwick's drinking, however, was to lead to serious trouble. In 1906 his wife died, leaving him with a young son. He was still working at Coppice Colliery during the winter months. In January 1907 he was involved in a struggle with a man named William Brown at Heanor after both men had been drinking. Later that night there was another struggle in which Brown was said to have produced a knife, Bestwick receiving a severe facial wound. Brown's body was later found, death having been caused by a knife wound, and Bestwick was charged with unlawful killing, being remanded in custody at Langley Mill Police Station. A few days later an inquest jury returned a verdict that Brown had met his death in a struggle with Bestwick, Bestwick acting in self-defence, which amounted to justifiable homicide. The manslaughter

83

charge was dropped, no further evidence being offered, and Bestwick was released.

Although Bestwick maintained his form there was more trouble to come in 1909. 'It cannot be said to be good for the team when one of its regular and important members has to be suspended and in the end dropped as the case was towards the end of the season with Bestwick, whose connection with the County ceased, the committee dispensing with his services,' was a contemporary view. Bestwick was dismissed because of his intemperance, his liking for a drink having been a source of concern to the Club for some time. It seemed a sad end to a remarkable career – but county cricket had not seen the last of Bestwick . . .

The 1905 season was also remarkable for the form of L. G. Wright, who at 43, made 1,855 runs with an average of 42.15. He made four hundreds, three of them in succession, which included his career-best 195 against Northamptonshire at Derby and 176 at Edgbaston. He was one of *Wisden*'s Five Cricketers of the Year.

Cadman advanced as an all-rounder in 1905 and Arthur Morton was also showing promise as a batsman and medium-pace off-break bowler, which would make him a second all-rounder for Derbyshire for many years to come. Morton and Cadman were to become synonymous with Derbyshire cricket as all-rounders who at the bread and butter level of the County Championship turned in many match-saving and a number of match-winning performances. Morton played for Glossop as an amateur and it was on the recommendation of Sir Samuel Hill-Wood that he was first chosen for Derbyshire in 1903. In his early days he was primarily a batsman. Stockily-built he relied on the old-fashioned virtues of length and direction when he bowled and his batting was described as steady, although he could hit powerfully when the occasion demanded.

Derbyshire won three (Yorkshire, Northamptonshire and War-wickshire) of their 20 Championship games in 1905, finishing 14th of the 16 counties. One of the saddest features of the summer was the poor form of William Storer. At 38 and in failing health he was not the force of old and he had a miserable start to the summer. He was dropped from the side, and retired at the end of the season. Another sad farewell in 1905 was that of Walter Boden, who died in hospital in September, six years after the death of John Cartwright, another major influence on the Club in its formative years.

Storer's retirement was to be followed by Bertie Lawton's resignation as captain after only two matches in 1906. Lawton had opened the bowling against Lancashire at Derby and when the next match began at Leicester there was a telegram awaiting him from one or more of the committee suggesting that he give the real bowlers a chance. In protest Lawton opened the bowling but took himself off after four overs, sending in his resignation as captain immediately. Ashcroft and Wright shared the captaincy afterwards, Wright taking over and leading the side in 1907. Lawton returned as skipper for 1908 and 1909, R. B. Rickman, an all-rounder who was born at Doncaster and educated at Sherborne, deputising when he was unable to play.

In general these were lean days. Joe Humphries shattered the County wicket-keeping record in 1906 with 76 dismissals. He was chosen as the specialist 'keeper for the 1907–08 MCC tour of Australia when Lilley declined an invitation, the party being led by A. O. Jones, of Nottinghamshire. A feature of Humphries' style was the manner in which he stood up to Warren and Bestwick, demonstrating not only his bravery but a high degree of skill. He appeared in three Tests and in the second at Melbourne was one of the heroes of a remarkable England victory. Needing 282 to win England had lost eight wickets for 209 but Humphries and S. F. Barnes took the score to 243 before Humphries was out for 16, England eventually winning by one wicket.

But highlights were few and far between. In 1906 Derbyshire finished last, winning two matches and losing 17 of their 20 games.

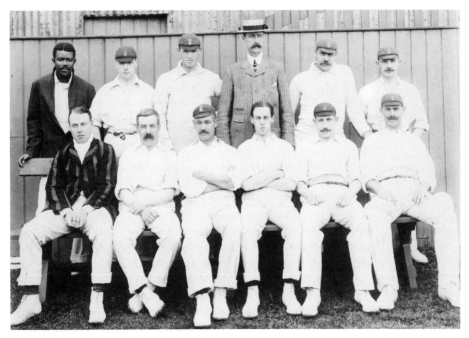

Derbyshire in 1906. Standing: C. A. Ollivierre, A. Morton, A. R. Warren, W. B. Delacombe (sec.), W. Bestwick, S. W. A. Cadman. Seated: G. M. Buckston, E. M. Ashcroft, L. G. Wright, F. C. Hunter, E. Needham, J. Humphries.

85

Some fine bowling by Warren and Bestwick and another of Ollivierre's all-too-rare days when nothing went wrong brought an innings victory over Leicestershire at Glossop. Opening with Cadman after the visitors had made 237 he made 157 in 175 minutes with 22 fours in a total of 509. Wright, who at Leicester carried his bat through a completed innings for the third time in his career, was also in good form in Derbyshire's second victory of the season, a five-wicket win over Sussex at Derby, Ashcroft making an unbeaten hundred and Bestwick taking 11 wickets in the game.

There was no respite in 1907, Derbyshire again finishing last with a similar record to 1906. The slow left-arm bowling of Fred Bracey (five for nine and six for 36) helped them to a 274-run victory over Northamptonshire at Derby and Hampshire were beaten by an innings on the same ground after Needham had made a century. He was to enjoy his most successful season in 1908, scoring 1,178 runs for the County, average 28.73, and making three hundreds against Essex, two of them in the same match at Leyton. This was the year Warren and Bestwick each took more than a hundred wickets in the Championship and their success was reflected in five victories which lifted the Club three places off the bottom. Hampshire (twice), Essex and Northamptonshire were beaten and there was a 36-run victory over Nottinghamshire at Queen's Park, only the second occasion Derbyshire had beaten their neighbours in the Championship.

These were heartening results but there was a disastrous season in 1909 when, with two victories against 15 defeats in 21 matches, Derbyshire finished next to the bottom of the table. Again there was little to cheer but the victories brought some fine individual performances to the fore. When Warwickshire were beaten by six wickets at Coventry Derbyshire owed much to John Chapman, who hit two sixes and 29 fours in making 198 in three and a half hours in a total of 436. Chapman was born in Gloucestershire and it was said he received some of his earliest cricket coaching from E. M. Grace, brother of W.G. In 1893, when he was 16, he went to Uppingham, gaining his school colours two years later as a forcing batsman and a fine fieldsman at cover. Business took Chapman to Russia in 1901, where he remained for a couple of years, and when he returned home he played club cricket, often for Sheffield Collegiates. In 1909 Chapman, now qualified by residence at Unstone in the Chesterfield district, made his Derbyshire debut at the age of 32.

He was one of several amateurs who flitted in and out of Derbyshire cricket at that time. Gilbert Curgenven and Tom Forester would return but Guy Sparrow, who made 64 in his first innings at Northampton in 1905, played in only two games. Fitzherbert Wright, great-grandfather of Sarah Ferguson, Duchess of York, appeared in a few matches, and left-handed batsman Richard Sale, whose son was to play for the County in 1949–54, showed promising form before a cartilage operation in 1912 left him unable to withstand the rigours of three-day cricket.

By contrast Leonard Oliver, another left-handed batsman, was to enjoy a long career. At 17 he was a member of the powerful Glossop team and made his County debut in 1908, eventually becoming a difficult batsman to dismiss and one with a variety of strokes, particularly on the off-side, who was always attractive to watch.

Bestwick was dismissed at the age of 34 after taking more than 900 wickets for the Club, a new County record. L. G. Wright announced his retirement from the first-class game at the age of 47, having had a poor season in 1909. It had been a memorable career, stretching back to 1883 and at the time of his retirement he held most of the County's individual batting records.

WORLD RECORD

SINCE THE PROBLEMS BROUGHT ABOUT BY Sam Richardson's term as assistant secretary Derbyshire's administration had been relatively untroubled apart from the ever-present shortage of cash.

But there was another crisis in 1907 which culminated in the departure of W. Barclay Delacombe who had been secretary for 18 years. Delacombe was a useful club cricketer who appeared in ten games for the County when required in 1894–1900. In 1907 he was asked to resign as secretary and as a parting shot burned all the Club's scorebooks and other records. Things had reached such a state financially that in 1906 an appeal for support had been launched by Lord Curzon of Kedleston in his single year as president. Many of his friends promised substantial subscriptions for a few years and there was an increase in membership. But in 1907 wretched weather and poor results resulted in poor support and Derbyshire plunged into yet another financial crisis. *Wisden*, incidentally, gave Delacombe a fulsome send-off, saying he resigned after doing much excellent work as secretary.

In January 1908 he was succeeded as secretary by R. S. T. Cochrane, but in July Cochrane was offered a good job in the brewing industry in London and resigned. On 4 August 1908 Mr W. T. Taylor was appointed secretary of Derbyshire CCC from a short list of five candidates. It was an appointment which secured the administrative stability of the Club for the next half-century.

William Thomas Taylor was born at Wirksworth on 14 April 1885 and he was to become something of a legendary figure in Derbyshire cricket as secretary of the club for 51 years and 149 days until he resigned in 1959. He was appointed to the committee and in 1962–72 he was one of the hon secretaries of the Club, finally leaving the management scene after a connection which lasted 67 years. He attended home matches until April 1976, a few months before his death at his Breadsall home in his 92nd year. The MCC had elected him an Honorary Life Member – the first and only time that a county secretary was so honoured while still in office – an office, incidentally, which was the longest secretaryship of any of the 17 first-class clubs.

As a cricketer he was no more than a useful club player but he appeared in four matches for the County. In his early years as secretary Will Taylor frequently travelled with the team to away matches, acting as scorer and twelfth man. He was to serve in the First World War, reaching the rank of Captain, and was badly wounded. He fought his way back to good health and was about to be promoted

Major when further injury ended the conflict for him. In later years he was to demonstrate his loyalty to Derbyshire, remaining with the Club even when he was invited to apply for the lucrative position of Lancashire's secretary in 1932. Had Guy Jackson been able to lead the MCC in South Africa in 1927–28 Will Taylor would have been manager.

Financially there was little improvement in 1910. The gates at Derby were deplorable and even fell away at Chesterfield. The donations which had followed Lord Curzon's appeal ran out after three years, subscriptions amounting to only £916. The Duke of Devonshire, who had been made president in 1909, made it clear at a meeting during the autumn that unless the subscription list was greatly extended the club would have to be wound up. Promises of further support were made by the Duke, Lord Curzon, S. H. Evershed and Charles Wright of Wirksworth and the meeting was adjourned with the hope that Derbyshire would participate in the County Championship the following year. At the adjourned meeting on 2 December 1910 the committee reported a generous response to their appeal and at the annual meeting of county secretaries at Lord's fixtures were arranged for the 1911 season.

A bazaar, organised by Mr Taylor and enthusiastically supported by the Duke of Devonshire, raised £1,635 and the crisis was averted. Of the Ninth Duke of Devonshire, Victor Cavendish (1868–1938), Mr Taylor said: 'No club could have had a better leader, and he was, in my opinion, the greatest friend Derbyshire cricket has ever had.'

The Eighth Duke (1833–1908) was the first of the Devonshires to become president of the Club (1893–94) and the Ninth Duke began a family association with the presidency that remains unbroken to this day, remaining president until his death. He was succeeded by Edward Cavendish (1895–1950), the Tenth Duke who was president from 1939 to 1950, and, in turn, Andrew Cavendish (born in 1920), the Eleventh Duke, who has been President since 1951.

On the playing field 1910 saw no improvement. Of 20 matches Derbyshire won two and lost 14, ending next to bottom. Thirty-two players represented the County in Championship games, only John Chapman, appointed as captain that year, Needham, Morton and Warren being ever-presents. Morton had a good year with 116 wickets at 22.67, Warren and Cadman also doing well, but the batting lacked substance. The two victories were gained over Leicestershire at Derby and at Leicester, where Needham hit a century before lunch and went on to make 159, and Oliver was unbeaten on 104, in a total of 464 for eight. Gilbert Curgenven, who had returned in 1909 after four years' absence, made 100 out of 185 in 90 minutes at Leyton but there were few other bright spots.

Derbyshire, then, had given their followers little cause for celebration by the time they met Warwickshire at Blackwell on 18, 20 and 21 June 1910. This was only the second first-class match to be staged on the Blackwell ground and one of only seven county matches ever to be played there, between 1909 and 1913. The colliery manager in the village, John Thomas Todd, 'J.T.', served on the County Club's committee and persuaded his colleagues to play matches there on an experimental basis. In 1914 Burton-on-Trent had its first match and Blackwell lost its annual fixture.

Warwickshire were a useful side – they were to win the Championship a year later – and they ran up a total of 429 for five on the first day, declaring at 504 for seven on the second day, Crowther Charlesworth making 216. Derbyshire were all out for 262, Fred Newton, a Yorkshireman by birth, but who had been brought up and learned his cricket in Grassmoor, making 87, and Frank Foster taking five for 62. Following on 242 behind Derbyshire were 51 for the loss of Newton by the close of the second day's play.

On Tuesday morning – the final day – they collapsed to 131 for eight, still 111 behind with only two wickets left and 40 minutes remaining before lunch. The ball had got up more awkwardly than on the Saturday or the Monday and the match seemed virtually over as Derbyshire's captain John Chapman, batting at number ten, joined Arnold Warren who had gone in at the fall of the sixth wicket. At that point of the season Warren was averaging 12 and his captain 15.21 so there seemed little cause for optimism. Warren used his height to good advantage, striking the ball hard, and with Chapman overcoming his indifferent start and beginning to play well 73 runs were added in 40 minutes. The lunch score was 204 for eight and now only 38 runs were needed to avoid the innings defeat.

After lunch Warwickshire made a big effort to finish the game. The ninth-wicket pair scored quickly, however, with Warren making the lion's share of the runs. The partnership passed 100 and when the total reached 242 the innings defeat was saved, amid cheers from the spectators. Warren had been first to his 50, Chapman soon following him, and at 264 the partnership reached 133, establishing a new County record for the ninth wicket, passing the 132 by Sam Cadman and Arthur Morton against Warwickshire at Glossop in 1904.

Chapman was now beginning to take over the role of senior partner, for Warren suffered a knee injury and was in some discomfort against Foster's pace. It handicapped his stroke play and running between the wickets, but although some runs were missed as a result of this, the partnership continued to flourish. The bowling was changed repeatedly, but the only chance offered was a difficult one to short-leg by Warren when he had made 60.

Chapman drove Quaife for a huge six into the nearby allotments, 300 was exceeded and the previous best English ninth-wicket record of 193 established by W. G. Grace and S. A. P. Kitcat against Sussex at Bristol in 1896 was broken. Soon the world record of 232 made by C. Hill and E. Walkley for South Australia against New South Wales at Adelaide was also broken. Chapman reached his century after two hours. Warren's century came in two hours 35 minutes with a four through the slips off the bowling of Phillips and at four o'clock when the players left the field for refreshments the score was 369 for eight, Derbyshire now leading by 127, and the partnership having added 238.

After the break runs continued to be scored freely until, with the stand worth 283 in 175 minutes, Warren fell to a brilliant slip catch by Phillips off Field's bowling for 123. He had hit 14 boundaries. Derbyshire were now 414 for nine and wicket-keeper Joe Humphries joined Chapman who had now passed 150. Sixteen runs were added for the last wicket before Chapman was bowled by Foster for 165 (two sixes and 19 fours).

Chapman and Warren's record stand of 283 has remained unbroken, the nearest approach to it being in 1921 when J. W. H. T. Douglas and S. N. Hare added 251 for the ninth wicket

John Chapman (left) and Arnold Warren. Derbyshire's captain and fast bowler shared a world record ninth-wicket stand of 283 against Warwickshire in Blackwell in 1910.

DERBYSHIRE *v* WARWICKSHIRE

Played at Blackwell Colliery Ground, 18, 20 and 21 June 1910

MATCH DRAWN

WARWICKSHIRE 504 for eight declared (Charlesworth 216, Quaife 88, Kinneir 87) and 63 for two.

DERBYSHIRE 262 (Newton 87, Higson 36, Jelf 33, Foster 5–62).

SECOND INNINGS

E. Needham	c Charlesworth b Foster	34
F. A. Newton	lbw b Quaife	21
J. Handford	c Foster b Field	16
S. W. A. Cadman	b Foster	0
A. Morton	b Santall	13
C. F. Root	run out	34
T. A. Higson	c Charlesworth b Field	2
A. Warren	c Phillips b Field	123
H. F. D. Jelf	c Charlesworth b Field	0
J. Chapman	b Foster	165
J. Humphries	not out	8
Extras		14
Total		430

BOWLING	O	M	R	W
Foster	26.4	4	119	3
Phillips	9	0	27	0
Quaife	12	2	47	1
Santall	22	4	66	1
Field	29	5	124	4
Charlesworth	4	1	16	0
Baker	2	0	7	0

Umpires: White and Moss

The ninth-wicket stand of 283 between Warren and Chapman remains a world record for the ninth wicket.

for Essex against Derbyshire at Leyton before being parted 32 runs short of the Blackwell record.

Fred Root's eight appearances for the County were among the most interesting features of the summer. Root was never a regular member of the side and eventually joined Worcestershire, changing his style of bowling and enjoying remarkable success with a method based on leg-theory and in-swing. He had formed the theory which led to his new tactics while still with Derbyshire, feeling the method might prove to be the means of combating the superiority of bat over ball which then existed, but he tended to blame Derbyshire for not encouraging him to bowl in this fashion. And yet many years later Lt Col R. R. C. Baggallay, who captained Derbyshire in the two seasons preceding the First World War, recalled that Sam Cadman was one of the first bowlers to introduce the 'off in-swinger' and for his bowling he used to have a field on the leg-side.

George Beet also made his first-class debut in 1910 as a wicket-keeper and useful batsman and even early in their careers the junction of their names 'Beet-Root' opened up all sorts of possibilities for seekers of cricketing curiosity. Beet and Root were members of the same team in 14 first-class games between 1912 and 1920 but the junction appeared only once on a scorecaard, in 1913 when H. P. Chaplin of Sussex was caught Beet bowled Root at Derby.

Beet was very dependable behind the stumps but he was unfortunate in that his pre-war career coincided with Humphries's long tenure as wicket-keeper. Then when he looked like establishing himself, Beet was supplanted by Harry Elliott. In later years he became a first class umpire, standing in a Test match in 1946.

Derbyshire in 1911 finished 14th in the Championship, winning two games and losing 13, with two clubs below them. They received a tremendous shot-in-the-arm when Lancashire were beaten at Old Trafford by two runs. It was Derbyshire's first win at Manchester since 1885 and their first victory over Lancashire since 1895. Magnificent bowling by Warren (seven for 61) gave them a lead of 53 on the first innings and Lancashire needed 308 to win. Tom Forester took five for 36 as they were bowled out for 305. Warren was also prominent in the second win of the season, by 59 runs at Northampton with six for 88 in the first innings, Forester having six for 39 when Northamptonshire, set 207 to win, were all out for 147. Derbyshire almost clinched success at Southampton when, set 365 in their second innings, they reached 344, Morton and Oliver scoring hundreds. Cadman (1,036 runs, average 29.60) was the leading runmaker although Chapman headed the averages and Warren (79) took the most wickets.

Archie Slater's form was one of the most encouraging features of 1911. He was the son of Henry and brother of Herbert, who had played for the County in earlier years. A batsman and medium-pace bowler, Slater was to become a fine all-rounder, not far short of Test class, but league cricket proved the greater attraction than the county game for much of his career. Although he was a regular member of the side until the outbreak of the First World War he did not return as a full-time player until 1927, remaining for four years. Another promising batsman, Archie Wickstead, was to fail to receive further invitations to play for the Club in 1912. Thus a possible lengthy career in the game was lost.

Funds received a boost in 1912 when 'an anonymous well-wisher', later identified as the Hon C. H. Lowther, donated £300 but a poor summer hit gate receipts. Of 18 Championship matches two were won and Derbyshire rose to fifth from the bottom, twelfth position being their highest placing since 1904.

It was mid-June before a victory was recorded, when Leicestershire were beaten by 83 runs at the Ivanhoe Gardens ground in Ashby-de-la-Zouch. The home side wanted 181, and although the pitch had been affected by rain they made a good start and appeared well on their way to victory by lunch on the final day. But this was the celebrated occasion when Arnold Warren headed straight for the refreshment tent at the interval and downed several whiskies, returning to bowl like a man inspired! The years fell away, Warren finished with an analysis of 24.4-7-52-7, four of them clean bowled, and Leicestershire were all out for 97. Warren also bowled well in Derbyshire's other victory when Somerset were beaten at Derby on only the second occasion the clubs had met, the first being at Bath earlier in the summer.

In 1913 Jack Chapman was succeeded as captain by Captain Richard Romer Claude Baggallay, a 29-year-old batsman and wicket-keeper, although he never kept for the County. Baggallay was born at Kensington and educated at Marlborough. He was a useful club cricketer who joined the XIth (South Notts) Hussars, and when he became Adjutant of Yeomanry he came to live at Hargate Lodge, between Hilton and Egginton, thus establishing a residential qualification for the County. His term as captain opened remarkably, Derbyshire winning their first three matches of 1913, against Essex at Leyton, Hampshire at Southampton and Warwickshire at Derby. On Saturday 31 May almost 9,000 people (receipts £220) packed Queen's Park to watch the second day's play against Lancashire but the match was the first of seven consecutive defeats. A 21-run victory over Nottinghamshire at Chesterfield in the final game of the summer – their fourth win in 18 matches – enabled them to end the year in 13th place.

Oliver and Cadman led the batting, Morton, Forester and Cadman being the best bowlers, but the saddest feature of the summer was the virtual end of Warren's colourful career. He appeared in the first eight matches but his figures were only moderate. A year earlier he had bowled his side to victory after a spell in the refreshment tent but, of course, his liking for drink could work the other way. While there was never any doubt about Bill Bestwick's drinking, Warren, according to Will Taylor, was a little more subtle. A new captain, Warren's reputation for waywardness, his age (38), loss of form, all no doubt contributed to his being dropped from the side, and apart from a fleeting appearance in 1920 his career was over. Yet for all his ups and downs he was remembered by people in Codnor as a man who commanded general respect and in later days there was little or no indication that he drank.

During the autumn of 1913 an event occurred which was to have far-reaching consequences and, indeed, it laid the initial seeds for considerable future success. Although the financial situation had improved money was still scarce, and Mr Taylor told of his delight one morning early in 1912 when he was opening the Club mail and found three £5 notes sent by an anonymous donor. He later discovered that the sender was once again the Hon Christopher Lowther, whose mother was of Derbyshire birth. Lowther began to take a keen interest in the Club, making a number of donations, attending many home games and playing in club and ground matches.

'Young players were not coming forward and in the autumn of 1913 he invited me to meet him in London to discuss the future of the Club and how the playing strength could be improved,' Mr Taylor said. 'Incidentally, he entertained me to a very excellent lunch at Simpson's in the Strand. I expressed the view that the gap between the standard of local and county cricket was such that inexperienced players coming into the side had too great a test and the only solution was an engagement on the staff for a full season of promising young cricketers and a system of intensive coaching. He agreed and immediately set to work. He promised a very handsome annual subscription and obtained the services of Harry Blacklidge, a good all-round cricketer from the Surrey club as coach, and to play for the Club when qualified.'

Blacklidge started his duties in the newly formed nursery in 1914 and a number of young players were engaged. The first Nursery staff in 1914 included Fred Bracey, Harold Wild, Walter Reader-Blackton, Joseph Gladwin, Jim Horsley and Arthur Severn.

Joseph Gladwin was the father of the great Cliff of later fame and Severn a useful batsman who played in 1919 before leaving the County and going to live in Doncaster. Jim Horsley, a fast-medium bowler of great ability, made a major impact, although like Slater, his career was interrupted by spells in league cricket. He was born at Melbourne and played three matches for Nottinghamshire in 1913 before joining Derbyshire to take 56 wickets in his first season at 16.33 each. With Forester, Slater and Morton also doing well and Cadman, Root and Bracey available Derbyshire had a useful attack. This was supported by some steady batting, Morton scoring a thousand runs and Cadman, Oliver, Slater and the returned Gilbert Curgenven providing useful runs. Five matches were won in 1914 and Derbyshire finished in twelfth place. There was an innings victory over Worcestershire at Derby and a fine performance against Nottingham-shire at Chesterfield. Notts led by 49 on the first innings and needed 149 to win. Four wickets were down for 24 but George Gunn and Iremonger added 76. Gunn, who was last out, went on to make 79 before he was bowled by Root with a leg-break when he was expecting the ball to swing into him. Root and Forester each took four wickets, Derbyshire winning by five runs. Baggallay always referred to Forester as his workhorse – an accolade which can be illustrated by his bowling that season on the excellent pitch at Leyton: 35-14-89-7 and 55-21-124-7.

At Basingstoke Morton and Slater shared a fifth-wicket partnership of 191 to establish a new County record and there was a remarkable game against Lancashire at Derby in which Derbyshire made 524, six batsmen reaching fifty but nobody making a hundred. They were Chapman (88), Curgenven (86), Morton (80), Bowden (70), Oliver (55) and Horsley (55), with Horsley and Joe Humphries (46 not out) adding 93 in 80 minutes for the last wicket to establish a record which lasted for 72 years. Amidst all of this Bullough performed a hat-trick for Lancashire. Then in the next game against Yorkshire at Chesterfield Derbyshire collapsed in their second innings from 67 for four to 68 all out, Drake (five for 6) taking four wickets in four balls and Morton, first in and last out, making 50, or 73.5 per cent of the total. After a run of six defeats in seven games the rot was stopped with a six-wicket victory over Leicestershire in the first match played at Burton-on-Trent. Burton's emergence as a venue for county matches marked the end of Blackwell's place in the sun and it joined Long Eaton, Wirksworth and Glossop among the defunct areas of first-class cricket in the County. Derbyshire used three gounds at Burton, beginning on a club ground and later using Ind Coope and Allsop's Ground, which eventually came under the aegis of Allied Breweries Ltd. Two matches against the Universities were also played on the Bass Worthington ground.

Somerset at Chesterfield were another of Derbyshire's victims in 1914 and in the final game of the summer they gained a five-wicket victory at Worcester. Cadman made 119 not out in the second innings of 239 for five, putting on 141 with Slater (75) in 90 minutes after three wickets had gone for 14. By now the nation had been at war for four weeks, Baggallay having already joined his regiment in France. It was to be Derbyshire's final first-class game for five years.

So the war that was expected to end by Christmas halted county cricket for four seasons. With it ended the 'Golden Age', roughly spanning the period from 1895, when the Championship was increased, to the outbreak of the war.

In no way could it be called a Golden Age for the County: almost poverty stricken, with stories of acrimonious behaviour among some of their players, unfashionable and in some quarters unwelcome. Yet Derbyshire played much good cricket and when the era ended their prospects looked brighter than for many years.

Derbyshire 1914. Standing: A. J. Atfield (umpire), S. Cadman, A. Morton, J. Horsley, H. Wild, G. Beet, A. G. Slater, J. Bowden, A. A. White (umpire). Seated: J. Chapman, T. Forester, R. R. C. Baggallay (capt.), G. Curgenven, L. Oliver. In front: H. G. Blacklidge (coach).

97

JACKSON'S MEN

BY THE END OF THE FIRST WORLD WAR Bill Bestwick had been in the cricketing wilderness for nearly a decade. After parting company with Derbyshire he played for Shirebrook for a time before making his way to South Wales. Here he married his second wife, played league cricket and in 1914 headed the then second-class Glamorgan's bowling averages. The war years found him playing for Heanor Town in the Derbyshire Alliance, where he produced some startling figures. Clearly Bestwick, even in advanced years, still had much to offer his county. He made his peace with the Club and returned to play a full season's cricket in 1919 at the age of 44.

The chairman of the committee, Alderman R. B. Chambers, had managed to keep a subscription list going and club matters in order during the war, when the pavilion at Derby was used as a hospital by the Royal Garrison Artillery. R. R. C. Baggallay was appointed joint captain for 1919 with Jack Chapman, but owing to his military duties he was able to play in only three matches so the 42-year-old Chapman led the side.

The opening five matches brought three victories, at Leicester, Edgbaston and over Northamptonshire at Derby, Bestwick's bowling proving decisive in each game. But seven defeats in the last nine encounters left Derbyshire in joint ninth position. Oliver and Chapman scored the most runs, while Bestwick's 89 Championship wickets cost him 18.13 each and he was rewarded by being selected for the Players against the Gentlemen at Lord's.

While Bestwick was at Lord's Derbyshire took on the Australian Imperial Forces, a side drawn from prominent Australian cricketers who had served in the European theatre of the war. It was led by H. L. Collins, who was to captain the 1926 touring team, and included Jack Gregory, a great personality who was to form with Ted McDonald one of the fastest opening attacks in Test history on the 1921 tour.

A crowd of more than 2,000 saw Derbyshire dismissed for 181 on the first day, Gregory produced the fastest bowling seen on the County Ground at Derby that summer. But Derbyshire struck back quickly, Horsley dismissing Collins before he had scored and then, at 55 for four, bowling Murray and having Lampard and Stirling lbw to perform a memorable hat-trick. He took six for 55 in the AIF's total of 125.

Derbyshire began their second innings at 12.10 on Tuesday but by lunch seven wickets were down for 78. Southern had attacked the

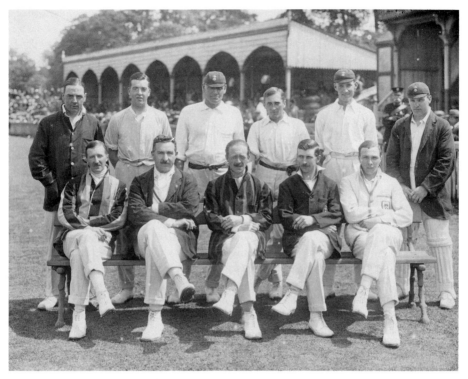

Derbyshire in 1919. Standing: A. Morton, J. Horsley, W. Bestwick, T. F. Revill, H. Wild, G. Beet. Seated: J. Chapman, T. Forester, R. R. C. Baggallay (capt.) L. Oliver, L. E. Flint.

bowling, however, twice driving Gregory to the boundary between cover and mid-off to reach 22 at the break. He continued to attack after lunch, being last out for 43, Derbyshire leaving the AIF 169 to win.

Horsley began from the pavilion end but Trennery and Collins took 19 off the first four overs. Trennery was caught by Beet, standing a long way back to Horsley, who at 26 swung the game in Derbyshire's favour by dismissing Collins and Pellew in the same over. Half the Australian wickets were down for 36 but Murray made 54 and Oldfield and Winning shared a thrilling last-wicket stand that carried the score from 105 to within 37 of the target. An ankle injury caused Horsley to withdraw from the attack and Ratcliffe, who had fielded superbly in the slips, came on to have Winning stumped with his eleventh ball. Derbyshire had won by 36 runs and they were the only county side to defeat the AIF that year. Horsley (eleven for 117) and Morton (seven for 120) bowled unchanged for all but the eleven deliveries sent down by Ratcliffe, Morton bowling unchanged throughout each innings.

Derbyshire had a respectable record in 1919 and it seemed the old days of prolonged failure were receding. It was not to be. Bestwick and Horsley followed Root, Slater and Bowden into league cricket. They were crippling blows and of 18 games in 1920 17 were lost, the remaining one – Humphries' benefit – being abandoned. John Chapman was appointed captain but Len Oliver led the team in most of the games, although Chapman played regularly. On more than one occasion it was difficult to field a full eleven and the selection committee had about as many meetings as there were matches.

'A panic policy was pursued by our selection committee, which was far too large and no fewer than 39 players represented the Club that season. If a young player coming in failed, he was immediately dropped and another youngster tried with the same result. The side was dispirited and completely lacking in fight,' said Mr Taylor.

Those models of consistency Morton and Cadman found themselves opening the batting and the bowling in some games. They were the only ever-present members of the team and had Humphries turned out in his benefit game 40 players would have represented Derbyshire in 18 games, half of them appearing in only one or two matches.

Of the 39 players who represented the Club in 1920 nine played in two games and ten in one – 19 players who appeared in no more than two matches each. Eighteen amateurs turned out and it was clearly no way to run a first-class cricket club. Obviously something drastic had to happen if Derbyshire were to remain first-class.

The first real steps towards a revival had been taken when the Nursery was reopened. The former Surrey player Street had taken over in 1919 but the scheme was worked for the next two years by Sam Cadman, who supervised coaching when he was not playing. In 1922 Fred Tate, the old Sussex and England bowler, was appointed and he was to hold the position for three years. In 1921, however, it was still operated on a 'part-time' basis with Cadman in charge.

But much more was needed than just the coaching of youngsters. Will Taylor recalled the crisis:

I remember Captain George Buckston, who had played before the war, telling me at the end of the 1920 season that unless there was a radical alteration in the general 'set-up' he believed the Club would cease, but if the committee so desired, he was prepared to undertake the captaincy for one year only in an effort to pull things together.

He was appointed to lead the side and only those intimately connected with the organisation of the Club can possibly realise the great services he rendered to Derbyshire cricket.

G. M. Buckston was only an average cricketer. He was educated at Eton, playing his cricket as a wicket-keeper and lower order batsman.

DERBYSHIRE
v AUSTRALIAN IMPERIAL FORCES

Played at Derby, 14 and 15 July 1919

DERBYSHIRE WON BY 36 RUNS

DERBYSHIRE	FIRST INNINGS		SECOND INNINGS	
*Mr L. Oliver	c Oldfield b Lampard	19	c Oldfield b Gregory	8
S. Cadman	b Gregory	8	b Gregory	8
†G. Beet	b Gregory	0	c Stirling b Collins	18
W. N. Malthouse	c Winning b Collins	30	b Gregory	9
A. Morton	c Lampard	36	b Gregory	1
Mr J. D. Southern	c Oldfield b Gregory	7	c Lampard b Gregory	43
T. F. Revill	b Winning	16	c Winning b Collins	0
H. Wild	st Oldfield b Trennery	31	c Gregory b Collins	2
A. Severn	not out	21	c Gregory b Collins	10
J. Horsley	st Oldfield b Stirling	0	lbw b Gregory	0
G. Ratcliffe	st Oldfield b Trennery	3	not out	5
Extras	b 1, lb 5, nb 4	10	b 2, lb 3, nb 3	8
Total		181		112

1st inns: 1-26, 2-26, 3-36, 4-84, 5-93, 6-121, 7-125, 8-175, 9-176, 10-181
2nd inns: 1-15, 2-18, 3-42, 4-47, 5-48, 6-50, 7-68, 8-100, 9-106, 10-112

BOWLING	O	M	R	W	O	M	R	W
Gregory	29	5	75	3	16.3	2	65	6
Collins	16	5	23	1	16	3	39	4
Lampard	17	2	47	3				
Winning	13	6	15	1				
Stirling	7	3	6	1				
Trennery	2.4	1	5	2				

AUSTRALIAN XI	FIRST INNINGS		SECOND INNINGS	
*Mr H. L. Collins	c Ratcliffe b Horsley	0	c Ratcliffe b Horsley	16
Mr J. M. Trennery	b Horsley	69	c Beet b Horsley	9
Mr E. Bull	c Malthouse b Morton	2	lbw b Morton	5
Mr C. E. Pellew	b Morton	15	b Horsley	0
Mr C. B. Willis	c Horsley b Morton	0	b Horsley	1
Mr J. T. Murray	b Horsley	0	b Morton	54
Mr A. W. Lampard	lbw b Horsley	0	b Horsley	0
Mr W. S. Stirling	lbw b Horsley	0	b Morton	0
Mr J. Gregory	b Horsley	28	c Wild b Horsley	5
†Mr W. A. Oldfield	not out	2	not out	26
Mr C. S. Winning	lbw b Morton	5	st Beet b Ratcliffe	10
Extras	b 2, nb 2	4	b 2, lb 2, nb 2	6
Total		125		132

1st inns: 1-0, 2-6, 3-42, 4-42, 5-55, 6-55, 7-55, 8-101, 9-118, 10-112
2nd inns: 1-19, 2-26, 3-26, 4-28, 5-36, 6-41, 7-42, 8-60, 9-105, 10-132

BOWLING	O	M	R	W	O	M	R	W
Horsley	19	6	55	6	21	6	62	6
Morton	19	6	66	4	22	2	54	3
Ratcliffe					1.5	0	10	1

Umpires: H. Mycroft and H. Shaw

*Captain †Wicket-keeper

Derbyshire became the only county to defeat the Australian XI of 1919.

He got his Blue at Cambridge in 1903 and made his County debut two years later. Buckston, who was the father of a future Derbyshire captain, R. H. R. Buckston, was 40 years old. He had played little first-class cricket and none for several seasons and his constitution was weakened by malaria. It was accepted that he would not have much playing success but it was hoped that his leadership would inject some morale, pride and self-respect into the Club.

He still had Cadman, Morton and Oliver from the pre-war days. Gilbert Curgenven, now 38, returned and Joe Bowden came back from the Central Lancashire League. At 36 Bowden was in the veteran stage but he was a solid batsman who became a dependable opener. But the master stroke was the re-engagement of Bill Bestwick. At 46 he was a burly, almost corpulent figure, a man who still enjoyed a drink and one far advanced in years for a bowler of his pace. However he had demonstrated in his solitary game in 1920 that the great ability he possessed was still more than a match for most county batsmen. There is no substitute for talent and Bestwick was soon to provide an ample demonstration.

There were, too, a number of promising youngsters, two of whom, Harry Elliott and Harry Storer, who had made their debuts in 1920, were to play key roles in the creation of Derbyshire's greatest-ever sides in the early and mid-1930s. Elliott was to become one of the finest of the County's long-serving wicket-keepers, indeed until the advent of Bob Taylor he was generally regarded as the best. Sir Archibald White, a former Yorkshire captain, recommended him to the County Club and Elliott became a virtual ever-present in the side for the next 16 years until 1937, when injury intervened. He went on two overseas tours, to South Africa in 1927–28 and India under D. R. Jardine in 1933–34 and played in four Tests, against the West Indies in 1928, one in South Africa and two in India. A useful batsman, Elliott became a most valuable senior professional to Derbyshire's amateur captains of the day and after the Second World War he returned to the County as coach. In 1947 he kept wicket in four matches, making him at 55 years 276 days the oldest player to appear for the County. He had some remarkable sequences of appearances – 194 consecutive matches for the County until 1928 when his Test debut at Old Trafford broke the run, and then 232 up to 1937 when he was injured.

In contrast to Elliott, Harry Storer's career took much longer to get under way. He was born at Liverpool – his father played soccer for Liverpool FC – but like Harry senior and his uncle William he was very much a man of the Ripley area. He quickly demonstrated outstanding talent at soccer and cricket, playing for Grimsby Town and then spending eight years as a wing-half with Derby County, being capped for England. In 1931 he was appointed manager of

Coventry City – which limited the time he could spare for cricket after that year – taking them to the Third Division (South) championship in 1935–36. He also managed Birmingham City to the Second Division title in 1948 and in 1955 was appointed manager of Derby County where he remained for seven years. It was to be a lengthy apprenticeship before he developed into a sound and reliable opening batsman, useful leg-spin bowler and occasional wicket-keeper. An outspoken character, Storer could be dour and uncompromising but he was also a man with a sense of humour. In 1929 he and Joe Bowden established a first-wicket record for Derbyshire by scoring 322 in the Essex match at Derby, Bowden getting 120. In six of the seven seasons between 1926 and 1932 he topped the County's batting averages.

Jimmy Hutchinson was another young professional who made his debut during that dreadful season of 1920. He became a useful middle-order batsman and medium-pace off-break bowler. But his forte was to be his magnificent fielding at cover point, perhaps the most outstanding fielder in that position in the County's history. Wilfred Carter was another useful batsman and occasional bowler who came into the side that year and Anthony Henry Mather Jackson, second cousin of Guy, who was to become the sixth Baronet, also showed promise as a fast-medium bowler and useful batsman.

Defeat in the opening match of 1921 at Birmingham brought Derbyshire's losing sequence to 25 Championship games out of the last 28. Two games were drawn and one abandoned – 25 defeats in 27 completed matches. The last Championship victory had been on 14 June 1919 and it was the twelfth consecutive defeat. The run ended at Worcester where some good batting by Cadman (91) and George Buckston, who opened and scored 71, followed by Bestwick's seven for 67 in the second innings, helped their side to an eight-wicket victory.

A thrilling game at Queen's Park saw Nottinghamshire beaten by 23 runs, Morton's eight for 79 in the second innings and thirteen for 128 in the match being decisive, and then came an encounter with Glamorgan at Cardiff in the first meeting between the sides.

It was preceded by an incident involving Bestwick. Derbyshire had gone down to the West Country to play three games at Bath, Bristol and Cardiff. Will Taylor recalled:

Bestwick occasionally suffered from a 'thirst' and as a result was unable to bowl or field much in Gloucestershire's second innings; Joe Bowden was also 'crocked' and I had to take a place in the field. We were still short and asked the Gloucester people if they could find us a substitute. They said they had a young player available whose name was Walter Hammond and who was a pretty good fielder. He turned out for us and caught a very fine catch and the other Derbyshire substitute caught a fairly good one!

At Cardiff Glamorgan made 168, Bestwick taking four for 71 but Derbyshire collapsed to 83 all out, 85 behind. Taylor continues the story:

> On the Sunday evening Bill was again *hors-de-combat* and this was reported to our skipper who decided to try him out first in Glamorgan's second innings. He commenced with that lovely run and beautiful action and in his first over bowled their opening batsman Whittington. He then continued throughout the innings and accomplished the memorable performance of taking all ten wickets (seven clean bowled and three in his last over in four balls) in 19 overs at a cost of 40 runs.

It was a remarkable performance and it indicates just why the County adopted a tacit policy of turning a blind eye to some of his drinking adventures. Derbyshire had accepted Bestwick for what he was – a magnificent bowler whose behaviour, because of his drinking, was sometimes erratic but who gave of his best on the field. When the County played away a member of the team – usually Arthur Morton – was given the job of accompanying him at all times lest his drinking prevented him taking his place in the side. On at least one occasion Bill gave him the slip by entering a shop and leaving by the back door. There was the legendary day in 1922 when Bestwick, absent from the ground at Worcester – Guy Southern had to be hurriedly summoned – turned up later and barracked his own side from the stand, clearly the worse for drink.

But, as Mr Taylor recalled, there was another side to this controversial figure. After he took all ten at Cardiff the committee decided that collections should be made for him during the next two games at Derby and Chesterfield. Will Taylor again:

> In those days, the players were paid match fees with a small retaining sum in the winter and Arthur Morton had been seriously injured in a motor-cycle accident early in June and was unable to play again that season. When I handed the proceeds to Bill, he counted out half and handing it to me said: 'Give this to 'owd Arthur, he needs it more than me.' This was a typical gesture on the part of this great-hearted cricketer, who, in spite of his peccadilloes, was, I consider, the outstanding personality in Derbyshire cricket during the whole time I have been associated with the Club.

Bestwick's splendid bowling meant that Derbyshire needed 192 to beat Glamorgan but they lost eight wickets for 116, Curgenven making 46. Then Carter, with an unbeaten 50, and Elliott added 77 and the remaining runs were obtained without further loss. In the return at Queen's Park Derbyshire won by three wickets, Bestwick taking his haul of Glamorgan wickets for the season to 23, and his seven for 39 in the second innings helped his side to a 172-run win over Leicestershire at Chesterfield. As a result of these five victories Derbyshire rose from bottom place to twelfth. Bestwick, who took nine for 65 in an innings at Edgbaston, finished with 147 Championship wickets at 16.72 each. *Wisden* commented: 'Naturally, he had not the speed of his younger days but he kept up something more than medium pace and retained his old accuracy.'

Buckston remained true to his word by retiring from the captaincy and from first-class cricket. A vote was taken to determine the leadership and this resulted in a unanimous decision to appoint Guy Jackson.

Guy Rolfe Jackson was born at Ankerbold, near Chesterfield and educated at Harrow where he gained a regular place in the school XI in 1914 as a left-handed batsman. During the war he served in Salonika with the Derbyshire Yeomanry, reaching the rank of Captain and being awarded the Military Cross, the French Légion d'Honneur and the Greek Military Cross, also twice being mentioned in despatches. He made his debut in 1919, playing five games for the County in a promising start. Jackson came from a family of coal owners and iron masters, for the Jacksons ran the Clay Cross Company which had been founded originally by George Stephenson to exploit the coal and iron in that area.

Six victories in 22 matches lifted Derbyshire to eleventh place in 1922. It was in this season, against Warwickshire at Derby on 5 June, that the celebrated occurrence of Bill Bestwick and his son Bob bowling to William Quaife and his son Bernard took place. The two Bestwicks bowled to the two Quaifes for six overs from opposite ends, the only occasion in first-class cricket that father and son have bowled to father and son. Bestwick finished the season with 92 wickets, Morton taking 100 in one of his best all-round years.

By now more new faces were appearing, among them Leslie Townsend who was to become one of the finest all-rounders to play for Derbyshire. A week's trial in 1920 and a hundred for the second team at Edgbaston in 1921 led to a first-team place in 1922. Morton taught him how to spin the ball, Bestwick gave him some good advice. Townsend became a reliable player with plenty of powerful strokes, his off-driving being especially good. A right-arm medium-pace off-break bowler with a nice, easy action, Townsend was also a good fieldsman and he was to play a key role in Derbyshire's great years of the next decade.

This was also the era of the Hill-Woods. Samuel Wood had captained the County at the turn of the century. The surname was changed to Hill-Wood in 1912 and the baronetcy conferred on Sir Samuel in 1921. Four of his sons were to play for the County: W.W., B.S., C.K.H. and D.J.C.H. W.W., Wilfred William Hill-Wood, later to become Sir Wilfred, gained his blue in a strong Cambridge side, making 81 in the 1922 Varsity match. He was a batsman with an awkward, crouching stance, developed to offset a habit of drawing away from the ball, but it served him well. He had only one full year with the County, making 961 runs in 1923, although he did not play his final game until 1936.

His brother Basil, who was to be the second baronet, was a fast-medium bowler who turned in some useful performances in 1919–25. Incidentally dressing room humour was just as sharp in the 1920s, W.W. being known to the pros as 'whisky and water' and B.S. as 'brandy and soda'. The remaining two Hill-Woods came later, Charles, the younger son, a fast-medium left-arm bowler who gained a blue at Oxford in three years, 1928–30, also did reasonably well for the County in 18 games in the same seasons. His elder brother Denis, a steady opening batsman, also got his blue at Oxford in 1928 but made only five appearances for Derbyshire in 1928–29. At this time, incidentally, Sir Samuel Hill-Wood was in his final years as Conservative MP for High Peak. He became chairman of Arsenal Football Club in 1927, remaining so until his death in 1949, when Denis succeeded him until his death in 1982.

The regular appearances of W. W. Hill-Wood and the return from league cricket of Jim Horsley strengthened Derbyshire in 1923. Horsley's seven for 48 in the Whitsun game at Edgbaston followed by Guy Jackson's unbeaten 82 helped Derbyshire to a four-wicket victory and Bestwick's match analysis of 53.4-16-118-13 enabled his side to defeat Leicestershire at Ashby-de-la-Zouch. Bestwick and Horsley also bowled well in an innings victory over Northamptonshire at Chesterfield. The remaining win of the season – four victories lifting Derbyshire to tenth – was over Glamorgan at Queen's Park where Hill-Wood's batting played a significant part. Hill-Wood (107) and Bowden (114) shared in a then-record opening partnership of 206 at Bath.

It was in 1923 that Derbyshire first played at Buxton, the only English ground on which county cricket is staged at an altitude of more than 1,000 feet. The Park Ground was landscaped in the 1860s mainly at the expense of the Duke of Devonshire but the square was not laid until 1876. More improvements were carried out but generally the vagaries of the weather often proved too much for everybody's efforts, there being a high incidence of rainfall at that altitude.

Derbyshire now looked a useful outfit but in 1924 they finished bottom of the table, losing 13 out of 24 games and failing to win any. The most notable newcomer in 1924 was Stan Worthington, although he appeared only once that year, making his debut at Trent Bridge. Worthington joined Bolsover Colliery as a trainee electrician and soon worked his way into the first team which played in the powerful Bassetlaw and District League. Here he was noticed by the County's coach Fred Tate and he went to Derbyshire on a month's trial in April 1923. Burly and powerfully built, Worthington was destined to become one of the great names of Derbyshire cricket. He was, in his early days, principally a fast-medium bowler who was able to move the ball into the bat. He had the ability to keep going for long spells on the hottest days, producing the occasional ball that would beat the best batsmen. As time passed so his batting improved to a remarkable extent and in 1926 he was to rise in the order from tenth when the season started to seventh. It was to be as a hard-hitting batsman that he made his mark in county and Test cricket. He could, on his day, punish any type of bowling and he occupied any position in the batting order, although his greatest days were at number three. Standing 6 ft, Worthington ultimately made the fullest use of his excellent physique, mainly as a front-of-the-wicket player who drove with splendid vigour and scored well on the leg-side. He was an excellent fieldsman

Derbyshire in 1924. Back row: H. Storer, W. Bestwick, W. Carter, J. Horsley, H. Elliott, J. Hutchinson. Front row: A. Morton, A. H. M. Jackson, G. R. Jackson (capt.), S. Cadman, J. Bowden.

and his bowling at a pace just above medium was to be a great asset in the late 1920s.

Derbyshire's crying need at this time was for batsmen and in 1925 they were able to make use of Garnet Lee, a quality all-rounder who had not been retained by Nottinghamshire after the 1922 season. Lee was a sound, hard-hitting batsman, strong on the leg-side who could either open or go in lower down. He also bowled leg-breaks and googlies and although 38 he added ability and experience to a team which, nevertheless, might already be said to have enough veterans. Bestwick (50), Cadman (48) and Morton (40) were hardly in the first flush of youth.

Indeed Bestwick was to spend much of the summer coaching young players in the Nursery and he played in only seven matches. The lion-hearted bowler was given a testimonial that year and he headed the averages once again, taking seven for 20 against Leicestershire at Burton-on-Trent when he nearly won the game for his side. At the end of the summer he retired, having taken 1,452 wickets at 21.27 each in 321 matches for the club, then easily a County record. Afterwards he became an umpire, standing in three Tests before his death from cancer at the age of 63 in 1938.

The first priority in 1925 had been to win a Championship game. Derbyshire had not won since 27 July 1923 and when they failed to win any of the first four games in 1925 the run was extended to 34 Championship encounters and 35 first-class games. The run ended on 5 June 1925 when Worcestershire were beaten at Stourbridge. It was Derbyshire's longest period in terms of games without a victory.

Five victories – against Essex at Leyton, where Morton made 131, one of four consecutive hundreds he scored on the ground in 1922–25, Worcestershire (twice), Somerset and Glamorgan – raised them four places in the table.

Yet another new ground was introduced to county cricket in 1925 when Derbyshire met Nottinghamshire at the Rutland Cricket Ground, Ilkeston, situated close to the county border. The ground had been laid out by the corporation and enlarged from the original ground presented by the Duke of Rutland. Situated in picturesque surroundings it had a spacious pavilion and a terrace with seating for 3,000 spectators. Rain ruined the game but 7,000 people watched the first day's play, the experiment of staging the local derby there proving a success.

Cadman took charge of the Nursery, much good work being done with the young players by the Rev Henry Ellison, Rector of Aston-on-Trent and a man who became a tower of strength as hon secretary from 1930. H. R. N. Ellison, who played once for Nottinghamshire in 1897, had a flair for spotting young players and with Cadman he played a big part in developing Derbyshire's fine sides of the 1930s.

Of the first ten games in 1926 Derbyshire failed to win any but the rot was stopped with a six-wicket victory over Gloucestershire at Bristol. The victory can be seen as a turning point. There was no great significance in defeating a moderate Gloucestershire side but from that point almost 40 years of respectability and no little success was to result. Far from struggling for the remainder of the summer Derbyshire went on to win five games and finish eleventh in the Championship.

Townsend and Worthington had developed into useful all-rounders and Slater returned from league cricket for the 1927 season. Jackson's men got off to a magnificent start with a 64-run victory over Kent at Chatham – the first time Derbyshire had beaten Kent since 1881, although there had not been regular fixtures for much of the time. There was a win over Essex at Ilkeston and Somerset were beaten at Taunton. Some fine bowling by Lee at Swansea helped Derbyshire to a three-wicket victory over Glamorgan and there was a third consecutive win when Somerset were beaten at Chesterfield. By 21 June Derbyshire were second in the table with five victories. A win over Northamptonshire followed and then came a thrilling two-wicket win over Warwickshire in the August Bank Holiday match at Derby.

Garnet Lee produced a prodigious all-round performance in the nine-wicket victory at Northampton, taking five for 65 and seven for 78 in 43 overs to finish with match figures of 77-27-143-12 and scoring 100 not out in a total of 419 for six.

In winning eight of their 24 games and losing only three Derbyshire finished in fifth place, the best season in their history to that point. Recognition of Derbyshire's talents came when Guy Jackson was appointed by the MCC to lead the 1927–28 side to tour South Africa, Harry Elliott being selected as one of the wicket-keepers. Jackson led the MCC South African XI v The Rest of England at Scarborough before the tour, but he was unable to make the South African trip, because of ill-health caused by malaria contracted during the war and which still affected him from time to time.

Jackson's link with the mining industry led to the discovery of the greatest slow bowler to appear for the County. During the 1926 strike Jackson took his side to play Creswell Colliery and was impressed by the spin of 24-year-old Tommy Mitchell, who had been born in the village. Asked to join the groundstaff Mitchell refused an initial offer of £3 a week because he could earn more in the pits, but he accepted when it was increased to £4. A mercurial character who wore spectacles, Mitchell became a highly skilful leg-break bowler who gave the ball plenty of air, and later in his career he added the googly to his repertoire. He was a fine fieldsman, usually in the covers and to his own bowling, but he was no batsman. Mitchell was an artist with the ball, temperamental, occasionally inconsistent, but on his day was a man who could bowl out anybody. He was probably the best leg-spinner in England after Tich Freeman's best days ended.

Another youngster making his way into county cricket via the Bassetlaw League and the Derbyshire ground staff was Denis Smith, a left-handed batsman who was to score more runs for the County than anybody else. At 16 he played for the Somercotes village club and soon attracted the attention of the County Club. Smith could hit the ball very hard but initially he did not possess many strokes. The careful coaching of Sam Cadman ironed out this weakness and a spell in the Bassetlaw League assisted in his development.

Interestingly, in July 1925 Smith was opening the club and ground's innings against Loscoe Colliery with Albert Alderman with Stan Worthington going in number three – an order which a decade hence would appear regularly on first-class scorecards. Alderman, like Mitchell, made his debut in 1928, a year after Smith. His career developed alongside that of Smith's. Fair-haired and of medium build, he became a solid and dependable opening batsman and a splendid fieldsman in the deep. He was to prove the perfect foil for the tall, elegant, left-handed Smith in later years. Alderman also played soccer for Derby County and Burnley.

In a 1928 summer of high scores Derbyshire won six matches and slipped to tenth place. Perhaps the most significant aspect of the season was a tacit agreement that Derbyshire were now socially acceptable again. Sussex were added to the list of games, MCC were met at Lord's for the first time in 21 years and Oxford University were played for the first time. In 1929 – the first time Derbyshire met Middlesex in a first-class match – Mitchell struck form early on, taking ten wickets in a five-wicket victory over Hampshire at Portsmouth and eleven for 129 in another success at Edgbaston. Harry Storer made two centuries and Stan Worthington took a career-best eight for 29 in a win over Sussex at Derby; then Hampshire were beaten by an innings at Queen's Park. At Burton-on-Trent Derbyshire gained their third consecutive win and their fifth in eight games when Somerset were routed by an innings, Mitchell again proving the match-winner.

For three weeks Derbyshire headed the Championship table, apart from one Saturday when Lancashire led by a single point. After a rain-affected game against the South Africans at Derby there was a 116-run win over Worcestershire at Stourbridge, the fourth consecutive Championship win and their sixth in nine games.

Kent ended the run of triumph at Queen's Park, and although Worcestershire were beaten at Ilkeston and there was a comfortable win at Bath the impetus was lost. Four consecutive defeats after mid-July ruined their chances, despite a win over Northamptonshire in

August and a good win at Southend. Nottinghamshire, saved by the rain at Ilkeston, won the Championship, Derbyshire finishing seventh with ten wins. They also beat Oxford University at The Parks.

Lee's leg-spin now took second place to Mitchell but another slow bowler, the 19-year-old Tommy Armstrong, made his first appearance. Armstrong's left-arm spin was never able to command a regular place in a side which was to be dominated by pace and Mitchell's leg-spin.

Seven of 28 games were won in 1930, ninth place being achieved. There was a remarkable performance by Archie Slater in the ten-wicket victory over Somerset at Chesterfield. The westerners were routed for 54 and 70, Slater taking seven for 31 and seven for 17, including three wickets in four balls. Second innings hundreds by Smith and Townsend helped Derbyshire to a 199-run victory at The Oval – their first win over Surrey since 1904.

Derbyshire's search for pace bowling continued and this led to Alf Pope's debut in 1930. Pope was a hard-hitting batsman and fast-medium bowler. Like his brother George, who was two years younger, and who was to make his debut in 1933, he was a very fine all-rounder. The Pope brothers were to become synonymous with Derbyshire in the 1930s. The family moved to Chesterfield when George was two, their father being in the sports ground business which gave the cricketers a fine working knowledge of the pitches on which they played. George developed as a similar type of all-rounder to Alf, although he was a better batsman. A third brother, Harold, was to play a few matches for the County as a leg-spin bowler in 1939–46. But it was George and Alf who really made the grade, George to the England side. Alf was slightly the quicker bowler, and both men were tall and aggressive cricketers who added greatly to the strength of the fine team that was being built.

At the end of the 1930 season Albert Widdowson, who had been groundsman at the County Ground, Derby, for 41 years, retired, and Harry Williams, who had been groundsman at Queen's Park, Chesterfield, was his successor.

An even greater matter for regret was Guy Jackson's resignation as captain after nine successful years. Following his resignation he was to play in a number of games until 1936, and was later chairman of the committee in 1942–60 and a member of the MCC committee in 1934–38. Derbyshire played 232 matches during his nine-year term as skipper of which he missed only 12. His captaincy covered a greater period than any other, the runners-up being S. H. Evershed and D. B. Carr, although Carr was to skipper the side in more matches: 223 to 220.

Jackson was succeeded by Arthur Richardson, 23 at the time of his appointment and only a few weeks past his 24th birthday when he first led out the team as official captain. He was born at Quarndon and educated at Winchester. A right-hand batsman, he made his debut for Derbyshire in 1928, leading the side when Guy Jackson was injured.

Arthur Walker Richardson was to captain Derbyshire in 1931–36 and his son G.W. played for the County in 1959–65 as a hard-hitting batsman and occasionally a devastating left-arm pace bowler. A. W. Richardson served on the committee until 1974, having much to do, along with Edgar Wassell, in the reconstruction of the County Ground in 1955 when the old pavilion was demolished and the grandstand taken into use.

One of Richardson's first acts as captain was to take Leslie Townsend and Harry Williams to his father's leatherworks in Eagle Street and ask Leslie if he could fix up an indoor practice net inside a large, empty warehouse. Soon Derbyshire was one of the few counties with the equivalent of an indoor school. A great team was beginning to take shape, guided in the background by Sam Cadman's coaching. There was probably no finer coach of bowlers in the world than Cadman – he wintered repeatedly in South Africa where he had a coaching engagement – and his skill had a great deal to do with the advent of a marvellous attack.

As captain Richardson quickly earned the respect of Jackson's men, and after an indifferent start some fine bowling by Mitchell (six for 11 and six for 19 and match figures of 20.4-7-30-12) earned an innings victory over Sussex at Queen's Park. Hampshire were beaten at Chesterfield and Southampton and Worcestershire at Derby. Two victories over Northamptonshire followed, Townsend performing a hat-trick in taking eight for 45 at Northampton and Lee hitting three consecutive sixes off Jupp in his 141 not out in a total of 217 for six declared. The seventh and final win of 1931 was over Glamorgan at Queen's Park, Derbyshire rising two places in the table to seventh.

In 1931 A. F. Skinner made his debut. He was born at Brighton but his father came to Derby as assistant clerk to the county council. Educated at The Leys School, Cambridge, Alan Skinner missed a chance of a blue in 1934 because of injury, but he became a forcing batsman, strong in cutting both square and late. Only 18 when he made his debut, he was a good fieldsman, particularly in the slips.

The 1931 summer was very wet, and with an economic depression prevailing the finances suffered. Gate money was down and since the war there had been a profit in only two years, 1921 and 1930. But the gates had improved generally since Derbyshire began to field a winning team, with home matches at Derby, Chesterfield, Ilkeston, Buxton and Burton-on-Trent. The departure of Slater and Hutchinson reduced the staff and it was in 1931 that Harry Storer was

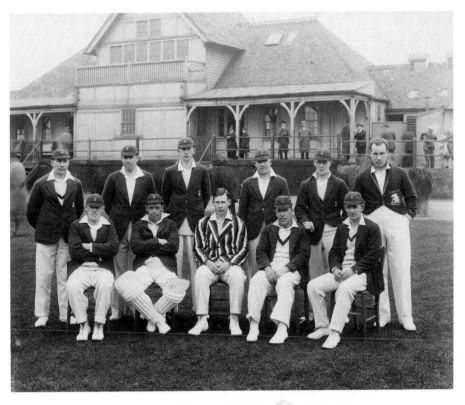

Derbyshire in 1931, on the threshold of their great decade. Standing: A. E. Alderman,
L. F. Townsend, D. Smith, J. M. Hutchinson, T. Mitchell, T. S. Worthington. Seated: H. Storer,
H. Elliott, A. W. Richardson, G. M. Lee, A. G. Slater.

appointed manager of Coventry City, his appearances in first-class cricket being limited afterwards. At least it opened the way for Charlie Elliott to receive an extended run. Elliott, who was born at Bolsover in 1912, was a nephew of Harry Elliott and became a reliable opening batsman after the Second World War, a superb close-to-the-wicket fieldsman and a useful off-break bowler. Charlie won greater renown as a first-class umpire, standing in 42 Tests between 1957 and 1974. Chairman of the cricket committee, an England selector, elected an honorary member of the MCC and awarded an MBE for his services to the game, Charlie Elliott became one of the most respected and influential figures in the cricket world and a man who devoted almost a lifetime of service to the Club. Yet in the beginning it was far from easy. In 21 games in 1932 his record was only modest, but it brought him rich experience and as a bonus a place in cricket history alongside another newcomer that year, Bill Copson.

113

Potentially William Henry Copson was the greatest of all Derbyshire's fast bowlers. He had been working underground at Morton Colliery when during the General Strike in 1926 he joined his colleagues in a game of cricket on the local recreation ground. Copson, who had not played cricket as a boy because the school he attended had no facilities for the game, quickly discovered that he was a natural bowler and soon he was playing in the Derbyshire League. In 1931 the Morton secretary, Mr Fred Marsh, recommended him to the County Club.

Under the guidance of Sam Cadman, Copson made rapid progress. Slightly built, with red hair, he had long arms and shoulders toughened by his years in the pits. He took an easy run up to the wicket and hesitated slightly before releasing the ball. Right-arm fast, he was able to obtain a great deal of pace out of even the most lifeless of pitches and could swing the ball late either way with a disconcerting break-back. In spite of his comparatively slight frame he generated great pace off the wicket from a fairly short run and his break-back on the greenish pitches at Derby was lethal. Had Copson had the physique and strength of a Bill Bestwick he would have been an England bowler for many years but his magnificent potential was to be handicapped by illness and injury.

Nevertheless his arrival was timely. On 8 June 1932 he made his

Bill Copson. With better health, he might have been the greatest of all in Derbyshire's long line of pace bowlers.

debut at The Oval and with his first ball he had Andy Sandham caught for a duck by Charlie Elliott and his career was on its way. Hobbs made 67, Surrey got 315 but Copson sent back Sandham, Jardine, Tom Shepherd and Fender to return 25-7-43-4. After three matches at The Oval, Southampton and Tonbridge he had taken 17 wickets at 16.70 each and won his county cap.

Alf Pope was also showing promise and he had a magnificent game at Ilkeston where Nottinghamshire were beaten by seven wickets, the first win by Derbyshire over their local rivals since 1921. Pope took six for 54 in the visitors' 244, then Richardson, who opened regularly that summer, made 90, adding 165 for the third wicket with Denis Smith (81). Pope took his match analysis to ten for 109 and Derbyshire, needing 180 to win, got home for the loss of three wickets.

There was a resounding victory over Essex at Chesterfield by an innings and 171 runs where Derbyshire declared at 487 for nine, Lee and Worthington adding a record 212 for the sixth wicket. Victories over Northamptonshire at Queen's Park and Leicestershire at Ashby-de-la-Zouch, coupled with a nine-run win over the Indians at Ilkeston, gave Derbyshire three successes in the last four matches of the season. The late surge lifted them to tenth, with six wins.

Leslie Townsend achieved a double in the Championship, 1,350 runs (average 30.68) and 104 wickets (18.63). Mitchell's bowling – he had taken a hundred wickets in each of four consecutive seasons after making a relatively modest start to his career in 1928 – was rewarded by his selection for the 1932-33 'bodyline tour' of Australia and New Zealand under Jardine's captaincy. He played in only the fourth Test at Brisbane and the second Test against New Zealand at Auckland. Perhaps Mitchell's greatest achievement was at Sydney in the second match against New South Wales when he bowled Bradman for one after dismissing Fingleton on the first day.

There was a win over Somerset at Ilkeston to get the team under way in 1933 and, after some good bowling by Copson and Mitchell, victory over Kent at Derby. A third consecutive victory followed, over Leicestershire at Chesterfield in two days, Lee (107) and Alf Pope (72) sharing a record stand of 170 for the seventh wicket. Storer (232, 20 fours) became the first Derbyshire player to make two double centuries when his side ran up a total of 455 for seven declared against Essex at Derby, an eight-wicket victory resulting, and the double over Leicestershire was completed, Townsend making 233. Harry Elliott, captaining the side in Richardson's absence, went in as nightwatch-man at number three and made 94, sharing a record third-wicket partnership of 222 with Townsend. Elliott declared at 508 for seven in reply to Leicestershire's 346, and Mitchell's six for 36 in the second innings proved decisive.

Derbyshire's season settled into one of positive cricket which usually brought results, wins and losses being evenly split. Townsend's six for 64 and eight for 26 brought a 71-run victory over Gloucestershire at Chesterfield. But at Portsmouth in May Derbyshire collapsed from 41 for one to 47 all out, Boyce taking six for five in nine overs, the game being drawn. Against Nottinghamshire at Ilkeston Derbyshire needed 313 to win but lost by 57 runs despite Worthington's fastest-ever century for the Club in 60 minutes. He made 108 in 70 minutes, including four sixes, on a worn pitch.

Runs piled up in this summer of entertaining cricket: 513 for eight against Worcestershire at Chesterfield, Worthington making an unbeaten 200 and Derbyshire winning by an innings and 234 runs; 448 for eight declared against Warwickshire at Derby (victory by 317 runs) and then a magnificent win at Lord's over Middlesex, the first time Derbyshire had won a county match at headquarters.

Northamptonshire were beaten at Queen's Park and the eleventh victory – a new Club record – came in the return at Northampton. Derbyshire scored at 77 an hour to declare at 538 for three, Lee making 128 and sharing in a first wicket partnership of 150 with Alderman (62). Then Townsend (142) and Smith (129 not out) added 177 for the third wicket. Worthington (70 not out) then helped Smith add 112 in 50 minutes and Derbyshire got home by an innings and 184 runs.

These wins earned Derbyshire sixth place. The summer proved to be a personal triumph for Leslie Townsend. He shattered L. G. Wright's old record with 1,954 runs in the Championship, averaging 44.40 and making six centuries, including one double hundred, another record. In all matches for the County he made 1,966 runs, and in all first-class games 2,268 (average 44.47), thus becoming the first Derbyshire batsman to exceed 2,000 runs in a season. In the Championship he took 87 wickets at 16.61 each, 90 in all games for the County, and completed his third double with the help of end-of-the-season festival matches. He was chosen as one of *Wisden's* Five Cricketers of the Year and was to play in all three Tests on Jardine's 1933–34 tour of India. Elliott also got into the party when Ames withdrew and, after his best season to date with Derbyshire, when he established a new record with 89 dismissals, he played in two Tests.

Derbyshire's place in the top six had been earned the hard way. Only three times in their history had they aspired to these heights, in 1895 and 1927, when they finished fifth, and in 1933 when they were sixth. There had still been no win over Yorkshire since 1905 at Derby, and none over Lancashire since 1911 at Old Trafford. Indeed, since the Championship was reorganised Derbyshire had won only three times against the 'Roses' counties, in 1894 and 1895 over Lancashire at Derby and during the same years at Sheffield and Leeds, the 1894 games not being part of the Championship, since Derbyshire did not rejoin until the following year. Of the other 'Big Six' counties Kent had been beaten at Chatham in 1927, Ilkeston in 1930 and Derby in 1933, Middlesex at Burton-on-Trent in 1930 and Lord's in 1933, Nottinghamshire at Queen's Park in 1921 and Ilkeston in 1932 and Surrey at The Oval in 1930. Gloucestershire, who mounted a strong challenge for the Championship in 1929–31, had been beaten in 1922, 1926 and 1933; Sussex, fourth in 1931 and runners-up in 1932 and 1933, in 1929, 1930 and 1931.

Lancashire and Yorkshire apart, Derbyshire had thus proved themselves a match for every other county, winning at least once against all of them in the 1930s.

THE GLORY YEARS

APART FROM AN ISOLATED SEASON WHEN Nottinghamshire headed the table, the County Championship had been dominated by Lancashire and Yorkshire since Middlesex's two successes immediately after the First World War. Of the last 12 Championships Yorkshire had won seven and Lancashire four. In the early 1930s there had been a strong challenge from Gloucestershire, who were only deprived of the honour in 1930 by the anomalies of the scoring system.

Kent and Nottinghamshire were still strong, Essex and Warwickshire had improved, but in 1934 Sussex, able to field a powerful team, seemed the most likely to end the domination of the northern counties. Middlesex, undergoing transition, would become a very good side in later years but Sussex alone appeared as a threat to Lancashire and Yorkshire in 1934.

Derbyshire seemed likely outsiders. They were thoroughly tested at the start of the 1934 season, Lancashire having the best of a drawn match at Ilkeston and Sussex winning a tremendous struggle at Hove by two wickets, collapsing to 97 for eight against Copson and Mitchell when set 95 to win.

Warwickshire were beaten by two wickets in the Whitsun game at Derby but Copson suffered a strain and had to miss six matches, Richardson and Mitchell also missing games through injury. But Mitchell bowled well in a victory at Northampton, Worthington hitting 147, and took eleven wickets in the game against Yorkshire at Chesterfield, twice dismissing Sutcliffe on the Saturday when 21 wickets fell, Derbyshire being defeated by 102 runs.

There followed a historic win at Trent Bridge, the first time Derbyshire had beaten Nottinghamshire at their headquarters. Copson, Mitchell and Storer were absent, but Derbyshire got home by 28 runs. There was a win at Leicester, but by the end of June Derbyshire seemed well out of the title hunt with only 76 points out of a possible 180 from their first 12 games.

The tide turned dramatically early in July. Somerset were beaten at Chesterfield and Kent at Tunbridge Wells. Mitchell took thirteen for 88 at Stourbridge, including eight for 22 in Worcestershire's second innings of 48, Derbyshire winning by an innings. Derbyshire's 306 contained an unbeaten 70 from Elijah Carrington, a batsman who had a good defence and a fine range of off-side strokes. For a time Carrington looked like establishing a regular place in the middle order but despite a good season in 1935 he faded later on.

The Australians cruised to a nine-wicket win at Chesterfield, Bradman (71) being caught at the wicket off Townsend and Mitchell taking seven for 105, bowling which led to his recall for the fourth Test at Leeds. He had been selected for the first Test at Trent Bridge but had taken only one wicket for 108. He fared even worse at Headingley where Bradman (304) added 388 for the fourth wicket with Ponsford, Mitchell finishing with nought for 117 in 23 overs.

Before the Leeds Test he had taken six for 56 and seven for 57 in the 278-run win over Middlesex at Derby, Derbyshire's fourth consecutive victory in the Championship. He also took ten wickets in the win over Hampshire at Derby, Worthington making 154, and this surge of form left Derbyshire with an outside chance of taking the title. They forced Yorkshire to follow on at Sheffield but the game was drawn and then came a crucial match at Old Trafford against Lancashire, who at that time were chasing Sussex hard at the top of the table. But Derbyshire collapsed against the spin of Hopwood and were beaten by 135 runs – a serious setback to their Championship hopes.

They bounced back at Weston-super-Mare with an innings win over Somerset, Townsend making 106 not out and taking six for 66 and five for 64. But defeat by Middlesex at Lord's ended their title bid, although they did not allow the season to fade completely. They defeated Nottinghamshire at Ilkeston to record their first-ever double over their neighbours and, on the last day of the season, established a record 12 wins with a success against Leicestershire at Queen's Park.

Lancashire won the Championship, Sussex having led until 14 August but suffering from having won only one of their last 12 games after 17 July. Derbyshire finished third, their highest-ever placing, the top three positions being:

	P	W	L	Won 1st inns	Lost 1st inns	No Dec	Pts	%
Lancashire	30	13	3	10	4	0	257	57.11
Sussex	30	12	2	7	8	1	243	54.00
Derbyshire	28	12	6	6	3	1	223	53.09

Finances apart, Derbyshire faced the 1935 campaign brimming with confidence after their success in 1934. As in the previous season they faced a tough opening encounter, this time with Yorkshire at Chesterfield. Carrington (74) helped Smith put on 202 for the fourth wicket in two hours, Smith hitting a six and 25 fours in making 189, Derbyshire reaching 382. Yorkshire replied with 328, then Alderman made a hundred and Richardson set the visitors 266 to win in 195 minutes but rain intervened and the match ended in a draw.

It was a good start and it was followed by some splendid cricket. Surrey, 60 all out in their first innings, were beaten in two days at The Oval, and Leicestershire were crushed with a day to spare at Derby. Victory over Essex at Brentwood followed.

This took Derbyshire to the top of the table and they consolidated their position with an innings victory over Hampshire at Chesterfield. Smith (four sixes and 31 fours) made 225, he and Townsend adding 235 for the third wicket. At Leicester Mitchell gave a marvellous display of high-class spin bowling. After Derbyshire had made 140 he took the first six wickets as Leicestershire finished Saturday's play at 68 for six. On Monday he captured the final four to finish with 19.1-4-64-10, all ten in an innings, five bowled, one lbw, three caught by Worthington and one stumped. Rain intervened when Leicestershire, needing 245 to win, were 111 for three.

Copson returned after a spell in which he was out with an injury to rout Somerset at Derby, the westerners being dismissed for 89 and 35, Copson taking five for 15 and Townsend three for 1. The following match against Lancashire at Old Trafford proved to be one of the best games of the summer. Derbyshire made 227 and Elliott then held four catches in Lancashire's 168. Set 320 to win in four and a half hours Lancashire reached 153 for three by tea but some inspired bowling, fielding and wicket-keeping brought Derbyshire victory by seven runs. The win – a triumph for Elliott (caught eight and stumped two in the match) came with five minutes to spare and was Derbyshire's first since 1911 over their oldest rivals.

Still leading the Championship table, Derbyshire met Nottinghamshire at Ilkeston. It was the high noon of the border clashes between the counties. The majority of the players on both sides were born within a 20-mile radius and the local derby spirit was reflected in a Saturday gate of 8,000. Needing 186 to win on a wearing pitch Derbyshire lost Storer to Larwood without a run on the board but Alderman (76 not out) gave a splendid display and they won by seven wickets. It was their seventh win in eleven games and Derbyshire maintained their position at the top, ahead of Yorkshire and Kent.

But with Mitchell and Copson injured Derbyshire were punished by Surrey at Chesterfield, a drawn game costing them the lead. Yorkshire, in the midst of a run of six consecutive victories, moved to the top on 5 July. Defeats at Bristol and Trent Bridge pegged Derbyshire back but an innings win over Kent at Queen's Park and a ten-wicket victory over Gloucestershire at Burton-on-Trent brought them briefly back into contention. But the revival was halted by Sussex, who outplayed them at Derby, winning by seven wickets.

It was all very disappointing after the fine start, but Derbyshire stormed back into the race with a superb run of victories which began against Northamptonshire at Chesterfield on 29 July. They then travelled to Hove for a crucial match against Sussex, who had won eight consecutive Championship matches. Sussex made 194, but although Worthington made 91 Derbyshire's lead was only 19.

Copson responded with six for 42 and Derbyshire needed 226 to win. Half their side went for 99 but an unbroken sixth wicket partnership of 128 between Skinner (64 not out) and George Pope (60 not out) saw them home to a brilliant victory by five wickets. In the meantime Yorkshire collapsed to an astonishing defeat at the hands of Essex, being routed for 31 and 99.

Derbyshire gained their twelfth win of the summer when they beat Warwickshire at Derby. After being dismissed for 85 and trailing by 101 on the first innings at Northampton they gained a comfortable victory as a result of a hundred by Townsend and some fine bowling by Mitchell and Copson. Then in a bowlers' match at Chesterfield Essex were beaten and a new record of five consecutive wins was established.

So the stage was set for a classic battle at Scarborough in the midst of the holiday season in a match which might well decide the Championship. Derbyshire had to win to stand any realistic chance of overhauling Yorkshire. The side was at full strength – Richardson, Smith, Worthington, Alderman, Skinner, Townsend, the Popes, Elliott, Mitchell and Copson – and they started well. Yorkshire lost half their side for 131 but Sellers (73) with help from Wood, Smailes and Verity, steered them to 304, a good score on a lively pitch. Derbyshire collapsed on Thursday against Jacques who took three quick wickets. Trying to pull a no-ball from him Worthington received a fractured jaw and lost several teeth and took no further part in the match. All out for 133 Derbyshire fared little better in their second innings, making only 174, Yorkshire winning by ten wickets.

With only a very slim hope of taking the title Derbyshire prepared for the run-in before the season ended. They were on the receiving end at Dover when Kent hit 560, Ashdown striking 47 boundaries in his unbeaten 305. Alf Pope took ten wickets during the 80-run win at Bournemouth and the summer finished with a victory at Taunton. Runners-up to Yorkshire, Derbyshire enjoyed their best-ever season with 16 victories. *Wisden* reported:

> Had they made 'safety-first' their policy, they might have ousted Yorkshire. As it was Derbyshire, acknowledged as exponents of attractive cricket, continued to hold victory as the highest prize, and if at times this urge caused their downfall the County gained tremendously in popularity and respect among both supporters and rivals.

It was a year of record-breaking for Mitchell (160 Championship wickets, which exceeded Bestwick's 147 in 1921, and 171 in all first-class games at 20.16, including three costly ones in the second Test against South Africa at Lord's). Elliott in his testimonial year caught 69 batsmen and stumped 21, his total of 90 surpassing his 1933 record. The Popes made progress and Denis Smith had a marvellous season with 1,767 runs (average 42.07) in all county games and 2,175 in all first-class cricket. Selected for the Trent Bridge Test he was forced to miss the game because of a cracked rib but he scored 36 and 57 in the third Test at Headingley, sharing an opening partnership in the second innings of 128 with Bakewell. In the fourth Test at Old Trafford he made 35 and nought, being left out of the side for The Oval game. For the Rest of England against Yorkshire at The Oval he made 78 out of a total of 112, 69.6 per cent of the total, nobody else reaching double figures.

Smith was selected to tour Australia and New Zealand in the winter with an MCC side led by E. R. T. Holmes. It was not an official Test tour but Smith played in three representative games in New Zealand and did well on the tour.

Gates increased by nearly £1,000 to £4,549 and the loss was cut to £155 so on all fronts the County had cause to celebrate in 1935. The top three positions were:

	P	W	L	Won 1st inns	Lost 1st inns	No Dec	Pts	%
Yorkshire	30	19	1	3	7	0	321	71.33
Derbyshire	28	16	6	4	2	0	266	63.33
Middlesex	24	11	5	6	1	1	202	56.11

The dream of ultimate success appeared to be rudely halted in the opening games of the 1936 season. Captained by W. W. Hill-Wood in his final match for the County, Derbyshire hung on for a draw at Southampton and after a win over Oxford University they were soundly beaten by Kent. Captain N. A. McD. Walker, adjutant to the Sherwood Foresters, who played only twice for the County, led the side in Richardson's absence at Gravesend but the skipper returned for the Surrey match at Derby. Again things went wrong and on the final day Surrey, needing only 94 to win, were well placed at tea with around 50 required and eight wickets remaining. But Copson produced an amazing burst of 7-3-8-6, Surrey being all out for 77, Derbyshire winning by 16 runs. Copson's overall second innings figures were seven for 19 and in the match he took twelve for 52.

Copson bowled well in an innings victory over Sussex at Chesterfield, Leslie Townsend making 182 not out in a total of 387 and a third consecutive victory was earned when Gloucestershire were beaten at Bristol. It proved costly, however, for George Pope damaged a muscle and developed cartilage trouble which prevented him from playing again that season.

After a win at Northampton, Derbyshire beat Gloucestershire at

Derby, and began a vital match against Yorkshire at Chesterfield. Rain ruled out play on Saturday and on Monday Derbyshire lost three wickets for 18 before Townsend (101) and Worthington (80) added 154 in 135 minutes for the fourth wicket. Replying to a total of 253 Yorkshire lost seven wickets for 62 and were all out for 112, Mitchell taking six for 60. Forced to follow-on under the two-day rule, they reached 102 for one, the game ending in a draw. It was a useful performance, but Derbyshire then crashed to a two-day defeat at the hands of Somerset at Ilkeston in the next match.

They retained second place, however, ahead of Nottinghamshire and behind the leaders, Kent, and recovered their form at Edgbaston. Charlie Elliott made 97 in a total of 318 and Townsend (five for 44 and seven for 46) destroyed Warwickshire, Derbyshire winning by an innings and ten runs. In the next game against Worcestershire at Chesterfield the side gained a three-wicket victory. Derbyshire had established themselves as firm contenders for the Championship and they did their hopes a power of good with an innings win at Worcester, the home side being routed for 64 and 47, Copson returning match figures of 31-8-54-12, consisting of five for 38 and seven for 16.

Nottinghamshire now led the table from Derbyshire and Kent but the margin was close as Derbyshire began the first of two matches in the Chesterfield Festival, their opponents being Warwickshire and Hampshire. It was the first-ever cricket week held by the County. Worthington (163) dominated Derbyshire's 381 against Warwickshire and Derbyshire won by an innings and 159 runs.

It was their ninth win in 15 games, and with Nottinghamshire restricted to five points by Middlesex and Kent not playing, Derbyshire, on the evening of Tuesday 7 July 1936, moved to the top of the Championship table.

Derbyshire had 158 points from 17 games, second placed Kent having 137 from 16 when the teams met at Burton-on-Trent on Wednesday, 15 July. Bill Copson missed this vital encounter, having been chosen for the Players at Lord's. At Burton rain interrupted Wednesday's play but more fine batting by Leslie Townsend put Derbyshire in a strong position by Thursday evening. He made 115, adding 106 with Skinner for the third wicket. Derbyshire made 268, Freeman and Wright, turning the ball appreciably, getting rid of the last seven batsmen for 78. Kent made a bad start but Woolley scored 61 out of 94 and although Pope took five for 48 the lead was restricted to 84. By the close of Thursday's play Derbyshire had made 50 without loss and on Friday Richardson declared, setting Kent 289 to win. Anxious to recapture top place they went for the runs. Fagg made 46 but Pope, Worthington and Townsend each took three wickets and they were all out for 147, Derbyshire winning handsomely by 141 runs. Had Kent won they would have replaced Derbyshire at the top of the table; defeat left them with much to do.

Derbyshire's victory over Kent gave them a comfortable lead at the top . A drawn match with the Indians at Derby gave them valuable respite before two more crucial encounters against Yorkshire at Sheffield and Nottinghamshire at Ilkeston.

Yorkshire won the toss and put their opponents in. Derbyshire owed everything to Stan Worthington, who opened the innings and exacted due revenge on Jacques, who had caused such havoc at Scarborough a year earlier. He hit 21 fours in making 135 out of 216, the next best score being 17 by Skinner. Copson struck early, getting rid of Sutcliffe for a duck and by the close Yorkshire were 102 for four. Rain washed out Thursday's play and the battle now centred on first innings points. Yorkshire just scraped ahead, being all out for 218, Copson taking six for 60 and Alf Pope four for 58. So Copson's remarkable run of success continued. Poor health had dogged his progress in 1935 and the club had sent him to Skegness to recuperate. Specialists dispelled doubts about his condition and it was found he was suffering from a strained sacro-iliac joint at the lower extremity of his back. As part of the treatment for this Copson trained with Chesterfield FC and his form in 1936 fully justified the efforts both he and the club had made to get him fully fit.

Derbyshire faced another severe test against Nottinghamshire at Ilkeston, both sides being weakened by Test calls, Nottinghamshire supplying Hardstaff and Derbyshire Worthington to the England team for the second Test against India at Manchester. Invited when Leyland withdrew from the side, Worthington made the most of his opportunity by scoring 87. Retained for the final game at The Oval he became the first Derbyshire batsman to score a century in a Test, hitting 128, most of his 19 fours being scored in front of the wicket, and sharing in a fourth-wicket partnership of 266 with Hammond. It was a magnificent display in which at times he outscored Hammond, driving and pulling to good effect and square-cutting perfectly. Both Worthington and Copson were selected for the MCC tour of Australia in 1936–37 under the captaincy of G. O. Allen and each had their finest season in 1936.

Had he been able to maintain his 1935 form Denis Smith would surely have been in contention with Worthington for a Test place. He had been dropped down the order for a time after an indifferent run but was restored to open the innings at Ilkeston. He stayed nearly three hours for 59, Derbyshire being 154 for six by the close. On Monday they were all out for 187 and then came a thrilling battle for first-innings lead, won by Derbyshire, with Nottinghamshire getting within five runs of their target, Mitchell taking six for 87. Smith (36) and Alderman (53) gave their side a good second-innings start, the score reaching 94 for two. But the last eight wickets crashed for 31, Voce taking six for 43 and Larwood three for 29 and Derbyshire were all out for 125. Needing 131 to win Nottinghamshire began shakily but they survived several missed chances and won by six wickets. The defeat left Derbyshire still with a clear lead at the top of the table but their neighbours and nearest rivals had narrowed the gap.

Derbyshire ran into more trouble at Chelmsford against the Essex pace attack. On Saturday half the side were out for 29 and the innings was over in two hours for 80. Essex took the lead for the loss of only two wickets, making 219 in all and leading by 139. Alderman held his side together in their second knock against the leg-spin of Peter Smith, but he was out shortly before the close on Monday, Derbyshire ending the day at 195 for seven, a lead of only 56.

On the last morning Alf Pope hit well but Essex needed only 102 to win. They reached 51 for three without looking in any difficulty but an amazing spell by Tommy Mitchell turned the whole course of the match. In 30 balls he took six for 25, Essex being all out for 81. Derbyshire's 20-run victory, their eleventh success in 21 games, became all the more significant when it was learned that Nottinghamshire had won at The Oval.

Again Derbyshire had demonstrated an ability to come from behind and win at a crucial time. Defeat at Chelmsford would not have cost them the leadership but it would have made them vulnerable. As it was they maintained a comfortable margin ahead of Nottinghamshire, with Yorkshire now third and Kent fourth.

Mitchell was again in good form at The Oval, where Denis Smith made his first hundred of the season and Alderman took a superb one-handed catch on the boundary to dismiss Barling in a drawn game. Elsewhere Middlesex and Yorkshire won, Nottinghamshire had to be content with first innings points but Kent, now on the slide, had dropped to fifth place, being overhauled by Middlesex.

Again, though, Derbyshire's response to the challenge was positive. A crowd of 7,000 watched them dismiss Leicestershire for 117 at Derby and eventually go on to win by nine wickets after more good bowling from Copson and Mitchell. The game ended in two days, the third occasion this had happened in four Championship games at Derby. It was their twelfth win in 23 games, Yorkshire now being in second place and Nottinghamshire third. At this stage Derbyshire needed 51 more points from five games to be certain of winning the Championship.

They were hot favourites but faced a crucial match against Nottinghamshire at Worksop in their next encounter. Worthington

ESSEX *v* DERBYSHIRE

Played at Chelmsford, 1, 2 and 4 August 1936

DERBYSHIRE WON BY 20 RUNS

DERBYSHIRE	FIRST INNINGS		SECOND INNINGS	
A. E. Alderman	c sub b Farnes	0	c Wade b Farnes	79
D. Smith	b Stephenson	8	b Stephenson	15
T. S. Worthington	c Wade b Stephenson	13	c Wilcox b Smith	42
L. F. Townsend	c Wilcox b Farnes	0	lbw b Smith	8
Mr A. F. Skinner	lbw b Nichols	19	lbw b Smith	7
C. Elliott	b Farnes	4	b Smith	4
H. Elliott	lbw b Stevenson	11	b Smith	14
Mr A. W. Richardson	b Nichols	2	c Wade b Stephenson	14
A. V. Pope	lbw b Farnes	9	b Stephenson	33
T. B. Mitchell	b Farnes	0	c Wade b Nichols	6
W. Copson	not out	9	not out	3
Extras	b 1, lb 4	5	b 7, lb 4, nb 4	15
Total		80		240

BOWLING	O	M	R	W		O	M	R	W
Nichols	9	2	27	2		18	3	51	1
Farnes	13	6	20	5		27	5	56	1
Stephenson	11.3	4	27	3		18.5	4	56	3
Eastman	3	2	1	0					
Smith						24	3	62	5

ESSEX	FIRST INNINGS		SECOND INNINGS	
Mr L. G. Crawley	b Copson	6	b Copson	1
Mr D. R. Wilcox	lbw b Pope	9	lbw b Townsend	15
M. S. Nichols	lbw b Copson	21	c Townsend b Pope	10
J. O'Connor	c Alderman b Townsend	87	b Mitchell	21
Mr B. H. Belle	b Mitchell	0	lbw b Mitchell	10
Mr C. T. Ashton	lbw b Copson	10	lbw b Mitchell	0
P. Smith	b Pope	6	b Townsend	8
Mr J. W. A. Stephenson	b Townsend	20	lbw b Mitchell	0
L. C. Eastman	c Mitchell b Copson	31	lbw b Mitchell	6
T. H. Wade	not out	6	c Skinner b Mitchell	8
Mr K. Farnes	c Alderman b Pope	11	not out	1
Extras	b 10, lb 1, nb 1	12	lb 1	1
Total		219		81

BOWLING	O	M	R	W		O	M	R	W
Copson	31	8	64	4		13	6	20	1
Pope	27.1	11	40	3		7	1	16	1
Townsend	19	7	38	2		15	8	19	2
Worthington	5	2	5	0					
Mitchell	11	1	60	1		5	0	25	6

Umpires: H. G. Baldwin and G. Brown

Derbyshire's recovery which kept their Championship hopes alive.

was absent at The Oval – his place was taken by George Langdale, a forcing left-hand batsman who made his County debut as a 20-year-old amateur. He later played for Somerset and became a Bassetlaw League official. Nottinghamshire were without Larwood, Voce and Hardstaff and Derbyshire had the best of the match, setting a target of 337 on the final day. But a chanceless display by Keeton and Harris, who shared an unbroken opening partnership of 215, saved the game for Nottinghamshire.

The game was highly significant. Derbyshire, who took five points to Nottinghamshire's three (in drawn matches there were five points for the side ahead on first innings and three for the other side), extended their lead over their neighbours but Yorkshire closed the gap with a crushing win over Somerset at Sheffield. Tension was mounting and it showed in Derbyshire's visit to Eastbourne to meet Sussex. Eighty-eight behind on the first innings Derbyshire lost half their side for 125 and only stubborn batting by the two Elliotts saved the game and three points. The title moved a little nearer and now Derbyshire faced what was on paper their easiest game of the summer against Northamptonshire at Chesterfield.

Northamptonshire were at the beginning of a spell in which they failed to win a match between 14 May 1935 and 29 May 1939, during

Harry Elliott.

which they lost 61 out of 99 games. But they gave Derbyshire a real fight after being 65 behind on the first innings. Bakewell and Brookes then shared a fourth-wicket partnership of 211, Bakewell scoring a magnificent 241 not out. It meant Derbyshire needed 347 to win and nerves took over.

It was now that Arthur Richardson, who had not had a particularly good season with the bat, played one of his most vital innings for the County. Points were vital and it was a time for survival. His unbeaten 27, with 41 from Skinner, plus support from Alf Pope, helped Derbyshire recover from 54 for five to 173 for seven, five more points being earned.

Tragedy stalked the game. Mitchell suffered a broken thumb, which put him out for the remainder of the season, but infinitely worse was to follow. Returning home from Chesterfield R. P. Northway and A. H. Bakewell of Northamptonshire were involved in an accident when the car in which they were travelling overturned near Kibworth in Leicestershire. Northway died and Bakewell's right arm was so badly broken that he never played first-class cricket again, his epic display at Queen's Park being his final innings.

Yorkshire, restricted to three points at The Oval, and Nottinghamshire, beaten at Clacton, fell away and Middlesex, their title bid coming a little too late, beat Kent. By the evening of Tuesday 25 August 1936 Derbyshire were assured of at least a share in the Championship. They had 224 points from 26 games (57.43 per cent), Yorkshire having 210 from 28 (50 per cent). Middlesex were now third and Nottinghamshire fourth. It meant that Derbyshire needed only three points from their remaining two games to become Champions. If they lost both of these and Yorkshire won both their remaining matches the two counties would be level at 53.33 per cent. Only Yorkshire could equal Derbyshire, who had led since 7 July and been in second place since June.

So, needing only to avoid defeat to become Champions, Derbyshire travelled to Wells to meet the unpredictable Somerset team. Yorkshire met Sussex at Hove. On the Wednesday Derbyshire were all out for 216, Smith making 93, but as the match progressed they took a firm grip. Alf Pope (five for 35) and Copson reduced Somerset to 146 all out and then 50 from Richardson helped leave Somerset a target of 271 on the final day. Half the side were out for 140, but Arthur Wellard, missed off Armstrong when he had scored a single, turned the game Somerset's way. He drove Armstrong for five consecutive sixes and scored 86 out of 102 in 62 minutes, including seven sixes and eight fours; 74 in 15 scoring strokes. Although Copson took six for 81 in 30 overs of sustained pace (Armstrong had one for 64 in eight overs!) Somerset won the game by one wicket to perform the double over Derbyshire.

It was a disappointment, but the news was received that Yorkshire, who had led by 103 on the first innings, had failed to beat Sussex, so on Friday 28 August 1936 Derbyshire became the Champion County. They had crowned a glorious period in their history and were now at the summit of county cricket.

Defeat at the hands of Somerset, while a fate not unknown to Champions, was not, perhaps, the best way of winning the title but it had been a magnificent game of cricket at Wells. Derbyshire, who had failed to win any of the last four matches, sealed the title in style with an innings victory over Leicestershire in their final game at Oakham. Replying to a total of 151, Smith (169) and Worthington (102) shared a second wicket partnership of 209, their side winning by an innings.

In all matches Worthington made 1,519 runs for the County (average 37.97), his full first-class record being 1,734 (41.28). Leslie Townsend (1,454 runs, 34.62), Smith (1,333, 31.73) and Alderman (1,145, 26.02) were the others who exceeded a thousand runs.

Copson, with 140 Championship wickets and 153 at 12.54 each in all Derbyshire games, led the bowlers. In all first-class cricket he took 160 wickets at 13.34, with only Larwood and Verity ahead of him in the national averages. Mitchell (121 at 21.42) and Alf Pope (99 at 18.13 and 13th place in the national lists) were other key bowlers, while Townsend finished with 63 wickets at 20 apiece. That magnificent attack, minus George Pope for most of the season, was supported by Elliott's splendid wicket-keeping. The fielding, perhaps, was not quite at its best, *Wisden* saying it left much room for improvement, but the close catching of Smith, Worthington, Townsend, and when he was available, Alan Skinner, played its part in the success.

In a wet summer the batsmen did not reveal the same powers of runmaking as in recent seasons but they usually ensured an adequate total made at a pace quick enough to enable the bowlers to do their work. Five of Derbyshire's victories were by an innings, a mark of their superiority, and there were four doubles.

Will Taylor lost no time in making arrangements for a civic reception:

It was suggested to me that when the Championship was won there should be a public reception for the team on their return to Derby following the match against Leicestershire at Oakham and I immediately set to work.

The Drill Hall was booked and I made contact with our president, the Duke of Devonshire, who was grouse shooting at Bolton Abey and who came post haste to Derby. The Mayors of the five towns in the county where we played were invited and were present. All arrangements were made for refreshments, and always having the financial position in view, the band of the Sherwood Foresters was booked for a dance after the reception of the team and a charge made to non-members of the Club. Everything went according to plan and we had a wonderful evening.

The reception was held on the Tuesday evening. Arthur Richardson said that whenever he had asked the team for extra effort in a crisis he had always received it. Will Taylor read one or two of the handful of telegrams he had received – congratulations from Brian Sellers, captain of Yorkshire, and one from Maurice Turnbull of Glamorgan on a success gained without having to use them as fodder. The Welsh county finished second from the bottom and Derbyshire did not meet them in the mid-1930s, possibly because of the distance they had to travel.

Wisden said that Derbyshire's triumph was gained on sheer merit:

Their cricket, reflecting as it always did the true spirit of the game, caused delight to thousands of enthusiasts up and down the country.

Magnificent bowling – they possessed probably the deadliest and best varied attack of any side in the country – team-work rather than individual brilliance, and a will-to-win spirit no matter the position of the game, were the salient factors which made Derbyshire stand out head and shoulders above most of their rivals.

Richardson recalled the Championship side in an interview with Gerald Mortimer, of the *Derby Evening Telegraph* 35 years later:

Copson and Tommy Mitchell were at the heart of the Championship victory. Two killers, both positive bowlers and both likely to run through a side. Their personalities were as different as their bowling styles.

Bill gave nothing away. Tommy was always tempting them with his leg spinners and was liable to be hit. But he was equally liable to get wickets and get them quickly.

Unfortunately, we lost George Pope in May of 1936 with cartilage trouble after he had really developed during the previous two seasons. But his brother, Alf, did wonderfully well.

He was a most willing player. I would sometimes tell him that he might have to bowl until close of play and he would just say; 'I like bowling, skipper.' and come bounding in for hours.

I wanted Leslie Townsend to make runs, so I did not use his off-spinners nearly as much as Guy Jackson had done. He became a perfect complement to Stan Worthington.

Stan enjoyed fast bowling; Leslie was infinitely happier against spin. I pushed Stan up the order and, therefore, he did not bowl much. I was more interested in specialists rather than all-rounders.

Stan Worthington was a wonderful cricketer. There were times, watching from the edge, when it was hard to tell if it was Stan Worthington or Wally Hammond at the crease. I cannot pay a bigger compliment than to compare him and Hammond.

Denis Smith was a most beautiful hitter. He was inclined, like all hitters, to be erratic, but his record over the years provides an answer to that.

So, with Albert Alderman an unassuming opener and a fine fielder, the top batting was good enough. With Copson and Mitchell in the side, we did not need too many runs and, as a result, the games were always open.

Alan Skinner has never been given the credit due to him. He did not win a blue at Cambridge, but he was one of the best amateur cricketers in the country.

He scored a lot of his runs down to third man and those who did not know him thought he was snicking the ball. In addition he was a superb catcher. I owe him a great debt for the way he filled in when Harry Storer went off to manage Coventry City.

Harry, I am sure, would have played for England if he had not always had football at the back of his mind. He and Arnold Hamer are the only two complete players I have seen play for Derbyshire.

Harry Elliott, of course, was a great wicket-keeper and a wonderful influence on the side. Think of the best regimental sergeant-major you have ever known – that was Harry Elliott.

It was a privilege for me to play in company with such fine cricketers and such wonderful people.

The professionals shared the feeling. They presented him with a silver cigarette case inscribed with the signatures of the Championship team and the simple dedication: 'To the skipper, from the lads.'

Alan Skinner also recalled that marvellous season with affection:

The side had a magnificent attack, both in depth and variety, for all sorts of wickets, and we fielded well with plenty of good close-to-the-wicket experts. It was, of course, not a great batting side, but we were in the first three of the Championship for four years so it could not have been all that bad! We had a number of batsmen who could score quickly and this meant that in uncertain weather our bowlers had time to get the opposition out twice and we could usually finish a match without a contrived ending.

Actually, I always felt the 1935 side played better cricket. So far as I can recall we had a better record and were a bit unlucky not to win the Championship that year.

Derbyshire, the County Champions, 1936. Standing: H. Elliott, L. F. Townsend, W. H. Copson, J. Bennett (masseur), H. Parker (hon. scorer), A. V. Pope, D. Smith, C. S. Elliott. Seated: H. Storer, T. S. Worthington, A. W. Richardson (capt.), T. B. Mitchell, A. E. Alderman.

Yorkshire were always our toughest opponents during those seasons, although, oddly enough, I usually managed to make a few runs against them. It is interesting to compare the Championship attack with bowlers like Jackson and Gladwin in later years. I should say there was little to choose between these two and Copson and Pope, but the latter had the advantage of being supported by Townsend, Mitchell and George Pope, when he was fit, and this helped to maintain the pressure.

Derbyshire did not play Glamorgan or Middlesex in 1936, meeting all of the remaining 14 counties in home and away matches. They won six games on their opponents' grounds and seven at home, three each at Derby and Chesterfield and one at Burton-on-Trent. Two of the four defeats occurred at Ilkeston.

There had been a change of groundsman for the Championship summer, Harry Williams' spell ending on 5 October 1935 when he moved to Old Trafford. He was succeeded by Harry Fletcher, who

1936 COUNTY CHAMPIONSHIP TABLE – FINAL POSITIONS

	Played	Won	Lost	Won on 1st inns	Lost on 1st inns	No result	Points possible	Points obtained	Percent-age
Points awarded	—	15	—	5	3	4	—	—	—
Derbyshire	28	13	4	5	5	1	420	239	56.90
Middlesex	26	10	4	8	3	1	390	203	52.05
Yorkshire	30	10	2	12	4	2	450	230	51.11
Gloucestershire	30	10	7	4*	8	1	450	203	45.11
Nottinghamshire	28	8	3	9	8	0	420	189	45.00
Surrey	30	9	7	6	6	2	450	191	42.44
Somerset	26	9	10	2	3	2	390	162	41.53
Kent	28	9	9	4	5	1	420	174	41.42
Essex	26	8	8	5	5	0	390	160	41.02
Hampshire	30	7	5	9	9	0	450	177	39.33
Lancashire	30	7	6	7	5	5	450	175	38.88
Worcestershire	28	7	9	4	7	1	420	150	35.71
Warwickshire	24	4	8	2	7	3	360	103	28.61
Sussex	30	4	10	7	6	3	450	125	27.77
Leicestershire	24	2	5	8	8	1	360	98	27.22
Glamorgan	26	1	12	6	5	2	390	68	17.43
Northamptonshire	24	0	9	5*	9	1	360	61	16.94

*Including ten points for a win on the first innings in a match played under the Laws for one-day games.

had been groundsman to the Burton Gentlemen CC on The Meadows where Bass and Allsop also had grounds. Derbyshire played their early matches at Burton on pitches prepared by Fletcher who spent 15 years there. He had only a short term at Derby for he became ill during the 1937 season and died in October, aged 55. Alfred Pope carried on until on 26 January 1938 the 21-year-old Walter Goodyear was appointed, after spending eight years learning his trade at Chesterfield under Tinker Simpson and Harry Williams. When Williams came to Derby Goodyear took over at Queen's Park.

Derbyshire's scorer in their Championship year was Harry Parker, who had succeeded W. J. Piper in 1927, Piper ending a period of 35 years as scorer. Charles H. Wright, of Heanor, had scored in away games in the early 1920s, Harry Parker undertaking this job in 1925. He was born at Codnor, but spent much of his life in Ripley, where he was manager of the lamp wick factory of James Crossley and Co Ltd for 32 years.

Arthur Richardson left at the end of the season, resigning as captain after six highly successful years to concentrate on business. He was succeeded by Robin Buckston, who was born at Kensington in 1908 and educated at Eton and Cambridge University. In the 1927 match against Winchester, Buckston and E. R. Sheepshanks (a future Reuter correspondent who died covering the Spanish Civil War) added 144 for the last wicket after nine had fallen for 108, Sheepshanks making 116 and Buckston 39 not out. He was a useful batsman and a capable wicket-keeper, whose contribution to Derbyshire cricket was to be considerable. Captain in 1937–39 Buckston served as hon secretary and succeeded Guy Jackson to be chairman of the Club in 1960–65. He was also chairman of the selection committee and a great supporter of the Club. A schoolteacher in Bournemouth, his home was at Sutton-on-the-Hill.

As in the previous season Derbyshire made a slow start in 1937. There was a defeat at Worcester before the first victory at Chelmsford. Wins over Kent at Derby and Somerset at Ilkeston put Derbyshire in touch with the early leaders and these were followed by a 202-run victory over the New Zealand tourists at Derby. After making 241 Derbyshire gained a lead of 75, Mitchell taking five for 101. Smith (85) and Alderman (112) shared a first-wicket partnership of 165 in the second innings and the tourists, needing 403 to win, were all out for 200, Mitchell taking five for 75.

There was an innings victory over Leicestershire at Chesterfield, where Mitchell took six for 50 in the visitors' 130 and then Smith (121) and Alderman (175) began Derbyshire's reply with 233 in three hours. Buckston declared at 470 for six, Alderman and Worthington (72) adding 149 for the second wicket, which fell at 382! This was followed by a good win at Taunton, in which Bert Rhodes took six for 38 in the second innings.

A. E. G. 'Dusty' Rhodes began his career as a fast-medium bowler, but after the Second World War he turned to leg-breaks and googlies, although still bowling occasionally in his quicker style. Rhodes was also a useful, hard-hitting batsman.

Rhodes' early opportunities in 1937 arose because of an illness to Bill Copson which kept him out of several games, and was followed by a knee injury which put him out of the side for nearly a month. When Copson returned for the Warwickshire match at Derby on 17 July he had taken only 38 wickets at 21 each.

Earlier in the season Warwickshire had made 523 for seven against Derbyshire at Edgbaston with R. E. S. Wyatt (232) and Tom Dollery (128) sharing a fourth-wicket partnership of 253. But at Derby it was a different story. The home side won the toss and Copson and Rhodes opened the attack, Alf Pope recalling later that it was 'about the only time I never used the new ball'.

Copson began the attack from the Nottingham Road end with Rhodes operating from the old pavilion end. 'This was always the case,' said Alf Pope. 'Bill would have the benefit of bowling down the hill and usually bowled into the wind. When Bert came off after four overs I remember taking over at the pavilion end.'

Copson quickly made inroads into the Warwickshire batting. He took two wickets without conceding a run in his first two overs and, in five overs, three for five as Warwickshire crashed to 18 for five, Pope taking the other two wickets. Copson bowled Ord, his fourth victim, in his seventh over and dismissed Dollery and Mayer with the fifth and sixth balls of his eighth over. His hat-trick came when he bowled Fantham with the first delivery of his ninth and he finished the innings by bowling Hollies with his next ball to take four wickets in four balls. Warwickshire were all out for 28. Copson had taken eight wickets for 11 runs in eight overs and two balls, two of which were maidens. Pope had two for 5 in four overs and there was much speculation about what might have happened to Warwickshire if he had opened the bowling with Copson instead of Rhodes.

Copson had bowled at great speed and obtained devastating lift from what was described as a good wicket although it had some early life. He made the ball swing appreciably both ways and batsmen forced to play late defensive strokes seemed powerless to cope with him.

Derbyshire made 227, Copson hitting seven boundaries in his season-best 30 not out and then bowled Kilner with his second ball to take his sequence to five wickets in six balls. When he bowled Santall for the second time that day his sequence stood at six wickets in 13 deliveries. He finished the match with eleven for 93, Derbyshire winning by five wickets.

An innings victory over Nottinghamshire at Chesterfield, Derbyshire's fourth consecutive win and their tenth in 19 games, left them on 27 July with an outside chance of retaining the title. Although there were nine-wicket wins over Northamptonshire at Chesterfield and Sussex at Derby, where Worthington was forced to retire with cramp caused by a pad strap being too tight, when on 238 – he made 491 for once out against Sussex in 1937 – the chance was soon gone as Middlesex and Yorkshire fought out a titanic battle for the title, Derbyshire finishing third. It was an excellent all-round season for George Pope, in which he made 1,318 runs (average 35.62), with three hundreds, and took 92 wickets in all first-class matches.

Injuries had much to do with the inconsistency which prevented Derbyshire from making a realistic bid for the title. Mitchell broke a finger and later a thumb, Copson took 76 first-class wickets at 18.39 compared with his 160 in 1936 and this disturbed the 'brimstone and treacle' (as A. A. Thomson so aptly put it) combination of the Championship season. Nevertheless Smith (1,914 runs in all games) and Worthington (1,774) remained at the forefront of the country's runmakers and Alderman had his best season.

During the 1937–38 winter George Pope and Stan Worthington toured India with Lord Tennyson's side, Pope doing well with 58 wickets at 15.93 each. It was not an official Test tour but it

DERBYSHIRE *v* WARWICKSHIRE

Played at Derby, 17 and 19 July 1937

DERBYSHIRE WON BY FIVE WICKETS

WARWICKSHIRE	FIRST INNINGS		SECOND INNINGS	
W. A. Hill	c Smith b Copson	0	b Mitchell	105
N. Kilner	c Skinner b Copson	7	b Copson	0
F. R. Santall	b Copson	0	b Copson	1
J. Buckingham	b A. V. Pope	9	b G. H. Pope	7
Mr R. E. S. Wyatt	b A. V. Pope	1	c Smith b Mitchell	30
H. E. Dollery	b Copson	7	c Skinner b Copson	98
J. S. Ord	b Copson	1	c Worthington b Mitchell	9
Mr P. Cranmer	not out	2	lbw b G. H. Pope	6
J. H. Mayer	b Copson	0	not out	14
W. E. Fantham	b Copson	0	c G. H. Pope b Mitchell	4
E. Hollies	b Copson	0	lbw b Mitchell	0
Extras	lb 1	1	b 9, lb 7, w 1	17
Total		28		291

BOWLING	O	M	R	W	O	M	R	W
Copson	8.2	2	11	8	32	4	82	3
Rhodes	4	0	11	0	5	2	12	0
A. V. Pope	4	1	5	2	21	1	56	0
G. H. Pope					14	5	26	2
Mitchell					31.5	5	80	5
Townsend					2	1	2	0
Worthington					5	0	16	0

DERBYSHIRE	FIRST INNINGS		SECOND INNINGS	
D. Smith	b Mayer	6	c Cranmer b Mayer	32
A. E. Alderman	run out	8	lbw b Mayer	15
T. S. Worthington	b Hollies	5	c Buckingham b Mayer	18
Mr A. F. Skinner	lbw b Mayer	13	not out	12
L. F. Townsend	c Santall b Wyatt	52	b Mayer	2
G. H. Pope	b Mayer	8	c Dollery b Mayer	6
A. Rhodes	run out	58	not out	7
A. V. Pope	b Mayer	4		
H. Elliott	b Wyatt	9		
T. B. Mitchell	st Buckingham b Mayer	21		
W. Copson	not out	30		
Extras	b 12, lb 1	13	lb 1	1
Total		227	(five wkts)	93

BOWLING	O	M	R	W	O	M	R	W
Mayer	23	7	83	5	12.4	0	39	5
Wyatt	18.4	6	48	2	9	0	44	0
Hollies	11	1	42	1	3	0	9	0
Fantham	2	0	22	0				
Santall	5	0	19	0				

Umpires: E. Robinson and C. W. L. Parker

In this match Copson took four wickets in four balls and six in 13.

demonstrated that he was on the verge of international honours and indeed he was invited to Nottingham for the first Test against Australia in 1938 but was left out of the side. Nevertheless he enjoyed another marvellous summer and his spirited bowling, in which consistently good length and swerve provided the basis of his attack, and his aggressive batting brought him 1,040 runs and 103 wickets in all games.

Again in these glory years Derbyshire enjoyed a successful summer, winning eleven games and finishing fifth, only marginally short of third or fourth position. Again they went flat out for victory, 19 of their 28 matches ending with a decision and though never in the Championship hunt they continued the run which saw them in the first six for six consecutive seasons.

Another win in 1938 would have placed Derbyshire joint third, and with the Championship-winning team still virtually intact there seemed no reason why a title challenge could not be mounted in 1939. The power of the side was demonstrated when Oxford University were shot out for 72 and 47, Copson taking five for 12 and five for nine, including four wickets in five balls and a hat-trick in the same sequence. But there was a humiliating setback at Bramall Lane when, after dismissing Yorkshire for 83 (Alf Pope four for 37, George six for 44 bowling unchanged) Derbyshire were routed for 20. Smurthwaite (five for 7) who achieved little else that summer, and Smailes did the damage, Alf Pope being the top scorer with six! Derbyshire fared little better at the second attempt, being all out for 97, Smailes taking all ten. Derbyshire's 20 was their lowest score since 1888.

There was an exciting match at Cheltenham, however, when Gloucestershire were beaten by one run. The home side began their second innings needing 261 for victory and they got a good start. But although they claimed the extra half-hour 14 were still needed with three wickets left at the close of the second day's play. On the third morning Scott hit Mitchell for a boundary but was caught and bowled in his next over. Goddard took two twos off Copson and then fell to a catch by Leslie Townsend at mid-off and when Lambert joined Neale four were wanted. Each got a single before Neale skied Mitchell and was caught by Smith.

With war clouds looming Derbyshire journeyed to Taunton and ran into trouble against Somerset. Trailing by 77 on the first innings they were left to get 260 to win. Smith was out for 27 but a partnership of 188 between Leslie Townsend and Alderman changed the whole course of the game. Alderman made 55 and Derbyshire, 262 for three, won by seven wickets. Townsend mixed sound defence with powerful hitting in a four-hour stay during which he made an unbeaten 142, his best score.

Ten victories and eight defeats left Derbyshire in ninth place in what became an ordinary season after the heady summers of the past six years, but it was a fine year for Bill Copson. Chosen to make his Test debut at Lord's he took five for 85 and four for 67, *Wisden* commenting that 'he bowled keenly and if a trifle short of a length, always commanded respect'. In the second Test at Manchester his figures were two for 31 and one for 2, but he did not play in the final game against the West Indies at The Oval. Taking twelve wickets at 15.41 each, he headed the England bowling averages but the only other hint of representation for Derbyshire's players came with George Pope's selection for the 1939–40 tour of India which was cancelled because of the war.

So an era ended. Despite the hint of decline in 1939 that fine team would probably have gained more successes in the early 1940s had cricket continued. Six seasons would be lost to the war before what remained of it regrouped for the 1946 season.

LAST OF THE VINTAGE WINE

DERBYSHIRE FACED THE RESUMPTION OF county cricket in 1946 with the elderly remnants of the Championship-winning side and a lot of unknown quantity.

The war had allowed little scope for organised cricket, and one-day fixtures with Nottinghamshire were Derbyshire's only attempt at wartime games. Derby, the home of Rolls-Royce, was a target for the Luftwaffe and there were barrage balloons and anti-aircraft gun emplacements at the County Ground.

Captain G. R. Jackson had been appointed chairman of the committee and by 1945 a deficit of £800 in 1939 had been turned into a credit balance of £750. An appeal was launched to raise £10,000 to reconstruct the club.

George Pope, who would probably have become a regular member of the England side during the early 1940s, played in three of the Victory Tests against the Australians in 1945. The 18-year-old Reptonian, D. B. Carr, also played in one of the Lord's games.

Derbyshire's new captain, G. F. Hodgkinson, had only Bill Copson remaining from the principal members of that much-vaunted pre-war attack. Gilbert Hodgkinson was never anything more than a good club cricketer. He served as a captain with the Sherwood Foresters and was with the Highland Division in France, where he received a severe head wound. While in hospital near Fécamp he became a prisoner of war but received excellent treatment from a German surgeon and recovered from his wounds. He was repatriated via Sweden in 1943 in a prisoner exchange but *Wisden* in 1941 had published his obituary in its list of 'Deaths in the War 1940'. Fortunately for his family they had received a letter from him three months after he was posted missing.

When the war was over Hodgkinson was asked by Guy Jackson if he would captain Derbyshire. He accepted, although his greengrocery business meant that he was not available for a full season. In the event he captained the side in only 15 of the 27 first-class matches, Worthington, the vice-captain, deputising when he was absent.

In 1945 Derbyshire had arranged eight one- or two-day matches on a home and away basis. They held Yorkshire to two draws, Cliff Gladwin taking eight for 27 at Queen's Park, serving notice that he was likely to be Bill Copson's new-ball partner when Championship cricket resumed. Gladwin was 30 before he took his first first-class wicket but he finished the 1946 season with 109 wickets at 18.36 each. He also scored 566 runs – at almost 6 ft 3 in he had a long reach and could drive well – and the career of one of Derbyshire's greatest-ever bowlers was under way. He mixed in-swing with off-breaks that summer; in 1948–49 he developed a leg-cutter on the plumb South African pitches and with a high-armed action and light-footed run up to the wicket he became a magnificent bowler. Gladwin took a relatively short run up and with his burly build he was able to keep going for long spells, bowling his in-swingers and possessing a thorough knowledge of batsmen's strengths and weaknesses. He used the crease well to vary the angle and kept an accurate mental note of his bowling analysis. He played in eight Tests. It might have been many more had he not been a contemporary of Bedser. Fifteen wickets at 38.06 each was a somewhat modest return but he performed well as stock bowler during the South African tour and in the first Test at Durban he was involved in one of the most thrilling finishes in Test history. England were set 128 to win and had collapsed to 117 for eight when Gladwin joined Bedser.

As he walked out to bat he made his famous remark to Dudley Nourse, the Springbok captain: 'Cometh the hour, cometh the man.' Bedser levelled the scores off the sixth ball of the final over bowled by Tuckett. With one run needed to win Gladwin faced the last two balls, hitting out and missing the seventh. He and Bedser conferred and decided to run for anything off the last ball. Gladwin swung and missed, the ball struck his left thigh and bounced a yard or two in front of him, and the batsmen galloped to safety. England had won by two wickets and the bruise on Clifford Gladwin's left thigh became a temporary showpiece.

Throughout most of his career Gladwin was to have the assistance of Alan Revill's magnificent fielding in the leg-trap, a position in which he first fielded in 1947 after Copson had missed several chances in that position in one game. With an upright stance Revill was a hard-hitting batsman who scored most of his runs in front of the wicket, a world-class fieldsman and a useful off-break bowler.

Another newcomer in 1946 was Eric Marsh. A nephew of Stan Worthington he had worked as a miner before and during the war. In 1938 he was knocked unconscious in the Markham Colliery disaster which claimed more than 70 lives but recovered to take part in the rescue operations. A slow left-arm bowler and left-hand batsman, Marsh was a useful all-rounder. Once in 1948, when Derbyshire's twelfth man, he was summoned by Eddie Gothard to bowl, that great umpiring character Alec Skelding allowing the field to be set before intervening, Denis Smith also pointing out the error. At the end of the 1949 season Marsh was invited by John Eggar, then Master-in-charge of cricket at Repton, to coach at the school, a position he held for many years.

Eggar, too, made his debut for the County in 1946. A dogged

batsman he was to become a great asset to the club between 1946 and 1954 but was to appear in only 31 games, mainly during the August holidays. Another amateur, Pat Vaulkhard, was an aggressive batsman who played regularly for Derbyshire only in 1946 and in 1950, when he was captain.

Three defeats came in the first four games of 1946, and not until the 12th game on 5 July against Surrey at Derby was a victory registered. The Champions of a decade earlier had floundered in or around bottom place but the Surrey match brought a change of fortune. Smith made 140 and with Derbyshire needing 123 for victory Revill and Marsh saw them home by two wickets, sharing a vital partnership which clinched the points with only minutes to spare.

Four more wins in five games later on, over Sussex in the first county match at Abbeydale Park, Dore, at Southampton and Edgbaston and over Glamorgan at Chesterfield, lifted Derbyshire to respectability by early August. But they failed to win any of their last seven games and finished 15th with five wins and 12 defeats.

There was a remarkable performance at Trent Bridge where Denis Smith (who was the regular wicket-keeper from July) and Pat Vaulkhard shared a record fourth wicket partnership of 328, beating by 20 that of Davidson and Storer who had put on 308 at Old Trafford 50 years earlier. Three wickets had fallen cheaply but Vaulkhard made 264, only ten short of Davidson's record individual score in the Manchester game. He struck two sixes and 31 fours in an innings which lasted just over seven hours. Hodgkinson declared at 529 for nine and Nottinghamshire followed on 264 behind but rain limited play to 50 minutes on the final day and the match was drawn.

Smith (1,391 runs, average 35.66) was the leading batsman, Leslie Townsend being the only other player to register a four-figure aggregate. Of the bowlers Copson (93 first-class wickets) was still probably the fastest bowler in the country for a few overs, and Rhodes, mainly in his quicker style, took 75 wickets at nearly 30 apiece, but there was little other support for Gladwin. Only Armstrong of the slower bowlers was really impressive, and he headed the averages with 28 wickets at 17.60 each. During his career he played the equivalent of only two seasons, and the feeling remains that more might have been made of his skills by the club.

Although the bowling lacked depth, the batting was causing most concern. The Smith-Alderman combination which had produced eleven pre-war century opening partnerships, six of them in 1937, endured for only two games in 1946, Townsend being the regular opener with Smith and then Alderman as his principal partners.

Gilbert Hodgkinson thoroughly enjoyed his cricket but as he pointed out: 'At the end of the 1946 season, the Club realised I couldn't do too many jobs, for I had a living to earn, and very rightly appointed Eddie Gothard as skipper. He was able to devote more time to it than I was.'

Gothard was born at Burton-on-Trent and made occasional appearances for Staffordshire, playing in every game when they won the Minor Counties Championship for the sixth time in 1927. Although 42, he proved to be immensely keen, very fit, and an active fieldsman at mid-off or mid-on, where he hustled around with his spectacles fixed to his temples with adhesive plaster. A slow-medium seam bowler he was to produce a couple of astonishing performances during his two seasons in county cricket. As a captain he was a strict disciplinarian, but his sense of humour and understanding enabled him to get the best out of his men.

His hand was strengthened immeasurably in 1947 by the return of George Pope, who at 36 was still a formidable all-rounder. His power was badly needed in the middle-order and his in-swingers and leg-cutters added an extra edge to the attack. His return to share the new ball with Copson took a lot of the strain off the veteran fast bowler, who could now be used in shorter spells, and also allowed Gladwin to be used as first change. In a batsman's year the pace trio was probably the best in the land: Pope took 114 wickets, Gladwin 117 and Copson 89. All three played for England against the South Africans, Pope at Lord's, Gladwin at Old Trafford and The Oval and Copson at The Oval, where he opened the England attack with Gladwin.

At the start of the season Derbyshire looked like turning back the clock to the glory days. Defeat in the opening game at Canterbury was followed by a two-wicket victory over Worcestershire at Chester-field, a win at Birmingham and an innings success against Northamp-tonshire at Derby. Hampshire inflicted a seven-wicket defeat at Portsmouth but there followed one of the most amazing matches in Derbyshire's history when Somerset were beaten by an innings and 125 runs in one day at Chesterfield on 11 June 1947.

It was the first Championship match to be completed in a day since Lancashire beat Somerset in 1925 and Pope's in-swingers, bowled with great accuracy on a lively pitch against what *Wisden* described as 'irresolute batsmen' proved decisive. He bowled unchanged in both innings and his figures of six for 34 and seven for 16 were all the more remarkable because he conceded 24 runs before taking a wicket. When Derbyshire batted Vaulkhard's 84, including three sixes, proved the decisive innings. Eddie Gothard recalled that day with mixed feelings!

It was a great win but the only comment from the secretary, Mr W. T. Taylor, was 'we've lost two days gates'. I did not take very kindly to the remark at that time and it was only when I

Derbyshire in 1947. Back row: H. Elliott (coach), A. E. G. Rhodes, A. C. Revill, W. T. Taylor (sec.), L. F. Townsend, G. O. Dawkes, C. Baker (scorer). Seated: C. S. Elliott, A. E. Alderman, T. S. Worthington, E. J. Gothard (capt.), D. Smith, G. H. Pope (on ground), E. Marsh.

became aware of the financial struggle the club had had over so many years and for which he was largely responsible for overcoming that I fully understood and sympathised with his feelings.

Derbyshire were now second in the table but their challenge faltered. Lancashire beat them by three runs at Buxton after Gladwin (nine for 119) had been deprived of an opportunity to take all ten by Cranston's declaration on the second morning with one wicket remaining. Gloucestershire and the eventual winners Middlesex forged ahead but the cricket was seldom dull. Led by Bill Blaxland, Derbyshire, all out 32 in their second innings (Ian Smith six for 1, including a hat-trick) only just failed to beat the South Africans, the Springboks getting home by three wickets, and the Essex pair, Frank Vigar and Peter Smith, added 218 for the last wicket at Chesterfield in a remarkable display.

With Smith injured (Alderman also kept wicket in a few games) Harry Elliott came out of retirement to keep in four games, but any wicket-keeping problems were to be solved by the arrival of George

143

DERBYSHIRE *v* SOMERSET

Played at Chesterfield, 11 June 1947

DERBYSHIRE WON BY AN INNINGS AND 125 RUNS

SOMERSET	FIRST INNINGS		SECOND INNINGS	
F. S. Lee	lbw b Pope	16	c Elliott b Gladwin	1
H. Gimblett	c Vaulkhard b Gladwin	3	c Smith b Pope	2
M. Coope	b Pope	13	b Pope	3
H. T. F. Buse	c Alderman b Rhodes	23	c Smith b Gladwin	4
R. J. O. Meyer	b Pope	0	c Revill b Pope	0
A. W. Wellard	b Pope	4	c Elliott b Pope	0
G. W. L. Courtenay	b Pope	1	c Smith b Pope	3
W. T. Luckes	lbw b Rhodes	1	b Rhodes	11
J. Lawrence	lbw b Rhodes	0	c Townsend b Pope	5
M. Tremlett	b Pope	1	b Pope	1
H. Hazell	not out	2	not out	8
Extras	b 1, lb 2, nb 1	4		
Total		68		38

BOWLING	O	M	R	W	O	M	R	W
Pope	21	11	34	6	9.1	2	16	7
Gladwin	10	6	10	1	8	3	14	2
Rhodes	10.2	2	20	3	1	0	8	1

DERBYSHIRE	FIRST INNINGS	
A. E. Alderman	c Buse b Meyer	12
L. F. Townsend	st Luckes b Hazell	37
C. S. Elliott	c and b Hazell	46
P. Vaulkhard	b Wellard	84
D. Smith	c Wellard b Hazell	5
G. H. Pope	c Wellard b Hazell	2
A. C. Revill	lbw b Hazell	2
E. Marsh	b Lawrence	0
C. Gladwin	b Buse	35
A. E. Rhodes	c Wellard b Buse	0
E. J. Gothard	not out	2
Extras	lb 5, nb 1	6
Total		231

BOWLING	O	M	R	W
Wellard	11.2	2	35	1
Buse	3	2	3	2
Meyer	14	4	45	1
Lawrence	11	0	71	1
Hazell	18	1	64	5
Tremlett	2	0	7	0

Umpires: W. Elliott and C. N. Woolley

Derbyshire's one-day Championship victory, the first in the Championship since 1925.

Dawkes from Leicestershire. He began a Derbyshire career in which he was unlucky never to keep wicket for England – he was a contemporary of Godfrey Evans – and with his hard-hitting batting and fine keeping to the County's pace attack, he provided years of entertainment until his retirement in 1961. Standing nearly 6 ft Dawkes was one of the tallest of wicket-keepers.

The events of that glorious summer continued to unfold. At Trent Bridge, scene of so many huge scores in those days, Nottinghamshire were dismissed for 191 on the Saturday, Elliott and Townsend beginning Derbyshire's reply with 126 for the first wicket before Townsend was out for 76. Joined by Eggar, Elliott pushed the score along and by the close Derbyshire were 204 for one. On the Monday the runs continued to come at a rate of one a minute, both players reaching their centuries by the lunch interval. Elliott pulled the leg-spinner Harvey into the Trent Bridge car park for six and with a hook for four he reached his 200. At 475 for one, Eggar skied a ball from Winrow and Stocks ran in from mid-on to take the catch. The pair had put on 349 for the second wicket – the highest-ever partnership for any Derbyshire wicket – and Eggar was out for 173. In the next over Elliott played forward to Stocks and was leg before for a chanceless 215 in six hours, Gothard declaring at 496 for three. But Winrow and Harvey, in an unbroken sixth wicket stand of 303, saved the game.

Still the year was not yet done and in the penultimate game, Middlesex came to Derby. They won comfortably by 212 runs but not before Gothard, who had taken only one first-class wicket before this game, created a sensation by performing a hat-trick. Fairbairn was caught by Rhodes, Edrich caught and bowled and Robins held off a defensive stroke. Remarkably, in that great era of Derbyshire pace, Gothard's hat-trick – he took only six Championship wickets in the whole season – became one of the principal talking points. But the new bowler had no opportunity to shine in the last game of the summer at Worcester, Copson and Gladwin routing the home side for 56 and Derbyshire winning their eleventh match to finish the season in fifth place.

Tucked away in the 'also batted' and 'also bowled' section of Derbyshire's averages for 1947 is the name of L. Jackson: 0, 0; 13-2-46-1 – modest figures which nonetheless heralded the start of a great career. Leslie Jackson progressed in the time-honoured fashion of Derbyshire pace bowlers to the coal face and the Bassetlaw League. After some good performances here he was invited to join the Derbyshire ground staff on the recommendation of Harry Elliott. He made his first-class debut against Kent at Dore, opening the bowling with Copson when Gladwin was playing in the third Test and Pope was absent. Between 1947 and 1963 he was to take 1,733 wickets at

17.36 each, 1,670 of them for his County at 17.11 each, a record for any Derbyshire bowler.

Tall and wiry at 6 ft, Jackson was of a lively fast-medium pace, bordering on fast, and his bowling could be decidedly hostile. He was able to move the ball either way, often late, and make it lift awkwardly off a good length. His run-up was comparatively short, ten or twelve paces, and his action was not of the textbook for the arm tended to be a little low. Yet on most pitches and certainly on any with 'green' in them he was a deadly proposition. He was a natural bowler and if the purists felt he did not make the most of his height by bringing his arm over a little nearer to his ear he could direct them to the opinion of Alf Gover, the old Surrey and England fast bowler. Just before the 1949 season began he attended a fortnight's course run by Gover, who was full of praise for Jackson's attitude and ability and recommended only minor changes in his style.

Ten times he took more than a hundred wickets in a season, three times he appeared for the Players at Lord's but only twice was he chosen for England, against New Zealand at Old Trafford in 1949 and Australia at Headingley in 1961. That Jackson should have played in more than two Tests is beyond doubt. Hindsight suggests he would have been a good choice for the 1948–49 tour of South Africa in lieu of Maurice Tremlett as support for Bedser and Gladwin; had there been an MCC tour in 1949–50 he would surely have been picked. He was unlucky not to play against the West Indies in 1950 and although he struggled against injury that August he should have had John Warr's place in the 1950–51 Australian party led by Freddie Brown. Instead he toured India with a Commonwealth side but returned home after only two matches with an elbow injury which required an operation keeping him idle until well into the 1951 season. By the early 1950s the great era of pace also produced Tyson, Statham, Trueman, Loader and Moss, in addition to the established Bedser and Bailey. Yet he returned in 1961 to play a notable part in England's win at Leeds and in another era would surely have been a regular member of the Test side.

Eloquent tribute was paid to him by his County skippers such as Guy Willatt and Donald Carr, the latter recalling how one day in the dressing room after a hard day in the field he noticed a dark stain on Jackson's socks – blood from a burst blister. Said Carr: 'I asked him why on earth he hadn't told me about it, as I should have let him go off the field. His reply was "Well Skipper, you told me to bowl, so I went on bowling." What more could a captain want from any player?'

Yet for all his fame Jackson never lost touch with his background, returning to the mines each winter (he lost a brother in the 1950 Creswell colliery disaster). Later he had a surface job and after he retired he became a National Coal Board chauffeur. With the arrival of Les Jackson, Derbyshire's pace bowling tradition and its relationship with the coal mines reached its zenith. Hence the story that when the County needed a fast bowler they sent somebody along to the nearest colliery and whistled down the mine shaft.

Hostility, allied to the age-old principles of line and length, backed by splendid fielding and wicket-keeping were the hallmarks of the side. In 1948 the County could choose from four high quality fast or fast-medium bowlers – Copson, George Pope, Gladwin and Jackson – a redoubtable quartet though the four of them never appeared together in a County match. Copson was 40, Pope 37, Gladwin 32 and Jackson 27, so none of them were in the first flush of fast bowling youth – but then these were not the fast men of long, bounding run-ups and extreme pace. That they were all highly capable can be seen from their performances in 1948: Pope achieved the double (1,152 runs, 100 wickets) in 21 matches, still the joint-quickest for 60 years, Gladwin took 128 wickets, Jackson 65 and Copson, who missed much of the season through injury, 31 at 19 each. With Rhodes – who performed five hat-tricks during his career, four of them for his County – taking 75 wickets, although at 28 each, the attack was as good as any in the country and it resulted in another splendid season for Derbyshire.

It began with a victory over Somerset at Taunton, where Denis Smith raced to a century in 90 minutes. There was a fine batting display at Portsmouth where Pope (207 not out) and Rhodes (105 not out) shared a record unbroken stand of 241 for the seventh wicket, Hampshire only just avoiding defeat. Three consecutive victories followed, over Kent at Gillingham, Northamptonshire at Chesterfield and by 301 runs over the eventual Champions Glamorgan at Derby, Pope taking seven for 34 in the second innings.

Leading the Championship table, Derbyshire gained an 11-run victory over Somerset at Ilkeston and Leicestershire were beaten at Ashby-de-la-Zouch, Smith and Alderman recalling memories of their glory days with a second-wicket partnership of 209 and Gladwin taking eight for 56 in the second innings.

Then, at Chesterfield, the weather dealt Derbyshire a cruel blow in their match against Yorkshire. Glamorgan now led the table, Derbyshire being second and Yorkshire third. Both sides were depleted by injuries and Test calls, Yorkshire being without Hutton, Yardley and Coxon and Derbyshire minus Townsend, Vaulkhard and Copson. Brian Sellers – one of the selectors who had spurned the claims of Pope and Gladwin – won the toss and Yorkshire batted. After an hour they were 18 for six, Elliott holding two spectacular catches at silly mid-on and in the gully. Pope, from the pavilion end, was whipping the ball across from leg to off, Gladwin kept a nagging

DERBYSHIRE *v* YORKSHIRE

Played at Queen's Park, Chesterfield, 26, 28 and 29 June 1948

MATCH DRAWN

YORKSHIRE	FIRST INNINGS		SECOND INNINGS	
H. Halliday	c Dawkes b Pope	5	b Pope	0
E. Lester	c Elliott b Gladwin	0	c Dawkes b Pope	3
W. Watson	run out	4	c Revill b Gladwin	0
J. V. Wilson	c Elliott b Gladwin	2	lbw b Jackson	8
K. Smales	b Pope	1	c Dawkes b Pope	6
R. Aspinall	c and b Gladwin	5	c Revill b Pope	0
A. B. Sellers	b Pope	8	not out	0
J. P. Whitehead	b Pope	7		
T. F. Smailes	b Pope	7	not out	16
J. H. Wardle	not out	2		
D. V. Brennan	lbw b Pope	0		
Extras	lb 1, w 1, nb 1	3	b 1, lb 1, nb 2	4
Total		44	(for 6 wkts)	37

BOWLING	O	M	R	W	O	M	R	W
Pope	14.1	9	12	6	17	11	13	4
Gladwin	14	3	29	3	10	8	5	1
Rhodes					10	5	12	0
Jackson					3	2	3	1

DERBYSHIRE	FIRST INNINGS	
C. S. Elliott	lbw b Whitehead	62
A. Alderman	b Wardle	20
D. Smith	c Smales b Wardle	22
E. Marsh	run out	0
G. H. Pope	c Watson b Wardle	73
A. Revill	b Wardle	12
G. Dawkes	c Sellers b Wardle	68
A. E. Rhodes	c Wilson b Wardle	1
E. J. Gothard	lbw b Wardle	7
C. Gladwin	b Wardle	4
L. Jackson	not out	0
Extras	b 4, lb 3, nb 1	8
Total		277

BOWLING	O	M	R	W
Aspinall	13	1	49	0
Whitehead	15	5	46	1
Wardle	37.4	13	87	8
Smailes	14	4	38	0
Smales	16	6	49	0

Umpires: H. Elliott and B. Flint

Rain prevented Derbyshire's first victory over Yorkshire for 43 years.

length and by ten past one Yorkshire were all out for 44, Pope taking six for 12 and Gladwin three for 29. Keen fielding and aggressive pace bowling on a pitch that was not really difficult had given Derbyshire a splendid chance of winning their first game against Yorkshire for 43 years. With 14,000 people watching the first day's play they made 277, Pope top-scoring with 73, and then got three Yorkshire wickets down for 15 by the close. But rain washed out the second day and on Tuesday only 90 minutes' play was possible, the match ending in a draw despite Pope's superb all-round performance.

Defeats by Sussex and Middlesex damaged Derbyshire's hopes and the match against Gloucestershire seemed to be slipping away at Chesterfield for the first two days. On the final day, needing 278 to win, Derbyshire were 199 for eight when Gothard joined Pope. He was suffering from a pulled thigh muscle and needed a runner but he defended well in an unbroken stand of 81 to bring victory by two wickets, Pope making 125 not out. A win in the return at Bristol and a ten-wicket win over Sussex at Burton-on-Trent, Pope taking eight for 38 in the second innings, put Derbyshire back on top of the table. There was a setback at Colchester but an innings win over Nottinghamshire at Ilkeston kept Derbyshire on top before Gothard produced another of his amazing performances by bowling Bradman in the match against the Australians at Derby. Again there was a huge crowd – 14,000 – and the Don had made 62 when he tried to hook Gothard, appeared to pull the ball on to the ground and from there on to his wicket. Recalled Gothard:

> I had been trying to bowl little away swingers but sometimes I managed to produce a ball which came back and this is what happened on this occasion. It was a very hot afternoon with no breeze to carry the ball but it moved off the pitch. Bradman had moved across to play the ball through mid-wicket and he was outside his off-stump when he played the stroke. It was a bit optimistic to describe it as a hook, considering the pace at which I bowled.

So, like W. G. Grace, K. S. Ranjitsinhji, P. B. H. May and M. C. Cowdrey, Bradman never made a hundred against Derbyshire. In four innings in the County, once not out, he scored 183 runs, highest score 71, average 61. Including the matches in Australia, Worthington took his wicket three times and Townsend, Mitchell and Gothard once each.

Les Jackson made a big impression in this match, taking four for 103 in the tourists' 456, Pope and Copson being absent through injury. When Derbyshire batted Denis Smith made 88 which was then a County record against the Australians, who won by an innings.

Bradman is bowled by Eddie Gothard for 62 at Derby in 1948. The Don had four innings in Derbyshire – in 1930 at Chesterfield, when he was caught at the wicket off Worthington for 44 after sharing a second wicket stand of 106 with Ponsford (131); in 1934 at Chesterfield when he again fell to Elliott behind the wicket off Townsend for 71 and made six not out in the second innings; and at Derby in 1948 on the day after his unbeaten 173 in Australia's 404 for three to win the Headingley Test.

Derbyshire had mounted their strongest Championship challenge since 1936 but they were soon to run out of steam. Defeats by Surrey and Nottinghamshire cost them the leadership but by 18 August they were level with Glamorgan on 148 points after a victory over Leicestershire at Chesterfield, although the Welsh county had a game in hand. But they failed to take any points from their final two games and had to be content with sixth place, with eleven wins and six defeats, the last seven games bringing only one victory.

An injury to Pope, which prevented him from playing in the last five games, had much to do with this and in November he left county cricket, going to live in Jersey because of his wife's health, although he was to continue in the leagues, and in 1966 he became a first-class

Derbyshire v the Australians at Derby, July 1948. Glorious weather attracted a record first-day crowd estimated at 14,000.

umpire. The dour but consistent Elliott was the only batsman apart from Pope to score a thousand runs in the Championship. Smith, who became the County's leading run-scorer by exceeding Townsend's career aggregate, reached a thousand in all games.

In 1948 Eddie Gothard resigned the captaincy after two eventful years.

The new captain for 1949 was David Skinner, the younger brother of Alan. Thus the strict amateur tradition was maintained. Skinner was a useful lower-order batsman and off-break bowler, although he bowled only occasionally.

One by one, now, the stars of the 1930s were fading and on the hard, dry pitches of the parched summer of 1949 Derbyshire sometimes wore a jaded look. The season began well enough with victories over Somerset at Derby and Leicestershire at Ashby-de-la-Zouch (Revill 156 not out) in the opening games. Some appalling batting displays led to a number of defeats, although Lancashire were beaten at Buxton and the pace of Copson, Jackson and Gladwin paved the way for an eight-wicket victory over Essex at Westcliff. A century from Rhodes and some fine pace bowling undid Somerset at Taunton. At Bradford John Eggar stayed seven and a quarter hours in making 219 out of a second innings total of 491 but the match was still lost. Gladwin made a hundred at Trent Bridge, there was a close finish at Lord's when Middlesex ensured a share of the Championship with a three-wicket win (when Gladwin, after being run out, accidentally put his bat through the dressing room window) and the final game at Burton-on-Trent was won after Essex had been bundled out by the pace bowlers for 58 in their second innings. Six wins and 13 defeats left Derbyshire in 15th place, only three places off the bottom.

Copson, Jackson and Gladwin were probably the best pace trio in the land but on the prevailing good pitches 14 scores of more than 300 were made against Derbyshire while the side was bowled out for less than a hundred on seven occasions. Revill, Elliott, Smith and Rhodes reached a thousand runs and Gladwin missed the double only by 86 runs. Skinner, in his year of captaincy, set a fine example in the field and averaged 14 with the bat.

The batting was headed by Eggar, with 501 runs in seven games and another Repton schoolmaster, Richard Sale, a left-handed batsman and former Oxford blue hit a fine 146 at Old Trafford. In this match Derbyshire made 421 for seven declared, Eggar making 68 and Carr 72, so there was plenty of scope for headlines about Repton masters' caning attacks.

Carr's form in 1949 was a revelation in that he suddenly blossomed as a batsman after being primarily a slow left-arm bowler of high promise for a number of years. He was born in Wiesbaden when his father, a regular officer in the Royal Berkshire Regiment, was stationed in Germany. Donald and his two elder brothers Douglas and David spent their boyhood in India and Hampshire but in 1936 their father retired from the army and became Bursar at Repton School, Donald following his brothers as a pupil in 1940. He became captain in 1944, two years after he had first appeared for the school team, and during his three years in the side it was unbeaten until the final game against Rugby in 1944. Under the guidance of the master in charge of cricket, L. B. Blaxland, and the professional, Garnet Lee, he soon developed into one of the best schoolboy all-rounders of his day. In 1944 he captained The Rest against the Lord's Schools and also the Public Schools against a Lord's XI. Leaving Repton at Christmas he joined the army on New Year's Day 1945 and that summer, at 18, played for England in a Victory Test at Lord's. In April 1948 he went to Oxford University but was unable to gain a blue because Kardar was established as the slow left-hander, so he changed to unorthodox spin, with chinamen and googlies, and also concentrated on his batting.

In 1949 Carr hit three centuries for the University, played in eight games for Derbyshire, and in all first-class cricket made 1,210 runs (average 31.02). He became a Derbyshire regular in 1952, captained the side in 1955–62 and was secretary of the Club in 1960–62. Donald Carr managed three MCC Test tours abroad and was MCC assistant-secretary in 1962–74 and secretary of the Test and County Cricket Board and the Cricket Council from the early 1970s until he retired in 1986. He gained three blues at Oxford, being captain in 1950, was vice-captain of the MCC team which toured India in 1951–52 and led the MCC 'A' team in Pakistan in 1955–56. During the tour of India he captained England at Madras and he played in two Tests, his best innings being 76 in the first Test at Delhi when he and Alan Watkins shared a match-saving partnership of 158 when England faced defeat.

Carr – also a good soccer player who appeared for Pegasus in two Amateur Cup finals – was an attractive and free-scoring batsman, with pulls, cuts and the on-drive among his best strokes. He also became a world-class close-to-the-wicket fieldsman. In 1949 he was emerging as a possible England batsman of the future and it was during that season that Jackson and Gladwin appeared in Tests against the New Zealanders. They also opened the North's attack in the Test trial at Edgbaston, Jackson taking six for 37 and Gladwin two for 11 in the South's first innings of 85.

Yet despite the success of Derbyshire's fast bowlers and the promise of Carr it was clear that the need for sweeping changes had arrived. The first step taken by the committee was to appoint a new captain to succeed David Skinner and it was decided that the position should be held jointly by Pat Vaulkhard and another Repton schoolmaster, Guy Willatt, who would take over in August. Willatt fractured a finger in his first game as captain and Vaulkhard remained captain for the whole season.

Then came the registration of two batsmen, Arnold Hamer and John Kelly. Kelly was a stylish opening batsman from Lancashire who, as Cyril Washbrook's understudy, had found opportunity limited. Of the two new batsmen Kelly had appeared to be the better prospect but it was Arnold Hamer who was to become one of the finest openers ever to play for the County. At 33 he had little experience of county cricket but had received a thorough grounding in the leagues. Hamer had been given a trial with Yorkshire before the war, appearing in two first-class games in 1938. During the war he continued in the Huddersfield League before joining Spen Victoria in the Bradford League, where George Pope was a colleague. Later he played for Pudsey St Lawrence and in 1949 he established a new Bradford League record with 1,106 runs (average 73.73) in his final season prior to joining Derbyshire.

With sandy hair and ruddy complexion and being a trifle bow-legged, Hamer looked and was a rugged opening batsman, a forceful player who liked to get on top of the bowling and who was capable of hammering the first ball of any match to the boundary. He possessed a sound defence and drove firmly, particularly on the off-side. His age, the war, restricted opportunities with Yorkshire, all combined to prevent him from reaching the heights earlier in his life which could have led to a place in the England side. As it was his consistency brought him more than 15,000 runs for Derbyshire between 1950 and 1960, with a thousand runs in each of ten consecutive seasons and 19 hundreds. He was a safe fieldsman and a useful off-spin bowler.

By contrast Derek Morgan began his career with Derbyshire at 21 and was destined to play more matches for the County than anybody else, 540 between 1950 and 1969. Only Denis Smith scored more runs for Derbyshire than Morgan's 17,842, only Jackson, Gladwin, Bestwick and Mitchell exceeded his 1,216 wickets, no fieldsman surpassed his 563 catches. In eight seasons he made more than a thousand runs and he scored nine hundreds, seven in three consecutive years, 1962–64. He is the only Derbyshire player to score more than 15,000 runs, take more than a thousand wickets and hold more than 500 catches.

Yet Morgan never achieved a double, which indicates his consistency in producing such excellent career figures. He could count himself unlucky that he never played for England – he surely would have done if his career had spanned more recent times – but he was 12th man in five Tests, testimony to his splendid fielding, especially close to the wicket at backward short leg. As a batsman he was no great stylist but his application gradually resulted in him moving up the order and he produced his thousand runs a season quite regularly in his best years. As a fast-medium bowler his mixture of outswing and break backs could be lethal in the right conditions. To crown his career he was captain of Derbyshire from 1965 to 1969.

Guy Willatt was born at Nottingham and like Pat Vaulkhard and Rev Granville Payton, who made two appearances for Derbyshire in 1949, previously played for the County of his birth before transferring across the Erewash. Willatt was educated at Repton and Cambridge University, gaining his blue in 1946 and captaining the light blues in the following year.

His move to Repton in September 1950 came after a period as a master at Edinburgh Academy and he was specially registered to play for Derbyshire that summer. Willatt became the regular captain in 1951, continuing until the end of the 1954 season. Later appointments as headmaster of Heversham Grammar School in Westmorland and Pocklington in Yorkshire took him away from the County but he returned after his retirement and became chairman of the cricket committee in 1985, succeeding Charlie Elliott. Willatt was a solid, dependable left-handed batsman and a fine fieldsman in the covers who made hundreds for four first-class sides – Cambridge University, Nottinghamshire, Scotland and Derbyshire. In 1947 and 1952 he represented the Gentlemen at Lord's and he obtained a soccer blue at Cambridge.

With Dick Sale and John Eggar from the Repton teaching staff and ex-pupil Donald Carr available the Repton link had never been stronger, particularly as Eric Marsh was appointed professional in 1950, succeeding former players Wilfred Carter (1929–30), Garnet Lee (1941–45) Harold Pope (1947) and Albert Alderman (1948).

Derbyshire's 'new-look' team began the 1950 season with a defeat at The Oval, although Kelly made 74 in his second innings for the County. By June they had won only one of their first six games and a long and bitter struggle to avoid last place seemed likely. The victory had been over Northamptonshire at Derby when, set to score 227 in 200 minutes, they obtained the runs with nine minutes to spare after an unbroken partnership of 105 between Revill (108 not out) and Rhodes for the fifth wicket.

On 3 June Derbyshire began a match with Yorkshire at Bradford and a fine innings of 122 not out by Denis Smith, in which he struck two sixes and 12 fours, helped his side to a total of 289. Les Jackson dismissed Hutton for nought in the first over and some skilful leg-break bowling by Rhodes gave Derbyshire a lead of 60. Vaulkhard declared and set Yorkshire to score 299 in 160 minutes. Hutton made a century in 73 minutes and he and Lowson began with an opening stand of 123 in 52 minutes. But wickets fell steadily to Rhodes's cleverly flighted leg-spin and googlies and Derbyshire won by 79 runs, Rhodes taking six for 74 and, in the match, ten for 126. It was Derbyshire's first victory over Yorkshire since 1905, a spell of 45 years, and the main protagonists had been Smith and Rhodes, both of whom had been members of the fine pre-war sides, although almost everybody played their part. The last eight Yorkshire wickets had fallen in 45 minutes for 37 runs.

The victory boosted morale, particularly as Yorkshire were to finish third in the table. Worcestershire were beaten at Ilkeston but five of the next seven Championship matches were lost before Lancashire, joint Champions in 1950, were beaten at Old Trafford by 93 runs. Derbyshire trailed by 36 on the first innings but 109 from Revill helped them set a target of 238 and on a wet pitch Lancashire never looked like getting the runs. Eight victories in 28 games earned Derbyshire fifth position, a remarkable achievement in a summer of rebuilding.

Guy Willatt became captain for the 1951 campaign. Injuries played havoc with the side. Not until the end of July did Willatt have all his bowlers available and only one victory came in the first 15 games. Somerset were beaten at Frome and there were further wins at Portsmouth and Folkestone and an innings victory over Nottingham-shire at Ilkeston. A win by an innings over Leicestershire at Burton-on-Trent, where Alwyn Eato took five for 14 in the visitors' first innings of 45 left Derbyshire in eleventh position, with five victories.

Eato, described by Donald Carr as 'on his day one of the quickest and most hostile bowlers I have seen' received only limited opportunities between 1950 and 1955 because of the presence of Jackson, Gladwin and Morgan. He did well in Bassetlaw League cricket with Worksop, particularly in the late 1950s.

The big discovery of 1951 was Edwin Smith who in his second game for the County, at the age of 17, took eight for 21 in Worcestershire's second innings at Chesterfield with his off-spin bowling. On a worn pitch he took eight of the last nine wickets to fall, Willatt holding three catches and Hamer two. Smith was spotted by Harry Elliott when he held a coaching session at Clay Cross. After a game with the junior team in 1950 he was invited for a month's trial in the following spring and taken on to the staff. He made his debut against Hampshire at 17 years, five months and four days. The youngest player to represent Derbyshire is Fred Swarbrook, who made his debut against Cambridge University at Ilkeston in 1967 at the age of 16 years and six months. So Smith is the youngest to play in a Championship game.

Smith's family nickname of 'Tat' had nothing to do with Roy Tattersall, then one of the country's leading off-spinners but it remained with him throughout his cricket career. Boyish and rosy cheeked Smith turned the ball sharply but suffered by being generally the solitary spinner in a seam-dominated attack, which meant that he was often used in a defensive role.

His arrival was another step in the reconstruction of the side which had begun in 1950. The changes marked a new era especially as Denis Smith announced his retirement in 1951 although he was to play in one game the following season. In a remarkable career he had established a record aggregate for the County of 20,516 runs (average 31.42), with 30 centuries, also a record. In all first-class matches he made 21,843 runs (average 31.66), and hit 32 hundreds.

Smith was appointed County coach in 1952, Harry Elliott becoming an umpire once again. He was to coach Derbyshire's youngsters for the next two decades. He was a hard taskmaster, grudging with his praise. He once said: 'They said I was too harsh with them, but they were men, not boys. They didn't want mollycoddling and they learned to fight back at me in the nets. This taught them how to fight back in the middle and nobody could hold their hands out there, could they?'

A word of encouragement for young players from Smith was worth a volume of fulsome praise from others. The pipe, the faded England blazer, the County cap and his tall, gritty figure became a familiar sight on Derbyshire's grounds in an association with the Club which was to cover 44 years. Perhaps his character is best typified by a comment he made about his 189 against Yorkshire at Queen's Park in 1935, an innings he regarded as a turning point in his career. 'I remember thinking that day "these beggars can't bowl, I'm going to give them some stick".' 'These beggars' included Bill Bowes and Hedley Verity.

His retirement meant that the era of the vintage eleven which won the 1936 Championship was over. Charlie Elliott remained until 1953, Bert Rhodes, who made his debut in 1937, finished a year later. The remnants of that great side almost pulled off another title in 1948 and Smith in particular continued to give the County's followers a glimpse of how things used to be until 1951. The veterans and the newcomers who were introduced as they grew older and retired produced a team which beat every other county except Middlesex between 1946 and 1951.

OH MY JACKSON
AND MY GLADWIN . . .

THE RUN-STEALERS OF FRANCIS THOMPSON'S evocative poem have few parallels in the minds of most Derbyshire followers.

Perhaps of all the batsmen Wright and Kirsten will be the pair that flicker to and fro as memories of their crucial partnership in the NatWest final of 1981 mellow, just as those of Hornby and Barlow did in Thompson's mind 80 years ago.

The bowling, though, is a different matter. Those great pairings of Hulme and Davidson, Warren and Bestwick, Copson and the Popes, Jackson and Gladwin, Rhodes and Brian Jackson, Ward and Hendrick, Holding and Mortensen – any of these have served to arouse a host of memories down the generations. And while it seems invidious to nominate any pair greater than the others the Jackson-Gladwin combination must rank first simply because it was the most successful of a highly successful strain.

By 1952 they were approaching their peak. Astutely led by Guy Willatt Derbyshire were spearheaded by perhaps the most feared new-ball attack in the Championship – and this in an era of fast bowling riches unsurpassed in English cricket.

Willatt has told of the apparently grim but so successful method adopted by his side in those memorable years. Writing at the time of the Club's centenary in 1970 he compared Derbyshire to the Nottinghamshire he had known at Trent Bridge, where the sun always shone and the scoreboard seemed to show 280 for three on a summer's afternoon:

> At Derby (or Chesterfield) it was quite different. As I look back, a certain damp greyness seems to pervade all. The score at tea is more likely to be 180 for eight as the batsmen of either side struggle for survival and all is aggressive hostility and combative drama.

In Derbyshire, he found, the bowlers reigned supreme and this demanded a different mental approach and certain tactics which in footballing terms would then in 1970 be known as 'The Method':

> There was an absolute concentration on economy and 'the buying of wickets', or the giving away of easy runs, was a luxury that a County with Derbyshire's batting resources just could not afford. Technically speaking then Derbyshire bowlers (with notable exceptions) have been just below fast and just above slow. For to aim for maximum speed or subtleness of flight could lead to the

occasional loose delivery – and that was a sin and a crime. A nagging accuracy, a war of attrition would in the long run deliver up the enemy more cheaply.

Not that the tactics were purely defensive, for hostile fields were set, populated by an arc of close fieldsmen confident of their own safety because they were confident of the accuracy of the bowlers. ' "Method" cricket it is then (before the word was invented), gritty, purposive, combative, intensely competitive,' he wrote.

In 1952 Jackson took 108 wickets in the Championship and Gladwin 151; in all first-class matches Jackson had 119 and Gladwin 152. Morgan (921 runs, 71 wickets and 38 catches) gave them admirable support, Revill established a new County record with 42 catches and 45 in all games, Carr and Elliott each held 33. Behind the stumps Dawkes held 51 catches and stumped 12 batsmen. With Rhodes taking 83 wickets this was a superb side. Elliott headed the averages with 1,559 runs, average 34.76. Willatt made the number three position his own; he, Revill and Hamer also exceeding 1,400 runs. At Stourbridge Gladwin took seven for 43 and nine for 41 (16 for 84 in the match). At Ilkeston hundreds by Hamer and Carr enabled Derbyshire to declare at 529 for seven against Nottinghamshire and force victory in a run of twelve undefeated games which mounted a strong Championship challenge. But Surrey beat them by six wickets at Chesterfield and the season ended with eleven victories and fourth place. There was also a fine performance against the Indians, who were shot out for 86 at Queen's Park, Jackson (six for 39) and Morgan (three for 35) bowling unchanged. Rain intervened with the tourists 115 for three in their second innings, chasing a target of 373.

In 1953 Edwin Smith took five for 36 in the Australians' second innings at Chesterfield, the match being drawn, Gladwin taking nine for 143 in the match, and in the following game there was a remarkable performance against Surrey at Derby.

By lunch on the first day the Champions, unbeaten since August 1952, had collapsed to 46 for eight, Gladwin having taken five for 21 and Jackson three for 25. Surridge improved matters but the fast bowlers operated unchanged in dismissing Surrey for 81, Derbyshire being 132 for three by the close. Facing a deficit of 143 Surrey began well but slid to an innings defeat against the bowling of Gladwin and Carr, Morgan brilliantly running out Fletcher to start the collapse, the match ending in two days.

Joint sixth in 1953 with nine wins Derbyshire by 1954 had emerged as one of the most dangerous sides in the country. It was a side which was rich in team spirit. Ken Shearwood, one of Carr's Pegasus colleagues, recalled that when he kept wicket in his only first-class

DERBYSHIRE *v* SURREY

Played at The County Ground, Derby, 20, 22 and 23 June 1953

DERBYSHIRE WON BY AN INNINGS AND 1 RUN

SURREY	FIRST INNINGS		SECOND INNINGS	
D. G. Fletcher	b Jackson	3	run out	24
E. Bedser	b Gladwin	0	c Elliott b Jackson	2
B. Constable	c Morgan b Gladwin	7	b Gladwin	20
P. B. H. May	b Jackson	0	b Carr	30
T. Clark	lbw b Gladwin	16	c Carr b Gladwin	19
R. Pratt	c Dawkes b Jackson	1	c Willatt b Gladwin	3
J. C. Laker	b Gladwin	0	c Morgan b Carr	12
W. S. Surridge	c Dawkes b Jackson	51	c Dawkes b Carr	7
A. Bedser	c Dawkes b Gladwin	0	b Carr	16
G. Kirby	c Revill b Jackson	1	c Carr b Gladwin	1
J. W. McMahon	not out	2	not out	1
Extras		0	b 5, lb 1, nb 1	7
Total		81		142

1st inns: 1-0, 2-10, 3-10, 4-12, 5-25, 6-26, 7-31, 8-33, 9-46, 10-81
2nd inns: 1-4, 2-42, 3-51, 4-102, 5-102, 6-115, 7-124, 8-124, 9-126, 10-142

BOWLING	O	M	R	W	O	M	R	W
Jackson	20.4	8	34	5	8	3	8	1
Gladwin	20	6	47	5	20	3	58	4
Morgan					8	1	28	0
Smith					8	1	13	0
Carr					12.5	3	28	4

DERBYSHIRE	FIRST INNINGS	
C. Elliott	c Laker b Surridge	16
A. Hamer	b McMahon	43
G. L. Willatt	c Constable b McMahon	16
A. C. Revill	c Clark b Laker	31
D. B. Carr	c Laker b Surridge	43
J. Kelly	c Clark b Laker	1
D. Morgan	c Pratt b Laker	8
G. Dawkes	c A. Bedser b Surridge	15
C. Gladwin	not out	20
E. Smith	c Fletcher b A. Bedser	4
L. Jackson	c Constable b A. Bedser	11
Extras	b 10, lb 6	16
Total		224

1st inns: 1-29, 2-57, 3-93, 4-140, 5-141, 6-162, 7-184, 8-191, 9-200, 10-224

BOWLING	O	M	R	W
A. Bedser	26.3	8	53	2
Surridge	26	2	78	3
McMahon	31	18	33	2
Laker	21	6	41	3
E. Bedser	4	2	3	0

Umpires: E. A. Roberts and P. Corrall

Derbyshire's two-day defeat of the Champions.

Derbyshire v Gloucestershire played at Queen's Park, Chesterfield in 1954.

match for the County in 1949 he and the other two amateurs, David Skinner and Laurie Johnson, stopped at different hotels, changed in a different room and ate at a different table to the professionals, although he believed the food was the same. It was an old-fashioned amateur-professional segregation which Willatt eliminated during his term as captain.

The season began well with victories at Derby over Leicestershire, Gravesend and Westcliff in the opening three games. Scotland were beaten at Buxton in the first meeting between the sides but six Championship matches passed without a win, three being lost, one of them, crucially, against Surrey at Derby. Then came a thrilling victory at Cardiff. Jackson and Gladwin bowled unchanged in the Glamorgan first innings of 55; set 381 to win Glamorgan got to within six of the target before Gladwin settled the issue with his 1,000th wicket for the County. The sequence was extended to five consecutive victories, Lancashire being routed for 36 at Buxton, Kent beaten at Chesterfield and wins at Horsham against Sussex and Yeovil against Somerset following.

A setback at Worcester followed but by 20 July Derbyshire (116 points from 16 matches) were leading contenders for the Championship behind Yorkshire (142 from 19) and Warwickshire (124 from 19), the Champions Surrey being well down the list with 92 from 16. Derbyshire then faced the Championship leaders Yorkshire at Headingley. They made a poor start after being put in by Yardley. With the score at 12 Trueman dismissed Kelly, Willatt and Revill without addition. Carr was fourth out at 53 before Morgan helped Hamer add 131 for the fifth wicket. Hamer carried his bat for 147 (one six, 21 fours), Jackson helping him put on 41 for the last wicket, the total reaching 272. By the close Yorkshire had made 44 for the loss of Lowson.

On Thursday morning Yorkshire collapsed once Hutton had been removed and at lunch were 100 for seven, 23 still being needed to save the follow-on. They failed by four runs, Morgan taking five for 23, but although Hutton was absent with a broken bone in his hand Watson batted well and the arrears were cleared for the loss of two second-innings wickets. At the close Yorkshire were 190 for four, a lead of 37.

On the final morning they were all out for 207, Morgan completing a match analysis of ten for 78. Fittingly he made the winning hit when Derbyshire were set 55 for victory. They lost four wickets in obtaining the runs, including that of Hamer, who failed by just five balls to achieve the feat of being on the field of play for the duration of the match.

This memorable victory was Derbyshire's first at Leeds since 1895 and it lifted them into second place with 132 points from 19 games, ten points behind Yorkshire and four ahead of Warwickshire, with two games in hand over each county.

Having disposed of Yorkshire, Derbyshire now entered upon another trial of strength at Edgbaston. Here, some splendid bowling by Jackson (five for 28), Gladwin, Morgan and Smith reduced Warwickshire to 106 all out, Fred Gardner, so often a stumbling block to Derbyshire bowlers, staying nearly four hours for 40. Derbyshire slumped in turn to 92 for seven by the close of play but Carr (62) and Gladwin (38) earned them a lead of 52 on a rain-affected second day, Warwickshire being 41 for the loss of Horner by the close. But rain washed out Derbyshire's victory hopes on the last day.

They hit back at Cheltenham, dismissing Gloucestershire for 43 and clinching first innings points before lunch with a score of 44 without loss! That game was won and when Worcestershire were beaten at Derby they were clear favourites for the title, despite Surrey's late surge. On 17 August, with four games left, they had 164 points from 24 matches, Surrey having 160 from 24. Yorkshire were still leading

YORKSHIRE *v* DERBYSHIRE

Played at Headingley, 28, 29 and 30 July 1954

DERBYSHIRE WON BY 6 WICKETS

DERBYSHIRE	FIRST INNINGS		SECOND INNINGS	
A. Hamer	not out	147	b Appleyard	34
J. M. Kelly	c Appleyard b Trueman	3	lbw b Trueman	4
G. L. Willatt	b Trueman	0	c Trueman b Wardle	9
A. Revill	c Lowson b Trueman	0	run out	0
D. B. Carr	c Trueman b Appleyard	22	not out	3
D. Morgan	c Wardle b Trueman	66	not out	1
G. O. Dawkes	c Close b Trueman	4		
C. Gladwin	b Trueman	2		
E. Smith	c Close b Appleyard	8		
R. Carter	b Appleyard	0		
L. Jackson	b Close	17		
Extras	lb 2, w 1	3	lb 4	4
Total		272	(for 3 wkts)	55

1st inns: 1-12, 2-12, 3-12, 4-53, 5-184, 6-190, 7-198, 8-221, 9-231, 10-272
2nd inns: 1-9, 2-46, 3-46, 4-53

BOWLING	O	M	R	W		O	M	R	W
Trueman	29	6	109	6		6	1	30	1
Appleyard	29	5	99	3		8	1	16	1
Wardle	16	8	28	0		2.2	1	5	1
Close	4.2	0	33	1					

YORKSHIRE	FIRST INNINGS		SECOND INNINGS	
L. Hutton	lbw b Gladwin	44	absent hurt	0
F. A. Lowson	c Dawkes b Morgan	14	lbw b Morgan	27
J. V. Wilson	lbw b Jackson	31	b Morgan	39
E. I. Lester	lbw b Morgan	1	c Revill b Gladwin	29
W. Watson	b Morgan	2	run out	73
N. W. D. Yardley	b Smith	3	c Dawkes b Gladwin	30
D. B. Close	c Jackson b Morgan	2	c Hamer b Morgan	4
J. H. Wardle	c Carr b Morgan	0	b Morgan	1
R. Booth	not out	8	c Dawkes b Morgan	0
F. S. Trueman	run out	10	b Gladwin	0
R. Appleyard	c Kelly b Jackson	0	not out	0
Extras	lb 4	4	b 1, lb 1, w 1, nb 1	4
Total		119		207

1st inns: 1-31, 2-70, 3-73, 4-81, 5-92, 6-95, 7-95, 8-100, 9-114, 10-119
2nd inns: 1-42, 2-115, 3-158, 4-190, 5-193, 6-197, 7-205, 8-206, 9-207

BOWLING	O	M	R	W		O	M	R	W
Jackson	25.4	8	46	2		13	5	39	0
Gladwin	30	16	44	1		24.3	8	48	3
Morgan	16	5	23	5		16	2	55	5
Smith	2	1	2	1		13	4	29	0
Carter						9	1	32	0

Umpires: H. L. Palmer and L. H. Gray

Derbyshire's first victory at Leeds since 1895.

with 170 from 26 but had only two matches remaining. In short, if Derbyshire won their remaining four games they would be Champions, no matter what anybody else did.

They made a magnificent start to their game against Middlesex at Queen's Park on 18 August. Middlesex had reached 32 for four before rain set in and ruled out any further play for the remainder of the game. Any lingering hopes of the title vanished in the rain. The final top three positions were:

	P	W	L	D	Tie	No dec	1st inns lead L	1st inns lead D	Points
Surrey	28	15	3	8	0	2	1	6	208
Yorkshire	28	13	3	8	1	3	0	5	186
Derbyshire	28	11	6	9	0	2	3	6	168

At the end of the season Guy Willatt resigned the captaincy, Donald Carr succeeding him as skipper.

On Wednesday, 11 May 1955, the Duke of Devonshire declared the new County Cricket Ground at Derby open and the first match played on a new square began against the South Africans. The new match centre and outfield was now on the side of the ground adjoining the Grandstand Hotel. A new press box and changing quarters in the converted old jockey quarters on the racecourse and the demolition of the 71-year-old pavilion also helped to give the ground a fresh look. Also opened in 1955, on 17 January, was the indoor cricket school, the ceremony being performed by MCC assistant secretary S. C. Griffith. In front of the grandstand, new terracing to accommodate 3,500 members had been prepared and with the Championship near-miss of 1954 a recent memory Derbyshire hoped for another season of success to mark the changes.

The high hopes were not materialised. Nine games were won but there were ten defeats and Derbyshire finished eighth.

The major problems were inconsistent batting and an injury which kept Jackson out for half the season. It had been hoped that Charlie Lee would fill the number three spot vacated by Willatt but he failed and the problem was never solved, although Carr tried Johnson, Morgan and Hamer in succession to Lee. Lee was a Yorkshireman, who was specially registered for Derbyshire and after 1955 he was never to look back, scoring a thousand runs in eight consecutive seasons. In 1963 he became Derbyshire's first professional captain since 1889 and he earned a reputation as a dour opening batsman who was capable of scoring quickly and a doughty fighter.

Laurie Johnson, too, overcame a moderate start to his County career to become one of Derbyshire's finest batsmen in the post-war

Gladwin bowling and the famous leg-trap poised like hawks waiting for the kill. The close fielding of Carr, Revill and Morgan in the leg-trap and the wicket keeping of Dawkes were features of the Jackson-Gladwin era.

period. He was born in Barbados and came to England to train as an engineer in the sugar industry, playing for Swarkestone CC. Johnson qualified by residence and did not score his first hundred until 1960. Chatterton took 181 innings to reach his maiden hundred, Johnson at 32, 230 innings. His greatest days were in the 1960s; he was a fine, forcing batsman with good footwork who cut and drove well and was a fine fieldsman at cover. Most of his runs were scored in front of the wicket, where he could hit the ball very hard indeed.

In 1955 it was Hamer who enjoyed his finest season to date with 1,639 runs for the County. At Trent Bridge he made his career-best 227, a magnificent innings which included five sixes and 27 fours. Seven wickets were down for 133 before Hamer and Edwin Smith (57) added 157 in 32 overs and 89 minutes.

In his first year as captain Carr also enjoyed a splendid year, with 1,659 runs in all first-class cricket and 1,462 for the County. His left-arm spin captured 45 wickets at just over 22 each. Thirty-eight catches capped the season and Carr was rewarded with the captaincy of the MCC 'A' team which toured Pakistan in 1955–56.

Edwin Smith made a big advance with 91 competition victims and 105 in all games at 17.65 each. In the victory over Scotland at Edinburgh Smith took five for 66 and nine for 46, match figures of 14 for 112 in 65 overs. In the second innings he took nine wickets in succession but was denied the tenth when Hamer claimed the last wicket.

Reprinted from the "Manchester Guardian," Wednesday, September 30, 1953

RECONSTRUCTION AT DERBY CRICKET GROUND

Any effort made by a sporting club to better the amenities at its ground is always creditable. But so numerous and so far-sighted are the alterations planned by the Derbyshire County Cricket Club for its ground at Derby that when they are completed players, officials, and spectators will have the benefit of first-class facilities.

As the club realised, the amenities of the present Derby ground are quite inadequate. The stand was built originally in 1884 by public subscription and was re-erected in its present position in 1887, but although various improvements were made from time to time even club officials considered it primitive. Thus, in the matter of accommodation alone the club was in a poor position when compared with most other county grounds, and this probably had some little bearing on the low attendances at matches at Derby, the average being only 2,000 for a midweek game and 3,000-4,000 for one beginning on a Saturday. Therefore, when the committee thought that things generally were settling down again after the war a meeting was held. The conclusions arrived at at this meeting could not have been easy to make.

First and foremost was the question of finance. This alone must have been a formidable problem. For instance, a decision had to be made as to whether just spectators' facilities were all that were to be improved or whether it was possible for the club to modernise other things. Happily it was found possible and agreed that no effort should be spared to bring the ground up to modern first-class standards in every respect. This was no light task, for, assuming that the building licences could be obtained, it involved the preparation and laying of a new playing pitch and surrounding area; almost complete reorganisation of stand accommodation and the building of new ones; installation of bath and shower facilities in the players' dressing-rooms; moving of the club offices to a more suitable place; and the provision of an indoor cricket school.

The fact that the ground is situated on the site of the old Derby racecourse, coupled with some of the carefully planned alterations, saved the club considerable expense. It can, for instance, still make use of the original grand stand and the old jockey quarters (to be modernised as the dressing-rooms), and the decision to lay the new wicket con-

siderably closer to the grand stand will bring spectators much closer to the actual pitch. The sites for the various new facilities can be seen from the map reproduced. The picture above shows a part of the present ground as seen from the racecourse stand. The new ground will form roughly an oval, one side of which will run along the racecourse stand and the other on the far side of where the pavilion now stands.

As will be seen the scheme has vast possibilities, but the question of finance and support will direct the final policy of the committee. An explanation of the plan is probably necessary to appreciate the following aspects:—

1. Under a new Derby Borough scheme Nottingham Road and Stores Road are to be doubled in width, thus giving first-class approaches to the ground.
2. The racecourse stand will hold under cover about a thousand and the new terracing to be built in front of this stand will hold about 2,500. But seated to capacity the area will accommodate 6,000.
3. The present pavilion holds only 500-600, very few of whom are under cover, the concrete stand holds 300, with no cover; and the seating on the popular side including the portable stands, also is without cover. Part of the old pavilion, the Eastwood balcony extension, will be placed at the north end of the ground and tiered seats placed underneath it. The accommodation there will then be 300 on ground level and 150 on top.
4. The portable stands will be resited round the new ground.
5. It is hoped to place the press box in or on the Eastwood stand at the north end of the ground, complete with all facilities. Should licences not be available it will be in the old judges' box in the meantime.

One of the most interesting of the club's decisions is that regarding the indoor cricket school: certainly this should repay it handsomely in future years. Three types of wicket will be provided: fast, medium, and a spinner's wicket, the organisation of which will be arranged by D. B. Carr and D. Smith, the coach, who have already visited three of the biggest schools in the country to gather information and ideas. The school will, of course, provide all the facilities necessary for indoor practice throughout winter and will be let or lent at the discretion of the county cricket committee to clubs and to the Derby and

District Cricket Association, which has a membership of over 150 clubs. The committee would also presumably lend the school for the coaching of schoolmasters and club coaches. This will be organised by A. Collard, the area representative of the M.C.C. Youth Advisory Council. Considerable help and instruction has been given in the last three years by J. D. Eggar and R. Sale, housemasters at Repton School, and by the county club's coach.

The whole scheme has been made possible by the support and encouragement of both the Derby Borough Council, owners of the actual playing field, and by Messrs. Truman, Hanbury, and Buxton, the owners of the racecourse stand and jockey quarters. This help is much appreciated, for the county committee has to provide pitches and changing rooms not only for Derbyshire C.C.C. but also for six local cricket teams which have the use of the grounds in summer and for the Derbyshire Amateurs Football Club and Derby Hockey Club in winter.

The total cost of the new ground may be some £5,000-£6,000. The club has a reconstruction fund of £4,000 and also has had a gift of £1,000 from its supporters' club, but finance is still one of its major worries if all its hopes are to be fulfilled. When they are, as undoubtedly they will be, it is to be hoped that its efforts are rewarded with better attendances and, perhaps above all, with the emergence from its school of some outstanding new players.

The schedule which the club has drawn up is as follows:

Winter, 1952/3.—Match wicket laid by W. Goodyear, Derbyshire C.C.C. groundsman, assisted by two members of Derby parks staff. This was paid for by the gift of an anonymous donor.

Winter 1952/3.—Outfield rough level and terracing dug out.

Summer, 1953.—Outfield drained, prepared, and seeded. Work carried out by En-Tout-Cas Company under the direction of W. White (formerly assistant at Old Trafford and head groundsman, Leicestershire C.C.C., 1936-9).

Autumn, 1953.—Completion of terracing &c. in front of grand stand (cost approximately £1,500). The Derby C.C.C. Supporters' Club has given £500 towards cost of outfield and terracing.

September/December, 1953.—Alterations to and modernising of jockey quarters, changing rooms, and club office. The cost will be about £800. The landlord will pay for alterations to jockey quarters and the club will pay rent for same.

November, 1953/February, 1954.—Preparations for the indoor cricket school, beginning with alterations to lean-to building in the paddock. The cost, about £1,000, has been promised by the supporters' club.

September, 1953/January, 1955.—Pull down old pavilion, re-erect Eastwood extension, prepare and turf old pavilion site.

Summer, 1954.—Agree to types and numbers of seats for grand stand.

Summer, 1955.—All work completed, ground ready for play.

H. M.

Eato had been expected to fill Jackson's place when he was injured but he was now in competition with three young pace bowlers, Brian Furniss, Derek Hall and Harold Rhodes, the 19-year-old son of Bert Rhodes. Hall, like Furniss, stood 6 ft 5½ in and he did well in 1955, bowling mainly in-swingers at fast-medium pace. Back problems proved his undoing and he was forced to leave county cricket because of this after the 1958 season.

Rhodes had been steeped in cricket from an early age, practising at the County Ground as a schoolboy and being taken on to the staff as a promising off-spin bowler and useful batsman. A sore spinning finger led to a change of style to leg-breaks and googlies and he turned to fast bowling when Derbyshire Club and Ground visited Repton School to play against the old boys, Repton Pilgrims. A young fast bowler who was due for a trial failed to arrive because of a car accident and the County coach, Denis Smith, suggested that Rhodes should open with the new ball. Rhodes was a tall man, 6 ft 2 in, and he was to develop genuine pace and obtain a great deal of bounce and lift by making full use of his height. He had a whippy, wristy action and differed from the traditional line of Derbyshire pace bowlers in that he was genuinely quick, the fastest certainly since Warren, allowing for Copson's hostility for a few overs.

The spotlight, though, was on Donald Carr and he left with the MCC party for the tour of Pakistan. The hosts won the unofficial series by 2-1, Carr averaging 20 on a tour of generally low scores and which was marred by an unfortunate incident.

After the third day of the third 'Test' at Peshawar, when both match and series were virtually settled, an MCC player (or players) teased the Test umpire Idrees Begh, giving him what was known to them as the 'water treatment' during horseplay in the hotel. The members of the Pakistan Cricket Board took the gravest view of the incident. MCC offered to cancel the remainder of the tour and recall the team if it was felt this would be in the best interests of restoring friendly relations but Pakistan urged that the tour should continue. It was a shattering experience for a team of young players touring in trying conditions and, as captain, Carr announced that he would take full responsibility. The MCC players and manager made it quite clear when they returned home that the umpiring had nothing to do with their rag. They thought that Begh was a willing victim and had not one or two other Pakistanis seen the incident all might have passed off without comment. Begh himself accepted the apology but his fellow-

A plan drawn up in 1953 for the reconstruction of the Derby ground. (Reproduced here by permission of The Guardian)

countrymen were less easily appeased and student demonstrations were staged urging the MCC to go home. Emptying jugs or containers of water over each other was a standing joke among the MCC players but it misfired badly in this case.

After the hot sun of Pakistan Carr returned to one of the wettest summers in memory in 1956.

The season, though, started well. There was a thrilling six-run victory over Yorkshire at Chesterfield, Rhodes, on leave from the army, taking five for 52. Yorkshire were set 221 to win and stood at 196 for five at one stage. Derbyshire were third in July. But none of the last nine games was won, four being lost, and they finished in 12th place, their lowest position since 1949.

With a hail of gloomy predictions ringing in their ears after the setbacks of 1956 the Derbyshire side began the 1957 season with a defeat at Bradford. But there was a victory in the next game at the Aylestone Road ground at Leicester by an innings, after Leicestershire had been dismissed for 57 (in 66 overs!) and 55, Smith taking six for 19. Then fine bowling by Jackson and Gladwin set the scene for another innings victory over Essex at Burton-on-Trent.

These two wins put the side in good heart for the match against Yorkshire at Queen's Park, which was Les Jackson's benefit game – the first time a Derbyshire player had been granted a benefit since Arthur Morton in 1924.

It was a fine game, Kelly's hundred marking the first day, which was watched by 11,000 people. By the close Yorkshire were 30 without loss in reply to Derbyshire's 292. The second day's crowd was rewarded by some fine batting by Close (120) and excellent bowling by Jackson, Derbyshire gaining a lead of 93. By the close, with Carr 59 not out, Derbyshire were 174 for five. On the final day Carr declared when he was eight short of his century, leaving Yorkshire 260 minutes to get 325 at 75 an hour. By lunch they were 62 for two but Jackson was to finish the match in style when he had Platt held in the slips with eight minutes remaining, taking five for 51 and six for 63.

Derbyshire continued to go from strength to strength. Hamer made 138 in the win over Sussex at Derby and in glorious weather they faced the Championship leaders, Lancashire, at Aigburth, Liverpool. Hamer (104) and Lee (73) began the game with a partnership of 158 in 109 minutes, Kelly got 68 and then Johnson (88 not out) punished the bowling, adding 105 in 58 minutes with Morgan. Carr declared at 417 for eight and then Morgan and Jackson bowled their side to an innings win, Derbyshire's fifth consecutive victory, which equalled the Club record.

Something of a reaction set in at Lord's in the next game, Derbyshire losing half their side for 89 but they recovered to make

223. More good bowling by Jackson earned them a lead of 96 and a fifth-wicket stand of 109 by Carr and Dawkes in the second innings left Middlesex to get 339 on the last day. They never recovered from a bad start and Derbyshire gained their sixth consecutive victory to establish a new Club record.

It was a remarkable run which had placed Derbyshire at the top of the Championship table. The side had remained unchanged – Hamer, Lee, Kelly, Revill, Carr, Dawkes, Johnson, Morgan, Smith, Gladwin and Jackson – and every member of the team had played his part. The run ended at Edgbaston when Warwickshire won the Whitsun fixture, and Derbyshire then ran into a lean spell. But that magnificent pace attack produced its most remarkable performance of the season against Middlesex at Chesterfield.

Gladwin demolished the visitors' first innings in damp conditions. They were 74 for four at the end of a curtailed first day and all out 102 when play on the Thursday eventually got under way. Middlesex began their second innings at 6 pm after Derbyshire had made 153 and were soon in dire straits against Jackson and Gladwin. Four wickets fell for one run, Gladwin having taken three without conceding a run in three overs. The fifth and sixth wickets fell at nine and extra time was claimed but rain stopped play at five past seven with the score 11 for six, Gladwin having five for five, giving him ten for 17 in the day. On the final morning nine wickets were down for 13 but a last wicket partnership of 16 by Bennett and Moss enabled Middlesex to total 29, leaving Derbyshire with an innings victory.

Jackson did well in an innings win over Leicestershire at Queen's Park, Kelly (127) and Carr (141) sharing in a new record third-wicket partnership of 246, but this was the only game Derbyshire won after the victory over Middlesex. Ten wins against eight defeats left them in fourth place, having held the lead for a week at the start of June when they were in the midst of their record run of victories.

Jackson (129 Championship wickets) and Gladwin (99) were again the pivots of the attack although Morgan had 937 runs, 94 wickets and 42 catches in all games. Kelly enjoyed his best year since joining the Club with 1,535 runs (average 30.70) while Hamer led the averages with 1,616 runs. He gave perhaps the finest display of his career at The Oval, carrying his bat for 112 in a total of 208 against the two Bedsers, Loader and Lock, hitting nine fours in a five-hour stay. Carr and Lee also exceeded a thousand runs but Revill was not re-engaged for the 1958 season.

Les Jackson began that season in prime form with seven for 18 at Oxford but he suffered a groin strain which affected him for the rest of the year. Nevertheless it was a marvellous summer for Jackson. He topped the national bowling averages with 143 wickets at 10.99 each,

Jackson, Gladwin and Middlesex 29 all out at Queen's Park, Chesterfield, in July 1957. At one point the London county stood at 13 for nine.

of which 126 were taken in the Championship. This was the lowest average of any bowler taking a hundred wickets in the 20th century. In an exceptionally damp summer Jackson was able to move the ball considerably although the persistent groin trouble meant that his bowling was never much above half pace. In his last eight Championship games he took 62 wickets at 7.70 each. In June he performed a hat-trick at Kidderminster, all three of his victims being caught behind by Dawkes. Similarly, Cliff Gladwin's hat-trick against the New Zealanders at Derby had the assistance of his principal henchmen – Morgan holding two catches and Carr one. The second of these wickets was his 1,453rd for the County, enabling him to pass Bestwick's County record in what was to be his final season, which yet again brought him a hundred wickets. There is nothing like going out at the top. Gladwin was to continue to take wickets in league cricket, open a sports shop and earn a reputation as a chrysanthemum grower in his retirement. With Rhodes establishing a regular place and Morgan enjoying a good season the side once again possessed one of the best pace attacks in its history, while the spin of Smith and Carr

DERBYSHIRE *v* MIDDLESEX

Played at Queen's Park, Chesterfield, 17, 18 and 19 July 1957

DERBYSHIRE WON BY AN INNINGS AND 22 RUNS

MIDDLESEX	FIRST INNINGS		SECOND INNINGS	
J. D. Robertson	c Dawkes b Gladwin	38	lbw b Jackson	0
R. A. Gale	c Kelly b Smith	8	c Dawkes b Gladwin	4
D. O. Baldry	lbw b Morgan	4	b Gladwin	1
W. J. Edrich	c Revill b Gladwin	10	c Carr b Gladwin	0
G. P. S. Delisle	b Morgan	0	b Jackson	6
F. J. Titmus	c Carr b Smith	22	c Morgan b Gladwin	0
J. T. Murray	c Dawkes b Gladwin	1	c and b Gladwin	0
D. Bennett	c Dawkes b Gladwin	13	not out	14
H. W. Tilly	c Jackson b Gladwin	0	lbw b Jackson	0
R. J. Hurst	c Carr b Gladwin	2	run out	0
A. E. Moss	not out	0	c Hamer b Morgan	2
Extras	b 4	4	lb 2	2
Total		102		29

1st inns: 1-24, 2-34, 3-55, 4-62, 5-86, 6-86, 7-93, 8-93, 9-99, 10-102
2nd inns: 1-0, 2-1, 3-1, 4-1, 5-9, 6-9, 7-13, 8-13, 9-13, 10-29

BOWLING	O	M	R	W	O	M	R	W
Jackson	6	4	4	0	11	6	7	3
Gladwin	25.2	14	23	6	14	8	18	5
Morgan	19	5	42	2	4.2	3	2	1
Smith	17	6	29	2	1	1	0	0

DERBYSHIRE	FIRST INNINGS	
A. Hamer	b Moss	5
C. Lee	c and b Titmus	33
J. M. Kelly	b Tilly	23
A. C. Revill	b Hurst	17
D. B. Carr	c Murray b Tilly	4
D. J. Green	c Edrich b Hurst	1
G. O. Dawkes	c Gale b Tilly	28
D. C. Morgan	c Bennett b Hurst	28
E. Smith	c Murray b Tilly	0
C. Gladwin	not out	5
H. L. Jackson	c Titmus b Hurst	0
Extras	b 4, lb 5	9
Total		153

1st inns: 1-12, 2-53, 3-82, 4-82, 5-87, 6-87, 7-137, 8-143, 9-149, 10-153

BOWLING	O	M	R	W
Moss	5	2	12	1
Bennett	2	0	4	0
Titmus	10	0	33	1
Hurst	21.1	10	50	4
Tilly	13	4	45	4

Umpires: A. Skelding and W. E. Phillipson

The triumph of Jackson and Gladwin over Middlesex.

captured useful wickets. But the batting in a wet summer was unreliable.

The two most notable successes of the season came over Hampshire, who were runners-up in 1958, and in one of these, at Burton-on-Trent's Ind Coope & Allsops Ground, there occurred one of the most amazing matches in the Club's history. Hampshire were top of the table at that stage and Ingleby-Mackenzie, their enterprising captain, sent Derbyshire in on a green but soft pitch on the Wednesday. Only 25 minutes' play was possible, during which time Derbyshire made eight for the loss of Lee.

Warm and sunny weather on Thursday, 14 August ensured a prompt start but the drying pitch resulted in a torrid time for the batsmen, with the ball lifting and kicking and conditions generally being unpredictable. Shackleton and Heath took full advantage and Derbyshire were all out for 74, Hampshire beginning their innings at 12.46 pm.

With his seventh ball Rhodes had Marshall taken brilliantly by Dawkes, one-handed diving to his right. Five balls later he produced a delivery to Gray which moved from middle and leg and took the off-stump. At seven Pitman was run out and in the next over Rhodes had Barnard caught at short leg. Horton was bowled by Jackson and at lunch Hampshire had lost half their side for 17. Jackson took the last four wickets in nine balls and Hampshire were all out for 23, Jackson taking five for 10 and Rhodes four for 12.

Derbyshire began their second innings at 2.48 pm and Charlie Lee and Jim Brailsford, a Chesterfield batsman who was playing one of only three games in which he appeared for the County, began with a partnership of 21. Four wickets were down for 40 before Carr and Morgan added 54 in 39 minutes but after tea the last six wickets fell for 13 runs and Hampshire were set 159 to win, with 90 minutes of the second day remaining.

The innings began at 5.30 pm and Marshall and Gray were soon back in the pavilion with only a single scored. Barnard was out at 6.50 pm, 15 minutes after Morgan had replaced Rhodes in the first bowling change of the match. Carr claimed the extra half-hour and Hampshire were dismissed for 55, Derbyshire winning by 103 runs with 17 minutes – and a full final day – remaining. A crowd of around 3,000 had seen 39 wickets fall in six hours 39 minutes, excluding the lunch and tea intervals. Not since 1880 had so many wickets fallen in one day and the match had lasted seven hours two minutes. At the end of the game Carr presented Rhodes and Jackson with their County caps. Rhodes put down Derbyshire's success to the fact that he and Jackson were just that bit faster than Shackleton and

DERBYSHIRE *v* HAMPSHIRE

Played on Ind Coope & Allsops Ground, Burton, 13, 14 and 15 August 1958

DERBYSHIRE WON BY 103 RUNS

DERBYSHIRE	FIRST INNINGS		SECOND INNINGS	
C. Lee	c Horton b Shackleton	8	c Horton b Heath	6
F. C. Brailsford	c Barnard b Heath	4	c Horton b Heath	14
D. J. Green	c Sainsbury b Heath	6	c Barnard b Shackleton	4
A. Hamer	c Pitman b heath	5	c and b Heath	7
D. C. Morgan	c Horton b Shackleton	3	c Marshall b Shackleton	46
D. B. Carr	c Burden b Heath	12	lbw b Heath	19
H. L. Johnson	c Harrison b Heath	4	c and b Shackleton	6
G. O. Dawkes	c Burden b Heath	19	b Heath	0
H. J. Rhodes	b Shackleton	0	c Sainsbury b Heath	2
E. Smith	not out	6	b Heath	0
H. L. Jackson	b Shackleton	4	not out	0
Extras	lb 2, w 1	3	lb 1, nb 2	3
Total		74		107

1st inns: 1-8, 2-13, 3-24, 4-27, 5-27, 6-35, 7-52, 8-56, 9-68, 10-74
2nd inns: 1-21, 2-25, 3-25, 4-40, 5-94, 6-100, 7-100, 8-106, 9-107, 10-107

BOWLING	O	M	R	W		O	M	R	W
Shackleton	16.4	8	36	4		18.2	4	52	3
Heath	16	5	35	6		18	4	52	7

HAMPSHIRE	FIRST INNINGS		SECOND INNINGS	
R. E. Marshall	c Dawkes b Rhodes	4	lbw b Jackson	0
J. R. Gray	b Rhodes	0	c Dawkes b Rhodes	1
H. Horton	b Jackson	5	b Jackson	8
R. W. C. Pitman	run out	0	c Carr b Rhodes	11
H. M. Barnard	c Morgan b Rhodes	5	c Carr b Jackson	16
A. C. D. Ingleby-Mackenzie	c Lee b Rhodes	2	b Rhodes	4
P. J. Sainsbury	b Jackson	4	c Dawkes b Jackson	4
L. Harrison	not out	2	c Jackson b Morgan	0
D. Shackleton	c Lee b Jackson	0	c Jackson b Morgan	1
M. Heath	b Jackson	0	b Morgan	4
M. D. Burden	b Jackson	0	not out	0
Extras	nb 1	1	lb 6	6
Total		23		55

1st inns: 1-4, 2-5, 3-7, 4-12, 5-17, 6-17, 7-23, 8-23, 9-23, 10-23
2nd inns: 1-1, 2-1, 3-13, 4-23, 5-32, 6-45, 7-46, 8-46, 9-55, 10-55

BOWLING	O	M	R	W		O	M	R	W
Jackson	8.4	5	10	5		15	8	16	4
Rhodes	8	3	12	4		9	1	29	3
Morgan						5.3	3	4	3

Umpires: J. S. Buller and H. G. Baldwin

The match in which 39 wickets fell on one day.

Heath and to Carr's astute captaincy in bringing Derek Morgan into the attack at just the right time.

The return game at Bournemouth, the final game of the season, also produced some fine cricket. Jackson had a match analysis of eleven for 65, taking six for 51 in Hampshire's first innings of 193. Derbyshire in reply were 35 for seven at one stage but Johnson made an unbeaten 34, Rhodes and Smith providing useful support, and the total was 107. When Hampshire batted again they had no answer to Jackson (five for 14) who took his analysis in two games against them in 1958 to 20 wickets at 4.55 each! They were all out for 61, leaving Derbyshire 148 for victory. Hamer (63) and Kelly (26) added 81 for the second wicket and although four wickets were down for 93 Derbyshire gained a five-wicket victory. It was their ninth win of the season and they finished fifth in the Championship table, with nine defeats.

Harold Rhodes had emerged as a worthy successor to Cliff Gladwin, and in the hot summer of 1959 he developed great pace in a memorable season. He appeared in two Test matches against the Indians that summer as England sought to rebuild their side. But for all Rhodes' success it was his new-ball partner Les Jackson who was yet again the dominant figure in the County's attack, with 140 first-class wickets, including nine for 17 in the opening match at Fenner's. Bill Richardson, son of Arthur Richardson, had a good first season. A hard-hitting right-hand batsman and aggressive fast-medium left-hand bowler, he was appointed captain of the Second Eleven but came into the side when Rhodes was absent. He hit 91 in his second match at Swansea and took eight for 54 in Kent's first innings at Chesterfield in his fourth game.

The season was notable for a record-breaking run of success by the captain, Donald Carr, who scored 2,292 runs (average 44.07). Carr hit 2,165 runs for the County, the first time anybody had reached this figure for Derbyshire. He made two centuries in the match at Canterbury, hit five hundreds, only one fewer than Leslie Townsend's record of six, and in August he scored 817 runs, the most in a month by a Derbyshire player.

Late in the season Ian Hall showed promise as a determined opening batsman and at 19 he became the youngest player to score a century for the County when he made 113 against Hampshire at Derby (Cadman was the oldest when he scored 125 not out at Northampton in 1924 when he was 47). A year later Hall, at 20, became the youngest to make a thousand runs in a season for the Club, Garnet Lee being the oldest at 46 in 1933. Incidentally the youngest to take five wickets in an innings and a hundred in a season was Edwin Smith, at 17 and 21 respectively. Hall became a dour and reliable opener, whose adhesive qualities were not always appreciated by spectators who demanded something more in the Denis Smith-Hamer mould.

Derbyshire flourished in the warmth of that 1959 summer, twelve wins earning them seventh position. After a victory at Trent Bridge, their seventh win in 12 games, they headed the table on 23 June but faded out of the picture as eight matches followed without a win.

They built on this success in 1960. Ten games were won and while they were never in contention for the title they earned fifth place, an unbeaten run of six games (three wins) to close the season lifting them up the table.

Johnson at last hit his maiden century and went on to add three more in a season which brought him 1,872 runs for the County (average 37.44), during which he made the number three position his own.

The going of Hamer and Kelly left gaps in the order, and opportunities for younger players to emerge. Derbyshire Second Eleven in 1960 won four games and finished fifth in the Second Eleven Championship. Captained by Kelly it contained batsmen such as David Millner, David Short, Ray Swallow, Gerry Wyatt, the wicket-keeper and batsman from New Mills who understudied Dawkes, but left when Bob Taylor joined the staff, and David Green, all of whom became fringe players with the first-team without getting established.

Others became regulars. Ian Buxton was to become fully established in 1961 as a most useful all-rounder, a batsman who could strike the ball very hard, despite a short back lift, and a medium-pace bowler of in-swing which could be deadly in the right conditions. He was also a good fieldsman in the leg-trap and a man who was to captain the side for three seasons, 1970–72. All of Buxton's 350 first-class matches were played for Derbyshire, placing him ahead of Alderman (318) and Harry Storer (302) in this respect. He also played soccer for Derby County as a centre-forward before going on to Luton Town, Notts County and Port Vale, his soccer career ending when he took over the captaincy of the cricket team.

Peter Eyre was another product of that interesting second team. Eyre was a forcing left-hand batsman and a medium-fast bowler who could, on occasions and when conditions suited, produce a match-winning performance. He became a valuable team man whose career was handicapped by shocking luck – glandular fever, a cartilage operation, brief doubt about his action which was happily resolved, and a scalp disease which left him permanently and prematurely bald.

Two imports, Bob Berry and Billy Oates, added to the 'roses' contingent in the squad. Berry, a slow left-hander, was capped by three counties, his native Lancashire, Worcestershire and Derbyshire, with whom he spent the last four years of his career. Oates, from Yorkshire, took time to settle but in 1961 emerged as a most attractive and free-scoring batsman who served the club well for several years.

Through all of these changes Les Jackson towered above the

remainder of Derbyshire's bowlers. In 1960 he took 150 wickets at 13.56 for the Club, 146 in the Championship and 160 in all games, sending down more than a thousand overs at the age of 39. Old enemies suffered. Eight for 44 against Middlesex at Burton-on-Trent and seven for 33 at The Oval satisfied the blood lust of the County's followers demanding retribution for real or imagined ills at the hands of the southern and London counties down the years.

On 31 December 1959 Will Taylor had retired, bringing to an end – or virtually so, for he remained closely connected with the Club for the remaining 16 years of his life – an era in Derbyshire cricket. As Ronnie Aird, then secretary of the MCC, wrote in tribute:

> He has endeared himself to a very large number of cricketers and cricket administrators, and particularly to his colleagues, the other secretaries of the first-class and minor county cricket clubs. The reason is not hard to discover, because a more considerate and kind-hearted man it would be difficult to find.

Donald Carr, assistant secretary since March 1953, succeeded him and his brother, Major Douglas Carr, took over as assistant secretary.

One feature of Will Taylor's work had been the smooth way in which the County Club, the Supporters Club and its Auxiliary Association had worked together over the previous seven years. The latter had played a wonderfully sustaining role in assisting Derbyshire cricket and had been responsible for the birth of the *Derbyshire Cricket Year Book* under the joint editorship of Frank Peach and Frank Dawn in 1954, the former being hon secretary of the Supporters Club, the latter occupying a similar post with the Derby and District Cricket Association.

Will Taylor could recall, in retirement, playing against William Storer, and batting against Arnold Warren and Bill Bestwick in the nets. He had a great regard for Guy Jackson, thought highly of Guy Willatt, the first regular post-war captain and a man who did much to pull the side together, and ranked Harry Storer as the best batsman. He did not like to separate the fast-medium bowlers, although he acknowledged that Les Jackson on performance was the best of them, and singled out Hutchinson, Alderman, Carr and Chris Wilkins (due to arrive in 1970) as the best fieldsmen. He thought the quality of the pitches on which club cricket was played in the county was one of the main reasons why batsmen had never been produced to the same degree as bowlers, although he felt at one time that Denis Smith might develop into a second Frank Woolley.

Clearly a man with such integrity and perception was an asset even in retirement. Within a few months he was playing an influential role in bringing another of the same name, though unrelated, to the

County Ground, one who was to serve with equal distinction though in another sphere.

Robert William Taylor was born at Stoke-on-Trent and in 1956 made his first appearance for Bignall End's first team in the North Staffordshire League. Two years later, still short of his 17th birthday, he made his debut for Staffordshire. He was capped in 1960 and in June made his first-class debut when he kept wicket for the Minor Counties against the South Africans. By now Cliff Gladwin, who was professional with Longton in the North Staffordshire League, had recommended him to his former County, and Club coach Denis Smith came to see him play. In July 1960 Will Taylor and Robin Buckston travelled to Wolverhampton to see Bob take four catches and make one stumping in Staffordshire's match against Durham. He duly joined Derbyshire, appearing in two Second Eleven games that year and being specially registered to play for the County in 1961.

Taylor made his County Championship debut five weeks before his 20th birthday. George Dawkes injured a knee at Old Trafford in the eighth match of the season and Taylor came into the side for the game against Sussex at Derby which began on 7 June 1961. Ken Suttle became his first victim, caught off Ian Buxton. This fixture marked the first step towards a world wicket-keeping record and ended a run of 289 consecutive Championship appearances by Dawkes which stretched back to 1950. Dawkes returned to play in five games towards the end of the season before breaking down again, Taylor once more taking over. He ended the summer with 53 victims in 17 games. His career was launched; in 1962 Dawkes, after a successful cartilage operation during the winter, hurt that same knee in a car accident and retired from first-class cricket, leaving behind the memory of his lusty batting and magnificent wicket-keeping, and not least those 254 catches off the bowling of Les Jackson.

Taylor kept wicket in 29 games in 1962, his 77 catches being the most by any Derbyshire wicket-keeper in a season, with 80 victims in all, a total he exceeded by three in 1963. At 21 he was one of the country's most promising stumpers and he was to remain the County's 'keeper until he retired in 1984. Only twice was his place in jeopardy. In 1964 a soccer injury (he had played as a part-time pro with Port Vale) caused him to miss the first seven games, Laurie Johnson taking over the gloves. Derbyshire, always seeking to strengthen their batting, were tempted to continue this arrangement and play the extra batsman but common sense prevailed and Taylor returned. Then in 1967 at Leicester he edged a ball from Jack Birkenshaw into his left eye and suffered a detached retina which kept him out for the last three weeks of that season. Bob Stephenson, from Derby, made 64 in his first match and kept so well that he put Taylor's place under pressure,

The old and the new. George Dawkes (right) passes on some friendly advice to his youthful successor, Bob Taylor, in 1962.

but Bob returned in 1968, Stephenson eventually moving to Hampshire and a successful career with the southern county.

For three seasons Taylor kept wicket to the bowling of Les Jackson; the two greatest names in Derbyshire cricket, one at the start of his career, the other nearing the end. William Storer was the finest wicket-keeper-batsman and arguably the best Derbyshire-born player. Some of the imports, Spofforth, Trueman, Holding etc., made a bigger impact on the world stage but Jackson was the finest bowler and the Staffordshire-born Taylor achieved more than any other Derbyshire-produced cricketer.

Jackson was to receive long overdue reward at the age of 40 in 1961 when he was chosen to replace the injured Brian Statham in the third Test against Australia at Headingley. It was his second Test, the previous one having been against New Zealand 12 years earlier.

England won by eight wickets in a match dominated by the uncertain pitch and by Trueman, who had a match analysis of eleven for 88. Jackson had two long spells in the first innings, bowling for an hour from the pavilion end before lunch and for another hour afterwards. At tea Australia were 183 for two when Jackson took the new ball at the pavilion end. They were all out for 237, Trueman taking five for 58 and Jackson two for 57 in 31 overs. In the second innings he flattened McDonald's leg-stump with his fifth ball, a vicious break-back, finishing with two for 26 in 13 overs. But he was not selected for either of the two remaining Test matches.

A blow on the foot in the first Championship match caused Jackson to miss seven matches and this cost him his customary hundred wickets, Rhodes alone achieving the feat for Derbyshire. Buxton's combination of in-swing, line and length seemed likely to emulate Rhodes but he had a lean August and ended with 83. Johnson, Carr, Oates – 1,288 runs, of which 855 came in 11 matches between 22 July and the end of the season – and Lee were the leading runmakers.

Derbyshire made a disappointing start but they rallied to win ten games and finish the season in seventh place in the Championship table. Their best win was at Trent Bridge when Nottinghamshire set them 324 to win in 328 minutes, a tall order with Johnson suffering from a cracked rib.

Hall left early but Swallow and Lee added 50 before a collapse to 81 for four. Buxton and Carr then put on 70 in an hour but the sixth wicket fell at 166, and Johnson came in at number eight at six minutes past three. He kept one end closed while Carr took up the challenge, scoring his second 50 in 43 minutes, by when 100 were needed in 100 minutes. Carr played a glorious innings of 143 (one six, 17 fours) being out at 291 after sharing in a seventh-wicket partnership of 125 with Johnson, the captain batting for 210 minutes. Johnson now took over the role of senior partner and he and Eyre hit off the runs, Johnson making the winning hit with five minutes to spare.

Another notable victory occurred at Lord's when Middlesex set a target of 269 in 220 minutes. Lee (five sixes and seven fours in 82) and Hall (52) began with 132 in 90 minutes and Johnson's unbeaten 73 included two sixes, one of which broke a window in the Tavern. With Carr and Oates lending support he steered Derbyshire to a fine win with 17 minutes to spare.

These wins against the clock indicated that Derbyshire's batting, certainly on good pitches, was equal to that of most counties and this was borne out in 1962. Six batsmen, Morgan, Lee, Buxton, Johnson, Oates and Hall, each scored more than a thousand runs in the Championship and Carr joined them with the help of outside games – seven being a record for the County.

Neil Harvey (left), captaining the Australians, and Donald Carr inspect the pitch at Queen's Park, Chesterfield, in May 1961. Rain ruined the game against the tourists.

Eight wins earned seventh position. Yet again Jackson proved a match-winner; six for 25 and five for 65 at Ilford, six for 26 and seven for 47 against Leicestershire at Derby after Carr had declared at 400 for eight. During the season he exceeded Gladwin's career record for the County.

At the end of the season Donald Carr left the Club, having been appointed assistant secretary of the MCC, and the end of his seven-year era as captain coincided with a sudden decline in Derbyshire's fortunes, although this could not be laid at the door of his successor, Charlie Lee.

Defeat in the first three matches set the pattern of the 1963 season. Injuries and a serious decline in the batting meant that 14 of the 28 matches were lost, with only two wins – a record which left the Club in bottom place for the first time since 1924. Not until 26 July, in their 16th Championship game of the summer, did Derbyshire taste victory over another county and this came about in sensational fashion against Sussex at Hastings. Lee had complained about the state of the pitch before the game started but Sussex's target of 70 had been reduced by seven by the close of the second day. But some fine bowling by Rhodes (six for 22) and Les Jackson (four for 16) reduced them to 56 all out, leaving Derbyshire the winners by 13 runs. Although Carr returned in August to make 136 in the return game only one more game was won, Rhodes again playing a major role with nine wickets in the victory over Hampshire at Chesterfield.

For all their lack of success Derbyshire had been among the pioneers of a new and revolutionary form of cricket – the one-day game. When it became known early in 1962 that the MCC had agreed to stage a knock-out competition – the Gillette Cup – between the counties in 1963 the Leicestershire secretary, Michael Turner, suggested to several Midland counties that they should stage their own local knock-out competition. As a result Derbyshire, Leicestershire, Northamptonshire and Nottinghamshire took part in a miniature series of 65-overs limitation, Northamptonshire being the eventual winners. Derbyshire were beaten by seven runs at Leicester in May 1962, making 243 (Lee and Carr beginning with an opening partnership of 110) in reply to Leicestershire's 250 for five in a splendid match.

Their first game in the new competition sponsored by Gillette brought a six-run win at Bournemouth. Derbyshire made 250 for nine in 65 overs, Hall getting 61 and Morgan an undefeated 59. Hampshire were bowled out for 244, with Les Jackson returning figures of 15-6-24-1 at the age of 42 to demonstrate what a force he would have been in limited-overs cricket. Derbyshire did not survive the second round, however, being beaten at Old Trafford by Lancashire.

Carr and Dawkes had gone; now at the end of the 1963 season Jackson left. Another era was over. The period between 1952 and 1963 brought 108 Championship wins. A high proportion of these victories had been due to the bowling of Les Jackson. He left an indelible memory.

THE RHODES AFFAIR

AS LES JACKSON'S INDIAN SUMMERS bore rich fruit dark clouds had gathered over the career of Harold Rhodes, which was blighted by controversy.

Rhodes in 1960 appeared on the verge of a lengthy spell in the England side. Within a few months – although it was not realised fully at the time – the death knell had sounded on his Test career and his future as a county cricketer was, for a time, placed in jeopardy.

He became a victim of the great throwing controversy which dominated world cricket in the 1960s. For some years throwers had been infiltrating the game after successful attempts to remove them half-a-century earlier. A campaign gathered pace after the 1958–59 MCC tour of Australia when the actions of several Australian bowlers came under close scrutiny. An MCC sub-committee had urged umpires to inspect certain bowlers' actions in 1958 but nobody was called for throwing. At the umpires' suggestion a list of bowlers with suspect actions was drawn up in 1959 and their counties warned. That summer three bowlers were no-balled, umpires Paul Gibb and Syd Buller being the chief protagonists. By now the crux of Law 26, which dealt with the subject, was a definition of a throw, the key factor being a sudden straightening of the bowling arm, whether partial or complete, immediately prior to the delivery of the ball.

Such was the background. Rhodes, who had played in two Tests in 1959, was selected for the MCC side which met Surrey at Lord's and there was another early opportunity to impress the selectors when Derbyshire met the South Africans at the County Ground on 7 May 1960.

The main interest in that game centred on Geoff Griffin, the Springboks' fast bowler who had been no-balled for throwing in their domestic season. Seven first-class umpires were to find fault with his action on the 1960 tour but he bowled 29 overs against Derbyshire and neither umpire – Paul Gibb nor Ron Aspinall – called him for throwing. Instead Rhodes was no-balled by Gibb three times on the first evening and a further three times on the second day. Gibb was not satisfied with Rhodes' action, saying later that there was something different about it and, as the law stood, he was entitled to call him.

It was a shattering experience for the Club and for the young fast bowler. Years later Ted Dexter was to write that some players had thought his action odd when he played in the 1959 Tests. But neither Rhodes nor the Club had received any indication of doubt existing about his bowling before Gibb's dramatic intervention from square-leg.

Harold Rhodes. In 1960 he appeared on the verge of a long Test career, but he became a victim of the great throwing controversy which dominated cricket for a decade. Rhodes' action – his arm had an unusual backward extension of the elbow joint – was eventually declared fair after what amounted to an eight-year trial.

It was to be several years before the phenomenon was explained. Medical examinations and X-rays were to show that Rhodes had an unusual backward extension of the elbow joint. His arm was over-extended in the latter part of its delivery swing beyond the normal 180 degrees by some ten degrees. This hyper-extension, as it became known, made his action appear occasionally suspect to the naked eye but, in fact, he was bowling perfectly naturally. It was this hyper-extension which gave the illusion of a throw caused by his arm bending back beyond the straight.

Rhodes, himself, while acknowledging that he had a whippy wrist-action (permissible under the laws) was adamant that he did not bowl unfairly. 'My action was sideways on, I delivered the ball from very close to the stumps and I could also bowl a good out-swinger which could be achieved as a result of a textbook action,' he wrote in his book, *The Harold Rhodes Affair*. And in his foreword to that book Fred Trueman contrasted Harold's sideways-on action with the open-chested style of the acknowledged chuckers, whose left foot was splayed out towards cover and gully and not pointing down the pitch in the orthodox manner.

For years, though, there was to be controversy. Those six no-balls effectively ruled Rhodes out of Test cricket in 1960, despite his 91 wickets at 17 apiece. The English authorities, anxious to be seen to put their own house in order while endeavouring to stamp out throwing elsewhere, could scarcely pick Rhodes. He was to become a virtual sacrificial lamb.

He was not included in the MCC side of promising young players which toured New Zealand in 1960–61, although it would have been the ideal way in which to blood a young fast bowler. He did visit the West Indies with E. W. Swanton's team that winter and returned to find himself in the MCC team to meet the Australian tourists at Lord's early in the 1961 season. That year there was a throwing truce which existed in matches involving the Australians prior to 7 June – and Rhodes was the only bowler to be reported under the terms of this, umpires having been instructed not to call people with suspect actions but to submit a report. Charlie Elliott and Frank Lee were the umpires at Lord's – the game in which Rhodes' bowling was considered doubtful – and it was believed Elliott reported him and Lee supported the move.

The next step was a change of action to a slinging type with the arm well behind the back, reminiscent of Les Jackson. After missing three games Rhodes returned to perform a hat-trick against Oxford University at Buxton. Then on August Bank Holiday Monday he was again no-balled by Gibb in Derbyshire's game against Northampton-shire. Gibb called three consecutive deliveries from square-leg in his third over. After taking a magnificent catch on the boundary, Rhodes was brought back into the attack with Arthur Jepson standing at square-leg, Jepson finding nothing wrong with his bowling.

Rhodes eventually reverted to his original action and finished the summer with 109 wickets at 21 each, having delivered 1,040.5 overs.

In January 1962 he was filmed at the County Ground and then

Derbyshire in 1962. Standing: H. L. Johnson, I. W. Hall, C. Lee, T. G. Ryde (scorer), H. J. Rhodes, W. F. Oates, I. R. Buxton, R. W. Taylor. Seated: D. C. Morgan, G. W. Richardson, D. B. Carr (capt.), H. L. Jackson, E. Smith.

visited a number of countries with an International XI before returning to a relatively quiet 1962. The throwing controversy seemed to be dying away now as far as Rhodes was concerned. In 1964 he found difficulty in adjusting to the new front foot rule which determined a no-ball. As he toiled away in the final home game of the season at Chesterfield in a Somerset total of 403 with Syd Buller umpiring, a recall to the Test side appeared a distant dream.

Indeed, Derbyshire suffered that year from turning out a modest pace attack in relation to past standards. With Les Jackson having retired, Rhodes' new-ball partner was the unrelated Brian Jackson. Jackson, born in Cheshire, was specially registered in 1963, his first of six successful years in his brief career with Derbyshire. He was an aggressive bowler with a high, whirlwind action who could slant the ball in at a good pace and also move it away. John Arlott described him as bowling 'a grudging length' – an ideal description of a ball which is too short to drive but not short enough to play comfortably off the back foot, an ability possessed by legions of Derbyshire seamers.

Mike Page had a fine first season with the County, scoring 990 runs. Twelve players – Garnet Lee, Arnold Hamer, Chris Wilkins, Brian Bolus, Lawrence Rowe, Eddie Barlow, John Wright, Peter Kirsten, David Steele, John Hampshire, Peter Bowler and Steve Goldsmith – have made a thousand runs in their debut seasons with the County, but all had played first-class cricket elsewhere. Blackpool-born but Hull-raised, Page had played none, and his initial summer was also marked by a fine 52 not out against the Australians at Derby, when Laurie Johnson made an unbeaten 101 – the first century by a Derbyshire player against the Australians. Runs for Hull in the Yorkshire League had attracted Derbyshire's attention and Page was specially registered for the 1964 season. He became a fine, stylish batsman, with a good technique and elegant strokes. A good player of spin, Page could battle it out on difficult pitches but he never quite made the most of his ability, otherwise he might well have played for England. He was also a good fieldsman, excelling at bat-pad early in his career; his 49 catches in 1967 smashed the County record. Another newcomer in this period was John Harvey. A product of the Lord's ground staff he made his debut in 1963 as an attractive batsman and fine cover fieldsman.

There was an early exit in the Gillette Cup at Northampton, and Derbyshire finished 12th in the Championship table, with five victories and nine defeats. Charlie Lee bade farewell to the club at the end of the season and was succeeded as captain by Derek Morgan. During his career Lee shared 11 century stands for the first wicket with Arnold Hamer, equalling the County record established by Denis Smith and Albert Alderman.

Morgan's qualities of leadership were to be put to the test almost immediately when the controversy surrounding Harold Rhodes' action was dramatically fanned into life after Derbyshire were beaten at Lord's in the second round of the Gillette, despite a record undefeated partnership of 74 in 26 overs for the ninth wicket by Taylor and Rhodes in 1965.

There was some acrimony in this game and it spilled over into the Championship encounter with Middlesex at Chesterfield a fortnight later. By now the press was pushing Rhodes' claim for a place in the England side against New Zealand but one or two Middlesex players were said to have discussed a possible protest about his bowling, even to the point of asking Derbyshire to leave him out of the team. He responded with six for 24 in a Middlesex total of 85, Derbyshire winning by five wickets. Then came a bombshell. Although the umpires, Tom Spencer and Hugo Yarnold, had been satisfied with his bowling the Middlesex captain Fred Titmus reported Rhodes to Lord's. Later another captain – unnamed – made a similar report.

Derek Morgan leads Derbyshire out to field against Surrey in 1964. On Morgan's left is Edwin Smith and immediately behind are Laurie Johnson, Brian Jackson and Peter Eyre.

Worse was to follow. A film had been taken of Rhodes bowling in the Gillette game at Lord's and on the evidence of this MCC felt his action was still suspect. Doug Insole, chairman of the Test selectors, wrote to Derbyshire saying that in view of this he could not be considered for the England team. No action was taken on the comments made by Titmus and the other unidentified captain – and Rhodes then took six for nine in Leicestershire's 36 all out at Loughborough.

187

Rhodes was now top of the national bowling averages and this sort of form should have guaranteed him a place in the Tests against New Zealand and South Africa and in the MCC party which toured Australia in 1965–66. Instead he was filmed again, this time at Buxton, before the controversy reached its climax in Derbyshire's match against the South Africans at Queen's Park.

Everything went well on the first day. The tourists were all out for 149, Rhodes, with umpire Jack Crapp at square leg and Syd Buller at the bowler's end, taking four for 35. Derbyshire's openers Ian Hall and John Eyre had made 75 without being parted by the close. But on the Monday Derbyshire were all out for 143. Brian Jackson bowled the first over and then at ten past three on 28 June 1965, Rhodes prepared to bowl his first over from the pavilion end with Buller at square leg.

Buller watched the first ball from square-leg and then crossed over to point, square of the wicket on the off-side. It was the classic manoeuvre of an umpire who was considering no-balling a bowler he thought was delivering the ball unfairly. After watching two balls from point Buller returned to square leg and no-balled the next two deliveries. Morgan asked him if he felt that Rhodes was throwing every ball and Buller replied: 'Yes'. Rhodes finished the over by sending down three leg-breaks off a short run and did not bowl again in the innings.

The crowd, angry at the way it considered Rhodes was treated, subjected Buller to abuse for the rest of the afternoon and he was slow-handclapped off the field at the tea interval, two policemen falling in alongside him as he walked towards the pavilion. The sensational headlines over the next couple of days obscured the fact that Derbyshire had beaten the South Africans by seven wickets, their first-ever victory over the Springboks and their first over a full-scale touring side since New Zealand were defeated in 1937.

The controversy raged on with Derbyshire followers unable to understand how 29 umpires – including Gibb and Buller – had stood in matches in which Rhodes had bowled during the past three and a half years and found no fault. There were mutterings that the Queen's Park no-balling was designed to save the Test selectors' embarrassment, that Rhodes would not have been called had he been having only an average season. Indeed, Ian Woolridge in the *Daily Mail* described the incident as a 'ceremonial calling – for there is no doubt that Buller's action was no spur-of-the-moment decision'.

Yet Buller was a great umpire, a fair and honest man, tough and conscientious, widely respected by the players. Rhodes believed he was as much a 'sacrificial lamb' as himself during the throwing controversy, led to believe that he was acting in the best interests of cricket during a crisis in which England had to be seen to be whiter than white and the interests of Commonwealth relations served. Rhodes may well have been unjustly treated but at the time many people were divided in their opinions about the legality of his action. There was something different about his bowling – a hyperextension which at the time was not appreciated. During the purge, the campaign against throwing, it was perhaps understandable that his bowling was viewed with suspicion. What rankled was the fact that the calling had taken place when he was taking wickets and on the verge of the Test team and not during the past three seasons when his record had been only moderate.

After the no-balling Rhodes was left out of the side for two matches (Peter Eyre was also absent, in his case for a much longer period, after his action had been reported to the MCC by Norman Oldfield, who umpired the Kent game at the end of May), returning to the team against Hampshire at Derby on 10 July.

Derbyshire had consistently backed their fast bowler and the Club did not waver in the face of the latest crisis. A statement was issued by Major Douglas Carr, the Secretary, after a two-hour committee meeting, which said:

> Members of the Derbyshire committee have found no evidence to cause them to change their former view regarding Rhodes' action, and he will therefore return to the County side on Saturday.
>
> It has been suggested that an informal discussion between Rhodes and some of the Test selectors might be of value, due to the unusual flexibility of his arm. In addition to this, some views on the Law regarding throwing and the administration of it are being forwarded to MCC as anything that can be done to help prevent similar occurrences with any bowler can do nothing but good.
>
> The committee wish to make it clear that they will always support their players to the fullest possible extent within the Laws of Cricket, realising that the umpire's decision on every occasion is final.

Press and TV cameras, a larger than usual crowd, many of whom moved around the ground to study Rhodes from various vantage spots, and umpires Cec Pepper and Sam Cook, both scrutinising him from square leg and point, added drama to the occasion. But Rhodes emerged unscathed, taking five for 57 in 30 overs and the first hurdle was behind him.

More trouble was ahead, however. Rhodes had passed the scrutiny of such umpires as Fred Price, Hugo Yarnold and Arthur Fagg, all noted for a tough line on throwing, but at Portsmouth Charlie Elliott, after studying his bowling closely, warned Morgan that if Rhodes continued bowling he would have to no-ball him. Derbyshire had already decided to leave him out of the next game at Trent Bridge where Buller and Bill Copson were the umpires 'to avoid putting additional strain on the captains, players and umpires concerned, pending the outcome of efforts to clarify the whole position'.

It was all the more tragic because Rhodes finished top of the national bowling averages with 119 wickets at 11.04 each in 24 first-class matches. Second was Brian Jackson with 120 at 12.42, each taking all their wickets for Derbyshire. In the Championship they each had 115 victims, Rhodes at 11.09 and Jackson at 12.37. They were match-winners in themselves, Rhodes the fastest bowler in the country, Jackson displaying great stamina and bowling a very good out-swinger, and they were well supported by Buxton, Smith and Morgan and by Bob Taylor, whose 86 victims in all first-class games placed him at the top of the wicket-keepers' lists. Unfortunately the batting did not match the outcricket and only two hundreds were made, both by Hall in the game at Folkestone, 101 in each innings. Consequently it was a mixed season of nine defeats and seven wins which found Derbyshire in ninth place in the table.

The controversy had become a saga. Rhodes was filmed repeatedly, bowling before members of the throwing committee, a special sub-committee set up to study the subject, in a black and white sleeve. He also bowled in a splint. Medical evidence, including a skeleton, was

John Arlott described Brian Jackson as bowling 'a grudging length', which illustrates perfectly the tradition of Derbyshire seam bowling. In 1965 Jackson – he was not related to Les Jackson – finished second to Harold Rhodes in the national bowling average.

produced, and various statements issued concerning his action, the gist being that it was basically fair although some members were not entirely satisfied with it on occasions. In July 1966 against Somerset at Burton-on-Trent he bowled with Buller at square leg for the first time since the South African game, the umpire crossing to point for one over and, after three maiden overs had been sent down by Rhodes, informing Morgan that he would have to no-ball him if he continued. He remained out in the cold as far as Tests were concerned, although the West Indian Charlie Griffith played in the 1966 series despite being called by Arthur Fagg. In 1967 Rhodes took 102 wickets at 15.53 each. By now the Law had a new definition, saying a bowler should not be debarred from straightening an over-extended arm nor using the wrist in the delivery swing, although this was rejected by the ICC that summer, albeit being allowed to continue in domestic cricket in 1968. In August 1967 there was another confrontation with Buller when Rhodes bowled with him at square leg at Northampton in the first innings. Nine wickets were down and he took the tenth with his third ball so another potential drama was averted. Then, in December 1968, after what amounted to an eight-year trial, Rhodes was at long last cleared. A Test and County Cricket Board sub-committee declared his basic action to be fair, issuing a statement which said:

> The sub-commitee have considered the bowling action of H. J. Rhodes in the light of the recommendation made by the International Cricket Conference concerning the definition of a throw. This definition does not allow any straightening of an over-extended arm prior to delivery. The committee decided by a clear majority that Rhodes's basic action is fair under this definition, but, as with every other bowler, umpires will be expected to interpret, in each and every case, the law as written.

By now Rhodes was 32. There is no doubt that the throwing controversy robbed him of a lengthy Test career, but what amounted to his final first-class season with Derbyshire in 1969 passed without incident. Prior to the start of the season he survived a road accident in Germany in which he received severe head injuries, and was not fully fit until the summer was well advanced. There was a final confrontation with Syd Buller, who stood at square leg while Rhodes bowled in a John Player League game at Ebbw Vale but said nothing about his bowling. Sadly, Buller died a year later, a man whom Rhodes himself has described as 'a magnificent umpire and an honest man'.

Rhodes was to leave Derbyshire at the end of the 1969 season, playing league cricket and appearing in one-day games for Nottinghamshire, but he returned in 1975 to play in one-day matches and one first-class match for his native County. That summer an unidentified captain and an umpire reported his action to Lord's, although nothing happened as a result. Had more than one captain or umpire been involved the matter would have gone before an adjudication committee. But his days in league cricket passed without incident and the abiding memory is of a most likeable man emerging from the whole affair with a great deal of respect and dignity.

It cast an unfortunate shadow over Derbyshire cricket in the 1960s, although with typically sharp dressing room humour Rhodes' colleagues, when they learned he enjoyed gardening, christened him Percy after the famous gardener Percy Thrower.

Eight wins in 1966 earned ninth place in the Championship, with Morgan and Harvey exceeding a thousand runs and Smith heading the bowlers with 87 wickets, two more than Morgan. The season had begun well with a seven-run victory at The Oval, their first win on the London ground since 1935. Needing 125 in the fourth innings Surrey reached 114 for six with Barrington going well but Smith had the Test star caught by Harvey and he and Rhodes polished off the tail, Smith taking nine for 70 in the match. Brian Jackson took eight for 18 as Warwickshire were routed for 38 at Coventry – the lowest score of the season.

In the Gillette Cup Derbyshire lost a thrilling match with Essex at Chesterfield, the visitors getting home by two wickets in the face of some hostile pace bowling by Alan Ward, who took three for 36.

It was the first indication that Derbyshire possessed in Ward possibly the most exciting talent ever unearthed by the Club, a talent which unhappily because of injuries and other factors was never to attain anything like its full potential. Recommended to the club by George Pope, Ward attended the County Ground for trials in August 1964, joining the staff the following year. Injuries and breakdowns held back his progress and Derbyshire kept him under wraps in his early years while he filled out and increased his pace. Ward was nursed through 1967 and the early part of 1968 before producing startling form towards the end of that season. He stood 6 ft 3 in and even at that early stage of his career word was going around that the County had discovered a player who was expected to be the fastest bowler in the country.

Ward had a fine, high action during which, however, he arched himself backwards in the last few strides thus placing his body under severe strain. Injuries were nearly always to be a problem, so, too, was temperament. Later on it was felt his action became too chest-on, and also that perhaps he placed too much stress on his frame by straining for pace too often instead of reverting to line and length for a time.

Emerging to challenge for regular places as batsmen were David Smith and Peter Gibbs, each of whom were to have a relatively brief career with the County but were destined to become one of the most successful pairs of openers Derbyshire have possessed.

Yorkshire-born Smith was specially registered in 1965, making his debut that year. A left-handed batsman he joined a Derbyshire contingent at Undercliffe in the Bradford League, where Jim Brailsford was pro and Les Jackson the leading bowler, in his formative seasons with the Club. Peter Gibbs had received a good grounding in first-class cricket with Oxford University. He was born in Cheshire and was in the Oxford eleven in 1964–66, also playing for Staffordshire. Smith was a determined and gritty batsman who had battled his way through several disappointments before breaking into county cricket, where he became a sound opener and reliable slip fieldsman. Gibbs was a stylist, with a particularly memorable stroke through the covers. In the end business took both away from Derbyshire cricket and in later years Gibbs became a successful playwright with numerous works screened on television.

Destined for a longer stay with the club was Philip Russell, who was later to become one of Derbyshire's most successful coaches. Russell displayed early promise as a batsman and medium-pace bowler, making his debut for the County in 1965, breaking a tooth and a finger when attempting a catch in his first game at Trent Bridge. It was as a bowler that Russell, always a deep thinker about the game, made his biggest impact, turning from seamers to off-cutters during the course of his career which was to be interrupted when he was not re-engaged in 1973. That summer he took 114 wickets at 8.84 for Langley Mill in the Notts and Derby Border League, where he first demonstrated a coaching ability that was to extend far beyond Station Road. Russell was to be particularly successful in one-day cricket and returned to the County in 1974 after a year's absence, his first-class career continuing until 1985.

There was an early opportunity for one of the young batsmen in 1967 when Ian Hall was forced to miss the first half of the season because of a leg injury received while playing soccer. When the opening game began against Leicestershire at Derby, Smith and Gibbs, who had opened in the final match of the 1966 season at Colwyn Bay, formed a new combination. Derbyshire won by nine wickets, their first victory at the County Ground since June 1962, and it was to herald a summer which brought four more victories, at Bath, at Chesterfield, where Gibbs (86) and Smith (114) shared an opening stand of 174 against Essex and Morgan returned a match analysis of eleven for 67, and in the following game at Cardiff when Morgan (eleven for 55) took his tally of wickets to 22 in successive matches. A four-run win at Northampton completed the set, 17 draws and only five defeats leaving Derbyshire sixth in the table. The Smith-Gibbs partnership flourished immediately with three century stands, Smith being the highest scorer in the Championship and making 1,337 runs in all games while Gibbs, who missed seven games, scored 916 runs.

There was a tribute to Walter Goodyear and the other groundsmen inasmuch as not one Derbyshire pitch was reported as unsuitable in a season when 15 counties were visited by Bert Lock, the newly appointed Inspector of Pitches.

Given this confidence in their own pitches the batsmen revelled in the summer of 1968, six making more than a thousand runs. Morgan led the averages, Smith and Gibbs put together three century opening stands and Page, Buxton and Harvey also reached four-figure aggregates.

For a long time. Derbyshire mounted a challenge for the Championship. There was an excellent five-wicket victory at Hove when Page (82) led a successful bid to make 271, and a 21-run win at Kidderminster followed soon afterwards. Buxton (five for eight and six for 25) took full advantage of a drying pitch at Derby as the double

Derbyshire 1968. Back row: D. H. K. Smith, J. Eyre, P. E. Russell, J. H. Harvey, F. W. Swarbrook, C. P. Marks. Middle row: T. J. P. Eyre, A. Ward, D. Smith (coach), P. J. K. Gibbs, M. Hendrick, F. J. Allen (masseur). Front row: M. H. Page, E. Smith, D. C. Morgan (capt.), D. J. Carr (secretary), H. J. Rhodes, A. B. Jackson, I. R. Buxton. (Raymonds News Agency)

was completed over Worcestershire. Gibbs, Smith and Harvey were capped during the nine-wicket win over Gloucestershire at Chesterfield and with only one defeat in their first 15 games Derbyshire were well in touch with the leaders. But three consecutive losses halted their challenge, two of these coming during Ilkeston's Festival Week. This was the final season before the formation of the John Player League and Derbyshire's split of home games had been virtually unaltered for many years. In 1968 Derby and Chesterfield each got five matches, Ilkeston two and Buxton and Burton-on-Trent one each.

The game against the Australians took place at Chesterfield and resulted in a most thrilling match which saw Derbyshire beaten by just eight runs when set 345 in seven hours. A magnificent 92 from Harvey almost clinched victory, the game being watched by 9,800 paying spectators with receipts of £2,479.

Buxton also witnessed a remarkable game against Somerset, Page and Morgan making hundreds in a total of 400 for four declared, Page suffering a broken nose while fielding and then returning from hospital, bandages and all, to see Derbyshire home to a two-wicket victory.

The climax to this entertaining season, however, was yet to come. Alan Ward came into the side in mid-August to replace Brian Jackson, who left at the end of the campaign to return to league cricket. Ward immediately generated fearsome pace, not least at Cardiff when Derbyshire met Championship-chasing Glamorgan. Peter Eyre (89) and Page (80) helped them to 247 and then Ward (six for 56) took full advantage of an end where the ball tended to 'fly' to give his side a 45-run lead. Gibbs made 86 and Morgan left Glamorgan 216 but with Ward and Rhodes taking four wickets apiece they never looked like getting the runs. Ward followed this with five for 50 against Hampshire at Derby and in four first-class games for the County took 26 wickets at 11.84. Derbyshire's six wins left them eighth in the table.

With Rhodes still capable of reaching a good pace there was much excited talk of what the new fast bowling combination might achieve in 1969. Ward made an early appearance at headquarters when he played for MCC v Yorkshire (dismissing Boycott for nought), Taylor keeping wicket in this game. Rhodes was recovering from his autobahn accident injuries and it was some time before the pair bowled in harness. But in July they caught Warwickshire on a lively Derby pitch, bowling unchanged in a first innings of 78, Ward having a match analysis of ten for 81 and Rhodes nine for 85 in their side's first victory of the season. Their fast bowling also had much to do with a win over Kent at Derby but there were only three victories in the Championship, Lancashire at Blackpool being the other victims, and Derbyshire finished 1969 second from the bottom.

Ward appeared in only 15 of the 24 Championship games, taking 56 wickets at 12.92 each. He was, however, selected for three Test matches against the New Zealanders in which he took ten wickets, and he finished at the top of the national bowling averages with 69 victims at 14.82. Rhodes, in his last season of Championship cricket, came seventh with 64 at 18.23 and the loss of his pace bowling and Morgan's all-round skill and experience left the Club short of resources for the new decade.

It also placed a question mark over the Club's policy of refusing to take advantage of the rule permitting the special registration of overseas players. Only Yorkshire and Derbyshire did not possess one in 1969, Derbyshire having preferred to develop their own players or specially register them from other counties.

Clearly after the indifferent performances in the Championship it was time for a fresh approach.

LORD'S '69

THE DISMAL FORM SHOWN BY DERBYSHIRE in 1969 had extended into the new John Player League competition which was staged for the first time that summer. Only five of the 16 games were won – Sussex at Hove were Derbyshire's first victims, Ward taking four for 12 in their dismissal for 63 – and they finished 15th in the final table with ten defeats.

Given this lack of form there appeared little prospect of progress in the Gillette Cup competition. For the past three summers Derbyshire had made an early exit, in 1968 ignominiously when they were beaten by ten wickets at Hove. They were not among the favourites to win the competition in 1969.

Nevertheless, there was a good start at Taunton in the first round when Somerset were beaten by three wickets, Fred Rumsey, the former England left-arm pace bowler, who had joined the Club as public relations officer, taking three for 19 and earning the Man of the Match award after Morgan had put Somerset in.

Still rank outsiders, Derbyshire faced Worcestershire at Derby in the second round and chased a target of 157. Gibbs and Smith gave their side another good start with a stand of 52 but five wickets were down for 108 and 49 were needed from 16.4 overs. Morgan batted brightly for 33 and a good display by Taylor helped Derbyshire to a four-wicket victory with 11 balls remaining.

In the third round for the first time, Derbyshire met Glamorgan at Cardiff and again Morgan's tactics of putting his opponents in proved successful. The Welsh county were all out for 117, Tony Lewis making 60 and Rhodes taking four for 18. Derbyshire were given another good start and at tea were 53 for one for the loss of Gibbs in 23 overs. Smith (49 not out) and Page saw them home to a comfortable nine-wicket victory in the 44th over, Rhodes being Man of the Match.

In the semi-final Derbyshire were drawn against Sussex, acknowledged masters of one-day cricket, twice winners and three times finalists in the previous six Gillette competitions. Heavy rain had fallen at Chesterfield earlier in the week and the water had seeped under the covers but groundsman Harold Graham and his assistants mopped up so well that a prompt start was possible on the morning of Wednesday 30 July 1969. Morgan won the toss on a warm, sunny day and chose to bat on a slow, spongy pitch. The game attracted a crowd of 10,582, the receipts being £3,520. Gibbs and Smith began with 34 for the first wicket but then Derbyshire met trouble, Page slipping on the damp turf and being run out at 51 and Gibbs lofting a ball to deep extra cover after making 44, the score now being 68 for three from 27.4 overs. Morgan defended grimly, Harvey stayed for three quarters of an hour, but when the innings closed at 2.45 pm the total was only 136 from 56.4 overs. The odds seemed heavily in favour of Sussex, a fact which the more vociferous onlookers made clear. The ill-informed barracking from sections of the crowd at this match illustrated an unwelcome by-product of the limited-overs games.

Seldom can a situation have been so misread. With the fourth delivery of his first over Ward caused Lenham to chop an in-swinger on to his leg stump and for five overs the score remained at one for one, the run, a no-ball, also having come in the first over. Suttle edged Rhodes to the boundary and then a ball from Ward splayed Cooper's stumps and Sussex were five for two.

Mere statistics cannot adequately illustrate the drama of that Wednesday afternoon. There have been many incidents of memorable pace bowling in the annals of Derbyshire cricket but the accuracy and hostility of Ward and Rhodes has never been surpassed. The hush as each bowler roared into the attack, was punctuated by bursts of relieved applause as maiden followed maiden and Parks and Suttle, Sussex's most experienced batsmen, hung on in the face of some keen fielding by Derbyshire in their baggy, Australian-style caps. For a long time it appeared the only other sound to be heard was the thud of the ball crashing into Suttle's pads as he struggled to cope with Rhodes. When the pace bowlers came off the score was ten for two after 14 overs, eleven of which were maidens. It was a memorable spell, Ward bowling down the hill from the pavilion end – he now had the choice of ends having succeeded Rhodes as the fastest bowler – and Rhodes from the lake end. Rhodes recalled that Sussex had one or two stroke players in their side who could become frustrated if they were bogged down so they set out to bowl straight, keep the ball well up and give them nothing. In seven overs he conceded only the edged boundary and Sussex, now needing 127 in 46 overs at 2.76 per over, collapsed against Eyre and Rumsey. Line and length proved the telling factors for Peter Eyre, whose six for 18 earned him the Man of the Match award from Don Kenyon, although he noted Gibbs' fine innings.

So at Lord's Derbyshire were to meet Yorkshire, who had beaten Nottinghamshire by 68 runs after being put in at Scarborough. The team was the same as in the four previous Gillette games and they faced in Yorkshire tough and uncompromising opponents who had beaten Surrey after being put in in the 1965 final. Norfolk, Lancashire, Surrey and Nottinghamshire had been their victims en route to Lord's.

The game proved something of an anti-climax. Morgan won the toss and asked Yorkshire to bat, understandable enough in view of the tactic which worked both at Taunton and Cardiff, but heavily criticised afterwards. Boycott was absent with a hand injury, Leadbeater had broken a finger in the previous match and played with his hand strapped. It all went wrong for Derbyshire. Woodford was out at 39 but Brian Close, the Yorkshire captain, and Leadbeater added 64 in 43 minutes before Close was out at 103 for 37. Page strained his side in holding the catch which dismissed Close, Edwin Smith taking his place in the field. Chances were either missed or mistimed strokes did not quite go to hand and Yorkshire, with Leadbeater making 76, reached 219 for eight, then the second highest score in the final.

Smith and Gibbs again began well, with 37 from 18 overs but the rate was never quick enough against some varied and accurate bowling in which Close played a major role. Ward was promoted to number four to try and accelerate the scoring rate but with Page affected by injury and Morgan unluckily run out the task was too great. With six wickets down for 112, 108 were needed from 20.2

Architects of victory. Alan Ward (left) bowling in the nets with Harold Rhodes looking on, while (right) Rhodes himself comes under the scrutiny of Derbyshire's coach, Denis Smith.

DERBYSHIRE *v* SUSSEX (GILLETTE CUP SEMI-FINAL)

Played at Queen's Park, Chesterfield, 30 July 1969

DERBYSHIRE WON BY 87 RUNS

DERBYSHIRE

P. J. K. Gibbs	c A. Buss b Suttle	44
D. H. K. Smith	c and b M. Buss	10
M. H. Page	run out	8
I. R. Buxton	c and b M. Buss	2
J. F. Harvey	c Greig b A. Buss	16
*D. C. Morgan	not out	26
†R. W. Taylor	b Bates	5
T. J. P. Eyre	c Graves b A. Buss	4
A. Ward	c Griffiths b Bates	7
F. E. Rumsey	b A. Buss	8
H. J. Rhodes	b A. Buss	0
Extras	lb 5, w 1	6
Total		136

Fall: 1-34, 2-51, 3-68, 4-71, 5-96, 6-101, 7-114, 8-127, 9-136, 10-136

BOWLING	O	M	R	W
Snow	9	1	23	0
A. Buss	10.4	1	27	4
M. Buss	12	1	23	2
Greig	5	0	16	0
Suttle	12	3	21	1
Bates	8	1	20	2

SUSSEX

L. J. Lenham	b Ward	0
K. G. Suttle	b Rumsey	5
G. C. Cooper	b Ward	0
†J. M. Parks	c Morgan b Eyre	16
A. W. Greig	c Smith b Eyre	6
*M. G. Griffith	b Rumsey	0
P. J. Graves	c Taylor b Eyre	2
J. A. Snow	c Taylor b Eyre	7
M. A. Buss	b Eyre	2
A. Buss	not out	7
D. L. Bates	b Eyre	2
Extras	nb 2	2
Total		49

Fall: 1-1, 2-5, 3-12, 4-27, 5-28, 6-29, 7-33, 8-40, 9-41, 10-49

BOWLING	O	M	R	W
Ward	8	5	11	2
Rhodes	7	6	4	0
Rumsey	9	3	13	2
Eyre	10.2	4	18	6
Buxton	1	0	1	0

Umpires: R. Aspinall and H. Mellows

Toss won by Derbyshire.

overs when Page fell and although Buxton did well the game was over at 6.41 pm, Derbyshire being dismissed for 150 in the 55th over.

Thousands of Derbyshire followers had made the trip to St John's Wood, 400 travelling on British Railways' first-ever cricket special. It was the wrong result for Derbyshire but 21,000 spectators had enjoyed the cricket on a fine sunny day and it was a memorable climax to a splendid Gillette run in an otherwise disappointing season.

CENTENARY AND BEYOND

AN OVERSEAS PLAYER MIGHT HAVE MADE all the difference to the Gillette final in 1969 and Derbyshire quickly learned their lesson from the failures of that season. The South African Chris Wilkins arrived as a 25-year-old attacking opening batsman anxious to improve his game. He had impressed in domestic cricket and there was a hope that if he proved successful it would give Derbyshire a lift and lead to a healthy accumulation of batting bonus points.

With Morgan and Rhodes gone, Ian Buxton succeeded to the captaincy, leading a side which had an added incentive to do well in 1970, Derbyshire's centenary year. The Duke of Devonshire began the centenary fund-raising subscriptions, along with some of the vice-presidents and committee members, with £2,300, and two luncheons at Chatsworth House resulted in donations of £4,800. More contributions raised the total to £9,000, Royal Crown Derby China and Webb Corbett pieces were sold or auctioned and a bumper 271-page edition of the *Year Book* was produced, but the response to the centenary appeal was not as generous as had been hoped.

Chris Wilkins, the exciting South African all-rounder, scored over 4,000 runs and took 47 wickets between 1970 and 1972. He drove with ferocious power and in 1971 added a fifth wicket 203 with Ian Buxton at Old Trafford. Wilkins was a fine cover fielder, brilliant slip and capable emergency wicket-keeper.

There was also a special centenary game played under John Player League rules at Chesterfield on 5 July 1970 between Derbyshire and an MCC team which was captained by Carr and included Les Jackson, Gladwin, Brian Jackson, Hamer, Lee, Willatt, Dawkes and Morgan. A hundred years earlier, on 21–22 July 1870, a Derbyshire XI had beaten MCC at Lord's; on this occasion the County won by 58 runs, but perhaps the most memorable aspect was Jackson and Gladwin once again opening the attack on a beautiful day before a large crowd.

That brought back more memories of pace but it was spin which proved the dominant factor in Derbyshire's attack early in 1970. Fred Swarbrook had first played three years earlier, and now he was to establish a regular place in the side as a slow left-arm bowler and left-hand batsman. He became a most useful 'bits and pieces' player, a bowler who did not turn the ball a lot but relied on line and length, and a dogged and determined little fighter of a batsman who proved very popular with the crowd. Sadly, after some consistent performances in the 1970s, Swarbrook lost control of his bowling, producing assortments of head-high full tosses and long hops which brought his career to a premature end after the 1979 season when he was still only 29.

By contrast Michael Hendrick, who also began to emerge at this time, went on to a career which touched the heights. He made his debut in 1969 but sore shins were to prove a handicap in 1970 and 1971, when his retention by the County hung in the balance for a time. The breakthrough was to come in 1972 and Derbyshire by then had a fine bowler, with a splendid physique, high and rhythmic action and superb control of line and length. He was able to move the ball either way off the seam and obtain a great deal of bounce from his height and his high arm action. He was sometimes criticised for failing to run through opposing sides in the manner of the old Derbyshire pace bowlers but the nature of the game was changing and counties, boosted by overseas stars, were stronger than in yesteryear. At his best he was a magnificent bowler, the equal of his glorious predecessors, such as on a day at Ilkeston in 1977 when he and Colin Tunnicliffe reduced a powerful Middlesex side to 54 all out. That Saturday morning Hendrick, with four slips, a gully, forward short leg and two backward short legs, evoked memories of Derbyshire pace at its best. Hendrick remained with Derbyshire until the end of the 1981 season when he joined Nottinghamshire.

A Gibbs century paved the way for Derbyshire's first win of the season, over Gloucestershire at Queen's Park and June began with consecutive victories at Worcester and over Sussex at Buxton. Ward (six for 30) routed the visitors for 75 en route to match figures of ten for 113, and on the Sunday he dismissed four batsmen with consecutive deliveries in taking five for 11 in the John Player League match between the counties at Derby. A four-wicket victory over Glamorgan at Derby was followed by a win at Northampton three weeks later. This was followed by a fine performance against Lancashire, the Championship leaders, at Derby. With Ward absent the visitors declared at 270 for nine, Smith and Gibbs making ten without being parted by the close of Saturday's play. On the Monday they took the score to 168 before Gibbs was out for 72 and then Smith (136) and Page (113) shared a second-wicket partnership of 175 in 125 minutes. At the close the score was 362 for three and on Tuesday morning Wilkins hit a rapid 96 before Buxton declared at 468 for five. Lancashire were all out for 204 and Derbyshire's ten-wicket victory carried them into third place in the Championship table, a point behind Lancashire and only seven behind Glamorgan, who had played three games more.

Four drawn matches followed before Derbyshire gained a six-wicket win over Warwickshire at Coventry, with Ward taking six for 69 in the first innings, despite Rohan Kanhai's brilliant 187 not out, and Swarbrook six for 48 in the second.

That win, on 11 August 1970, took Derbyshire to the top of the table with seven victories in 19 games, 176 points to Surrey's 172 from 19 and Yorkshire's 170 from 17. At that stage of the season they also stood third in the John Player League with nine wins in 13 games, eight points behind the leaders Lancashire.

Hopes were high of a double success in the centenary year but that was to prove the high point of the summer. Of the last five Championship games three were lost, Derbyshire remaining at the top until 21 August but ending in joint seventh place. In the JPL they finished third with 11 wins, leaving them nine points behind Lancashire, the Champions, and four behind Kent.

Wilkins hit two centuries and made 1,638 runs in all first-class games, 1,510 for the County. Using his long reach and powerful physique he set out to dominate the bowling from the start and gave some fine displays of scientific hitting.

Ward, who played at Lord's for England against the Rest of the World, was absent for five weeks with an ankle injury and was never fully fit after June. His four for 121 in 33 overs was achieved against a batting line-up of Richards, Barlow, Kanhai, Pollock, Lloyd and Sobers, with Engineer at number seven and Procter at number nine. Surely no Derbyshire bowler has ever operated against such an array of quality. Ward was selected for the MCC tour of Australia and New Zealand in 1970–71 but played in only two first-class games before returning home with a slight fracture of his right leg. Bob Taylor, who went out as reserve wicket-keeper to Alan Knott, earned his first

Test cap in February 1971 when he played against New Zealand at Christchurch.

By then the centenary celebrations were at an end. On Wednesday, 4 November 1970, just 100 years after the Club's formation, a dinner was held at the King's Hall, Derby. It was attended by some 250 members, players, guests and officials and produced an evening rich in memory and nostalgia. Sir Cyril Hawker, president of the MCC, proposed the toast to the Club and announced that Walter Goodyear had been selected as county cricket groundsman of the year by the county pitches committee and their sponsors, Watney Mann. All nine of Derbyshire's surviving past captains were present, with the playing span ranging from Jim Horsley and Garnet Lee down to Fred Swarbrook and Tony Borrington.

It was a heady evening but instead of success, lean days once again lay ahead for Derbyshire. Ian Buxton felt the success of the 1970 team only papered over the cracks. Three victories had been gained with only a little time remaining; had these matches been drawn then Derbyshire would have been next to the bottom. The need to strengthen the side would have been more apparent.

Although they had much the same team in 1971 the beginning of August found Derbyshire at the bottom of the Championship table with an unlikely record of one win, one defeat and 18 draws in 20 games. They finished last and it was to become familiar territory as they held the wooden spoon in 1972 and 1974 and only scraped clear by one point in 1973.

In 1971 Ashley Harvey-Walker made an unbeaten 110 in the second innings of his debut against Oxford University at Burton-on-Trent. An effortless stroke-player, he was to provide much entertainment over the next seven years, hitting three hundreds in a somewhat patchy career. Chris Wilkins continued to entertain, adding moderation to his hitting ability and scoring runs consistently. Nine hundreds flowed from his bat before he returned home after the 1972 season, the best being his 156 at Old Trafford (24 fours) in 1971 when he and Buxton shared a fifth-wicket partnership of 203, a new County record. Immensely strong, Wilkins struck the ball very hard in front of the wicket with a heavy bat and was a superb fieldsman, either in the covers or the slips, where he excelled.

Tony Borrington was an outstanding schoolboy batsman who scored heavily in local cricket and graduated into the County side through the junior, club and ground and second elevens. He was an aggressive player and an athletic fieldsman who gave some splendid displays, particularly in the one-day game. Borrington was beginning to establish himself in 1972 when another young batsman also took his initial steps in county cricket. Alan Hill did well in school and youth cricket before joining the staff in 1971 and making his debut a year later. He made a moderate start, a broken jaw putting him out for a long spell in 1974 just when he was running into form, and it was not until 1976 that he really emerged as one of the County's most consistent batsmen. That summer his 120 against Northamptonshire at Buxton was the first by a Derbyshire batsman in the John Player League. 'Bud' Hill became one of the finest Club men in the County's history, a gritty, determined opening batsman with a sound technique who did not twitch against fast bowling. He was sometimes barracked for his slow scoring (he made 103 for Orange Free State in South Africa in 1976–77 without hitting a single boundary!) but his 14-year career brought him a thousand runs in five seasons and 18 hundreds.

Hill's arrival in 1972 was overshadowed by a remarkable series of comings and goings at the end of that season. Harvey, Harvey-Walker, Russell and Swarbrook were not offered contracts, Gibbs, Hall and Eyre retired, Buxton resigned the captaincy and Wilkins returned to South Africa. Strenuous efforts were made to bring in big names. In two seasons only two games had been won in the Championship – only nine of 44 encounters were lost and Derbyshire's modern reputation of being better at saving games than winning them stems from this period – and something had to be done. Dennis Lillee, Peter Parfitt and Tom Graveney were all linked with the County that winter but none of them came; Fred Trueman played one-day games in 1972 but the long-awaited revival was some years away yet.

Brian Bolus, at 39, took over from Buxton as captain in 1973 and did a fine job in raising morale. Bolus had played in seven Tests after joining Nottinghamshire from Yorkshire, and he was still a batsman of class, either opening or lower in the order. Wilkins was replaced by the Indian off-spinner Srinivasaraghavan Venkataraghavan, a scorer's nightmare but a fine cricketer who had been a member of a successful Indian side with an attack including top-class spin. Venkat was a good close fieldsman and a useful batsman who produced some memorable spells of bowling in 1973–75 with the County, although he perhaps was the wrong type of overseas player to suit the needs of the day. Swarbrook was reinstated, as was Russell a year later, and waiting in the wings were off-spinners Bob Swindell and Geoff Miller, both of whom found their opportunities restricted because of Venkat. Swindell looked a promising prospect in 1972-77 but it was Miller who made the grade and eventually bridged the gap between Test and county cricket.

He had vast experience of school cricket, touring India and the West Indies and being chosen as the Outstanding Boy Cricketer of 1972. Miller, like so many of his predecessors, played in the Bassetlaw

League, with Chesterfield, and made his County debut at 20 in 1973. There was always the feeling that Miller would, one day, play for England; throughout his career there was also the feeling that his rich potential had never quite been fulfilled. He played in 34 Test matches, 25 one-day internationals and went on eight major tours. He was captain of Derbyshire in 1979-81, a quality batsman in the middle order, a superb off-spin bowler when at his best with a 'magic' ball capable of defeating any batsman, and a good fieldsman in the slips. Miller was the Best Young Cricketer of 1976, the year of his Test debut, and had the counties enjoyed similar programmes of matches during his career to those of earlier years he would probably have achieved doubles in 1976, 1977 and 1984. In short, he ranked among the best all-rounders and it was a pity that his final years with Derbyshire were not his happiest. He almost left after the 1981 season and was to do so in 1986 when he joined Essex.

Ironically he will be remembered not just for his, at times, world-class off-spin bowling but for the inordinate length of time he took to score his maiden century. It eventually came in May 1984 at Old Trafford in his 256th innings in first-class cricket at the age of 31. His inability to reach three figures before this had been a source of amazement on the county circuit. He had reached the nineties on five occasions, twice for Derbyshire, twice for England and once on a tour for England, including 98 not out in a Test against Pakistan in Lahore in 1977-78 and 98 in the Old Trafford Test against India in 1982.

But Miller's bowling was his forte. He learned the art of spin gradually and by playing alongside the best. In Australia in 1978-79 Miller changed his style by adopting a straighter run up to the wicket, bringing his left arm higher and bowling with greater control round the wicket. He developed a ball which drifted away from the batsman and found the confidence to tailor his loop to the situation, becoming an all-rounder who was always worth his place in the England team without ever quite getting fully established. The advent of John Emburey and a back injury were to limit his opportunities later on.

In 1973, Miller's best days lay in the future; a year later Lawrence Rowe, the talented West Indian, joined the Club for the 1974 season. Rowe was a player of world-class, with 214 and 100 not out on his Test debut, and 302 against England. But somehow the anticipated weight of runs never arrived, despite a relatively good season which brought him 1,059 in first-class games (though with no hundreds – 94 was his best) and an average of 36.51. He topped both first-class and one-day batting averages but this, his solitary season with the club, proved only a qualified success.

Colin Tunnicliffe, who became the club's commercial manager after his career ended, made his debut in 1973 after graduating through the Notts and Derby Border League as a left-arm fast-medium bowler. Tunnicliffe might have lacked the high quality of some of the earlier members of the line of pace bowlers but he was a good, honest professional and a valuable member of the side in later years, particularly in one-day games. Harry Cartwright also emerged during this period. Cartwright was a highly entertaining middle-order batsman and brilliant fieldsman who never quite realised an exciting potential. In many respects his career mirrored that of Tony Borrington in that their formative years were spent in a struggling side, with uncertainty surrounding the Club's future. Each took time out to prepare for their own future by spending two years in the teaching profession, each had his best days in the late 1970s and each left the game relatively early.

Alan Morris, from Staveley, was another stylish batsman who was pleasant to watch but could not quite bridge the gap. Keith Stevenson, a fast-medium bowler from Derby, also had his days of success before seeking wider opportunities with Hampshire.

There was now serious concern about the fast bowler, Alan Ward. He was still very much in the selectors' minds after his early return from Australia in 1970–71 and his solitary Test against Pakistan in 1971. He played for MCC against the 1972 Australians at Lord's but appeared in only five Championship games that year, a pulled muscle keeping him out. Michael Carey commented in *Wisden*:

> His absence seemed an inordinately long one for such an injury and, in the end, there appeared to be mental as well as physical barriers to be crossed. It is to be hoped that a fresh start, under a new captain and perhaps with more support, will spur Ward to the kind of achievement worthy of a bowler of his talents.

Carey's assessment was, unhappily, soon to be proved correct. On Monday, 18 June 1973 at Chesterfield Ward was sent off the field by his captain Brian Bolus for refusing to bowl that afternoon against Yorkshire, only the third time such a thing had happened in first-class cricket. After Derbyshire had made 311 Ward removed Boycott in his first over but although he bowled very fast he was erratic and was no-balled nine times. Jackie Hampshire, who was missed off him before he had scored, a difficult chance to Cartwright in the slips, overcame his discomfort against Ward's pace by launching a savage attack in which he took 19 runs off the fast bowler's third over after lunch. Nine overs from Ward cost 56 runs and he was not asked to bowl again until after tea when Bolus signalled that he wanted to bring him on at the pavilion end. Ward said he was unable to bowl, pointing out that he had lost his confidence, was having trouble with his run and was bowling a lot of no-balls. Bolus, who had previously left the field to talk to the Derbyshire secretary, Major Douglas Carr, then made a dismissive gesture and Ward walked off and left the ground before play ended. The following day he apologised but two days later announced that he was retiring from first-class cricket and his contract was cancelled by mutual consent.

Injuries and the presssure of the first-class game – 'When Brian Bolus asked me to bowl, something exploded inside me. I couldn't go on. People will never understand, but all I wanted to do was to get off that pitch' – led to a retirement which disappointed and saddened Bolus. It was a tragic waste of talent (Ward played in only ten of his County's 40 Championship games in 1972–73) but there was a happy return in 1974 when he produced the most consistent bowling of his career, taking 56 wickets at 20.96 each, including a career-best seven for 42 against Glamorgan at Burton-on-Trent.

If Ward's career was in temporary eclipse that of Michael Hendrick gathered momentum. At Trent Bridge in 1972 he took six for 7 in a JPL game and six for 43 in the Championship game six days later. Eight for 50 against Northamptonshire, seven for 65 against Somerset and, in 1973, eight for 45 against Warwickshire, all at Chesterfield, served notice that here was a fast-medium bowler of genuine quality. Sixty-six wickets at 20.53 earned him a place in the Young England side against the West Indies at Old Trafford and then in the Prudential Trophy international at Leeds, Bob Taylor keeping wicket in both that match and the one at The Oval. Taylor, who had toured Australia in 1971–72 with a World XI and appeared in one of the five representative games, accompanied Hendrick to the West Indies in Mike Denness' 1973–74 party. Neither played in a Test; Hendrick took 12 wickets at 26.66 in five first-class matches, while Taylor appeared in only three matches. Clive Taylor, in *Wisden*, put the Knott-Taylor situation of the 1970s in a nutshell, when he wrote of Knott:

> It was his batting probably that decided the selectors' vote in his favour at a time when Taylor was challenging strongly on wicket-keeping grounds. It remains a tragedy that a player of Taylor's class should play not one Test match and only three first-class games in three months.

In 1974 Hendrick took 65 first-class wickets at 19.81 and played in five Tests. Taylor and Hendrick went to Australia in 1974–75, Taylor again serving time as Knott's deputy. Hendrick played in the first Test at Brisbane, missed the second because of a throat infection and bowled only 22 balls in the third at Melbourne before pulling out with a hamstring injury. He appeared in the second Test against New Zealand at Christchurch but the hamstring injury took its toll in the

1975 season when, despite taking 68 wickets at 15.83, finishing second in the national averages and bowling well for MCC against the Australians at Lord's, he did not play in either the Prudential Cup or the Test series that summer.

Nevertheless, Hendrick's emergence as a Test player was an encouraging factor in Derbyshire cricket in 1974. In truth, though, it was a season of disaster perhaps epitomised by a selection policy which produced 17 different opening pairs during the season! Morale slumped, there was yet another cash crisis and as an economy measure the services of Edwin Smith, who succeeded Denis Smith as Club coach in 1972 following Denis' retirement, were dispensed with. To save expense the Second Eleven and club and ground sides, in addition to the position of coach, were dropped.

Derbyshire appealed to Derby Borough Council to take over maintenance of the County Ground at Derby but their request was rejected. The annual cost of running the ground was £6,500 net and this was the only other area in which economies could be made. The Council offered a grant of £100 per day, amounting to £1,200 in 1975, but it was not enough.

Although the Club offices remained at the ground the tenancy was given up on 5 May 1975, a Benson and Hedges game against the Minor Counties (North) and a Championship match against Worcestershire before that date marking the end, at least for the time being, of county cricket at Derby after 104 years.

The deficit in 1974 of £5,138 was lower than that of most County Clubs and less than half the previous year's loss, but further cash debts of £15,000 meant that Derbyshire were again fighting for their existence.

In his annual report, the chairman, Mr Ken Turner, made no attempt to conceal the extent of the problem:

> The immediate aim is survival, closely connected with a return to the successful playing days of a few years ago. Everything else for the moment must be subordinated to these two vital aims.

A survival budget was drawn up, with Derbyshire cricket at its lowest ebb since the disastrous days of 1920.

THE BARLOW SHAKE-UP

WITHIN A MONTH DERBYSHIRE FACED yet another crisis. Brian Bolus, out of form mainly because of business worries, resigned the captaincy following his team's elimination from the Benson and Hedges Cup in the qualifying stages.

On paper Bolus had a talented squad. There were fellow past and present Test players in Hendrick, Taylor, Venkataraghavan, Ward and Philip Sharpe, who joined the County from Yorkshire. A world-class slip fieldsman and experienced opening batsman, the 38-year-old Sharpe played in a dozen Tests in 1963–69. Mike Page, Harvey-Walker, Hill, Miller, Morris, Russell, Stevenson, Swarbrook, John Ward and Michael Glenn, a 6 ft 5 in fast-medium bowler, completed the full-time staff. Borrington and Cartwright were now teaching but were available for one-day matches. Ron Headley, at 35, joined the Club for limited-overs games. Headley, son of the great George, had enjoyed a long and successful career with Worcestershire as a left-hand opening batsman and had played in two Tests for the West Indies against England in 1973. He and Sharpe were destined to form a successful opening partnership in limited-overs matches.

The early weeks of the Championship programme found Derby-shire lingering in familiar territory at the bottom of the table. Bob Taylor, who succeeded Bolus as captain, underwent a baptism of fire in his early games at the helm. His first act as skipper was to tell an unhappy Bolus that he had been dropped from the side because of his indifferent form. Then Lancashire made 477 for five declared on the opening day of their match at Buxton. By close of play on Saturday evening Derbyshire had lost two wickets for 25.

Rain and a blizzard ruled out play on Monday, 2 June 1975, the spectacle of a cricket ground covered by an inch of snow in June making national news. Amazingly a start was made on Tuesday when Derbyshire were caught on a vicious, drying pitch which was described by Taylor as the worst he had played on. 'At times it was physically frightening,' he said. Harvey-Walker, mindful of the steep bounce, handed his false teeth to an umpire and Derbyshire crashed to one of their heaviest defeats, by an innings and 348 runs.

Buxton's wintry weather gave way to a prolonged spell of glorious sunshine in one of the hottest summers in memory. Fine bowling by Hendrick helped Derbyshire to their first win of the season in the Championship at Northampton and ten days later there was a splendid game against Warwickshire on the Allied Breweries ground at Burton-on-Trent. Derbyshire made 214 and Hendrick and Venkatar-aghavan bowled them to a first innings lead of 96. A fighting 81 from

Bolus heralded a return to form and favour and Warwickshire, needing 238 to win, were 35 without loss at the close of the second day. On the Friday Amiss made 96 but Warwickshire collapsed from 225 for six to 231 all out, Venkataraghavan taking six for 77 and Derbyshire winning by six runs.

The corner had been turned. An unbeaten 150 from Bolus and Miller's six for 43 got Derbyshire home against Nottinghamshire at Ilkeston, Venkataraghavan taking eight wickets in this match to add to the eight he had in the previous game at Cardiff, which was also won. But the most remarkable performance was yet to come. At Hove Fred Swarbrook, after making an unbeaten 69, took four for 42 in Sussex's first innings and followed it with nine for 20 in the second innings, a spell of nine for ten in 34 balls bringing victory by 179 runs. Five wins left Derbyshire in 15th place but well clear of the bottom in their most successful season since 1970.

Bolus headed the batting averages, he and Page exceeding a thousand runs. Hendrick topped the bowling, but the spinners were the leading wicket-takers, Swarbrook dismissing 71 batsmen and Venkataraghavan 68.

But it was the Gillette Cup which provided more prospect of glory in 1975. A second-round win at Taunton was Derbyshire's first in the competition since the semi-final victory over Sussex six years earlier. Nottinghamshire were beaten by six wickets and then Hendrick's four for 16 restricted Middlesex to 207 in the semi-final at Chesterfield when a much larger total looked a possibility. Headley (58) and Sharpe (55) gave Derbyshire a good start with 81 in 27 overs and the score reached 126 for one from 40 overs, 82 being needed from the last 20. But the middle order fell away and the innings closed for 183, Middlesex having four overs to spare. It was a disappointing end, with Lord's beckoning strongly at one stage, but the cup run indicated Derbyshire's improved form in the one-day game. In the JPL they had been second on 8 June, winning four of their first five games, but eventually finished ninth.

Taylor's first season as captain had been a success in that improvement had been made after a bad start. But more changes were in the offing. Twelve players were offered terms for 1976 but Mike Page was not given a contract. Taylor wanted him to stay for another year and the decision was criticised at the time because Derbyshire seemed to have left themselves short of resources. Page had done well in 1975, although he had not been a member of either the JPL or Gillette Cup sides and his record in the Sunday games was poor.

There were changes, too, in administration, when in September 1975 Major Douglas Carr left after 13 years. The job of the secretary had changed, the emphasis now being on fund-raising. David

Harrison (30), who had been assistant secretary for the past 18 months, was appointed as secretary/fund raiser. Already experienced in business Harrison had proved his ability to raise money. Immediately he became a man who was approachable to members and his appointment was in line with the changing nature of first-class cricket, with the conception of a secretary-manager combining these activities with public relations and fund-raising. Nomadic Derbyshire had played on eight grounds in 1975 – Derby, Chesterfield, Ilkeston, Buxton, two at Burton-on-Trent, the Trent College ground at Long Eaton and Darley Dale.

Despite the upheavals optimism was high for the new season and two new arrivals seemed destined to give the Club the shot-in-the-arm it had so badly needed. In February 1976 George Hughes, a man with a brilliant reputation in business, succeeded Ken Turner as chairman. He had a first-class honours degree at Cambridge in modern languages and a business background in banking, salesmanship and computers. At 38 he was chairman of Hughes International, a company with world-wide interests, and it was hoped that he would bring business and financial expertise into the running of the Club.

Then came a genuine cricketing coup. Venkataraghavan was released at the end of his three-year contract and, with Lawrence Rowe still registered at that time, there was one vacancy for an overseas player. The sacking of Page had been followed by the retirement of Brian Bolus. A batsman was the priority and the gap was filled by the 35-year-old South African, Eddie Barlow. One of the world's top all-rounders, Barlow played in 30 Tests for the Springboks in 1961–69, his international career being cut short by the 1970 ban on South Africa. In 1970 he appeared in all five matches for the Rest of the World against England and with a highest Test score of 201 at Adelaide, six hundreds and an average of 45, he was a man with vast experience of big-time cricket. Stockily-built and an aggressive cricketer, Barlow was a powerful batsman, confident and competitive. He was a more than useful bowler, with a good outswinger and an occasional ball which nipped back, and a good fieldsman at slip. In the recent seasons he had also proved himself a successful captain with Western Province. Suddenly Derbyshire's future looked exciting.

On the face of things Derbyshire did nothing spectacular in 1976. They won only four Championship games, the first not until their tenth game on 13 July when Somerset were beaten at Queen's Park after Ward had taken six for 52 in the second innings. Until then they had been bottom of the table and a defeat by fellow-strugglers Glamorgan put them back in the basement later that month. But a magnificent 217 by Barlow established a platform for Miller and Swarbrook to spin out Surrey at Ilkeston, Lancashire were beaten by

15 runs at Buxton after Derbyshire had followed on 151 behind, and Hill's 126 set up a five-wicket win at Bristol, where the target was 275 in 170 minutes. It was enough to lift Derbyshire to 15th place and in addition there were innings victories over the Universities, Sharpe making 228 at Oxford and 144 against Cambridge on the Bass Worthington ground.

These big scores enabled him to top the averages with 1,277 runs (34.51), Hill having 1,303 (34.28) and Barlow 1,162 (29.05) but in the Championship Sharpe's average declined to 26, his best effort being 126 against Yorkshire at Chesterfield when he and Hill (151 not out) shared an opening partnership of 228.

Hill, in fact, was an immediate beneficiary from Barlow's presence and from the Springbok's assumption of the captaincy which was vacated by Bob Taylor in June, Taylor feeling it was interfering with his wicket-keeping. Under Barlow's driving influence Hill became a more positive cricketer and it was a method which was to work with one or two other members of the team before his three-year stay ended.

The biggest advance was made by Geoff Miller, who scored 744 runs and took 74 wickets for the County in 20 games. With Swarbrook (65 wickets) he formed the most effective spin duo in the County's history if one regards Leslie Townsend as medium pace during his pairing with Mitchell. With Barlow topping the bowling averages Derbyshire had an extra option and it was reflected in the Gillette Cup, where Lincolnshire and Surrey were beaten before Derbyshire lost in the quarter final at Southampton. Hendrick and Ward were not quite at their best in 1976 but Keith Stevenson did well with 32 wickets and also bowled well in the one-day games.

Nobody was quite prepared, though, for the end of season bombshell which saw Ward and Sharpe released when the retained list was announced. Ward's sacking created a sensation for he seemed to have several years of cricket still ahead of him – he was 29 – although in the event he joined Leicestershire, where he was only a qualified success.

With new regulations limiting overseas players to two per county Barlow and the 22-year-old New Zealander John Wright were to be Derbyshire's two in 1977. Wright, a left-handed opening batsman, had come to England for trials with Kent in 1976. That summer he also played for Derbyshire 2nd which engaged in a few friendly games prior to re-entering the Second Eleven Championship in 1977. In one of these, against Nottinghamshire Second Eleven at Heanor, Wright made a splendid 159 not out and he was registered and contracted to Derbyshire when Kent indicated they were willing to release him.

Chesterfield had, by now, become Derbyshire's principal venue, with Ilkeston getting more than its usual ration of games in the absence of Derby. A JPL game was played on the small Heanor ground in 1976 but at long last the differences between the Club and Derby Borough Council were reconciled and county cricket returned to Derby in 1977 when three first-class games, a JPL and a Benson and Hedges match were played there.

With Barlow in charge, Philip Russell now taking on the responsibility for coaching youngsters, John Brown appointed as permanent coaching organiser and Charlie Elliott, then a current Test selector, chairman of the cricket committee, the Club had taken on a new shape. For the first time in 15 years it showed a profit, the balance sheet revealing that it was £18,435 in the black. Improvement in four key areas, membership, gate receipts, sponsorship and TCCB contributions, brought about the change and although total expenditure was up from £82,000 to £94,000, income also rose from £80,000 to £112,500.

Seven games were won and seventh place achieved in the Championship. After an indifferent start there was a superb performance against Middlesex, the reigning Champions, who were routed at Ilkeston, being 50 for nine at lunch on the first day, and put to the sword on the second. Tunnicliffe and Cartwright hammered 120 in 13.5 overs for the ninth wicket in 53 minutes. Edmonds conceded 80 runs from his last six overs, Tunnicliffe taking 24 from his last, and in all hitting five sixes and six fours. Derbyshire won in two days, their first innings victory in the Championship since 1968.

This fine win was the turning point of the 1977 season. Four consecutive victories, over Leicestershire at Burton-on-Trent, at Hove, Northampton and over Warwickshire at Chesterfield (Cartwright 141 not out, Stevenson seven for 68 in the second innings), put Derbyshire in fine fettle. A win over Worcestershire at Chesterfield in a game reduced to a single innings and an innings victory over Nottinghamshire at Ilkeston, where Borrington made 115 and Miller scored 66 and took six for 45 in the second innings, rounded off a fine season.

The Barlow shake-up had worked. Wrote Michael Carey in *Wisden*:

> At last in 1977 Derbyshire emerged, convincingly and recognisably, from the shadows of mediocrity that had engulfed them for years. Under the inspired leadership of Barlow, they played cricket that was largely positive and purposeful and their refreshing approach was reflected in a climb to seventh place in the county championship table.
>
> Unquestionably the key to the revival – which saw Derbyshire in

Derbyshire 1977. Back row: D. A. Harrison, J. Graham-Brown, K. Stevenson, J. G. Wright,
J. Walters, A. Harvey-Walker, R. Swindell, A. Morris, C. Beardmore (hon. scorer).
Front row: C. J. Tunnicliffe, A. J. Borrington, P. E. Russell, M. J. Hendrick, E. J. Barlow (capt.),
R. W. Taylor, F. W. Swarbrook, H. Cartwright, A. Hill. Inset: G. Miller.

fourth place in the Championship table at one stage – was Barlow.
Gerald Mortimer wrote in the *Derby Evening Telegraph*: 'Barlow has
led from the front and persuaded players to explore their potential,
persuaded them that, by working at their game, they can both give
and derive enjoyment.'

Alan Hill was coaxed, bullied and cajoled into using the full range of
strokes built on a sound, technical base. Geoff Miller was encouraged
and given the long spells necessary for a bowler of his type. Colin
Tunnicliffe, Tony Borrington and Harry Cartwright had enjoyed
their best season. Mike Hendrick, free from injury, became a
magnificent bowler, in the very forefront of world seamers.

Barlow had returned to South Africa after the 1976 season leaving
his players with a tough schedule of exercises to carry out during a
winter training programme. 'Woe betide anyone who was not up to
scratch when he returned the following April,' said Bob Taylor,
adding that card sessions during periods when rain halted play had
been replaced by training runs along the boundary edge. Barlow's
keep-fit routines pioneered a new trend on the county circuit as
Derbyshire became one of the toughest, most entertaining and athletic

fielding sides in the country. But there was always an underlying theme of enjoyment and fun. Players were there to entertain and enjoy their cricket. 'Eddie Barlow's captaincy at Derbyshire marked my happiest three seasons at the Club; he made it a pleasure to come to work,' wrote Taylor.

It was Barlow himself who touched on the kernel of his achievements. 'The guys have stopped wondering how we lost and started to be angry if we don't win,' he said.

Derbyshire's success was reflected nationally as Mike Hendrick finished second in the averages and top of the regular bowlers with 67 wickets at 15.94 each. He played in three Tests during that Queen's Silver Jubilee summer, taking 14 wickets at 20.71 each. At Leeds, where England regained the Ashes when Marsh was caught by Randall after skying a ball from Hendrick, he had four for 41 and four for 54. Geoff Miller played in two Tests, he and Hendrick being in the side for the third Test at Trent Bridge when the Queen visited the ground on the same day that she had been in Derbyshire.

Hendrick and Miller were selected for the England tour of Pakistan and New Zealand in 1977–78, Bob Taylor at last emerging as England's wicket-keeper at the age of 36 as Alan Knott threw in his lot with Kerry Packer's world series circus. Hendrick, ill during the Pakistan leg, appeared in just one Test in New Zealand in Wellington, where John Wright marked his debut with 55, the Kiwis beating England for the first time. Taylor and Miller appeared in all six Tests on the tour, sharing a partnership of 89 for the seventh wicket in Lahore when Miller batted six hours for 98 not out, and each enjoying success at Christchurch, where Miller made 89 and Taylor 45.

The Derbyshire influence had spread world-wide. Although Barlow was engaged with Packer during the winter, Western Province still remained strong and won the Currie Cup, Peter Kirsten scoring 579 runs and averaging 41.35 during the South African domestic season. Along with Allan Lamb and Garth le Roux, Kirsten had been brought to England by Barlow in 1977 and all three had played for Derbyshire Second Eleven, Kirsten making 534 runs in four games for an average of 133.50. It was to be the 23-year-old Kirsten who joined Wright and Barlow as Derbyshire's overseas contingent in 1978, although only two could play in the same side. In the event Wright joined the New Zealand tourists for the second part of a twin-tour season in June, leaving the South Africans a clear run in the side.

Kirsten was born in Pietermaritzburg, his father Noel keeping wicket for Border. He had a fine record as a schoolboy, came to England for trials with Sussex in 1975 and made 31 against the Australians, and then returned home to score heavily for Western Province and the South African Universities. Apart from his three hundreds in seven innings for Derbyshire Seconds in 1977, the dapper Kirsten – who also bowled off-spin – hit 527 runs (average 87.83) for Worksop in the Bassetlaw League. He joined Derbyshire with a first-class average of 42 and eleven hundreds under his belt. Four consecutive hundreds and six in seven innings in the 1976–77 South African season made Kirsten one of the most exciting prospects to emerge from the Republic.

With Barlow indicating that 1978 would be his final season as a player there was every hope that he would lead Derbyshire to success in at least one of the four competitions – Schweppes County Championship, Gillette Cup, John Player League or Benson and Hedges Cup.

LORD'S '78

BY THE SECOND WEEK OF JULY 1978 Derbyshire were on course for a unique treble in the one-day competitions.

They were safely over the first hurdle of the Gillette Cup and mounting a strong challenge in the John Player League. And to the delight of everybody connected with the Club they had reached the final of the Benson and Hedges Cup in which they would meet Kent at Lord's on Saturday 22 July.

Almost everything had gone right for them in a remarkable burst of success at the start of the season which brought eight wins in the first nine competitive games. This had put them among the early pacemakers in the JPL and a 43-run win at Bournemouth over a second-placed Hampshire side just above Derbyshire confirmed them as genuine title contenders.

The Schweppes Championship had seen a thoroughly workman-like victory at Old Trafford and an innings win over Glamorgan at Chesterfield, Peter Kirsten's magnificent 206 (five sixes, 21 fours) in only his fourth Championship game establishing a strong position.

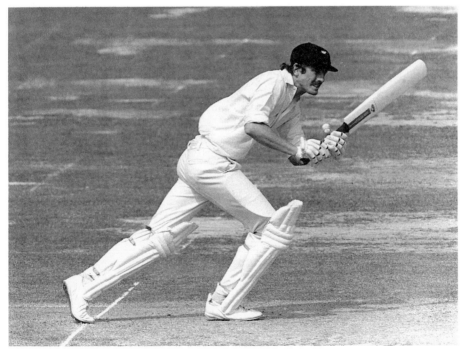

J. G. Wright, the Derbyshire and England batsman, seen here at Lord's in 1978. (Patrick Eagar)

Earlier Kirsten (58) and Wright (164) had given a taste of things to come with a second-wicket partnership of 112 against Pakistan at Chesterfield, after Wright and Hill had launched the innings with 156. Player-coach Philip Russell, captaining the side for the first time, held five catches in an innings to equal the Club record held jointly by Morgan and Lee. But with Test calls weakening the side the Schweppes form was uncertain, and after one defeat, by Surrey on a sub-standard pitch at Ilkeston, the Rutland Ground was banned until further notice, Ashley Harvey-Walker having achieved the unlikely figures of seven for 35 in the second innings and ten for 82 in the match with his occasional off-spin.

In the Benson and Hedges Cup, however, Derbyshire had looked invincible. They won all four of their zonal qualifying games, defeating Warwickshire at Ilkeston, where Hill (102 not out) and Barlow (75) shared a third-wicket stand of 153, Lancashire at Old Trafford, Gloucestershire at Bristol (Barlow six for 33) and Minor Counties West at Derby.

Alan Hill, who made 349 runs (average 58.16) in the seven B & H games that summer, maintained his form in the quarter-final against Middlesex at Derby. Rain halted play on the first day with Derbyshire 11 without loss from six overs, Hill becoming the first Derbyshire batsman to wear one of the new protective helmets which came into vogue in 1978. On the second day he took his score to 69 in a total of 154 in 52 overs. Although Gatting made 50 Middlesex were all out for 125, Barlow taking three for 22.

Derbyshire were rewarded with another home game in the semi-final in which they met Warwickshire at Derby. Once again the match went into the second day, rain, a far cry from the blazing summers of 1975 and 1976, reducing play to 36.5 overs on the Wednesday when Derbyshire made 119 for two, losing Kirsten to a catch at the wicket off Willis when the light was very poor. But an excellent 77 from Tony Borrington enabled them to make 203 for nine in their 55 overs. Humpage made a typically robust 78 but with Barlow taking three for 26, Hendrick two for 14 in 11 overs and Miller one for 18 in 11, Warwickshire were dismissed for 162 in 50.4 overs. Miller also scored 21 and held three catches but Borrington took the Gold Award.

Kent reached the final by defeating Yorkshire, Surrey and Essex and losing to Nottinghamshire in the zonal games and beating Nottinghamshire and Somerset in the knock-out stages. Vastly experienced, they were appearing in their third consecutive Benson and Hedges final and their seventh final at Lord's, including six in eight seasons. They had won the B & H Cup twice and were 4/7 favourites, with Derbyshire quoted at 11/8.

Derbyshire gained a psychological advantage, though, when they won an amazing JPL game at Maidstone on July 9. Kent, leaders and eventual Champions in the Schweppes, faced a moderate task after Derbyshire had made 164 for eight in 40 overs. Woolmer and Johnson had 93 on the board in 25 overs before the first wicket fell and Hendrick, who gave a magnificent performance, was bowled out by the 29th over. With ten overs left the target was 52 and at the start of the 38th Kent were 141 for four, 24 being required off three overs, Hendrick having finished and Tunnicliffe being off with a torn muscle in his side. But three men were run out in an over from Kirsten, Miller then taking two wickets in the 39th over and catching Underwood off Kirsten as Kent collapsed from 143 for four to 149 all out. With six wins in eight JPL matches Derbyshire were now second in the table, four points behind Hampshire with a game in hand.

Nineteen-year-old Alan Mellor, a slow left-arm bowler from Staffordshire took five for 52 on his first-class debut at Maidstone but the weekend at the Mote Ground proved costly. The Championship game was lost and Borrington received a chipped wrist bone to add to Tunnicliffe's injury. He had suffered a hair-line fracture of the skull after being struck by a ball from Clive Rice at Trent Bridge in the pre-helmet days. Incidentally, the metal grill of his helmet saved Philip Russell from serious injury that summer when he was struck by a pull from Malcolm Nash while fielding at short square-leg at Chesterfield. He received a cracked cheekbone and a bad cut.

Injury-hit Derbyshire now went off the boil a little. Barlow's five for 30 had bowled them to victory at Worcester in the first round of the Gillette Cup but the home side had their revenge in the JPL a week after the Maidstone game. Then came defeat by Middlesex at Derby in the second round of the Gillette, though again Derbyshire demonstrated their remarkable fighting qualities. Replying to a total of 199 they lost seven wickets for 43 but Hill (72), helped by Taylor and Russell, took the score to 146 before he was ninth out, the total eventually reaching 166. This setback occurred two days before the Lord's final.

For the final Derbyshire's main problem was one of selection. They decided to gamble with Borrington, who had the plaster removed from his wrist only on the Thursday before the match, but Tunnicliffe was not fit to play.

On the day of the match Derbyshire sprang a surprise by bringing in 26-year-old seam bowler Bob Wincer (not in the original squad of 13) to replace Tunnicliffe. Wincer had played most of his cricket in Yorkshire and had done reasonably well in half-a-dozen first-class games that season, although he had appeared in only one limited-overs match.

If Derbyshire were to win the Cup they would have to play to their full potential. They did not – or were not allowed to. Kent, vastly experienced in this form of cricket, outclassed them and won comfortably by six wickets.

Barlow won the toss and batted on an overcast morning. Although Borrington failed there was a hint of prosperity at 30 for one from nine overs. But Hill and Barlow fell, Shepherd swung the ball, and only three runs came in seven overs. It was not until the 22nd over that 40 was passed. Kirsten – the day had nothing better than a sizzling off-drive by him to the extra cover boundary – threatened for a while but 111 for four from 41 overs at lunch became 147 all out, which was nowhere near enough unless Kent collapsed. At tea they were 80 for three from 27 overs.

Hendrick was brought on at the pavilion end in a bid to break through. Woolmer edged his third ball to Barlow's right at first slip but he could not hang on to a difficult chance. The next ball was edged to Taylor, diving to his right, and he failed to take the catch.

So the buoyant optimism among the crowds pouring out of St John's Wood underground station in the morning had dwindled to silent acceptance of defeat as Kent coasted to victory. Russell had bowled magnificently and his could have been a match-winning spell if Derbyshire had scored another 40 or 50 runs or if somebody could have produced similar figures from the pavilion end. As in 1969 it had been a disappointing result but a marvellous day out.

After Lord's the season faded. Derbyshire did not win another JPL game and finished eighth. They won only one more Schweppes Championship match, beating Nottinghamshire at Derby, and ended in 14th place. There were glimpses of promise from A-level student Iain Anderson, an opening batsman who played for Burton CC. He shared an opening partnership of 182 with Hill at Worcester, making 75 in only his second game. John Lister, a 19-year-old batsman from Darlington, did well in his early appearances and Alan McLellan, who was born in Ashton-under-Lyne but learned his cricket in Australia, came in as Taylor's deputy and showed promising form. Lister, McLellan, Mellor and Wincer never became established, though, and were to be released after the 1980 season. Barlow, Harvey-Walker, Morris and Graham-Brown did not play for the County after 1978.

Ironically it was the success of their Test stars, Taylor, Hendrick and Miller, which helped lead to the inconsistency. Taylor played in all six Tests against Pakistan and New Zealand, Miller in five and Hendrick in two, being 12th man four times. In addition Miller and Taylor appeared in all four of the one-day Prudential Trophy internationals and Hendrick in one. Nonetheless, the fact that this trio and John Wright graced the Test stage in 1978 was an indication of the status of Derbyshire's modern cricketers.

Only two regular bowlers bettered Hendrick's 59 wickets at 15.16 each as he enjoyed yet another splendid season.

It was typical of the improvement among several players under Barlow's direction. The South African was now 38 and, at such an age, past his best as batsman, bowler or all-rounder. He also had problems with a back injury.

In an analysis of his going, Gerald Mortimer wrote in the *Derby Evening Telegraph*:

Derbyshire will miss him in three ways. His batting had passed its peak, but he was still a fine player, and, above all, a determined competitor.

Barlow bowled like an eternal optimist, expecting to take a wicket with every ball. He bowled a full length and always attacked. There were times when he turned games single-handed.

It was as a leader that he was most effective and, if his three years are not to be wasted, the pattern he laid down should be continued. What a pity Eddie didn't come to Derbyshire ten years ago.

Barlow was going but the principles had been established.

COME ON, DERBYSHIRE

IN THE TEST ARENA, DERBYSHIRE CRICKET had now reached its high noon. Bob Taylor, Mike Hendrick and Geoff Miller were all members of Mike Brearley's victorious England party which retained the Ashes with a 5-1 victory in Australia in 1978–79. Taylor and Miller played in all six Tests and Hendrick in five.

At 37, Taylor was now regarded as the first choice wicket-keeper in the continued unavailability of Alan Knott. He had set himself the highest standards of ability and physical fitness; neat and unspectacular he kept wicket with almost flawless efficiency to the point where a missed chance became news, a rarity to be discussed and analysed at length. Taylor's nudging and blocking style of batting was also beginning to pay dividends and in the 1978–79 series he scored 208 runs, average 26, with 97 in the fifth Test at Adelaide.

Hendrick, now 30, had put behind him the memories of 1974–75 when he returned home early with a hamstring injury. He had been told a few home truths by Eddie Barlow, who had made him realise that he was not doing himself justice by breaking down and he set about getting himself fully fit. 'Eddie always worked on the principle that if ever we came across a batsman who could hit the ball three miles, then Derbyshire would be able to fetch it quicker than any other team in the land,' he said. Hendrick's steadiness and consistency was seen by Brearley as an admirable foil to the more adventurous flair of Willis, Old, Botham and Lever. On the county circuit he was generally regarded as the best opening bowler of his type, although one school of thought suggested he bowled too short, which meant that he seldom had batsmen half-forward, half-back. On the 1978–79 tour Hendrick asked Ken Barrington why he was able to beat the bat so often without taking wickets consistently. He was never to take five in an innings in a Test and few of his wickets were obtained in front of the wicket. It was considered his stock ball was pitched a couple of feet too short and when it moved off the seam it did too much. Barrington encouraged him to bowl a slightly fuller, more attacking length, telling him: 'Pitch it up there and you'll have the batsmen in no-man's land!'

Hendrick's response to the criticism, incidentally, was to say that if he pitched the ball right up at his pace he would get hammered. Certainly his bowling on the tour belied the theories, his 19 wickets in the tests coming at 15.73 each, while 28 at 14.25 left him at the top of the first-class bowling averages.

Taylor (1977) and Hendrick (1978) had been among *Wisden's* Five

Left to right: Mike Hendrick, John Wright, Geoff Miller and Bob Taylor, on the only occasion when four Derbyshire players appeared at once in a Test match, during the 1977-1978 Test series.

Cricketers of the Year but Geoff Miller, at 26, had still not established himself in the England team despite a run of eleven consecutive Tests. Yet he was a most useful bits and pieces player and the balance of the team often looked wrong without him. Again, Barlow's influence shone through. Miller was moved up the Derbyshire order and given more responsibility as a bowler. In Australia, with 234 runs (23.40) and 23 wickets at 15.04 apiece – he headed England's bowling in the Tests – he at last became a regular, with five for 44 in the final Test at Sydney as his best performance.

Hendrick and Miller played their parts in the social life of the tour with their depiction of Derbyshire miners Arthur and Sam and their pub conversation ('Jackson and Gladstone, they were real baarlers; Gladstone used to baarrl big benders'). But it was Taylor and Miller who placed Derbyshire cricket at perhaps its highest peak in the story of the England-Australia series.

At Adelaide in the fifth Test, England, leading 3–1, were five ahead on the first innings but had collapsed to 132 for six on the third day when Taylor joined Miller a few minutes before lunch. It was very hot

225

CHAPTER EIGHTEEN

but in the first 20 minutes after lunch they added 27 runs, carrying the
score to 213 for six by tea. When Miller fell for 64 at 267 the
Derbyshire pair had added 135, only nine short of the seventh-wicket
record against Australia. By the close England were 272 for seven,
with Taylor on 69 and next morning he carried his score to 97 before
being caught behind off the last ball before lunch after batting for six
hours. Taylor recalled that he and Miller had constantly encouraged
each other during the partnership: 'we said to each other "Come on,
Derbyshire" as well as England.'

Miller (62) and Taylor (64) shared in another big stand against India
at Lord's in 1979 when they added 103 for the eighth wicket. Taylor
also helped Ian Botham put on 171 for the sixth wicket at Bombay in
1980 in a Test in which he held seven catches in an innings and ten in
the match, eight of them off Botham.

Taylor was to appear in 57 Tests – he returned to keep wicket for 73
overs in the Lord's Test against New Zealand in 1986 when he was on
duty for Cornhill and Bruce French was injured – Hendrick in 30 and
Miller in 34, besides being members of the same team in numerous
one-day internationals.

Although there were to be disappointments along the way – Knott,
Bairstow and Downton were preferred in 1980–81 – Bob Taylor's
career continued on its remarkable path until his retirement at the end
of the 1984 season. By then he had shattered John Murray's world
wicket-keeping record, exceeding his 1,527 victims while on the
1982–83 tour of Australia, a total he had raised to 1,649 by the end of
the 1988 season, during which he appeared at the Scarborough Festival
at the age of 47. His maiden – and only – hundred in first-class cricket
came against Yorkshire at Abbeydale Park in 1981 and his services to
cricket were acknowledged by the award of an MBE.

If that winter of 1978–79 cemented the Test careers of Taylor,
Miller and Hendrick it also heralded the arrival of a young batsman
who appeared capable of emulating them at the highest level. Kim
Barnett was born at Stoke-on-Trent and showed promise as a leg-spin
bowler while still attending Leek High School. Games for Stafford-
shire, Northamptonshire Second Eleven and Warwickshire Second
Eleven followed before he was selected for the Young England tour of
Australia, where he averaged 40 and made 89 in the Melbourne Youth
Test. Iain Anderson was also a member of the England party.

Barnett was attracted by the Derbyshire set-up which had been laid
down by Barlow and he joined the Club for the 1979 season, making a
big impression in his first season. A dazzling 96 against Lancashire at
Chesterfield when 18 demonstrated that Derbyshire had unearthed a
rare talent, and his 752 runs at an average of 25 in 23 games that year
justified the cricket writers' superlatives in describing his class.

For Derbyshire, though, the season did not go well. Grey haired and bespectacled David Steele, hero of the 1975 Test series against Australia, arrived as captain in succession to Barlow; another Staffordshire man along with Taylor and Barnett. But after an early victory at Hove it was soon evident that Derbyshire were drifting, highlighted by the game against Middlesex at Derby when Steele declined to chase a target of 215 in 177 minutes. He was jeered by the members and the Club issued a statement saying his action was not in accord with their policy of playing purposeful cricket. Steele later apologised, explaining that he was upset because of earlier short-pitched bowling at Derbyshire's tail-end batsmen. Later he gave up the captaincy, Miller taking over, although Steele remained a player of quality, finishing second to Wright in the batting averages and bowling more overs with his slow left-arm spin than anybody else. But just the one Championship game was won, the Club finishing second from the bottom in both the Schweppes and John Player League competitions. There was an early exit from the Gillette Cup but in the Benson and Hedges tournament Derbyshire reached the semi-finals, losing by only six runs to Surrey at Derby in Miller's first match as captain.

The 1979 season, however, proved only a minor hiccup. Barry Wood, another vastly experienced batsman, was recruited from Lancashire and with Wright and Kirsten in phenomenal form Derbyshire's batting was probably the strongest in their history. Kirsten scored 1,895 runs, average 63.16, with six hundreds, including three double centuries. Wright was not far behind with 1,504 (48.51) and all of the County's batting records seemed there for the taking. They began the 1980 season with an unbroken second-wicket partnership of 321 at Old Trafford and followed it with 253 against Northamptonshire at Derby. By the time Kirsten left after the 1982 season he and Wright had each made more than 7,000 runs for the County, averaging well over 40 and scoring more than 40 centuries between them. Kirsten indicated that he wanted a year off to pursue a business career in his homeland and to rest from year-round cricket in England and South Africa but he never returned. Both Kirsten (eight) and Wright (seven) exceeded Leslie Townsend's record of six hundreds in a season in 1982, and Kirsten's six double centuries for Derbyshire were a club career record. It was magnificent batting of the highest quality. Like all the great batsmen Kirsten possessed an ability to get into position early so that he appeared to have all the time in the world to deal with any type of bowling, and a range of stroke play allied to the concentration to make big scores. He was very quick between the wickets and his strokes, particularly the square cut and the cover drive, were masterpieces of precise timing and power. A useful off-spin bowler, he also captained the side on occasion, as, later on, did Wright.

Wright looked back with immense pleasure on the partnerships he shared with Kirsten:

> Peter was a great player and we enjoyed batting together. Our styles complemented each other. He is a right-hander and I am left, he is short and I am tall so he would be cutting balls I was going forward to.
>
> I am mainly a front-foot player but Peter likes to get on to the back foot. This contrast made it very difficult for the bowlers to adjust to a consistent line and length.

Unlike some of the great partnerships of past years they had no problems running between wickets and there were no difficulties caused by either of them attempting to hog the strike. 'We were good together, good mates, and I was very sorry when Peter left the club,' said Wright.

Four wins, over Hampshire at Chesterfield where Hendrick took seven for 19 in the first innings, at Northampton and over Somerset at Chesterfield and Surrey at Derby, lifted Derbyshire to ninth place, and although they fared poorly in the knock-out competitions they finished sixth in the JPL with eight victories.

By the start of the 1981 season Derbyshire had assembled a squad which was rich in experience. Miller, the captain, Wood his vice-captain, Borrington, Hendrick, Hill, Kirsten, Steve Oldham, a fast-medium bowler from Yorkshire, Steele, Taylor, Tunnicliffe and Wright had all been capped, while Anderson, Barnett, Walters, Brooks and the giant Dallas Moir, a slow left-arm bowler and aggressive batsman who was born in Malta but educated in his parents' native Scotland, were waiting in the wings. Paul Newman, a highly promising fast-medium bowler from Leicester, had made his debut in 1980. Capable of genuine pace, Newman showed exceptional promise under Russell's tuition in the nets and for a time he was spoken of as a possible England player.

It was an impressive looking side, marred only in the initial stages of the season by yet more uncertainty over the captaincy. Miller almost gave up the job after a defeat in the B & H Cup by Yorkshire in May but a number of players, among them Barry Wood, persuaded him not to resign. But in July he stood down because he felt the captaincy was affecting his form and for the fourth time in seven years Derbyshire underwent a mid-season change of captaincy. The 38-year-old Barry Wood – who now formed with John Wright one of the most formidable opening partnerships in the Club's history – became the sixth skipper in seven years. Charismatic and vastly experienced with Lancashire (1966–79) particularly in the one-day competitions, and with a dozen Test caps, Wood was to transform the side in remarkable fashion.

The Championship found Derbyshire in twelfth place with four wins, over Worcestershire at Queen's Park, where Wood and Wright began the second innings with a stand of 283 – Kent and Gloucestershire at Derby and Glamorgan at Swansea. Kirsten, Wood and Wright were the leading batsmen and with Hill, Steele, Barnett and Miller in support there was power and depth in this department. Steele led the bowlers and Newman, who played for the TCCB XI against the Sri Lankans, and Tunnicliffe also did well. Wright's 618 was a new County record in the JPL in which ten wins raised Derbyshire to fourth. Wright also made 144 against the Australians at Derby, the club's best against the tourists, and Kirsten and Steele's stand of 291 at Taunton was a new record for the third wicket.

Under Wood, Derbyshire's slump was halted and his quest for outright results evoked memories of the Barlow era. Throughout the summer Derbyshire looked a good side on Sundays and a capable one in the Championship. But it was the NatWest Bank Trophy which was to produce the glory.

Half a century of Derbyshire pace. From left to right: Alf Pope, George Pope, Les Jackson, Harold Rhodes and Mike Hendrick. All Derbyshire-born, they took a combined total of more than 4,200 wickets for the county. They were celebrating the diamond jubilee of the Nottinghamshire and Derbyshire Border League in November 1980.

LORD'S '81

ONLY THE MIDDLE-AGED AND THE ELDERLY could recall the solitary occasion when Derbyshire had won a major cricket trophy before Saturday, 5 September 1981.

That had been in 1936 when the County Championship was won. Since then they had flattered only to deceive, in the Championship in 1948, 1954 and 1970 and in the Lord's finals of 1969 and 1978. Too often, the County's followers had been forced to find solace in the mere avoidance of the wooden spoon yet there was genuine optimism at the start of the 1981 season.

When the NatWest quest began at Bury St Edmunds Derbyshire's main hopes appeared to rest in the John Player League in which they had a real chance of taking the title. Suffolk were duly defeated in the NatWest first round on July 11 and then came a four-wicket victory at Worcester in the second round when Wright (50) and Kirsten (84 not out and the Man of the Match award) set their side on the way to a total of 229 for six.

This win set up a local derby against Nottinghamshire in the quarter-final at the County Ground which attracted a crowd of more than 6,000. They saw Derbyshire, now led by Wood for the first time in the NatWest, dismissed for 164 and with Miller and Hendrick absent Nottinghamshire, at 75 for one after 28 overs, were well on course for victory. But Wood and Steele broke through, Oldham dismissed the dangerous Hadlee, and Derbyshire emerged as unlikely winners by 23 runs, leaving them with another home tie against Essex in the semi-final at Derby.

It had all the ingredients of a classic one-day encounter. Essex had beaten Derbyshire 17 days earlier in the JPL at Chelmsford but the counties were joint leaders on 16 August, three days before the semi-final. With four games left Derbyshire had their best-ever chance of winning the league but a defeat by Yorkshire at Queen's Park was a stunning blow. Two of the last three games were won but Essex took the title, eight points clear of Derbyshire, who were fourth.

Wood put Essex in in the NatWest semi-final on a green pitch on a gloomy morning. They made 149, Taylor holding five catches and stumping one batsman to become the first wicket-keeper to dismiss six batsmen in either a Gillette or NatWest Trophy match.

Derbyshire had done well but two shattering blows swung the game in favour of Essex. After ten balls the players went off for bad light and when they returned Wright fell at three and Kirsten at 12. Five minutes later bad light ended play for the day with Derbyshire 13 for two off 8.3 overs.

Overnight rain wet the outfield but the start was delayed only 30 minutes with Derbyshire needing 137 from 51.3 overs to win and go through to the final against Northamptonshire. Derbyshire quickly ran into trouble, losing Steele and Miller to leave them on 30 for four in the 15th over. Barnett joined Hill and took the score to 72 at lunch when 22 overs remained and 78 were required to win. Hill was run out in the 40th over at 74 and Wood and Barnett now embarked on a vital partnership. Barnett became bogged down for a while after Hill was out but he took a lovely four to mid-wicket off Gooch and when the last ten overs began Derbyshire, at 103 for five, needed 47 to win.

Wood, his injured ribs heavily strapped, helped Barnett push the score along mainly in ones and twos but 40 runs were still needed when Lever and Phillip returned to bowl the last eight overs. Wood mishooked Phillip to mid-wicket with 25 wanted from five overs, he and Barnett having added 51 in 16 overs. Barnett's 50 came in 150 minutes and he managed to turn one ball from Lever into a half-volley and despatch it for four before being bowled by Phillip as he gave himself a lot of room.

At 132 for seven Derbyshire needed 17 to tie with 15 balls left. Tunnicliffe fell and with six balls left the score was 139 for eight, with Taylor and Newman together. Fletcher had a ring of fieldsmen three

The NatWest Trophy winning side of 1981. Back row: P. N. Kirsten, K. J. Barnett, C. J. Tunnicliffe, S. Oldham, P. J. Newman, J. G. Wright, A. Hill. Front row: G. Miller, R. W. Taylor, B. Wood (capt.), D. S. Steele, M. J. Hendrick.

quarters of the way to the boundary to cut out easy twos on the large outfield but five runs came from Phillip's first four deliveries, 144 for eight, five needed to tie, six to win off two balls. But Phillip's fifth ball was short and Newman pulled it to the mid-wicket boundary, the ball bisecting two fieldsmen on the way. 148 for eight. One run would win it for Derbyshire on the basis of having lost fewer wickets and Fletcher brought all his fieldsmen in to save the single. After long consultations, Phillip bowled, Newman got a bat on the ball and with Taylor almost home, Hardie moved to the bowler's wicket as Phillip ran in the direction of point, collected the ball and turned. Instead of flicking it to Hardie, Phillip missed with his throw at the non-striker's end – Newman would have been out had he hit the stumps – and Derbyshire had reached the final, Barry Wood's seventh appearance in cricket's one-day showpiece.

Bob Taylor was Derbyshire's sole survivor of the 1969 Gillette side but David Steele had played in the Northamptonshire side which won the trophy in 1976.

There was a rehearsal of the game six days before the final when Northamptonshire visited the County Ground in a JPL match. Derbyshire were still in with a chance of winning the title and, with Wright making 82 and Tunnicliffe taking five for 24, they gained a comfortable victory.

It was a good omen. Steve Oldham, who had strained side muscles, was Derbyshire's only doubt. They had used only 13 players in the earlier rounds and Steele, Kirsten and Barnett had collected Man of the Match awards along the way. It augured well but Northamptonshire had an immensely powerful batting side, with Geoff Cook and Wayne Larkins among the most consistent opening pairs in the country and Richard Williams, Lamb, Peter Willey and Jim Yardley capable of making runs. They had won the Benson and Hedges Cup in 1980 and were at Lord's for the third time in three years.

All 4,000 tickets available to Derbyshire had been snapped up and the AA reported a steady stream of traffic out of Derby since early morning. More than a dozen specially chartered coaches left Derby and three coachloads left Chesterfield. The haze lifted and the sun was shining when Derbyshire took the field, Wood having won the toss and put Northamptonshire in to bat.

Hendrick began with three maidens from the pavilion end but Tunnicliffe's first over cost 12 runs, 21 coming from his first three, Wood and Newman taking over the attack after seven overs. They slowed the scoring rate but Northamptonshire passed 50 in the 16th over when Wood was hit over mid-wicket for six by Larkins, who raced to his own 50 out of 96 in the 27th over. The game was running away from Derbyshire.

Then, at 99 Larkins hit Wood to mid-wicket and Miller took a beautiful catch on the edge of the boundary, cutting off a potential match-winning innings. By lunch the score was 133 for one from 39 overs. A big score was in the offing.

The first real turning point of the match came in the second over after lunch when Allan Lamb played Newman into the covers and was sent back by Cook. A direct hit by Miller ran him out with the score on 137 and at 168 a superb catch by Alan Hill on the long-on boundary at the Nursery End accounted for Williams. He straight drove Miller and Hill took off to his left, 20 yards in front of the sightscreen.

At the start of the last ten overs Northamptonshire were 183 for three, which was better than Derbyshire could have hoped for at lunch. But they still had wickets in hand and Cook was in full cry as he completed a fine hundred with his ninth boundary in 51 overs. Hendrick's next two deliveries both went to the boundary and 15 runs came from the over.

The 200 went up in the 52nd over but Cook fell leg-before to Tunnicliffe for 111 and keen fielding by Derbyshire – three batsmen were run out – helped restrict Northamptonshire to 235 for nine, Wood using six bowlers.

It had opened the way for an interesting second session. With Sarfraz and Griffiths swinging the new ball Wright and Hill made a cautious start to the task of scoring nearly four runs an over to win the game. Wright drove Sarfraz through the covers and turned him to square leg for boundaries but survival and laying the foundations were paramount and there was nobody better than Alan Hill in this conext. He eventually fell in the 15th over at 41, leaving Wright and Kirsten to begin arguably the most crucial partnership they shared in their term with the County. Wright, playing very straight and correctly, Kirsten consolidating, were watchful to the extreme but they were still together at tea when the score was 67 for one from 25 overs, Wright 31 and Kirsten 18. With 35 overs remaining 169 were needed at 4.83 per over.

Five overs later the score had reached 87. One had the absolute conviction that as long as these two remained at the wicket Derbyshire would win. Even when they became bogged down in the face of some accurate bowling by Willey and Tim Lamb and only 29 runs were scored in the ten overs between 30 and 40 there appeared no cause for alarm as long as Wright and Kirsten stayed. At the end of the 40th over it was 116 for one, at the end of the 45th 146. Some of Derbyshire's followers were growing impatient but with those two in the middle and wickets in hand the odds were in the batting side's favour.

At the start of the 48th over Derbyshire, 154 for one, needed 82 from 13 overs at 6.30 per over. Mallender, from the Nursery End, dropped his first ball short and Wright pulled it magnificently for six into the tavern area. Four byes came from the next ball and those ten runs greatly simplified the task, 72 being needed now from 76 balls. But Wright fell leg-before in that eventful over and Kirsten suffered a similar fate from the last ball of the over. The overseas pair had added 123 in 33 overs. It was not quite quick enough to put the game in Derbyshire's pocket but it had established a platform as Wood and Barnett came together.

Suddenly, though, the task became difficult. With ten overs left, 62 were needed but Wood was bowled and Steele failed to score against his old County. Five wickets were down for 190 and time was running out. Miller and Barnett now added 22 from the same number of balls, Miller relieving the pressure with a pull for six off Sarfraz at a vital stage. Barnett was run out and at 213 for six Derbyshire required 23 from 17 balls. At the end of the 58th over it was 217, with Sarfraz to bowl his final over to Tunnicliffe. Two came, then Tunnicliffe slashed the Pakistan Test player through the covers for four and straight drove him for another four; 229 for six, seven needed to win off the last over, six to tie – and Derbyshire in that case would win if they lost fewer wickets than Northamptonshire's nine.

The light was now fading rapidly, a handicap for batsmen and fieldsmen. Griffith bowled from the Nursery End and Miller took two off the first ball and then a single. Tunnicliffe was forced to block the third but got a single off the fourth. Another single came off the fifth and with one ball to go one run was needed to tie the game and leave Derbyshire winners. Tunnicliffe was to receive, Cook set his field with great deliberation, the consultations seemingly endless. At last Griffith ran in to bowl, pitching the ball just outside leg stump. Tunnicliffe got something on it, bat or pad and with Miller hurtling towards him set off to the other end. The ball ran out on the on-side, Allan Lamb moved from mid-on and threw to the batsman's end, and Miller dived to safety fractionally before Cook took off the bails, nobody being able to turn and throw to the non-striker's end. Derbyshire had won off the last ball of all in semi-darkness – and the winning run was credited to Tunnicliffe, no signal for a leg-bye being received by the scorers.

Tunnicliffe's 15 runs came from eight scoring shots off the nine balls he received and at 7.38 pm Derbyshire had ended their near-half-century wait for a trophy.

For most Derbyshire followers the sight of Miller, bat held aloft in victory salute, was the first confirmation that the match had been won. 'Derbyshire, Derbyshire, Derbyshire' chanted to a Sousa beat in the tavern area all day long preceded the victory gathering in front of the pavilion, where pork pie sunhats of chocolate, amber and pale blue

Barry Wood holds the 1981 trophy aloft.

and with a Tudor rose and crown identified the followers of the winners. Not that identity was necessary. The events that Saturday evening were as heady as the champagne with which Bob Taylor sprayed the chanting hordes below the players' balcony and the Sousa chant broke out again as Barry Wood held the trophy aloft.

Wood described the victory as a triumph of character:

> Don't congratulate me. Congratulate all the lads in the dressing room. We have come of age this season. I talked about the will to win on Friday and that is the quality we produced. It was a team effort but I'm particularly pleased for people like Bob Taylor and David Steele, who have been in the game a long time. Bob especially. He has done 20 years with Derbyshire and never really sniffed a medal.

Taylor himself gave supporters full credit:

> All day they were behind us. They outshouted the Northampton-shire fans and gave us a terrific lift. I'm not ashamed to admit that

I'm a sentimental man, and the lump in the throat was accompanied by tears – tears of pride that we had at last won something for our supporters, and tears of relief that we had done ourselves justice in a final.

A jumble of memories came whirling in on me as I sat taking it all in: what would the likes of Charlie Lee, George Dawkes and Les Jackson make of all this diving around and slogging at 7.30 on a September evening?

Taylor, in his book *Standing Up, Standing Back*, nominated that side as the best Derbyshire team he played in:

It was a far cry from the days when we had good bowlers and orthodox batsmen who could not score fast enough. Our fielding was brilliant – with the likes of Barnett, Kirsten, Hill and Wood outstanding; we had spin from Miller and Steele; an accurate bowler who was also a number four batsman in Wood; a good pair of opening bowlers in Hendrick and Newman and the left-arm seamers of Tunnicliffe to give variety. We were also well led by Wood and the batting had the class of Wright and Kirsten backed up by the all-round efforts of Wood, Steele and Miller. It was a pleasure to be in that side.

The chairman of Derbyshire County Council, Councillor Sidney Collins, presented a plaque to the team in a ceremony at County Offices, Matlock, where a celebration luncheon was held.

Pieces of Royal Crown Derby were presented to the players at a civic reception at the Council House, Derby, by the Mayor of Derby, Councillor Miss Flo Tunnicliffe, aunt of Colin.

Saturday, 5 September 1981. A wonderful, memorable day.

DERBYSHIRE *v* NORTHAMPTONSHIRE NATWEST TROPHY FINAL

Played at Lord's, 5 September 1981

DERBYSHIRE WON, HAVING LOST FEWER WICKETS

NORTHAMPTONSHIRE

*G. Cook	lbw b Tunnicliffe	111
W. Larkins	c Miller b Wood	52
A. J. Lamb	run out	9
R. G. Williams	c Hill b Miller	14
P. Willey	run out	19
T. J. Yardley	run out	4
†G. Sharp	c Kirsten b Tunnicliffe	5
Nawaz Sarfraz	not out	3
N. A. Mallender	c Taylor b Newman	0
T. M. Lamb	b Hendrick	4
B. J. Griffiths	did not bat	
Extras	b 2, lb 9, w 1, nb 2	14
Total	(for 9 wkts)	235

Fall: 1-99, 2-137, 3-168, 4-204, 5-218, 6-225, 7-227, 8-227, 9-227, 10-235

BOWLING	O	M	R	W
Hendrick	12	3	50	1
Tunnicliffe	12	1	42	2
Wood	12	2	35	1
Newman	12	0	37	1
Steele	5	0	31	0
Miller	7	0	26	1

DERBYSHIRE

A. Hill	b Mallender	14
J. G. Wright	lbw b Mallender	76
P. N. Kirsten	lbw b Mallender	63
*B. Wood	b Sarfraz	10
K. J. Barnett	run out	19
D. S. Steele	b Griffiths	0
G. Miller	not out	22
C. J. Tunnicliffe	not out	15
†R. W. Taylor	did not bat	
P. G. Newman	did not bat	
M. Hendrick	did not bat	
Extras	b 5, lb 7, w 3, nb 1	16
Total	(for 6 wkts)	235

Fall: 1-41, 2-164, 3-165, 4-189, 5-191, 6-213

BOWLING	O	M	R	W
Sarfraz	12	2	58	1
Griffiths	12	2	40	1
Mallender	10	1	35	3
Willey	12	0	33	0
T. M. Lamb	12	0	43	0
Williams	2	0	10	0

Umpires: D. J. Constant and K. E. Palmer

Toss won by Derbyshire

A HOME AT LAST

VICTORY AT LORD'S WAS CELEBRATED throughout the County's sphere of influence, from Derby to Chesterfield, Burton-on-Trent to Buxton. Yet only a year earlier Derbyshire's followers had stood on the verge of crisis, with a rift threatening a north-south divide which placed the very bedrock of the club's support in jeopardy.

At the root of the problem was the uncertainty surrounding Derbyshire's plans for permanent headquarters. When they temporarily ceased playing at Derby consideration was being given to moving the headquarters to Chesterfield, with proposals for a new two-storey pavilion complete with banqueting rooms and indoor cricket nets in Queen's Park. These plans were turned down by Chesterfield Borough Council in June 1976.

County cricket returned to Derby in 1977 and around that time Derbyshire considered sites in Amber Valley, midway between its two major centres of support. One of these was in the Greenwich area of Ripley, not far from Derbyshire Police Headquarters at Butterley Hall which were officially opened when the Queen visited the County in July 1977. But Derbyshire did not pursue the idea and by 1978 Derby was back in the frame again.

The following year talks began with Derby City Council and John Smith's Brewery, who owned the Grandstand, over the future of the County Ground. A scheme was unveiled at the 1980 annual general meeting but there was a failure to reach agreement with Chesterfield Borough Council over the number of days' cricket to be played at Queen's Park. Consequently Derbyshire announced that they would follow Leicestershire's example and play all their home games at headquarters. When the 1981 fixtures were published all these were scheduled for Derby, although the full terms of the lease had not yet been agreed with the city council but planning consent had been obtained. It spelled the end of first-class cricket for occasional grounds such as Allied Breweries at Burton-on-Trent, the Rutland Cricket Ground at Ilkeston and the Park at Buxton. And, indeed, for Queen's Park, Chesterfield, where the first County match had been staged in 1898.

It would mean that Derbyshire would be able to concentrate all their resources on developing facilities at Derby. It was felt that this would make economic sense, particularly as Chesterfield's reputation of attracting the biggest crowds of all Derbyshire venues had been questioned in recent years.

But no more first-class cricket played amidst the sylvan beauty of Queen's Park under the gaze of the crooked spire? It seemed unthinkable and the Chesterfield Cricket Lovers Society was not slow to register a protest. David Harrison came under fire during a meeting at the Grosvenor Rooms when it was stated that the club had 2,700 members, the lowest of any first-class club in the country. Derby had 835 members and Chesterfield 690, with a further 205 said to come from the Sheffield area. It was also revealed that the average takings for a three-day match at Chesterfield in 1980 had been £1,226 compared with the Derby average of £337 but Queen's Park had had matches against the West Indies and Yorkshire.

In November Derbyshire's committee reconfirmed the decision to play all the games at Derby and Chesterfield Cricket Lovers Society began their campaign in earnest, around 30 members requesting a special meeting of the Club which was held at the Grandstand Hotel, Derby, on Monday, 15 December 1980.

The resolution to be voted on was: 'That 19 days' county cricket to be continued at Queen's Park, Chesterfield, in 1981 and subsequent seasons.'

Derbyshire's chairman Ron Palfreyman issued a warning that the majority of the committee would resign if they were defeated at the extraordinary meeting and the then Club captain Geoff Miller, who was born at Chesterfield, associated himself with the committee's views, saying it was in the players' interests to concentrate the resources on one ground.

The resolution was proposed by Brian Holling, secretary of Chesterfield Cricket Lovers Society. He said that originally the Society was told that Derbyshire's plans to develop the ground at Derby would not affect cricket at Chesterfield. There could be a big drop in membership if all the cricket was concentrated at Derby and he accused the County of being more interested in sponsors than members.

Mr Palfreyman said the resolution had ignored the financial implications of keeping cricket going on a nomadic basis within the County. The meeting was about the viability of the club – nothing more and nothing less.

Many votes were cast by post and the resolution was defeated by 861 votes to 703, a majority in favour of the Club of 158. It was bitterly disappointing for the Chesterfield members but the mandate had been given for a £500,000 development at the County Ground and the general view was that common sense had prevailed.

The meeting left a glimmer of hope for Chesterfield, however, with Mr Palfreyman saying negotiations would be resumed with the borough council. Eventually agreement was reached on eleven days' cricket being played at Queen's Park in 1981 and a Cricket Week was arranged in July when Derbyshire met Lancashire and Worcestershire.

Uncertainty remained. The 1981 annual meeting revealed a loss of
£41,804 and the gates for Chesterfield's Cricket Week were
disappointing. Agreement could not be reached with Derby City
Council over the lease and the County Club was told it could not buy
the ground. By August 1981 a Chesterfield headquarters scheme was
under consideration as the borough council suggested a Queen's Park
Sports Complex. Next came reports that Derbyshire might consider
moving to the Courtaulds Acetate – formerly British Celanese –
sports complex at Borrowash in Spondon.

With a loss of £47,374 in the year in which they won the NatWest
Trophy announced, Derbyshire cricket seemed to be losing its way,
but at long last terms were agreed with Derby City Council and the
development plans got under way. It was announced that a new
pavilion would be built at a cost of £120,000. The stone-laying
ceremony was carried out on 23 January 1982 by the Mayor of Derby,
Councillor Flo Tunnicliffe, and on 10 May the Duke of Devonshire
opened the Cavendish Pavilion (later renamed the Lund Pavilion after
Harry Lund, a benefactor of the Club), which came into use for the
first time during Derbyshire's nine-wicket victory over Somerset in
the first home game of the season.

The shoddy facilities for players and spectators alike at the County
Ground were soon to be consigned to the past. Sponsorship was
changing the face of cricket and the game in return provided its
followers with better conditions and entertainment. Derby's Cinder-
ella ground underwent an almost magical change, with a new
pavilion, new scoreboard, refurbished indoor school and new stands.
More improvements were made and the city had a cricket ground and
leisure complex which offered all-year-round facilities. Extensions
were made to the Lund Pavilion and bookings for various functions
throughout the year ensured it was used to the full. Derbyshire's
downtrodden image vanished in the 1980s as the partially tree-lined
Derby ground even offered protection from the wind in those quarters
where no building development had taken place!

Everywhere, it seemed, there was a wind, but one of change. David
Harrison became chief executive in April 1980 but on 13 July 1981 he
announced his resignation, ending his seven-year connection with the
Club. He was succeeded in November by Roger Pearman, Lichfield-
born and a former player with Middlesex and Bedfordshire. He had an
industrial and commercial background and had been director and
general manager of a subsidiary of Brengreen Holdings, where he was
responsible for all aspects of the company and its staff.

In March 1982 Barry Marsh succeeded Walter Goodyear as
groundsman at Derby. A former soccer player with Aston Villa and a
number of non-league sides, he had been captain of Langley Mill when

Philip Russell (who took over as full-time coach in 1980) played for the Millers, and had spent 18 years as groundsman at the Heanor Town Ground.

Farewells were also bid to two members of the successful NatWest team, meaning that the hopes of keeping that fine side together were dashed almost at once. Mike Hendrick, who had bowled well in the final despite not being match-fit, left to join Nottinghamshire. He had had only a modest season in 1981 by his standards, and at 32 seemed to feel ready for a change. David Steele also left, returning to Northamptonshire, and Geoff Miller, after initially wanting to leave, announced that he would remain with the Club.

Jackie Hampshire, the 41-year-old Yorkshire and England batsman, and a player of high pedigree, was released by his native county and joined Derbyshire for 1982. Hampshire, although in the veteran stage, was still a player of high class and his arrival was expected to offset the loss of Steele. Peter Hacker, a fast-medium left-arm bowler from Nottinghamshire, was specially registered for the 1982 season and with Paul Newman, then classed as one of the most promising fast-medium bowlers in the country, Oldham and Tunnicliffe, was to form the post-Hendrick pace attack.

The question of Bob Taylor's deputy was also on the way to being solved. Mike Deakin played in four games in 1981 but it was to be Bernie Maher who emerged as the great man's understudy. Maher had appeared for Middlesex Second Eleven and it was while he was at Loughborough University that he came to Derbyshire's notice. Maher was also a useful batsman and he made a spectacular debut for Derbyshire in 1981 at the age of 23. Against Gloucestershire at Derby he held five catches on the first morning of his county career.

Oldham's first innings six for 63 set Derbyshire on the way to victory over Somerset and Moir (five for 40) and Kirsten (121 not out) did well in a win over Leicestershire at Derby. Wright had formed a highly consistent opening partnership with Wood which produced a dozen century opening starts in all types of cricket between 1980 and 1983 but it was Iain Anderson who helped him establish a record against Yorkshire with 242 for the first wicket at Derby, Wright making 190 in a total of 473. Wright had previously carried his bat against Nottinghamshire for 141 at Chesterfield but his greatest performance that season came against Northamptonshire at Derby.

On the third day Northamptonshire set Derbyshire 347 to win in 305 minutes after acting captain George Sharp had declined to enforce the follow-on, expecting the ball to turn on the last day. It did, but Wood was set on a victory attempt and stationed ground staff youngsters around the boundary edge to save time by returning the ball. He and Wright began with 52 before the skipper was caught off

Steele for 28 but Wright and Kirsten (68) then added 125 in 34 overs, mastering any venom the pitch offered which, in the event, was not as much as anticipated. Wright reached his hundred in 174 minutes and at tea Derbyshire, 218 for two, needed 129 to win in two hours. Wright, who should have been stumped at 57, took successive boundaries off Griffiths with an on-drive, a hook, a square cut and an off-drive and although he lost Hampshire he found a willing partner in Kim Barnett. At the start of the last hour 69 were needed and with Barnett sharing in an unbroken stand of 114, Derbyshire reached 350 for three to win an improbable victory by seven wickets with 17 balls to spare. Wright's unbeaten 185 spanned six hours and he struck 33 fours. His finest innings for the County is generally considered to be his 96 against the West Indies attack of Roberts, Marshall, Garner and Collis King in 1980 at Queen's Park but this one ran it close. It was the highest fourth-innings total made by the County, beating the 344 at Southampton in 1911 and the winning 324 for seven at Trent Bridge in 1961.

Miller's eight for 70 and four for 68 and another Kirsten hundred produced a win over Leicestershire at Coalville and by 13 July Derbyshire were third in the table with four wins in 12 games, the only undefeated side in the Championship. But although Kirsten made two unbeaten hundreds in the match against Surrey at Derby and Barnett and Anderson scored maiden centuries, no more Championship games were won and Derbyshire ended eleventh.

Kirsten and Wright dominated the summer, Hampshire had a good first season and Dallas Moir took 76 wickets but Derbyshire faded after a good start. Something was wrong and as Gerald Mortimer (now responsible for the Derbyshire section in *Wisden*) commented in the Almanack:

By September, there was considerable unrest within the Club. Barry Wood's somewhat inflexible style of man-management caused increasing disquiet and he was openly critical of the committee who, while confirming him as captain, offered him a playing contract for only one year.

Wood found that full-time captaincy was a different matter from taking over for half-a-season, as had happened in 1981 when he led Derbyshire to victory in the NatWest Trophy. He was often in conflict with his players and performances inevitably suffered.

So, in a summer when Kirsten and Wright each exceeded Kirsten and Leslie Townsend's old record of six hundreds and both came close to reaching 2,000 runs in 21 Championship games, Derbyshire, once again, were under a cloud. Borrington and Hacker left at the end of the season and Moir also decided to leave county cricket at 25, although he changed his mind later. Wood had Barnett, Hampshire, Hill, Miller, Oldham, Taylor, Tunnicliffe and Wright remaining of his capped players to start the 1983 season – Kirsten had also left – but two youngsters who would make considerable impact in the 1980s had made their debuts. Roger Finney, a right-hand batsman and left-arm medium-pace bowler made a promising start and was to become a useful member of the attack who also scored well on occasion in the lower middle order.

John Morris, from Crewe, began his career as an 18-year-old and was to develop quickly into one of the finest batsmen Derbyshire has produced. Morris had played for Cheshire Schoolboys and it was after he played for the Kidsgrove and District League at Denton that he was recommended to Philip Russell. There had been previous trials with Warwickshire and Lancashire but Morris was encouraged by his reception at Derby in 1980 and decided to join the Club. He scored heavily for the second team, and in 1982 made his first-class debut.

Lancashire-born but New Zealand-raised Bill Fowler, a hard-hitting right-hand batsman and slow left-arm bowler, emerged in limited-overs cricket in 1982 and other newcomers for 1983 included fast-medium bowler Andrew Watts.

There was some talk that a few committee members would have liked to have seen Wood relieved of the captaincy and the office offered to Kirsten. Instead, the skipper received his vote of confidence – but only a one-year contract – in both cases on a

The great West Indian fast bowler, Michael Holding, spearheaded Derbyshire's attack in the 1980s. He is pictured here bowling to Peter Roebuck of Somerset in a John Player match at Heanor in August 1983.

243

unanimous vote and the South African returned home. With Wright likely to be unavailable for much of 1983 because of the New Zealand tour and Kirsten gone Derbyshire would clearly have a gap to fill but it was really a world-class fast bowler that was needed and the County went for the best in Michael Holding. Before his registration was approved Derbyshire had to satisfy the Test and County Cricket Board that he would play for the County for two seasons. He was to be involved in the World Cup with the West Indies until the final on 25 June and his debut for the County was to be further delayed by an ankle injury sustained when the crowd surged on to the pitch at Lord's. But at 29, the Jamaican-born fast bowler ranked among the best of all time, with a quite lovely action and, even off a short run, capable of generating extreme pace. In short, with memories of his magnificent fourteen for 149 in the 1976 Oval Test still fresh, Holding was quite simply the best and fastest bowler ever to be associated with Derbyshire.

His new-ball partner later that summer was, at the start of the season, virtually unknown and something of a curiosity. Ole Henrik Mortensen was born in Denmark and had made 17 appearances for his country, including among several visits to England one for the ICC Trophy in 1979. Ian Buxton saw him play in this competition and as a result he was invited to Derby for a fortnight's trial in 1981, when the County would have engaged him but could not as at that time players from the EEC countries were classed as overseas. By 1983 these rules had been changed and he was offered a contract for the summer, making an immediate impact in local and second team cricket, to such a degree that his first-class debut came at Trent Bridge at the end of May. Standing 6 ft 3 in tall, like Holding, Mortensen was fast and aggressive and seven for 12 for the second team at Lincoln served due notice of his ability. Nicknamed Stan, after the Blackpool and England footballer, Mortensen was to become a popular figure with the County's followers and, while he lacked Holding's pace, he proved an admirable foil to the Test star. Certainly Derbyshire's Dane whetted the appetite for the 1983 season and the County's attack of West Indian, Viking and Maltese-born Scotsman (Dallas Moir) looked full of potential, albeit a far cry from the days of whistling down mine shafts for fast bowlers, or spinners for that matter.

Viking and Caribbean, saga and calypso, but the major concern was how the 15 hundreds made by Wright and Kirsten would be replaced. Derbyshire lacked depth but Wood played in two one-day internationals in 1982 and Miller and Taylor in the five tests in Australia in 1982–83 so there still quality in the side. But within a week of the start of the season they found themselves thrown into another leadership crisis. Barry Wood suddenly resigned as captain, saying he found leading the side and maintaining his playing standards too demanding. So he followed Brian Bolus, Bob Taylor, David Steele and Geoff Miller in relinquishing the office, the fifth mid-season switch in nine years. Miller, mooted in *The Cricketer* a few months earlier as a potential England captain, took over the next few Championship and limited-overs games and, as a former skipper and England tour vice-captain, was favourite for the permanent job. Jackie Hampshire, who had captained Yorkshire, was another possibility, and Bob Taylor could also step in. Asking Peter Kirsten to return as captain could rule out the Holding signing and it was thought that to offer the position to any of the younger players such as Kim Barnett or Iain Anderson might handicap their development.

It emerged that Derbyshire were keen to reserve the appointment for a home-grown player, which made Miller clear favourite. Instead the club named Kim Barnett as Wood's successor.

He led the side for the first time at Trent Bridge, and was just 22 years 315 days old on the first day of his first-class captaincy – the youngest skipper in Derbyshire's history and the youngest on the current Championship circuit.

CHAPTER TWENTY-ONE

THE BARNETT APPROACH

KIM BARNETT'S APPROACH TO CAPTAINCY quickly endeared him to
Derbyshire's followers. His was not an easy baptism, as a young player
yet to establish himself fully in a team which included four men with
vast experience of the game and captaincy in Wood, Miller, Taylor
and Hampshire. Plenty of sound advice available, then, but also a need
for flair and a streak of ruthlessness if the ripples of discontent hanging
over from 1982 were to be eliminated. A new committee had worked
wonders for the Derby ground development project; now it was time
to translate these deeds into playing success.

In the event Wood did not remain long, his contract being
terminated by mutual consent in July, a sad ending to a brief era which
included those moments of 1981 Lord's magic. But the question
remained uppermost in members' minds: was Barnett capable of
doing the job or had he been pitched in too soon? Hindsight tells us he
had not but informed thought inside the Club in 1983 also never had
any doubt. Here was a young man who had played for England
Schools in India, Young England in Australia, a Derrick Robins side
on a tour of New Zealand, been on a Whitbread scholarship to
Australia, and appeared for Young England against Australia at
Worcester in 1980. And perhaps most significantly, he had encoun-
tered Eddie Barlow while playing for the Boland in the South African
Castle Bowl. Barlow had encouraged him to adopt a positive
approach to the captaincy issue whenever it cropped up in the future
and with that other shrewd cricket brain Philip Russell, now cricket
manager in all but name, to press his claims, the Barnett appointment
had more substance than many people appreciated at the time.

Nevertheless, there was much to do. At the start of the 1983 season
Barnett had a career average of 24.43, had made only two centuries in
first-class games for the County and his best season's aggregate was still
the 752 he made in 1979, his debut season. Seldom used, his leg-spin
had captured only 18 expensive first-class wickets. But there had been
an innings of great moment on 4 July 1982 in a John Player League
game at Derby when Barnett, opening with John Wright under
Kirsten's captaincy against Lancashire, had shared a stand of 132 and
gone on to make 111 before being run out. It was a new experience for
a young middle-order batsman who had found his opportunities
limited by the wealth of class above him on the Derbyshire scorecard.
Wood was injured, so Barnett, used to middle-order slogging in one-
day games, seized a chance to play a long innings, credit again being
due to Russell for suggesting the promotion.

Towards the end of the 1983 season Barnett began to go in first regularly in the Championship, rapidly becoming one of the most adventurous and entertaining openers in the game. With effortless and crisp timing, a glittering array of forceful and attacking strokes either side of the wicket, he could shred a county attack. Perhaps a little impetuous outside the off-stump, where he played the percentages, with hundreds of runs coming from square cuts or superb cover drives to compensate for the occasional edge, he was still capable of digging in when the occasion demanded. Few players, if any, in Derbyshire's history have looked better than Barnett in full cry. He became Anderson's opening partner and, with Hill, the trio each scored more than a thousand runs, Mortensen coming through with 66 wickets in a summer of success for the relatively new faces. Barnett's captaincy even came under fire for being too aggressive at times as he backed his fast bowlers with umbrella fields, but it was a positive, refreshing start to the new era.

There was a win at Trent Bridge in a game reduced to a single innings but three heavy defeats followed before another victory was recorded, at Bath. Then came a fine win over Yorkshire at Abbeydale Park, the first over the White Rose county since 1957. Barnett made a brilliant 95, while Mortensen took eleven for 89 and Moir nine for 159 in the match. Boycott carried his bat through the second innings, his side falling 22 runs short. Hill made centuries in victories over Worcestershire at Derby and Warwickshire at Edgbaston and by 15 July Derbyshire were sixth in the table. A two-wicket win at Swansea and a victory over Nottinghamshire at Derby completed the season's successes, seven wins leaving Derbyshire ninth.

The lithe Holding, dubbed 'Whispering Death' by players on the circuit, glided in with that beautiful long approach to the wicket which culminates in one of the most fluid and lovely actions the game has seen. Mortensen roared in opposite, and thus was forged one of the fastest opening attacks in the County's history. With Newman in support it routed Nottinghamshire for 53 at Derby on a pitch often described as a graveyard for fast bowlers, a theory which needed reassessing now. With Doxey Walker's Queen's Park pitches winning high praise for their pace and bounce and regarded as perfect cricket wickets, Barnett's dream of a West Indian-type pace-dominated attack was close to fulfilment. Oldham and Tunnicliffe left at the end of the 1983 season but replacements of sharper pace would soon follow.

First, though, there was a season of setback. In 1984 Wright, Barnett (1,703 runs in the Championship) and Hill dominated the batting with support from Morris, Miller, Fowler and Hampshire, but the bowling was depleted by Holding's absence with the West Indian tourists and a

Paul Newman, who proved an admirable foil to Holding and Mortensen in the 1980s.

troublesome back injury to Mortensen. It left spin dominant, with Geoff Miller enjoying a fine season which produced 891 runs and 86 wickets, and Moir taking 65 wickets and also scoring 534 runs, which included his maiden hundred.

Derbyshire did not win until their 16th championship match of the season on 27 July when Lancashire were beaten at Buxton. Then came an unexpected victory at Trent Bridge, after Derbyshire had followed on 222 behind. Consistent batting enabled them to make 381 and then bowl Nottinghamshire out, Moir's six for 60 in the second innings proving decisive. Wright's 177 paved the way to a total of 475 and an innings win over Sussex at Derby, Moir and Miller again bowling well, and the summer ended with a fine win over Hampshire at Derby, Barnett and Fowler making hundreds and Wright, Hill and Morris leading the chase to make 277 in 58 overs.

Although they won three of their four games, Derbyshire failed to survive the qualifying stages of the Benson and Hedges Cup and they lost at Leicester in the NatWest after beating Cumberland at Kendal. Four Championship wins had earned them eleventh place; in the JPL a similar number left them bottom of the table. But there was one amazing performance against Kent at Derby. Needing 256 for victory Derbyshire appeared to have lost the game with the score at 142 for eight in the 28th over. Moir then hammered 79 off 50 balls in 49 minutes, hitting four sixes and six fours. He and Taylor established a new JPL record of 105 for the ninth wicket in eleven overs, Taylor winning the game with two balls to spare when he hoisted Ellison for six.

Barnett hit six hundreds in the Championship, Wright played superbly on a limited contract, but the big advance was that of John Morris, who made three inter-county centuries. He showed a wide range of strokes and an ability at only 20 which was almost awe-inspiring.

Yet the most significant event came late in the season, when Bob Taylor played his final match for Derbyshire. Twenty-three years after Ken Suttle had been caught at the wicket, Mark Nicholas was stumped at Derby and the Championship career of a great player had ended. The Hampshire batsman was one of 1,304 who had fallen to Taylor in Derbyshire matches and it is a record which is likely to endure as long as cricket is played in the County. After announcing his retirement a few weeks before the end of the season Taylor enjoyed something of a royal progress around the counties, with spectators at away games generous with their applause. Had he retained his England place he might well have continued for longer but the selectors chose Paul Downton because of his superior batting that summer and Taylor left the first-class game at 43. He was not completely lost to the County, of course, for he continued as second team captain and coach to the juniors, eventually joining the general committee.

Jackie Hampshire, whose career had been handicapped by injuries in the past couple of seasons, also retired, but the basis of Derbyshire's side remained largely unchanged. Bernie Maher was pencilled in as Taylor's successor, with competition from Chris Marples, from Chesterfield. Marples, who kept goal for Chesterfield FC, had played for Grassmoor and Chesterfield in the Bassetlaw League and graduated through Derbyshire's junior and second team sides.

Bruce Roberts, who had made his debut with a second-innings 80 against Leicestershire at Chesterfield in 1984, was now emerging as a batsman of rich promise. Roberts, fair-haired and looking like a young Eddie Barlow, was born in Zambia and brought up in Zimbabwe, the fact that he had an English mother enabling

Derbyshire to register him as an Englishman. After learning his cricket in South Africa, Roberts, who hits the ball very hard, played with Horwich in the Bolton League, Sheffield Collegiate and Langley Mill before joining Derbyshire.

Alan Warner joined Derbyshire in 1985 from Worcestershire. Warner had impressed Derbyshire with his sharp pace when playing against the County in the past and although erratic at this stage of his career, he was to become a useful member of the side both as a bowler and hard-hitting tail-end batsman. Also adding to the cosmopolitan atmosphere of the dressing room at this time was Rajeshwar (Reg) Sharma, who was born in Kenya. Sharma, a batsman and useful off-spin bowler, had been educated in Kent and after trials with that county and Gloucestershire, he joined Derbyshire in 1985.

With £45,000 development plans announced at the new pavilion and a £26,000 profit in 1984 Derbyshire cricket appeared to have turned the corner at long last. Bowlers of the quality of Holding, Mortensen, Newman, Finney, Warner, Miller and Moir, with the addition of Barnett's leg-spin, gave the attack a healthy look but 1985 was to produce one of the most humiliating defeats in the Club's history. On 3 July they met Durham, of the Minor Counties, in the first round of the NatWest Trophy and crashed to a seven-wicket defeat – only the fifth time such an upset had occurred. Durham sent Derbyshire in to bat but apart from Barnett (53) nobody got to grips with the bowling and they were all out for 171. It was an uninspired display and with John Lister, a former Derbyshire player, making 42, Durham never looked like being defeated, cruising home with 26 balls to spare. Yet in the Benson and Hedges Derbyshire reached the quarter-finals, losing to Essex in what became a 20-over game at Chelmsford. In the John Player League, eight victories took them to fourth place. There was a victory at Knypersley over Worcestershire, where Derbyshire struck 18 sixes in making 292 for nine and a fine win at Edgbaston, where Barnett's unbeaten 82 led a charge to score at 7.5 runs per over in a 30-over game.

It was July before Derbyshire registered a Championship victory, Glamorgan being beaten at Derby, and there was a thrilling victory at Worcester when Wright (117) and Anderson (94) shared a second wicket partnership of 193 and their side made 336 for seven to win by three wickets. Some fine bowling by Holding and an unbeaten hundred by Morris brought the third victory of the season when Warwickshire were beaten at Chesterfield, Derbyshire ending in 13th place. Derbyshire had finished strongly, with Barnett and Roberts the leading run-getters and Holding and Finney heading the bowlers, but it was not the best of seasons.

It did, however, bring recognition for Barnett, who was appointed vice-captain of the England B touring team which visited Sri Lanka in 1985–86. Unfortunately illness compelled his early return after he had played in only four games, although in one of these he made 51 before retiring ill in the second 'Test' at Colombo. It was a debilitating illness which did not help Barnett's cause in the 1986 season, although his form remained good throughout that summer.

Fowler and Moir had now left the staff but there was promise in the form of Jamaican-born Devon Malcolm, who had joined Derbyshire just before the start of the 1984 season. Malcolm had come to England in 1980 and showed good form as a fast bowler in Sheffield cricket circles. Bespectacled, the 6 ft 2 in Malcolm had first played for the County in 1984 and he was to become one of the fastest of Derbyshire bowlers, although his bowling has tended to lack rhythm.

The 1986 season's first victory, over Yorkshire at Abbeydale Park (now a Yorkshire ground but once a Derbyshire venue) brought a new record. Alan Hill made a superb 172 not out and, with Martin Jean-Jacques (73) shared a new tenth-wicket record partnership of 132. Jean-Jacques, who was born in Dominica, had been spotted in the West Indies by Tony Pope and this was his first-class debut. In his third match he took eight for 77 in Kent's first innings at Derby, Derbyshire winning by 28 runs after Morris had made a dazzling 191. The Holding–Mortensen combination then set up a thrilling victory over Middlesex at the County Ground when some splendid pace bowling left the batsmen 289 to win, the runs being obtained with one wicket to spare. Another run-chase succeeded at Abergavenny and a fifth victory, which earned 11th place, came in a one-innings match at Taunton.

All four Benson and Hedges qualifying games were won but Kent won the quarter-final at Derby. The NatWest Trophy saw a record-breaking performance against Cornwall at Derby when Anderson (134) and Hill (153) shared a second-wicket partnership of 286, Derbyshire reaching 365 for three in their 60 overs. But they were eliminated in the next round by Surrey at Derby. Seven victories came in the John Player League (in which Barnett made 700 runs), ninth place being achieved.

By now Barnett (1,502 runs in 1986) and Morris (1,703) were ranked among the most promising and exciting batsmen in the country. Each had a sound technique and a wide range of strokes, each was capable of that touch of the unorthodox which can bewilder an attack and make nonsense of a run chase. Often too much depended on them, for Iain Anderson could not reproduce the form of three years earlier, although Bernie Maher showed great character in fighting back to regain the wicket-keeping place he had lost to Chris Marples and emerge as an opening batsman who averaged nearly 40. Marples was not retained after the 1986 season, Lancashire-born Karl Krikken coming in as reserve 'keeper. Alan Hill also retired, although he remained with the Club as second-team captain, and Geoff Miller left to join Essex. It was a sad end to a long career with the County, Miller feeling a fresh start might revitalise his career as he and Derbyshire drifted apart.

Miller's going at the end of the 1986 season was followed by an attempt to sign Ian Botham, who left Somerset and eventually joined Worcestershire. Geoff Boycott was also offered a two-year contract by Derbyshire but the former Yorkshire and England opening batsman turned this down and Peter Such, Neil Mallender, Alan Butcher and Colin Wells were also linked with the County as the bid to strengthen the squad continued, but no new signings were made.

Yet the talk of new players looked like nonsense after the opening game of the 1987 season in which Sussex were beaten at Chesterfield. Bruce Roberts, whose form over the past few years had been inconsistent, made a marvellous 184, with two sixes and 25 fours, John Morris helping him add 176 in 41 overs for the third wicket. Batting of this class had been rare in Derbyshire cricket and Roberts never looked back, heading the averages with 1,643 runs and enjoying a splendid season. There was an innings victory over Warwickshire at Derby and an exciting three-run win at Old Trafford. Hampshire were beaten on the tiny Heanor ground after a Roberts hundred and a good innings by Finney led the run chase and then came the first tie in Derbyshire's history at Bristol. Barnett made 110 before setting Gloucestershire 279 to win and Sharma (six for 80) took two wickets with the last two balls in their 2,219th first-class match. Derbyshire finished strongly with a win at Cardiff and a victory over Middlesex at Derby and with six successes they ended sixth in the Championship, their highest position for 20 years.

They had also done well in the Refuge Assurance Sunday League, mounting a strong challenge for the title with five wins and a tie in six games early on to lead in June. They remained in contention until the final game but a defeat by Somerset at Derby meant they finished fifth and out of the prize money. In the NatWest Trophy Derbyshire also threatened to take honours, defeating Cambridgeshire at Wisbech and then gaining a one-wicket victory at Canterbury before losing to Nottinghamshire in the quarter-final at Derby. Nevertheless, there was a success for the Club to savour in 1987 when the Bain Dawes Trophy, the one-day competition for second teams, came to the County Ground. Derbyshire headed the North Zone and then in the final at Southampton they defeated Hampshire by seven wickets in the 55 overs game. Mark Beardshall, a medium-fast bowler who made his debut in 1987, took four for 32, Paul Taylor took three crucial wickets, and then Andrew Brown (65) and Iain Anderson (58), like Taylor, both released by the County at the end of the summer, steered them to a seven-wicket win. The cup joined the ASDA Trophy in Derbyshire's honours cabinet, two victories having been recorded in this competition at Scarborough in 1982 and 1985.

No prize money, then, for Derbyshire in 1987 and after three profitable years the Club made a loss of almost £20,000. Chairman Chris Middleton had to field some testing questions at the annual meeting concerning the departure of Roger Pearman, the chief executive officer, who left the Club in April. Again, there was something of a mini-crisis in the air, for Roger Pearman had been at the helm during several years of development and prosperity and members were shocked by the parting of the ways between him and the Club. It was a controversial topic, a parting arrived at by 'mutual consent' although it cost Derbyshire a settlement of £20,000 and Mr Pearman also retained his Club car. Ian Edwards took over the duties of secretary, the chief executive position being scrapped.

That annual meeting was also told by cricket chairman Guy Willatt that other counties had the financial muscle to outbid Derbyshire where new recruits were concerned, which explained the failure to sign Trevor Jesty that winter. But new players did arrive and 1988 was to prove the wisdom of obtaining the services of Peter Bowler, an opening batsman from Leicestershire, and Steve Goldsmith, a middle-order batsman from Kent. Bowler had made a hundred on his debut for Leicestershire and he was to repeat the feat for Derbyshire at Fenner's with an unbeaten 155, sharing an opening stand of 238 with Barnett (151). Bowler quickly established himself as a solid and dependable opening batsman, scoring 1,725 runs and making four hundreds, Goldsmith also exceeding a four-figure aggregate in his debut season for the Club. But Derbyshire ran into problems over another newcomer when the Test and County Cricket Board fined them £2,000 for signing fast-medium bowler Simon Base while he was still under contract to Glamorgan. It was a heavy fine, the TCCB considering that Base was subject to a verbal contract with the Welsh county and he was not allowed to play for Derbyshire until 1 July.

With Finney troubled by injury – he reverted to bowling slow left-arm in 1987 and announced his retirement at the end of the 1988 season – and Holding and Mortensen also running into injury problems, Derbyshire failed to maintain their form in the Championship and finished 14th with four victories. Barnett's dream of an imposing battery of pace looked set to be realised with Holding, Mortensen, Malcolm, Newman, Warner, Base, Jean-Jacques, Beardshall and Frank Griffith on the books but by the season's end the lack of life in the pitches at Derby and Chesterfield had defeated them all. The pitches were criticised although groundsmen Barry Marsh and Doxey Walker had received high praise for the quality of the wickets. Yet only Glamorgan finished with fewer bowling bonus points than Derbyshire. A summer of sunshine, with hard, fast pitches offering plenty of bounce while encouraging stroke-play, could have made all the difference, but amidst the damp of 1988 it was an ideal almost impossible to attain.

The season – in which each county was to play six four-day Championship games – began well. Cambridge University were beaten by an innings and with Newman taking eight for 29 in the second innings there was a five-wicket win at Headingley. Essex, who featured among the Britannic Assurance Championship contenders, were also given a fright at Queen's Park when, after Derbyshire had trailed by 156, Bowler carried his bat for 159 and enabled them to build up a lead of 185. Essex slumped to 111 for nine by the close and with Derbyshire doing well in the Benson and Hedges competition it was a heartening start to the new season.

At the beginning of June Derbyshire gained a second Championship win in an intriguing game at Horsham. They needed 178 in a minimum of 50 overs and were set on the way by a marvellous 71 off 81 balls by Morris. Four were needed off the last over; two from the last ball. Sharma swung and got a bat on the ball and the batsmen scrambled the runs. But it was more than a month before another Britannic win was registered, Northamptonshire being beaten at Derby after two innings forfeitures and some splendid bowling by Mortensen. The fourth victory was at Weston-super-Mare, where Warner and Malcolm put paid to Somerset's hopes by routing them for 82 in the second innings.

That was Derbyshire's last Championship success in a season which ended disappointingly. There was promise in the batting of Tim O'Gorman, grandson of former music hall performer Joe O'Gorman, sadness in the back injury which had prevented Roger Finney from bowling in-swing and which eventually led to his premature retirement at a time when he ranked among the Championship's best all-rounders, and a sense of unreality as the much-vaunted attack was punished for 614 at Trent Bridge, the first time Derbyshire had conceded 600 for 76 years. Derbyshire's form also slumped in the Refuge Assurance League, 13th place and only five wins being their final offering.

Mortensen, struggling with a back injury, bowled magnificently to head the averages with 34 wickets at 13.64; Holding, beset by hamstring problems, remained a force in the longer versions of the limited-overs game but had a less successful time in the Championship. But for Kim Barnett, 1988 was a breakthrough year as England,

Ole Mortensen. The Dane bowled magnificently in 1988, heading Derbyshire averages despite problems with a back injury.

once again heavily defeated by the West Indies, searched for new blood. He had always demonstrated class but the selectors needed convincing about his ability to play a long innings. A year earlier he had made a dazzling hundred at Trent Bridge; in less demanding circumstances he had delighted a Scarborough holiday crowd with 158 off 165 balls in an ASDA trophy game against Lancashire. Now came perhaps his finest innings, 175 at Derby off a Gloucestershire attack including Lawrence, Curran and Alderman. It took 237 minutes, was made off 200 balls and contained 28 fours. It was made out of 258 and for the second time in his career he completed a hundred before lunch. With Roberts (69) – out of form to such an extent that he was later dropped in the order, Bernie Maher taking over the number three spot – he added 185 in 44 overs. Lunch at 174 for one was a far cry from some of the traditional Derbyshire batting collapses of the past.

In terms of figures Barnett exceeded even this majestic effort with an unbeaten 239 at Leicester. It was the perfect hint to the selectors and he was duly selected for the fifth Test at The Oval against the West Indies only for a hand injury incurred while fielding in a Refuge Assurance League game to compel his withdrawal. His chance came in the Lord's Test against Sri Lanka, in which he made 66 and 0 despite another scare when he broke his nose, again while fielding in a Sunday League match. He followed this by taking England's Man of the Match award for his splendid 84 in the Texaco Trophy match against Sri Lanka at The Oval and selection for the subsequently cancelled England tour of India followed as a matter of course.

Barnett needs only time and freedom from injury to exceed Denis Smith's career records of 20,516 runs and 30 centuries, but Morris, aged 25 at the start of the 1989 season, is on a similar course providing that marvellous ability can be translated into consistently good scores in the manner of Barnett.

The one player who would have unquestionably shattered all records left at the season's end, John Wright, still in magnificent form in 1988, announced his retirement from the county game although he remained captain of New Zealand. Wright, whose opportunities had been limited by sharing the overseas place since Holding's arrival, was awarded an MBE for services to cricket in the Queen's Birthday Honours and it was Barnett who said everything there was to say about the award: 'It could not happen to a nicer man.'

With Holding remaining for the final year of his contract in 1989, Wright's announcement left a vacancy for an overseas player and Derbyshire fended off stiff competition from other counties to sign the highly promising West Indian fast bowler Ian Bishop for the 1989 season. Bishop, who was a member of the West Indian party which toured England, was young and raw but generated a lot of pace and at 21 could view the prospect of a summer's cricket with Michael Holding with considerable enthusiasm.

Holding, Mortensen, Malcolm, Bishop etc., the line-up of pace was no longer home-spun. Derbyshire's staff now included only one County-born cricketer, batsman Chris Adams, who had scored heavily at Repton and made his debut at The Oval at the age of 18. But the fact that Derbyshire were able to sign Bishop at a time when several allegedly more fashionable counties were in the hunt was a heartening pointer to future prosperity.

LORD'S '88

GONE, THEN, WERE THE DAYS WHEN the Derbyshire executive could summon a fast bowler from the nearest coal mine, for there are few mines left in the County now.

But the tradition of pace, though cosmopolitan, had never been richer and it was to be borne out by one of the greatest displays of fast bowling in the County's 118-year history by Michael Holding. At 34 the West Indian might have been in the twilight of his career and his performances in the first-class game – 24 wickets at 34.45 – were not impressive. But on that Wednesday morning in the NatWest Trophy at Hove the years rolled away and fieldsmen and batsmen alike greeted the spectacle with something approaching awe.

Holding's majestic performance climaxed the early weeks of an unbroken run of success in the Benson and Hedges Cup and the NatWest Trophy. Barnett's battery of pace and the quality of batting available meant that Derbyshire had as good a chance as anybody of winning a Lord's final and in the Benson and Hedges Cup they fully demonstrated their power.

Derbyshire 1988. Back row: F. A. Griffith, K. M. Krikken, T. J. G. O'Gorman, D. E. Malcolm, S. Base, P. D. Bowler, M. Wakefield, C. J. Adams. Middle row: S. W. Tacy (scorer), M. Jean-Jacques, R. Sharma, A. E. Warner, B. J. M. Maher, M. Beardshall, S. C. Goldsmith, I. Edwards (secretary), J. D. Brown (Youth Coaching Organiser). Front row: B. Roberts, P. G. Newman, J. E. Morris, A. Hill, K. J. Barnett (capt.), P. E. Russell (coach), R. J. Finney, O. H. Mortensen. Absent are M. A. Holding and J. G. Wright.

CHAPTER TWENTY-TWO

In each of the four zonal games Barnett won the toss and put the opposition in to bat. Scotland were beaten at Glasgow, the rain ruined the Warwickshire match at Derby when it was interestingly poised and there was a victory over Leicestershire at Derby. At Aigburth, in the crucial third game of the qualifying stage, Derbyshire needed 258 for victory and they were given an excellent start by Barnett (85) and Bowler (64) who put on 140 (to be followed by one of 114 against Leicestershire). Derbyshire wobbled in mid-innings and when Holding joined Morris the score was 197 for five in the 48th over. With five overs remaining 44 were needed but Holding struck three sixes and Derbyshire got home by five wickets with 14 balls to spare.

The pace attack, though minus Mortensen, was seen at its best in the quarter-final tie against a powerful Middlesex side which fancied its chances of victory at Derby. Again Barnett won the toss and sent in the opposition and Holding destroyed the top order with three for 4 in his first three overs, reducing Middlesex to eight for three. Malcolm, now reckoned the fastest bowler in England, took four of the last five wickets and finished with five for 27 as Middlesex crashed to 110 all out in 46 overs. Rain meant the game going into a second day but Barnett, with an unbeaten 69 off 88 balls and including nine fours, steered his side to a nine-wicket victory, Bowler helping him put on 93 for the first wicket.

Paul Newman, one of the three survivors from the 1981 NatWest side (Wright and Barnett were the others), summarised Holding's value to the Club:

Our batting has flair right down the order and I suppose I am now one of the senior players. I am also a bit wiser and don't come charging in off 30 yards.

The physical demands of bowling fast day in, day out are tremendous. Michael Holding has now tailored his style but encourages Devon Malcolm to let fly while he is still young. When Michael says anything, the rest of us listen and learn.

Glamorgan in the semi-final at Swansea, though, were a different proposition. They had beaten Derbyshire in a Sunday game at Newport, had a potential match-winner in Matthew Maynard and the pitch was expected to favour spin rather than pace. Derbyshire, put in, struggled on a slow pitch but reached a useful 217 for eight; Glamorgan began well but declined from 70 for one to 116 for five, Maynard losing his wicket when his helmet came off and rolled into his stumps as he forced Holding into the covers. The batsman brushed his headgear during his follow-through and it was to prove a turning point, Derbyshire winning by 14 runs as the game went into Friday, Holding taking five for 31.

258

So they reached the final against Hampshire, an unsung side minus Greenidge and Marshall but one which had accounted for Worcestershire and Essex in away games en route to Lord's.

First, though, Derbyshire were to meet Sussex at Hove in the first round of the NatWest. Paul Parker won the toss and elected to bat. Sussex collapsed to 27 for six, all of the wickets to Holding and they were all out for 134 in 46.1 overs. Holding, who accounted for Parker, Imran Khan and the Wells brothers, all of whom failed to score, finished with an analysis of 10.1-2-21-8. Eight for 21 included nine no-balls and in earlier times it would have been eight for 12. It was a world record for limited-overs cricket and all of the wickets fell to catches in an arc between wicket-keeper and gully. It was classic fast bowling down the slope – although Holding modestly insisted that he was no longer a truly fast bowler – in which he got steep lift and made the ball climb from only just short of a length: a marvellous exhibition.

Some sensible batting by Barnett, Morris and Maher took Derbyshire into the next round and there was much interested speculation about what might happen if Hampshire's strong batting side came up against Holding and Derbyshire's quintet of pace on a fresh pitch at Lord's early in the morning.

But a week before the game Holding withdrew from the attack in a Championship game against Middlesex with hamstring problems. He bowled eight accurate overs in the NatWest second round match in which Cheshire were beaten at Chester's Boughton Hall, Mortensen taking five for 15, but this game did not end until the Friday evening before the final – hardly the ideal preparation.

So to Lord's and, from Derbyshire's point of view, a disappointing replica of the 1978 game. Mark Nicholas won the toss and sent Derbyshire in. They began well, too well, perhaps, with 25 from five overs. Then Steve Jefferies, who had played for Derbyshire against Pakistan in 1982, caused havoc with his left-arm in-swing from the pavilion end. Soon 27 for no wicket became 32 for four; Morris and Maher gave a hint of a recovery but despite Morris' 42 it was not to be and Derbyshire were humbled for 117. Barnett had little choice but to opt for an umbrella field of four slips and a gully. Malcolm worked up a tremendous pace from the pavilion end and when Terry left at 10 there was just a chance if two or three wickets fell quickly. But Nicholas remained, Robin Smith played beautifully for 38 off 27 balls before Goldsmith, running 45 yards, held a wonderful diving catch at very fine leg from a fierce hook off Warner, and Hampshire cruised home to a comfortable victory. Had Barnett won the toss and fielded first it might all have been so different, even though the pitch did not favour sheer pace and Derbyshire had no equivalent of Jefferies (Finney in his old style, comes to mind). Barnett had no doubts, saying that his bowlers thought they could have bowled Hampshire out for 80 when the ball was moving about in the morning.

Derbyshire, though, were not yet done with Nicholas and his men. They met them in a Sunday game at Portsmouth and, put in again, were bowled out for 133. In turn Hampshire struggled but won by four wickets. The Championship game ended in a draw but on the following Wednesday the teams clashed at Derby in the quarter-final of the NatWest Trophy. Again Nicholas won the toss and sent Derbyshire in. Barnett (32) before falling victim to Jefferies for the third time in the one-day encounters and Maher (44) got them to 146 for three but the total was only 191 and despite a late burst by Mortensen Hampshire won by four wickets, with 16 balls to spare.

So Hampshire had made it 3-0 in one-day games in 1988, winning the toss on each occasion. Lord's, though, might have been so different. But at least rain did not ruin the day, everybody got home early and there was always Goldsmith's catch!

DERBYSHIRE v HAMPSHIRE
(BENSON AND HEDGES CUP FINAL)

Played at Lord's on 9 July 1988

HAMPSHIRE WON BY 7 WICKETS

DERBYSHIRE

*K. J. Barnett	b Jefferies	13
P. D. Bowler	c Nicholas b Jefferies	4
B. Roberts	c Nicholas b Jefferies	0
J. E. Morris	run out	42
S. C. Goldsmith	lbw b Jefferies	0
†B. J. M. Maher	b Ayling	8
M. A. Holding	c Turner b Cowley	7
P. G. Newman	b Connor	10
A. E. Warner	b Jefferies	4
O. H. Mortensen	not out	0
D. E. Malcolm	b Connor	0
Extras	lb 14, nb 3, w 12	29
Total (46.3 overs)		117

Fall: 1-27, 2-28, 3-29, 4-32, 5-71, 6-80, 7-101, 8-114, 9-117, 10-117

BOWLING	O	M	R	W
Connor	7.3	1	27	2
Jefferies	10	3	13	5
Andrew	9	0	25	0
Ayling	9	2	21	1
Cowley	11	2	17	1

HAMPSHIRE

V. P. Terry	c Roberts b Malcolm	2
C. L. Smith	c Maher b Mortensen	20
*M. C. J. Nicholas	not out	35
R. A. Smith	c Goldsmith b Warner	38
D. R. Turner	not out	7
S. T. Jefferies		
J. R. Ayling		
†R. J. Parks	did not bat	
N. G. Cowley		
C. A. Connor		
S. J. W. Andrew		
Extras	lb 8, nb 5, w 3	16
Total (31.5 overs)	(for 3 wkts)	118

Fall: 1-10, 2-44, 3-90

BOWLING	O	M	R	W
Holding	11	2	36	0
Malcolm	7	2	25	1
Newman	3	1	11	0
Mortensen	5	1	19	1
Warner	5.5	0	19	1

Umpires: D. J. Constant and N. T. Plews

Derbyshire won the toss

*Captain; †Wicket-keeper

TOMORROW'S WORLD

SPONSORED CARS EMBLAZONED WITH cricketers' names are a far cry
from the days when Nudger Needham wore everyday clothes under
his whites during the final session of the day at Derby in readiness for a
quick dash to the old Nottingham Road railway station to catch the
6.35 pm train.

A far cry, too, is the modern County Ground from the windswept
wilderness of yesteryear – albeit of fond memory – when players and
spectators alike endured Spartan conditions. Yet those memories are
rich, of golden days at Derby when the sun blazed down, of
Chesterfield, a lovely ground at any time of the year, of Ilkeston and
the recollection of the annual clash with the old enemy from across the
Erewash. They are enduring memories and enduring is not an
inappropriate term with which to describe the story of Derbyshire
cricket. It has endured many trials and tribulations, with the perennial
headlines about batting collapses and the yearly cash crisis. Sometimes
the wonder has been that it has survived at all, let alone produced so
many superb cricketers.

It is unlikely now that Derbyshire will ever again field a County-
born side capable of winning the Championship, at least not in the
foreseeable future. Since the early 1970s the supply of County-born
players has dwindled to such an extent that the 18-year-old Chris
Adams, from Whitwell, who made his first-class debut at The Oval in

*Kim Barnett receives the Man of the Match award at The Oval on 4 September 1988, after the
England v Sri Lanka one-day International. (Allsport)*

1988, was the only County-born player remaining on the staff, he and Geoff Miller being the only Derbyshire-born players in the Championship – after the end of the season. In that context Derbyshire cricket has never been so poorly represented. Traditionalists may blanch at this but it is a situation not unique to Derbyshire and, indeed, not unique to cricket. Take a look at the staffs of any organisation – sporting, business, a school, a factory – and the chances are that many people were born far beyond the town or the county in which it is situated. A couple of decades ago most of them would probably have been born locally.

Kim Barnett, Bob Taylor, Arnold Hamer, Ole Mortensen and others are or were no less committed to Derbyshire cricket because they happen to have been born elsewhere. And the club has not forgotten its responsibility to the bedrock of the game in the County. In October 1988 it announced that it had received a £10,000 donation from John Paul Getty junior, specifically to help youth cricket in the County.

'We will do all we can to make the best use of an extremely generous donation from one of cricket's greatest benefactors,' said the Club chairman Chris Middleton. 'He is particularly interested in school and youth cricket and this is the main purpose of the £10,000.'

Chris Middleton, who watched Derbyshire as a schoolboy and has been a keen follower of the Club ever since, gave much of the credit for the Getty donation to Bob Taylor. 'He made the initial contact and, in these areas, Bob is worth ten other committee men,' he said.

Therein is the nub of the matter. Dressing-room accents may be cosmopolitan but Derbyshire cricket has not strayed from its heritage and the commitment is as great as ever. It has a chairman and a secretary who, though born in Sheffield and Staffordshire respectively, are steeped in Derbyshire tradition. It has a groundsman and coach who played together for Langley Mill in the old Notts and Derby Border League. Its main sponsors, Bass, have been local brewers since 1777, only 20 years after that first mention of the game in the County in the *Derby Mercury*. And its committee is a healthy blend of business parochialism and past players with vast experience of the game at a variety of levels, in Taylor's case as a player and Charlie Elliott's as an umpire and Test selector, at the very summit.

In short, Derbyshire cricket is in good hands and is looking eagerly to its future.

It is a healthy sign.

STATISTICAL SECTION

BIOGRAPHICAL DETAILS
OF DERBYSHIRE CRICKETERS

NAME AND EXTENT OF CAREER	BIRTHPLACE	DATE OF BIRTH	DATE OF DEATH
Archibald Ackroyd *1924–1925*	Heanor	18. 5.1897	25. 6.1968
Christopher John Adams *1988*	Whitwell	6. 5.1970	
Albert Edward Alderman *1928–1948*	Allenton	30.10.1908	
Michael Henry John Allen *1964–1966*	Bedford	7. 1.1933	
Richard Allsop *1872–1874*	Wirksworth	10. 6.1849	20. 3.1908
Iain Stuart Anderson *1978–1987*	Derby	24. 4.1960	
William Norris Antliff *1880*	Bottesford	23. 8.1848	29. 4.1909
Thomas Riley Armstrong *1929–1950*	Clay Cross	13.10.1909	
Dr. Edward Maynard Ashcroft *1897–1906*	Chorlton	27. 9.1875	26. 2.1955
Thomas Attenborough *1871–1874*	Ilkeston	7.1833	21. 1.1907
Richard Romer Claude Baggallay *1912–1919*	Kensington	4. 5.1884	12.12.1975
William Bagguley *1905*	Ruddington	9. 9.1886	18. 4.1936
Henry Bagshaw *1887–1902*	Foolow	1. 9.1859	31. 1.1927
Frederick Arthur Barber *1907–1920*	Ilkeston	13. 5.1887	4. 6.1943
Edgar John Barlow *1976–1978*	Pretoria, S. Africa	12. 8.1940	
Alan Sedgwick Barnes *1878*	West Derby	9.10.1850	17. 5.1915
Kim John Barnett *1979–1988*	Stoke-on-Trent	17. 7.1960	
George Bainbridge Barrington *1880–1887*	Pimlico	20. 4.1857	29. 3.1942
Frank Arthur Barrs *1900–1901*	Repton	24. 4.1871	16.12.1963
Arthur Barton *1901*	Shipley	30. 9.1874	19. 1.1949
Simon John Base *1988*	Maidstone	2. 1.1960	
Mark Beardshall *1987*	Barnsley	10. 1.1962	
Edward Henry Rilands Bedford *1924*	Aston	7. 6.1903	9.10.1976
George Beet *1910–1925*	Somercotes	24. 4.1886	13.12.1946
Gordon Alfred Beet *1956–1961*	Heanor	5. 5.1939	
George Hector Cook Beet *1928–1932*	Somercotes	30. 5.1904	22. 8.1949
Geoffrey Foxall Bell *1914–1920*	Stapenhill	16. 4.1896	17. 1.1984
John William Bennett *1895–1896*	Lower Whitfield	22. 2.1864	10.11.1928
Michael Bentley *1957*	Rotherham	14. 2.1934	
Robert Berry *1959–1962*	Manchester	29. 1.1926	
John Albert Berwick *1895–1901*	Northampton	30. 7.1867	31. 7.1946
Robert Saxton Bestwick *1920–1922*	Heanor	29. 9.1899	3. 7.1980
William Bestwick *1898–1925*	Heanor	24. 2.1875	2. 5.1938
James Billyeald *1871*	Hyson Green	20. 1.1835	8. 7.1890
Dr. Frank Miller Bingham *1896*	Alfreton	17. 9.1874	22. 5.1915
William Birkett (or Burkitt) *1898–1901*	Coal Aston	27. 2.1874?	2. 5.1934?
Henry Blackwell *1895–1898*	Wirksworth	16.12.1876	24. 1.1900
Lionel Bruce Blaxland *1925–1947*	Lilleshall	25. 3.1898	29. 4.1976
Albert Blount *1912–1926*	Morton	8. 8.1889	11.11.1961
Timothy Walter Boden *1920*	Sherborne	19. 5.1901	5. 9.1969
Walter Boden *1874*	Derby	6. 8.1837	16. 9.1905
Arthur Paul Boissier *1901–1906*	Bloxham	25. 1.1881	2.10.1953
John Brian Bolus *1973–1975*	Whitkirk	31. 1.1934	
Jesse Boot *1895*	South Normanton	18. 3.1860	1. 3.1940

NAME AND EXTENT OF CAREER	BIRTHPLACE	DATE OF BIRTH	DATE OF DEATH
Anthony John Borrington *1971–1980*	Spondon	8.12.1948	
Herbert Bostock *1897*	Ilkeston	4. 5.1869	20. 2.1954
Daniel Bottom *1894–1901*	Whitwell	2.10.1864	16. 2.1937
John James Bourne *1898*	Church Gresley	2.11.1872	23.12.1952
Joseph Bowden *1909–1930*	Glossop	8.10.1884	1. 3.1958
Peter Duncan Bowler *1988*	Plymouth	30. 7.1963	
Herbert Edgar Bowmer *1909–1911*	Wirksworth	4. 7.1891	1. 6.1966
Frederick Cecil Bracey *1906–1914*	Derby	20. 7.1887	28. 3.1960
Leslie Bradbury *1971*	Matlock	19. 4.1938	
George Bradley *1875*	Derby	29. 4.1850	24. 4.1887
Frank Collis Brailsford *1958*	Hepthorne Lane	26. 8.1933	
James Brelsford *1883–1886*	Brimington	19.12.1855	24.12.1924
David Charles Brooke-Taylor *1947–1949*	Bakewell	15. 6.1920	
Geoffrey Parker Brooke-Taylor *1920*	Bakewell	25.10.1895	13. 1.1968
Joseph Brooks *1895–1896*	South Normanton	10. 9.1870	15.5.1937
Kevin Graham Brooks *1980*	Reading	15.10.1959	
Ian Broome *1984*	Bradenstoke	6. 5.1960	
Andrew Mark Brown *1985–1986*	Heanor	11.11.1964	
George Arthur Buckley *1921*	Skegby	3. 2.1889	1.12.1935
George Moreton Buckston *1905–1921*	Hope	12. 3.1881	24.11.1942
Robin Henry Rowland Buckston *1928–1939*	Kensington	10.10.1908	16. 5.1967
George Joseph Burnham *1912*	Nottingham	5.11.1878	7. 3.1971
John William Burnham *1871–1876*	Nottingham	6. 6.1839	20. 4.1914
Matthew Burrows *1884*	Chesterfield	18. 8.1855	29. 5.1893
Joseph Parkin Burton *1901*	Somercotes	10.12.1873	25. 1.1940
Oswald Burton *1901–1905*	Gorton	21. 8.1874	4. 7.1944
Walter Butterfield *1896*	Keighley	6. 8.1870	19. 7.1954
Ian Ray Buxton *1959–1973*	Cromford	17. 4.1938	
Noah Buxton *1902–1911*	Codnor	6.11.1876	26. 5.1967
Samuel William Anthony Cadman *1900–1926*	Denton	29. 1.1877	6. 5.1962
Robert McKenzie Carlin *1905–1908*	Eastwood	24. 2.1871	10. 3.1950
Donald Bryce Carr *1946–1963*	Wiesbaden, Germany	28.12.1926	
Elijah Carrington *1934–1937*	Blackwell	25. 3.1914	
Horatio Stratton Carter *1946*	Hendon	21.12.1913	
Reginald Carter *1953–1955*	Whitwell	7.11.1933	
Wilfred Carter *1920–1926*	Annesley	19. 6.1896	1.11.1975
J. or W. Cartledge *1878*	Burton-Joyce or Woodseats	c1857	8. 9.1907
Harold Cartwright *1973–1979*	Half-Way	12. 5.1951	
John Chapman *1901–1920*	Frocester	11. 3.1877	12. 8.1956
Alfred Charlesworth *1898*	Simmondley	9. 5.1865	4.12.1928
Joseph Chatterton *1884–1886*	Thornsett	14. 2.1867	7.11.1886
William Chatterton *1882–1902*	Thornsett	27.12.1861	19. 3.1913
Charles Chester *1899*	Eastwood	7. 2.1869	9. 2.1940
Charles Cyril Clarke *1929–1933*	Burton-on-Trent	22.12.1910	
John Morton Clayton *1881–1883*	Chesterfield	17.11.1857	1. 4.1938
Alfred Henry John Cochrane *1884–1886*	Mauritius	26. 1.1865	14.12.1948
Terence George Owen Cole *1913*	Llanrhaiadr	14.11.1877	15.12.1944

267

NAME AND EXTENT OF CAREER	BIRTHPLACE	DATE OF BIRTH	DATE OF DEATH
Enoch Cook *1878–1879*	Sandiacre	23. 4.1845	14. 4.1927
John Cooke *1874*	Wirksworth	7. 3.1851	22.11.1908
Archibold Henry Hedges Cooper *1902*	Cowley	14. 8.1878	13. 1.1922
Herbert Cooper *1905–1910*	Dukinfield	25.12.1883	6.12.1963
William Henry Copson *1932–1950*	Stonebroom	27. 4.1908	13. 9.1971
Bertie Oswald Corbett *1910*	Thame	15. 5.1875	30.11.1967
Cornelius John Corbett *1911–1924*	Thame	3. 8.1883	10. 4.1944
Edwin Coupe (Coup) *1885–1887*	Ripley	9. 6.1861	1. 8.1892
James Arthur Cresswell *1923–1927*	Marehay	16. 3.1903	
John Louis Crommelin-Brown *1922–1926*	Delhi, India	20.10.1888	11. 9.1953
William Cropper *1882–1887*	Brimington	27.12.1862	13. 1.1889
James Cross *1897*	Leyland	6. 2.1862	22. 3.1927
Joseph Cupitt *1905*	Barrow Hill	25. 9.1867	6. 5.1932
Gilbert Curgenven *1901–1922*	Derby	1.12.1882	26. 5.1934
Henry Grafton Curgenven *1896–1897*	Derby	22.12.1875	14. 2.1959
Dr. William Grafton Curgenven *1872–1878*	Plymouth	30.11.1841	18. 3.1910
Arthur William Cursham *1879–1880*	Wilford	14. 3.1853	24.12.1884
Frank Davidson *1897–1899*	Brimington	1.10.1872	7. 6.1951
George Arthur Davidson *1886–1898*	Brimington	29. 6.1866	8. 2.1899
Joseph Davidson *1871–1874*	Brimington	9. 8.1846	3.12.1901
John William Davis *1920*	Ironville	10. 4.1882	29.10.1963
George Owen Dawkes *1947–1961*	Leicester	19. 7.1920	
Michael John Deakin *1981*	Bury	5. 5.1957	
Irvine Dearnaley *1905–1907*	Glossop	18. 2.1877	14. 3.1965
William Barclay Delacombe *1894–1900*	Georgetown, Ascension Is.	20. 7.1860	14.10.1911
Roger Thomas DeVille *1963–1964*	Uttoxeter	21. 1.1935	
Stanley Patrick Dickinson *1909*	Norton	7. 3.1890	25. 6.1972
James Joseph Disney *1881–1887*	Butterley	20.11.1859	24. 6.1934
Dr. Francis Dixon *1885*	Derby	31. 7.1855	20. 8.1943
Kenneth William Cecil Dobson *1920*	Barrow-on-Trent	28. 8.1900	6. 3.1960
Frank Dudley Docker *1881–1882*	Smethwick	26. 8.1862	8. 7.1944
Ludford (Charles) Docker *1881–1886*	Smethwick	26.11.1860	1. 8.1940
Ralph Docker *1879*	Harborne	31. 8.1855	7. 7.1910
Stephen Doughty *1880–1886*	Staveley	16.10.1865	11.11.1929
John (Thom Clarke) Eadie *1882*	Burton-on-Trent	25. 9.1861	19. 8.1923
William Stewart Eadie *1885–1899*	Burton-on-Trent	27.11.1864	20. 9.1914
George Burrill Earl *1883*	Melbourne	7. 8.1859	20. 4.1933
Alwyn Eato *1950–1955*	Duckmanton	15. 2.1929	
John Drennan Eggar *1946–1954*	Nowshera, India	1.12.1916	3. 5.1983
Charles Standish Elliott *1932–1953*	Bolsover	24. 4.1912	
Harry Elliott *1920–1947*	Scarcliffe	2.11.1891	2. 2.1976
William Ellis *1898–1906*	Whitwell	28. 8.1876	22. 1.1931
Robert Else *1901–1903*	Leawood	17.11.1876	16. 9.1955
Edward Estridge *1874*	Hounslow	28. 4.1843	30. 8.1919
Charles Evans *1894–1895*	Whittington Moor	19. 2.1866	14. 1.1956
Henry Evans *1878–1882*	Stoneyford	8. 7.1857	30. 7.1920
Thomas Evans *1883*	Stoneyford	3. 6.1852	2.12.1916
Edward Evershed *1898*	Stapenhill	3.11.1867	18. 2.1957

NAME AND EXTENT OF CAREER	BIRTHPLACE	DATE OF BIRTH	DATE OF DEATH
Sydney Herbert Evershed *1880–1901*	Burton-on-Trent	13. 1.1861	7. 3.1937
Wallis (W) Evershed *1882–1884*	Stapenhill	10. 5.1863	8. 5.1911
Percy George Exham *1883*	Cork, Ireland	26. 6.1859	7.10.1922
John Arthur Eyre *1908*	North Wingfield	25. 7.1885	12. 6.1964
John Richard Eyre *1963–1967*	Glossop	13. 6.1944	
Thomas John Peter Eyre *1959–1972*	Brough	17.10.1939	
Mark Andrew Fell *1985*	Newark	17.11.1960	
Roger John Finney *1982–1988*	Darley Dale	2. 8.1960	
John Fisher *1921–1922*	Hodthorpe	4. 8.1897	22. 6.1964
Charles Barnett Fleming *1907*	Derby	28. 2.1887	22. 9.1918
Henry Fletcher *1907–1908*	Clay Cross	25. 7.1882	27.10.1937
Thomas Fletcher *1906*	Heanor	15. 6.1881	29. 9.1954
Joseph Flint *1872–1879*	Wirksworth	23. 4.1840	2.11.1912
Louis Edward Flint *1919–1920*	Ripley	10. 1.1895	3. 4.1958
Edward Francis Walwyn Foley *1871*	Derby	6.10.1851	21.10.1923
Neville Montague Ford *1926–1934*	Repton	17.11.1906	
Thomas Forester (Forrester) *1902–1920*	Clay Cross	21. 9.1873	27.12.1927
Rev. Arthur Francis Emilius Forman *1877–1882*	Gibraltar	26. 7.1850	13. 2.1905
Frederick Gerald Forman *1911*	Chellaston	30. 8.1884	8.12.1960
Thomas Foster *1873–1884*	Mill Town	15.12.1848	22. 3.1929
William Henry Foulke *1900* (Foulk at birth, Foulkes at death)	Old Park	12. 4.1874	1. 5.1916
William Peter Fowler *1983–1985*	St. Helens	13. 3.1959	
Michael Campbell Frederick *1949*	St. Peter, Barbados	6. 5.1927	
Charles Redfern Freeman *1911*	Overseal	22. 8.1887	16. 3.1956
George Frost *1872–1880*	Wirksworth	16.10.1848	12.12.1913
John Henry Frost *1874*	Wirksworth	30. 1.1847	1.11.1916
Walter Fullwood *1946*	Holmewood	8. 2.1907	1.1988
John Brian Furniss *1955–1956*	Baslow	16.11.1934	
William Roy Genders *1946*	Dore	21. 1.1913	28. 9.1985
Peter John Keith Gibbs *1966–1972*	Buglawton	17. 8.1944	
Dr. Ian Gibson *1957–1961*	Glossop	15. 8.1936	3. 5.1963
John Dudley (Harwood) Gilbert *1930–1936*	Chellaston	8.10.1910	
Clifford Gladwin *1939–1958*	Doe Lea	3. 4.1916	10. 4.1988
Joseph Gladwin *1914–1919*	Doe Lea	6. 9.1890	8. 9.1962
Michael Glenn *1975–1976*	Belper	14. 6.1956	
Steven Clive Goldsmith *1988*	Ashford	19.12.1964	
John Goodall *1895–1896*	London	19. 6.1863	20. 5.1942
George William Goodwin *1921*	Chesterton	7. 9.1898	
Edward James Gothard *1947–1948*	Burton-on-Trent	1.10.1904	17. 1.1979
Thomas Gould *1896–1897*	Brassington	26. 9.1863	30. 3.1948
James Martin Hilary Graham-Brown *1977–1978*	Thetford	11. 7.1951	
George Grainger *1909–1921*	Morton	11.11.1887	17. 8.1977
David John Green *1953–1960*	Burton-on-Trent	18.12.1935	
George Green *1903–1907*	Hasland	13. 4.1880	25.11.1940
Dove Gregory *1871–1872* (real name Gregory Dove)	Sutton-in-Ashfield	9. 2.1837	21. 5.1873

NAME AND EXTENT OF CAREER	BIRTHPLACE	DATE OF BIRTH	DATE OF DEATH
George Robert Gregory *1899–1910*	Pilsley	27. 8.1878	28.11.1958
Frank Alexander Griffith *1988*	Walthamstow	15. 8.1968	
Peter John Hacker *1982*	Lenton Abbey	16. 7.1952	
Bert Hall *1902*			
Derek Hall *1955–1958*	Bolsover	21. 2.1932	13. 3.1983
Ian William Hall *1959–1972*	Sutton Scarsdale	27.12.1939	
John Peter Hall *1895–1897*	Worksop	20. 8.1874	9.11.1925
Thomas Auckland Hall *1949–1952*	Durham	19. 8.1930	21. 4.1984
Walter Hall *1882–1886*	Whitfield	27.11.1861	23. 4.1919
Thomas Haydn Hallam *1906–1907*	Pilsley	12. 4.1881	24.11.1958
Arnold Hamer *1950–1960*	Huddersfield	8.12.1916	
John Harry Hampshire *1982–1983*	Thurnscoe	10. 2.1941	
Joseph (William) Hancock *1897–1900*	Old Tupton	26.11.1876	23. 5.1939
James Handford *1910*	Hayfield	1. 2.1890	14. 8.1948
Raymond Leslie Hanson *1973*	Chesterfield	12. 4.1951	
Solomon Hardy *1898*	Ilkeston	18. 5.1863	5. 7.1931
John Frank Harvey *1963–1972*	Cambridge	27. 9.1939	
Ashley John Harvey-Walker *1971–1978*	East Ham	21. 7.1944	
George Hay *1875–1886*	Staveley	28. 1.1851	4.10.1913
Francis Rhead Heath *1924–1925*	Swadlincote	30.10.1894	19. 9.1967
John Stanley Heath *1924–1925*	Swadlincote	30. 8.1891	1. 9.1972
Michael Hendrick *1969–1981*	Darley Dale	22.10.1948	
William Hickton *1871–1878*	Hardstoft	24.12.1842	25. 2.1900
Thomas Atkinson Higson *1899–1910*	Stockport	19.11.1873	3. 8.1949
Thomas Atkinson Higson jnr *1932–1935*	Whaley Bridge	25. 3.1911	
Alan Hill *1972–1986*	Buxworth	29. 6.1950	
Maurice Hill *1966–1967*	Scunthorpe	14. 9.1935	
Basil Samuel Hill Hill-Wood *1919–1925*	Chelsea	5. 2.1900	3. 7.1954
Charles Kerrison Hill Hill-Wood *1928–1930*	Hoxne	5. 6.1907	21. 9.1988
Denis John Charles Hill Hill-Wood *1928–1929*	Hoxne	25. 6.1906	4. 5.1982
Wilfred William Hill Hill-Wood *1919–1936*	Chelsea	8. 9.1901	10.10.1980
Amos Hind *1876–1877*	Calverton	1. 2.1849	27. 4.1931
Gilbert Frank Hodgkinson *1935–1946*	Derby	18. 2.1913	7. 1.1987
J. Hodkinson *1882*	Findern?		
Arthur Hogg *1905–1906*	Ripley	20. 6.1877	21. 4.1956
Stanley Mitton Holden *1910–1920*	Chesterfield	25. 1.1886	10. 5.1971
Michael Anthony Holding *1983–1988*	Half Way Tree, W.I.	16. 2.1954	
James Horsley *1919–1925*	Melbourne	4. 1.1890	13. 2.1976
Thomas Douglas Hounsfield *1938–1939*	Hackenthorpe	29. 4.1910	
Edward Outram Houseman *1897*	Dronfield	19. 3.1869	10. 4.1942
Thomas Howarth *1873*	Glossop	10. 4.1845	12.10.1897
Albert Howcroft *1908–1910*	Cliffe	27.12.1882	7. 3.1955
Norton Montrésor Hughes-Hallett *1913–1914*	Melbourne	18. 4.1895	26. 5.1985
John Joseph Hulme *1887–1903*	Church Gresley	30. 6.1862	11. 7.1940
Rev. William John Humble *1873–1876*	Sutton Scarsdale	9.12.1846	1. 7.1924
Joseph Humphries *1899–1914*	Stonebroom	19. 5.1876	7. 5.1946
Samuel Walter Hunt *1936*	Doe Lea	9. 1.1909	2. 8.1963
Frederic Cecil Hunter *1905–1907*	Glossop	23. 8.1886	21. 7.1926
Colin Noel Bickley Hurt *1914*	Darley Dale	16.12.1893	31.12.1972

NAME AND EXTENT OF CAREER	BIRTHPLACE	DATE OF BIRTH	DATE OF DEATH
James (Metcalf) Hutchinson *1920–1931*	New Tupton	29.11.1896	
Albert Brian Jackson *1963–1968*	Kettleshulme	21. 8.1933	
Anthony Henry Mather Jackson *1920–1927*	London	9.11.1899	11.10.1983
Geoffrey Laird Jackson *1914*	Birkenhead	10. 1.1894	9. 4.1917
Guy Rolfe Jackson *1919–1936*	Ankerbold	23. 6.1896	21. 2.1966
Herbert Leslie Jackson *1947–1963*	Whitwell	5. 4.1921	
Leonard Jackson *1877–1882*	Norton Woodseats	8. 4.1848	21. 3.1887
Martin Jean-Jacques *1986–1988*	Soufrière, W.I.	2. 7.1960	
Stephen Thomas Jefferies *1982*	Cape Town, S.A.	8.12.1959	
Henry Francis Dönhoff Jelf *1910–1911*	Aldershot	27. 8.1877	18. 4.1944
Hon. William Monk Jervis *1873*	London	25. 1.1827	25. 3.1909
Hubert Laurence Johnson *1949–1966*	Pine Hill, Barbados	8.11.1927	
Duncan Alexander Johnston *1882*	Edinburgh	25. 6.1847	22.10.1931
Henry Guy Bowen Jordan *1926*	Buxton	10. 6.1898	5.10.1981
Frederick William Keeton *1876–1880*	Mosbrough	26.10.1855	27.11.1911
John Martin Kelly *1950–1960*	Bacup	19. 3.1922	13.11.1979
Richard Kenward *1899*	Hastings	23. 5.1875	24.12.1957
Peter Noel Kirsten *1978–1982*	Pietermaritzburg, S.A.	14. 5.1955	
George Richmond Langdale *1936–1937*	Thornaby-on-Tees	11. 3.1916	
Samuel Thomas Langton *1909–1910*	Parkgate	24. 1.1886	10. 7.1918
Albert Edward Lawton *1900–1910*	Dukinfield	31. 3.1879	25.12.1955
Charles Lee *1954–1964*	Rotherham	17. 3.1924	
Garnet Morley Lee *1924–1933*	Calverton	7. 6.1887	29. 2.1976
Colin Leech *1922*	Hayfield	30. 8.1889	6. 3.1961
Thomas Limb *1878*	Eastwood	25. 2.1850	21. 2.1901
Douglas Valentine Linathan *1920*	Woodhouse	29. 5.1885	17.12.1932
John Wilton Lister *1978–1979*	Darlington	1. 4.1959	
William Locker *1894–1903*	Long Eaton	16. 2.1866	15. 8.1952
Escott Frith Loney *1925–1927*	Bristol	21. 7.1903	19. 6.1982
Charles Lowe *1909–1912*	Whitwell	23. 6.1890	
George Lowe *1949–1953*	Mastin Moor	25. 5.1915	
Charles Harry Lyon *1902*	Rocester	18. 3.1878	3.12.1959
Rodney John McCurdy *1979*	Melbourne, Australia	30.12.1959	
John Archibald McDonald *1905–1906*	Belper	29. 5.1882	4. 6.1961
Alan James McLellan *1978–1979*	Ashton-under-Lyne	2. 9.1958	
Stuart Thomas McMillan *1922–1924*	Leicester	17. 9.1896	27. 9.1963
Bernard Joseph Michael Maher *1981–1988*	Hillingdon	11. 2.1958	
Devon Eugene Malcolm *1984–1988*	Kingston, Jamaica	22. 2.1963	
George Maltby *1905*	South Normanton	1.10.1876	30. 7.1924
Samuel Malthouse *1894–1895*	Whitwell	13.10.1857	7. 2.1931
William Norman Malthouse *1919–1920*	Whitwell	16.12.1890	10. 5.1961
Christopher Peter Marks *1967–1969*	Hanley	17. 7.1946	
Joseph Marlow *1879–1886*	Bulwell	12.12.1854	8. 6.1923
George (Smith) Marple *1901*	Chester	14. 8.1868	12. 8.1932

NAME AND EXTENT OF CAREER	BIRTHPLACE	DATE OF BIRTH	DATE OF DEATH
Christopher Marples *1985–1986*	Chesterfield	3. 8.1964	
George Marples *1905*	Attercliffe	30. 5.1883	30.12.1947
Arthur Marsden *1910*	Buxton	28.10.1880	31. 7.1916
George Allen Marsden *1894–1898*	Wirksworth	28. 6.1869	7. 1.1938
Frederick Eric Marsh *1946–1949*	Bolsover	17. 7.1920	
Joseph Marshall *1887*	Mosbrough	25. 7.1862	15. 1.1915
Edmund Anthony Jefferson Maynard *1880–1887*	Chesterfield	10. 2.1861	10. 1.1931
Alan John Mellor *1978–1980*	Horninglow	4. 7.1959	
Charles Middleton *1896–1903*	Leeds	21.12.1869	5. 2.1938
Geoffrey Miller *1973–1986*	Chesterfield	8. 9.1952	
David Millner *1960–1963*	Dove Holes	24. 7.1938	
Parvez Jamil Mir *1975*	Dacca, Pakistan	24. 9.1953	
Thomas Bignall Mitchell *1928–1939*	Creswell	4. 9.1902	
Keith Frederick Mohan *1957–1958*	Glossop	11. 6.1935	
Dallas Gordon Moir *1981–1985*	Imtarfa, Malta	13. 4.1957	
Derek Clifton Morgan *1950–1969*	Muswell Hill	26. 2.1929	
Alan Morris *1974–1978*	Staveley	23. 8.1953	
John Edward Morris *1982–1988*	Crewe	1. 4.1964	
Ole Henrik Mortensen *1983–1988*	Vejle, Denmark	29. 1.1958	
Arthur Morton *1901*	Salford	27. 3.1882	21. 2.1970
Arthur Morton *1903–1926*	Mellor	7. 5.1883	18.12.1935
Eric Claude Moses *1911*	Johannesburg, S.A.	18. 7.1893	10. 7.1971
Frank Mycroft *1894–1895*	Furnace	30. 6.1873	16. 9.1900
Thomas Mycroft *1877–1885*	Brimington	28. 3.1848	13. 8.1911
William Mycroft *1873–1885*	Brimington	1. 1.1841	19. 6.1894
Ernest Needham *1901–1912*	Newbold Moor	21. 1.1873	7. 3.1936
Joseph Needham *1883*	Flagg	9. 1.1862	30. 8.1889
Charles Niel Newcombe *1910*	Yarmouth	16. 3.1891	27.12.1915
Paul Geoffrey Newman *1980–1988*	Evington	10. 1.1959	
Frederick Arthur Newton *1909–1919*	Denaby Main	16. 9.1890	8. 8.1924
Charles Ernest Nornable *1909*	Norton	25.12.1886	21. 4.1970
William Farrand Oates *1959–1965*	Aston	11. 6.1929	
John O'Connor *1900*	Pinxton	23. 2.1867	13. 7.1936
Timothy Joseph Gerard O'Gorman *1987–1988*	Woking	15. 1.1967	
Stephen Oldham *1980–1983*	High Green	26. 7.1948	
James Oldknow *1901*	Denby	12. 3.1873	10. 9.1944
Leonard Oliver *1908–1924*	Glossop	18.10.1886	22. 1.1948
Charles Augustus Ollivierre *1901–1907*	Kingstown, St. Vincent, W.I.	20. 6.1876	25. 3.1949
George Osborne *1879–1883*			
Michael Harry Page *1964–1975*	Blackpool	17. 6.1941	
William Page *1881–1882*	Caverswall	29. 4.1847	27. 9.1904
William Ferguson Parrington *1926*	Sunderland	1.11.1889	7. 5.1980
Rev. Wilfred Ernest Granville Payton *1949*	Beeston	27.12.1913	
Frederick George Peach *1907–1925*	Repton	2.11.1882	15. 1.1965
William Peach *1905*	Timberland Fen	6. 5.1875	29. 1.1959
Lawrence Ivor Pearson *1946*	Darnall	25. 1.1922	
Hubert Selwyn Pink *1900*	Chapel-en-le-Frith	12.11.1878	25.11.1946

NAME AND EXTENT OF CAREER	BIRTHPLACE	DATE OF BIRTH	DATE OF DEATH
John Thomas Brown Dumelow Platts 1871–1884	Chellaston	23.11.1848	6. 8.1898
Alfred Vardy Pope 1930–1939	Tibshelf	15. 8.1909	
George Henry Pope 1933–1948	Tibshelf	27. 1.1911	
Harold Pope 1939–1946	Chesterfield	10. 5.1919	
George Porter 1881–1896	Kilburn	17. 8.1861	15. 7.1908
Richard Pratt 1923–1924	Lower Broughton	23. 6.1896	10.10.1982
William Prince 1898	Somercotes	28. 3.1868	1. 6.1948
Henry Fox Purdy 1906–1919	Brimington	17. 1.1883	21. 2.1943
John Henry Purdy 1896–1906	Brimington	23. 9.1871	19. 5.1938
Henry William Radford 1920	Derby	19. 6.1896	29.11.1972
George Ratcliffe 1887	Ilkeston	1856	7. 3.1928
George Ratcliffe 1919	Derby	9. 2.1882	31.12.1949
Walter Reader-Blackton 1914–1921	Shirland	4. 7.1895	1. 1.1976
Charles Regan 1877	Barnsley	11. 5.1842	17. 5.1921
Alan Chambers Revill 1946–1957	Sheffield	27. 3.1923	
Thomas Frederick Revill 1913–1920	Bolsover	9. 5.1892	29. 3.1979
Albert Ennion Groucott Rhodes 1937–1954	Tintwistle	10.10.1916	17.10.1983
Harold John Rhodes 1953–1975	Hadfield	22. 7.1936	
Arthur Walker Richardson 1928–1936	Quarndon	4. 3.1907	29. 7.1983
Bertram Harold Richardson 1950–1953	Ashton-under-Lyne	12. 3.1932	
George William Richardson 1959–1965	Marylebone	26. 4.1938	
John Richardson 1878–1883	Duckmanton	17. 3.1856	19. 2.1940
Samuel Richardson 1871–1878	Derby	24. 5.1844	18. 1.1938
Thomas Haden Richardson 1895	Tutbury	4. 7.1865	10.12.1923
Richard Binns Rickman 1906–1911	Doncaster	6. 5.1881	22.11.1940
William Rigley 1873–1882	Eastwood	24. 3.1852	15. 3.1897
Joseph Rimmer 1949	Langwith	26. 1.1925	
Bruce Roberts 1984–1988	Lusaka, N. Rhodesia	30. 5.1962	
Charles Frederick Root 1910–1920	Somercotes	16. 4.1890	20. 1.1954
Alfred Rose 1924	Glossop	15. 2.1894	21. 6.1985
Lawrence George Rowe 1974	Kingston, Jamaica	8. 1.1949	
Christopher Francis Baines Paul Rudd 1986–1987	Sutton Coldfield	9.12.1963	
Frederick Edward Rumsey 1970	Stepney	4.12.1935	
Philip Edgar Russell 1965–1985	Ilkeston	9. 5.1944	
Reginald Talbot Ryder 1903	Crewe	18. 6.1875	6.11.1923
Richard Sale 1908–1912	Broughty Ferry	21. 6.1889	7. 9.1970
Richard Sale jnr 1949–1954	Shrewsbury	4.10.1919	3. 2.1987
Thomas Gothard Selby 1885	North Wingfield	19. 2.1851	6.11.1924
Arthur Severn 1919–1920	Alfreton	23. 6.1893	10. 1.1949
Francis Joseph Shacklock 1884–1885	Crich	22. 9.1861	3. 5.1937
Wilfred Shardlow 1925–1928	Clowne	30. 9.1902	21. 6.1956
Rajeshwar Sharma 1985–1988	Nairobi, Kenya	17. 6.1962	
Philip John Sharpe 1975–1976	Baildon	12.12.1936	
Henry Shaw 1875–1884	Mansfield	21. 5.1854	8.11.1932
Kenneth Arthur Shearwood 1949	Derby	5. 9.1921	

NAME AND EXTENT OF CAREER	BIRTHPLACE	DATE OF BIRTH	DATE OF DEATH
Arthur West Sherwin 1908	Derby	22. 7.1879	10.10.1947
Charles Bakewell Sherwin 1907	Derby	9. 8.1877	8. 6.1950
Howard Sherwin 1937	Bolsover	22. 7.1911	
William Louis Shipton 1884	Buxton	19. 3.1861	21.10.1941
John David Short 1957–1960	Chesterfield	13. 6.1934	
Abraham Shuker 1874–1882	Stockton, Salop	6. 7.1848	11. 2.1909
Alan Frank Skinner 1931–1938	Brighton	22. 4.1913	28. 2.1982
David Anthony Skinner 1947–1949	Duffield	22. 3.1920	
Archibald Gilbert Slater 1911–1931	Pilsley	22.11.1890	22. 7.1949
Henry Slater 1882–1887	Heanor	23. 2.1855	20.11.1916
Herbert Slater 1907	Langley Mill	11.11.1881	2.12.1958
Alfort/Alfred Smith 1873–1880	Bury	7. 7.1846	21.12.1908
Denis Smith 1927–1952	Somercotes	24. 1.1907	12. 9.1979
David Henry Kilner Smith 1965–1970	Shipley	29. 6.1940	
Edwin Smith 1951–1971	Grassmoor	2. 1.1934	
Harry Watson-Smith 1920	Chesterfield	30. 9.1886	24. 6.1955
John Smith 1871–1878	Clifton, Ashbourne	27.10.1841	26.11.1898
Lemuel Strutt Tugby Smith 1909	Tibshelf	5. 6.1880	30.12.1927
Robert Posnett Smith 1871–1884 (later changed name to Stevens)	Sawley	1.11.1848	1. 5.1899
Willie Smith 1913	Gringley-on-the-Hill	12. 5.1885	8. 5.1964
Maurice Desmond Snape 1949	Creswell	7. 7.1923	
John Dunlop Southern 1919–1934	Derby	5.11.1899	7. 2.1972
Unwin Sowter 1871–1876	Derby	22. 4.1839	14. 4.1910
Guy Ratcliff Sparrow 1905	Aston	2. 7.1877	4. 1.1958
Harry Spencer 1895			4.12.1936
Ernest Stapleton 1902	New Basford	1. 1.1869	14.12.1938
David Stanley Steele 1979–1981	Bradeley	29. 9.1941	
Albert Steeples 1899	Somercotes	28. 7.1870	14. 8.1945
Richard Steeples 1897	Somercotes	30. 4.1873	2. 8.1946
George Robert Stephenson 1967–1968	Derby	19.11.1942	
George Stanley Stevenson 1904	Derby	20. 7.1876	25. 7.1938
Keith Stevenson 1974–1977	Derby	6.10.1950	
Michael Hamilton Stevenson 1950–1952	Chinley	13. 6.1927	
Harry Storer 1895	Butterley	24. 7.1870	25. 4.1908
Harry Storer jnr 1920–1936	West Derby	2. 2.1898	1. 9.1967
William Storer 1887–1905	Butterley	25. 1.1867	28. 2.1912
Henry Street 1887	Riddings	18. 4.1863	12. 3.1953
James Stubbings 1880–1885	Whitwell	27. 4.1856	17. 7.1912
Walter Stubbings 1900	Whitwell	4. 9.1870	28.11.1949
Henry Emanuel Sugden 1882	Edmonton	16. 7.1859	4. 9.1935
Frank Howe Sugg 1884–1886	Ilkeston	11. 1.1862	29. 5.1933
Walter Sugg 1884–1902	Ilkeston	21. 5.1860	21. 5.1933
Raymond Swallow 1959–1963	Southwark	15. 6.1935	
Frederick William Swarbrook 1967–1979	Derby	17.12.1950	
Robert Stephen Swindell 1972–1977	Derby	22. 1.1950	
Eric Sykes 1925–1932	Bolsover	23. 6.1906	
Cecil Frederick Tate 1928	Gillingham	1. 5.1908	

NAME AND EXTENT OF CAREER	BIRTHPLACE	DATE OF BIRTH	DATE OF DEATH
Francis Henry Taylor *1908–1911*	Wirksworth	14. 6.1890	6.12.1963
Jonathan Paul Taylor *1984–1986*	Ashby-de-la-Zouch	8. 8.1964	
Robert William Taylor *1961–1983*	Stoke-on-Trent	17. 7.1941	
William Thomas Taylor *1905–1910*	Wirksworth	14. 4.1885	17. 8.1976
William Holloway Thompson *1908*	Spondon	24. 6.1882	19.10.1954
Frederick Thornhill *1876*	Beeston	25. 9.1846	23. 7.1876
John Tilson *1871–1876*	Ilkeston	27. 3.1845	4.11.1895
Norman Douglas Todd *1906–1908*	Hetton-le-Hole	11. 6.1884	12. 5.1959
Dr. John Derek Williams Tomlinson *1946*	South Normanton	26. 3.1926	
William James Vincent Tomlinson *1920–1924*	Winshill	10. 8.1901	16. 5.1984
Harry Gillespie Topham *1881*	Ladbroke	17. 2.1862	28. 2.1925
Arnold Frederick Townsend *1934–1950*	Long Eaton	29. 3.1912	
Leslie Fletcher Townsend *1922–1939*	Long Eaton	8. 6.1903	
Colin John Tunnicliffe *1973–1983*	Derby	11. 8.1951	
Herbert Turland *1924*	Stapleford	29. 8.1894	
Allen Turner *1920*	Holmewood	24.10.1891	7. 1.1961
John Tye *1874*	Bulwell	10. 7.1848	19.11.1905
Patrick Vaulkhard *1946–1952*	Nottingham	15. 9.1911	
Srinivasaraghavan Venkataraghavan *1973–1975*	Madras, India	21. 4.1945	
Mark Wakefield *1987*	Rochdale	17.11.1968	
George Godfrey Walkden *1905–1906*	Derby	10. 3.1883	16. 5.1923
George Glossop Walker *1881–1898*	Harthill	14. 6.1860	11. 1.1908
Capt. Niel Alexander McDonald Walker *1931–1936*	Poona, India	22. 8.1895	10. 8.1960
Stanley George Walker *1932*	Pinxton	18. 5.1908	
William Alfred Wallis *1906*	Long Eaton	14.12.1878	12.11.1939
Conrad Adolphus Wallroth *1879*	Lee	17. 5.1851	22. 2.1926
John Walters *1977–1980*	Brampton	7. 8.1949	
William Walton *1887*	Glossop	7. 8.1862	16. 2.1925
Alan Ward *1966–1976*	Dronfield	10. 8.1947	
John Michael Ward *1973–1975*	Sandon	14. 9.1948	
Rev. Leonard Foster Ward *1866*	Oldham	24. 3.1886	1. 9.1945
Alan Esmond Warner *1985–1988*	Winson Green	12. 5.1957	
Arnold R. Warren *1897–1920*	Codnor	2. 4.1875	3. 9.1951
Horace Wass *1929*	Chesterfield	26. 8.1903	
Richard Martin Watson *1947*	Bakewell	31.12.1921	
Andrew Watts *1982–1983*	Chapeltown	4.10.1960	
David Webster *1975*	Sheffield	22. 5.1946	
Frederick Webster *1906*	Ecclesall	19. 1.1885	23. 3.1938
William Webster *1911*	Dinnington	1880	10. 3.1931
Christopher Whyatt *1976*	Old Whittington	12. 6.1954	
Archibald Wickstead *1911–1912*	Meltham Mills	6.11.1884	1. 2.1966
Albert Widdowson *1894*	Bingham	31. 3.1864	28. 4.1938
Harold Wild *1913–1920*	Hadfield	3. 2.1891	8. 8.1977
David Wilde *1971–1972*	Glossop	3. 7.1950	
Christopher Peter Wilkins *1970–1972*	Kingwilliamstown, S.A.	31. 7.1944	
Guy Longfield Willatt *1950–1956*	Nottingham	7. 5.1918	

NAME AND EXTENT OF CAREER	BIRTHPLACE	DATE OF BIRTH	DATE OF DEATH
Rev. Arthur Alfred Wilmot *1871*	Chaddesden	14. 2.1845	12. 5.1876
William Wilmot *1897–1901*	Denby	25.12.1869	19. 5.1957
Guy Denis Wilson *1902–1905*	Melbourne	30.11.1882	30.11.1917
Robert Colin Wincer *1978–1980*	Portsmouth	2. 4.1952	
Arthur John Wood *1911–1912*	Derby	7. 2.1892	1. 3.1951
Arthur Machin Wood *1879*	Pye Bridge	21. 2.1861	25. 8.1947
Barrie Wood *1980–1983*	Ossett	26.12.1942	
Lindsay Jonathan Wood *1986*	Ruislip	12. 5.1961	
Samuel Hill Wood *1894–1902* (later Sir Samuel Hill Hill-Wood)	Glossop	21. 3.1872	4. 1.1949
Albert William Woodland *1920*	Conisbrough	10. 6.1895	31. 1.1955
William Wood-Sims *1879–1886*	Ironville	10. 2.1858	30.11.1926
Kenneth Alexander Woodward *1909*	Liverpool	23.12.1874	24.12.1960
Thomas Stanley Worthington *1924–1947*	Bolsover	21. 8.1905	31. 8.1973
Frank Wright *1899* (or Francis Moult Wright)	Ilkeston	4. 5.1870	9.12.1943
Henry Fitzherbert Wright *1904–1905*	Swanwick	9.10.1870	23. 2.1947
James Wright *1898–1906*	Newbold	25. 3.1874	20. 8.1961
John Geoffrey Wright *1977–1988*	Darfield, New Zealand	5. 7.1954	
Levi George Wright *1883–1909*	Oxford	15. 1.1862	11. 1.1953
William John Wright *1932*	Danesmoor	24. 2.1909	12. 8.1988
Gerald Wyatt *1954–1960*	New Mills	4. 6.1933	
George Yates *1883*	Bolsover	21. 8.1858	21. 7.1933
John Henry Young *1899–1910*	Melbourne	2. 7.1876	2. 8.1913
John William Young *1894*	Clay Cross	24. 5.1863	9. 5.1933

CAREER RECORDS OF DERBYSHIRE PLAYERS IN FIRST-CLASS MATCHES FOR THE COUNTY

				Batting						Bowling				
Name	M	Inns	NO	Runs	HS	Avge	100s	Runs	Wkts	Avge	Best	5wI	Ct	St
Ackroyd A.	11	18	0	70	15	3.89	0	646	19	34.00	4/63	—	5	—
Adams C. J.	1	1	0	21	21	21.00	0						1	—
Alderman A. E.	318	529	52	12376	175	25.95	12	171	4	42.75	3/37	—	202	2
Allen M. H. J.	31	39	11	224	38*	8.00	0	1447	52	27.83	7/65	3	28	—
Allsop R.	3	5	0	42	33	8.40	0						3	—
Anderson I. S.	134	214	27	4611	112	24.65	2	1087	20	54.35	4/35	—	104	—
Antliff W. N.	2	4	0	17	5	4.25	0							—
Armstrong T. R.	58	83	33	314	28*	6.28	0	3239	133	24.35	7/36	7	18	—
Ashcroft E. M.	100	169	13	4530	162	29.04	8	1186	24	49.42	5/18	1	31	—
Attenborough T.	6	9	0	72	27	8.00	0	29	2	14.50	1/9	—	2	—
Baggallay R. R. C.	31	59	1	688	88	11.86	0						25	—
Bagguley W.	1	1	0	5	5	5.00	0						—	—
Bagshaw H.	123	215	9	5413	127*	26.28	7	2119	73	29.03	5/18	2	36	—
Barber F. A.	5	10	1	30	10	3.33	0	267	9	29.67	2/19	—	3	—
Barlow E. J.	60	98	8	2813	217	31.26	3	2108	98	21.51	5/63	1	81	—
Barnes A. S.	3	5	1	14	7*	3.50	0						—	—
Barnett K. J.	215	338	29	11412	239*	36.93	25	2886	65	44.40	6/115	1	143	—
Barrington G. B.	24	46	1	440	50	9.78	0	27	1	27.00	1/27	—	7	—
Barrs F. A.	3	5	0	68	58	13.60	0	29	1	29.00	1/17	—	—	—
Barton A.	3	6	0	24	7	4.00	0	61	0	—	—	—	—	—
Base S. J.	9	10	3	59	15	8.42	0	735	22	33.40	4/74	—	3	—
Beardshall M.	8	8	3	47	25	9.40	0	572	12	47.66	4/68	—	2	—
Bedford E. H. R.	1	2	0	3	3	1.50	0						—	—
Beet G.	47	87	9	1268	92*	16.26	0	27	0	—	—	—	58	11
Beet G. A.	6	7	2	36	17	7.20	0	100	2	50.00	1/42	—	3	—
Beet G. H. C.	5	9	1	102	35*	12.75	0						3	1
Bell G. F.	5	9	0	69	20	7.67	0						2	—
Bennett J. W.	16	25	2	257	43	11.17	0	701	35	20.03	5/8	3	7	—
Bentley M.	1	2	0	12	10	6.00	0						—	—
Berry R.	54	67	27	292	40	7.30	0	2906	97	29.96	6/100	3	35	—
Berwick J. A.	16	29	6	138	27	6.00	0	892	24	37.17	5/82	2	7	—
Bestwick R. S.	5	9	1	29	10	3.63	0	151	2	75.50	2/47	—	2	—
Bestwick W.	321	521	183	1605	39	4.75	0	30881	1452	21.27	10/40	104	89	—
Billyeald J.	1	2	1	15	11*	15.00	0						—	—
Bingham F. M.	1	2	0	17	11	8.50	0						—	—
Birkett W.	4	7	0	20	10	2.86	0	115	3	38.33	2/28	—	—	—
Blackwell H.	4	6	2	41	15	10.25	0	105	4	26.25	2/23	—	1	—
Blaxland L. B.	19	31	1	483	64	16.10	0	18	0	—	—	—	7	—
Blount A.	7	11	2	52	17	5.78	0	215	7	30.71	4/53	—	3	—
Boden T. W.	1	2	0	14	9	7.00	0						—	—
Boden W.	1	2	1	2	2*	2.00	0						—	—
Boissier A. P.	2	4	0	13	6	3.25	0	32	2	16.00	2/32	—	—	—
Bolus J. B.	64	117	14	3279	151	—	4	—	—	—	—	—	17	—

Name	M	Inns	NO	Runs	HS	Avge	100s	Runs	Wkts	Avge	Best	5wI	Ct	St
Boot J.	1	2	0	4	4	2.00	0						2	—
Borrington A. J.	122	203	24	4230	137	23.63	3	19	0	—	—	—	57	—
Bostock H.	4	6	2	75	36	18.75	0						1	—
Bottom D.	3	5	0	22	9	4.40	0	62	1	62.00	1/50	—	1	—
Bourne J. J.	1	1	0	6	6	6.00	0	103	3	34.33	2/63	—	—	—
Bowden J.	231	395	25	7613	120	20.58	4	54	1	54.00	1/0	—	75	—
Bowler P. D.	24	42	5	1725	159*	46.62	4	577	7	82.42	2/63	—	13	—
Bowmer H. E.	3	6	0	6	3	1.00	0						1	—
Bracey F. C.	77	132	54	562	28	7.21	0	3122	132	23.65	6/36	5	20	—
Bradbury L.	1							53	1	53.00	1/53	—	1	—
Bradley G.	1	2	0	1	1	0.50	0	17	0	—	—	—	—	—
Brailsford F. C.	3	5	0	41	14	8.20	0	2	1	2.00	1/2	—	1	—
Brelsford J.	8	14	1	56	16	4.30	0	482	24	20.08	5/31	1	4	—
Brooke-Taylor D. C.	15	26	1	375	61*	15.00	0						6	—
Brooke-Taylor G. P.	1	2	0	44	30	22.00	0						—	—
Brooks J.	5	7	4	8	6	2.67	0	190	2	95.00	1/22	—	1	—
Brooks K. G.	1	2	0	11	8	5.50	0						2	—
Broome I.	2	4	3	35	26*	35.00	0	82	2	41.00	1/17	—	1	—
Brown A. M.	4	6	1	146	74	29.20	0						4	—
Buckley G. A.	1	2	0	10	8	5.00	0	48	0	—	—	—	1	—
Buckston G. M.	33	65	2	829	96	13.16	0						1	—
Buckston R. H. R.	72	101	22	912	60*	11.54	0	10	0	—	—	—	16	1
Burnham G. J.	5	6	1	30	15	6.00	0						3	—
Burnham J. W.	6	11	0	55	31	5.00	0						2	—
Burrows M.	1	2	0	13	13	6.50	0	10	0	—	—	—	—	—
Burton J. P.	7	12	1	200	51*	18.18	0						4	—
Burton O.	3	4	4	21	9*	—	0	156	5	31.20	2/44	—	2	—
Butterfield W.	2	4	0	11	7	2.75	0	20	1	20.00	1/10	—	—	—
Buxton I. R.	350	579	86	11803	118*	23.94	5	12742	483	26.38	7/33	12	199	—
Buxton N.	7	14	2	40	7	3.33	0	171	5	34.20	2/14	—	1	—
Cadman S. W. A.	375	689	33	14055	126	21.43	8	20281	803	25.26	8/70	30	277	—
Carlin R. M.	15	28	1	306	37	11.33	0	208	5	41.60	2/53	—	5	—
Carr D. B.	337	564	52	14656	162*	28.63	18	7786	232	33.56	7/53	4	404	—
Carrington E.	50	77	4	1470	80	20.14	0	32	0	—	—	—	18	—
Carter H. S.	3	4	0	8	7	2.00	0	46	2	23.00	2/39	—	1	—
Carter R.	17	22	4	130	25	7.22	0	752	30	25.07	7/46	1	6	—
Carter W.	65	112	10	1812	145	17.76	2	707	16	44.19	3/12	—	26	—
Cartledge W. or J.	1	2	0	1	1	0.50	0						—	—
Cartwright H.	82	128	16	2384	141*	21.28	1	11	0	—	—	—	31	—
Chapman J.	113	210	15	3624	198	18.58	2	241	1	241.00	1/42	—	35	—
Charlesworth A.	7	10	1	92	23	10.22	0	47	0	—	—	—	2	—
Chatterton J.	11	22	2	108	21	5.40	0	119	5	23.80	1/9	—	3	—
Chatterton W.	196	351	31	7587	169	23.71	6	3078	128	24.05	6/46	3	176	4
Chester C.	1	2	0	0	0	0.00	0	9	1	9.00	1/9	—	1	—
Clarke C. C.	25	37	2	441	35*	12.60	0						8	—
Clayton J. M.	2	3	0	3	2	1.00	0	11	0	—	—	—	1	—
Cochrane A. H. J.	4	8	0	96	50	12.00	0	207	11	18.82	6/51	1	—	—

			Batting					Bowling						
Name	M	Inns	NO	Runs	HS	Avge	100s	Runs	Wkts	Avge	Best	5wI	Ct	St
Cole T. G. O.	6	11	0	171	36	15.55	0						3	—
Cook E.	8	15	2	92	23★	7.08	0						3	—
Cooke J.	1	2	0	6	6	3.00	0						—	—
Cooper A. H. H.	1	1	0	0	0	0	0	12	0	—	—	—	1	—
Cooper H.	15	28	4	216	23	9.00	0						7	—
Copson W. H.	261	341	99	1601	43	6.62	0	19380	1033	18.76	8/11	64	91	—
Corbett B. O.	1	2	0	1	1	0.50	0						—	—
Corbett C. J.	27	48	4	633	61	14.39	0	54	0	—	—	—	7	—
Coupe E.	13	26	3	195	33	8.48	0						2	—
Cresswell J. A.	21	34	13	160	28	7.62	0	1022	25	40.88	4/65	—	17	—
Crommelin-Brown J. L.	16	28	2	659	74	25.35	0	70	1	70.00	1/29	—	9	—
Cropper W.	56	107	4	1601	93	15.54	0	2844	170	16.72	7/25	8	26	—
Cross J.	9	15	4	82	29★	7.45	0	634	22	28.82	4/68	—	4	—
Cupitt J.	2	4	2	19	13	9.50	0	145	3	48.33	2/24	—	—	—
Curgenven G.	95	169	5	3440	124	20.98	3	1163	25	46.52	3/32	—	40	—
Curgenven H. G.	9	12	0	102	26	8.50	0	180	4	45.00	2/25	—	6	—
Curgenven W. G.	17	30	0	376	71	12.53	0						5	—
Cursham A. W.	9	15	0	106	40	7.07	0						3	—
Davidson F.	14	23	4	129	43	6.79	0	1094	43	25.44	6/36	2	11	—
Davidson G. A.	95	157	13	3881	274	26.95	3	7859	449	17.50	9/39	31	79	—
Davidson J.	4	6	3	14	8	4.67	0	96	6	16.00	3/33	—	2	—
Davis J. W.	1	2	0	9	8	4.50	0						2	—
Dawkes G. O.	392	608	86	9808	143	18.90	1	20	0	—	—	—	770	106
Deakin M. J.	4	6	0	45	15	7.50	0						9	—
Dearnaley I.	4	8	0	51	34	6.38	0						3	—
Delacombe W. B.	10	13	3	95	23★	9.50	0	44	0	—	—	—	2	—
DeVille R. J.	3	5	2	26	17	8.67	0	146	2	73.00	2/47	—	—	—
Dickinson S. P.	2	3	1	13	10★	6.50	0	45	1	45.00	1/38	—	—	—
Disney J. J.	53	94	28	370	27★	5.61	0						93	9
Dixon F.	1	2	0	15	15	7.50	0						—	—
Dobson K. W. C.	3	6	2	6	3	1.50	0	99	1	99.00	1/25	—	—	—
Docker F. D.	2	3	0	33	25	11.00	0						3	—
Docker L. C.	48	90	2	1769	107	20.10	1	280	9	31.11	3/38	—	16	—
Docker R.	2	4	0	9	6	2.25	0						2	—
Doughty S.	4	7	1	40	13★	6.66	0	79	4	19.75	3/28	—	1	—
Eadie J. T. C.	1	2	1	8	8★	8.00	0	6	1	6.00	1/6	—	—	—
Eadie W. S.	23	41	3	399	62	10.50	0	13	0	—	—	—	7	—
Earl G. B.	1	1	0	4	4	4.00	0						1	—
Eato A.	25	28	5	220	44	9.57	0	1429	50	28.58	5/14	1	7	—
Eggar J. D.	31	47	3	1385	219	31.48	3	149	1	149.00	1/2	—	16	—
Elliott C. S.	275	468	29	11965	215	27.26	9	526	11	47.82	2/25	—	210	1
Elliott H.	520	754	219	74.80	94	13.98	0	5	0	—	—	—	889	294
Ellis W.	18	32	2	361	58	12.03	0	120	0	—	—	—	7	—
Else R.	5	10	2	59	28	7.38	0	61	1	61.00	1/56	—	3	—
Estridge E.	1	1	0	4	4	4.00	0						—	—
Evans C.	9	14	2	157	31	13.08	0	526	19	27.68	4/46	—	7	—
Evans H.	5	10	0	41	10	4.10	0	252	19	13.26	7/47	2	4	—
Evans T.	2	4	0	78	35	19.50	0	91	3	30.33	1/22	—	1	—
Evershed E.	1	1	0	1	1	1.00	0						2	—

Name	M	Inns	NO	Runs	HS	Avge	100s	Runs	Wkts	Avge	Best	5wI	Ct	St
				Batting						**Bowling**				
Evershed S. H.	75	127	2	3126	153	25.01	4	117	5	23.40	5/19	1	33	—
Evershed W.	13	24	0	357	92	14.88	0	8	3	2.66	3/8	—	6	—
Exham P. G.	1	1	0	12	12	12.00	0						1	—
Eyre J. A.	1	2	1	2	1*	2.00	0						—	—
Eyre J. R.	48	84	4	1194	106	14.93	1	248	1	248.00	1/6	—	17	—
Eyre T. J. P.	197	264	49	3436	102	15.98	1	10305	359	28.70	8/65	8	83	—
Fell M. A.	5	8	0	98	27	12.25	0						—	—
Finney R. J.	114	168	29	2856	82	20.54	0	6297	202	31.17	7/54	8	26	—
Fisher J.	3	6	1	52	39*	10.40	0	15	0	—	—	—	—	—
Fleming C. B.	1	2	0	5	3	2.50	0						—	—
Fletcher H.	5	10	2	17	4	2.13	0						2	—
Fletcher T.	1	1	0	28	28	28.00	0	3	0	—	—	—	—	—
Flint J.	14	24	3	143	24	6.81	0	601	44	13.66	6/28	2	11	—
Flint L. E.	7	11	0	100	35	9.09	0	291	8	36.38	3/30	—	1	—
Foley E. F. W.	1	2	0	0	0	0	0						1	—
Ford N. M.	31	49	1	762	65	15.88	0	73	1	73.00	1/19	—	5	—
Forester T.	105	176	20	2556	87	16.58	0	6691	270	24.78	7/18	15	48	—
Forman A. F. E.	5	7	0	90	36	12.86	0	3	0	—	—	—	—	—
Forman F. G.	1	2	0	3	3	1.50	0						1	—
Foster T.	85	157	6	2485	101	16.46	1	208	8	26.00	2/18	—	61	—
Foulke W. H.	4	7	1	65	53	10.83	0	92	2	46.00	2/15	—	2	—
Fowler W. P.	49	78	11	1805	116	26.94	2	612	7	87.42	2/4	—	28	—
Frederick M. C.	2	3	0	98	84	32.67	0						1	—
Freeman C. F.	1	2	0	7	4	3.50	0						1	—
Frost G.	36	65	4	771	52	12.64	0						10	—
Frost J. H.	1	2	0	19	18	9.50	0						2	—
Fullwood W.	6	10	1	41	13	4.56	0						5	1
Furniss J. B.	4	5	1	9	6	2.25	0	259	7	37.00	3/52	—	2	—
Genders W. R.	3	6	1	62	24	12.40	0	22	0	—	—	—	2	—
Gibbs P. J. K.	145	260	13	7295	138*	29.53	9	288	4	72.00	2/54	—	77	—
Gibson I.	7	12	3	199	66*	22.11	0	128	3	42.67	1/6	—	7	—
Gilbert J. D. H.	11	11	0	106	25	9.64	0						2	—
Gladwin C.	332	457	130	5490	124*	16.79	1	27147	1536	17.67	9/41	99	123	—
Gladwin J.	3	5	2	8	5*	2.67	0	20	1	20.00	1/15	—	3	—
Glenn M.	7	7	4	23	11*	7.67	0	398	6	66.33	3/36	—	1	—
Goldsmith S. C.	24	39	4	1071	89	30.60	0	125	0	—	—	—	16	—
Goodall J.	2	3	0	38	32	12.67	0						2	—
Goodwin G. W.	8	16	1	224	53	14.93	0	205	7	29.29	4/23	—	1	—
Gothard E. J.	45	63	19	543	50	12.34	0	730	18	40.56	3/84	—	10	—
Gould T.	7	10	2	63	16*	7.88	0	225	9	25.00	4/45	—	5	—
Graham-Brown J. M. H.	17	22	2	219	43	10.95	0	457	9	50.78	2/23	—	5	—
Grainger G.	5	9	3	36	10*	6.00	0	348	7	49.71	4/91	—	1	—
Green D. J.	37	60	3	883	69*	15.49	0	1	0	—	—	—	17	—
Green G.	6	11	0	39	20	3.55	0	236	6	39.33	2/31	—	2	—
Gregory D.	4	7	3	19	10	4.75	0	255	25	10.20	6/9	3	3	—
Gregory G. R.	15	22	2	174	23	8.70	0	267	12	22.25	4/70	—	5	—
Griffith F. A.	5	7	1	105	37	17.50	0	347	10	34.70	4/47	—	2	—
Hacker P. J.	8	4	2	22	10*	11.00	0	677	25	27.08	5/51	2	3	—
Hall B.	1	2	0	10	7	5.00	0						—	—

Name	M	Inns	NO	Runs	HS	Avge	100s	Runs	Wkts	Avge	Best	5wI	Ct	St
				Batting				**Bowling**						
Hall D.	20	29	16	43	10*	3.31	0	1386	48	28.87	4/57	—	6	—
Hall I. W.	270	483	32	11666	136*	25.87	9	23	0	—	—	—	189	—
Hall J. P.	4	7	1	3	2	0.50	0	112	3	37.33	1/12	—	3	—
Hall T. A.	28	44	10	354	52	10.44	0	1882	70	26.89	5/57	2	15	—
Hall W.	11	17	4	146	43	11.23	0	376	14	26.85	6/47	1	9	—
Hallam T. H.	10	19	0	224	68	11.79	0						5	—
Hamer A.	290	507	19	15277	227	31.31	19	2271	68	33.40	4/27	—	159	—
Hampshire J. H.	57	87	12	2533	101*	33.77	2	30	0	—	—	—	38	—
Hancock J. W.	47	75	18	446	43*	7.82	0	2753	93	29.60	5/61	1	19	—
Handford J.	9	17	3	137	23	9.79	0	31	0	—	—	—	4	—
Hanson R. L.	1	1	1	1	1*	—	0						1	—
Hardy S.	1	2	0	10	9	4.50	0						2	—
Harvey J. F.	204	340	32	7425	168	24.11	4	21	1	21.00	1/0	—	84	—
Harvey-Walker A. J.	81	143	10	3186	117	23.95	3	1150	34	33.82	7/35	1	31	—
Hay G.	47	80	11	517	49	7.49	0	2193	137	16.01	6/16	6	33	—
Heath F. R.	4	6	1	72	17	14.40	0	47	3	15.67	2/4	—	1	—
Heath J. S.	6	9	1	69	28	8.62	0	268	7	38.29	5/54	1	2	—
Hendrick M.	167	168	64	1093	46	10.51	0	9968	497	20.06	8/45	21	110	—
Hickton W.	34	58	8	674	63	13.48	0	1846	129	14.31	6/15	9	18	—
Higson T. A.	21	38	2	422	46	11.72	0	1048	36	29.11	4/74	0	11	—
Higson T. A.	6	12	0	173	51	14.42	0						2	—
Hill A.	253	438	46	12043	172*	30.72	17	360	6	60.00	3/5	—	91	—
Hill M.	32	52	4	921	61	19.19	0	6	0	—	—	—	21	—
Hill-Wood B. S. H.	22	35	4	505	61	16.29	0	1406	45	31.24	6/74	1	8	—
Hill-Wood C. K. H.	18	22	4	359	72	19.94	0	1206	34	35.47	5/76	1	9	—
Hill-Wood D. J. C. H.	5	8	1	81	36	11.57	0	45	1	45.00	1/22	—	2	—
Hill-Wood W. W. H.	35	60	1	1519	107	25.75	1	1523	49	31.08	5/62	1	18	—
Hind A.	16	30	0	392	77	13.07	0	419	24	17.46	4/9	—	4	—
Hodgkinson G. F.	19	32	0	472	44	14.75	0						10	—
Hodgkinson J.	1	2	0	5	5	2.50	0	83	1	83.00	1/83	—	1	—
Hogg A.	3	6	0	5	4	0.83	0						—	—
Holden S. M.	4	6	2	13	6*	3.25	0	111	3	37.00	3/72	—	1	—
Holding M. A.	56	74	8	1205	80	18.25	0	4641	196	23.67	7/97	12	31	—
Horsley J.	84	127	30	1349	66	13.90	0	5058	264	19.16	7/48	19	45	—
Hounsfield T. D.	16	24	3	274	56	13.04	0						7	—
Houseman E. O.	1	2	0	4	4	2.00	0						2	—
Howarth T.	1	2	0	7	5	3.50	0						1	—
Howcroft A.	4	8	0	46	19	5.75	0						2	—
Hughes-Hallett N. M.	6	11	1	178	67	17.80	0	27	1	27.00	1/16	—	4	—
Hulme J. J.	133	215	28	2336	59	12.49	0	12607	508	24.82	9/27	32	74	—
Humble W. J.	6	10	1	77	19*	8.56	0						6	—
Humphries J.	276	482	122	5134	68	14.26	0	43	3	14.33	1/5	—	531	95
Hunt S. W.	5	5	0	48	17	9.60	0	3	0	—	—	—	—	—
Hunter F. C.	28	49	3	564	51	12.26	0	684	17	40.24	2/18	—	8	—

281

Name	M	Inns	NO	Runs	HS	Avge	100s	Runs	Wkts	Avge	Best	5wI	Ct	St
				Batting					**Bowling**					
Hurt C. N. B.	3	5	0	23	13	4.60	0	6	0	—	—	—	1	—
Hutchinson J. M.	255	415	37	7042	143	18.63	5	1238	31	39.94	3/44	—	96	2
Jackson A. B.	148	160	83	647	27	8.40	0	8602	456	18.86	8/18	17	28	—
Jackson A. H. M.	64	96	15	1199	75	14.80	0	1311	44	29.79	5/84	1	15	—
Jackson G. L.	4	7	0	39	19	5.57	0	126	7	18.00	3/52	—	4	—
Jackson G. R.	260	438	21	9741	140	23.36	9	208	3	69.33	1/10	—	104	—
Jackson H. L.	394	460	139	1966	39*	6.12	0	28589	1670	17.12	9/17	114	121	—
Jackson L.	5	10	1	97	28	10.78	0	189	7	27.00	2/19	—	2	—
Jean-Jacques M.	29	36	7	405	73	13.96	0	1995	58	34.39	8/77	1	9	—
Jefferies S. T.	1	2	1	14	14*	14.00	0	109	5	21.80	3/57	—	—	—
Jelf H. F. D.	10	20	0	230	37	11.00	0						3	—
Jervis W. M.	1	2	0	6	6	3.00	0							—
Johnson H. L.	350	604	65	14164	154	26.28	16	822	21	39.14	3/12	—	216	2
Johnson D. A.	4	8	0	65	31	8.13	0							—
Jordan H. G. B.	1	2	0	0	0	0.00	0							—
Keeton F. W.	3	6	0	33	9	5.50	0						1	—
Kelly J. M.	253	426	26	9464	131	23.66	9	89	1	89.00	1/21	—	119	—
Kenward R.	11	19	0	333	56	17.53	0						3	—
Kirsten P. N.	106	181	25	7722	228	49.50	20	1869	49	38.14	4/44	—	67	—
Langdale G. R.	4	7	1	77	29	12.83	0	141	2	70.50	2/29	—	1	—
Langton S. T.	3	5	0	14	6	2.80	0	42	0	—	—	—	1	—
Lawton A. E.	131	226	5	5554	149	25.13	8	2891	87	33.23	4/19	—	79	1
Lee C.	268	466	16	12008	150	26.68	8	721	21	34.33	2/9	—	201	—
Lee G. M.	229	386	26	9652	191	26.81	16	8002	313	25.57	7/67	18	87	—
Leech C.	1	2	0	38	26	19.00	0						1	—
Limb T.	1	2	0	0	0	0.00	0							—
Linathan D. V.	3	6	1	35	14*	7.00	0	78	1	78.00	1/15	—	2	—
Lister J. W.	5	10	0	205	48	20.50	0						1	—
Locker W.	16	30	0	511	76	17.03	0						4	—
Loney E. F.	25	37	7	511	39*	17.03	0	650	20	32.50	4/27	—	18	—
Lowe C.	5	8	2	25	17	4.17	0	90	2	45.00	1/20	—	—	—
Lowe G.	2	3	0	43	22	14.33	0						3	—
Lyon C. H.	2	2	0	6	4	3.00	0	6	0	—	—	—	—	—
McCurdy R. J.	1	—	—	—	—	—	—	50	1	50.00	1/50	—	—	—
McDonald J. A.	3	6	0	57	21	9.50	0						—	—
McLellan A. J.	26	24	8	99	41	6.18	0						41	2
McMillan S. T.	4	6	2	30	24	7.50	0	14	0	—	—	—	—	—
Maher B. J. M.	104	159	29	3061	126	23.54	4	151	3	50.33	2/69	—	223	12
Malcolm D. E.	50	53	14	239	29*	6.12	0	4095	129	31.74	6/68	3	11	—
Maltby G.	3	6	1	22	7*	4.40	0	20	0	—	—	—	1	—
Malthouse S.	9	12	2	118	38	11.80	0	67	0	—	—	—	3	—
Malthouse W. N.	7	13	1	116	30	9.67	0	69	0	—	—	—	2	—
Marks C. P.	14	21	2	216	39	11.37	0						6	—
Marlow J.	24	45	5	317	25	7.93	0	1237	60	20.62	7/46	6	23	—
Marple G. S.	1	1	0	6	6	6.00	0	17	1	17.00	1/17	—	—	—
Marples C.	26	39	8	580	57	18.70	0	48	0	—	—	—	54	5
Marples G.	2	4	0	11	6	2.75	0	116	1	116.00	1/53	—	1	—
Marsden A.	1	2	0	6	6	3.00	0						1	—
Marsden G. A.	30	46	6	417	37	10.43	0						12	—
Marsh F. E.	66	109	20	1627	86	18.28	0	1698	44	38.59	6/37	1	32	—

Name	M	Inns	NO	Runs	HS	Avge	100s	Runs	Wkts	Avge	Best	5wI	Ct	St
				Batting				**Bowling**						
Marshall J.	2	4	0	50	31	12.50	0						1	—
Maynard E. A. J.	37	68	4	558	84	8.72	0	53	2	26.50	2/34	—	12	—
Mellor A. J.	13	15	6	26	10*	2.89	0	653	17	38.41	5/52	1	4	—
Middleton C.	4	8	1	47	21	6.71	0	21	0	—		—		—
Miller G.	240	359	51	8087	130	26.25	2	16329	597	27.35	8/70	31	194	—
Millner D.	31	56	1	701	80	12.75	0	27	0	—		—	6	—
Mir P. J.	1	2	1	61	57*	61.00	0	58	2	29.00	2/37	—	—	—
Mitchell T. B.	303	390	102	2342	57	8.13	0	18630	1417	20.20	10/64	115	120	—
Mohan K. F.	10	17	2	163	49	10.87	0	23	0	—		—	4	—
Moir D. G.	71	84	11	1098	107	15.04	1	6600	195	33.84	6/60	9	63	—
Morgan D. C.	540	857	143	17842	147	24.99	9	30523	1216	25.10	7/33	35	562	—
Morris A.	47	77	4	1174	74	16.08	0	118	0	—	—	—	29	—
Morris J. E.	117	191	12	6261	191	34.97	13	453	3	151.00	1/13	—	40	—
Mortensen O. H.	86	99	53	461	74*	10.02	0	5831	252	23.13	6/27	11	26	—
Morton A.	1	2	0	0	0	0.00	0	14	0	—		—	—	—
Morton A.	350	610	56	10813	131	19.52	6	21958	966	22.73	9/71	62	124	—
Moses E. C.	3	6	0	16	9	2.67	0	40	1	40.00	1/16	—	3	—
Mycroft F.	2	4	0	7	4	1.75	0					—	4	—
Mycroft T.	16	31	9	159	24*	7.22	0	5	0	—		—	24	10
Mycroft W.	78	138	44	499	44*	5.31	0	6294	534	11.79	9/25	55	46	—
Needham E.	186	340	15	6550	159	20.15	7	82	0	—		—	135	1
Needham J.	1	2	1	9	6*	9.00	0					—		—
Newcombe C. N.	1	2	0	1	1	0.50	0	32	0	—		—		—
Newman P. G.	115	143	29	1834	115	16.08	1	8502	277	30.69	8/29	5	25	—
Newton F. A.	20	37	6	422	87	13.61	0	21	0	—		—	7	—
Nornable C.	1	1	0	8	8	8.00	0	72	5	14.40	3/24	—	—	—
Oates W. F.	121	211	14	4568	148*	23.19	2	577	13	44.38	6/47	1	54	—
O'Connor J.	9	14	5	55	17	6.11	0	619	24	25.79	5/56	2	4	—
O'Gorman T. J. G.	7	13	1	171	78	14.25	0						7	—
Oldham S.	70	59	23	436	39	12.11	0	5070	143	35.45	7/78	1	20	—
Oldknow J.	2	4	1	7	4*	2.33	0	162	4	40.50	3/123	—	2	—
Oliver L.	174	322	13	6303	170	20.40	6	328	5	65.60	2/20	—	69	—
Ollivierre C.A.	110	201	4	4670	229	23.71	3	414	10	41.40	3/34	—	108	—
Osborne G.	7	13	1	45	14	3.75	0	23	1	23.00	1/23	—	3	—
Page M. H.	254	451	47	11538	162	28.56	9	527	7	75.29	1/0	—	248	—
Page W.	3	6	0	50	19	8.33	0					—	—	—
Parrington W. F.	6	11	1	148	47	14.80	0					—	1	—
Payton W. E. G.	2	4	1	93	35*	31.00	0					—	1	—
Peach F. G.	12	24	1	258	61*	11.22	0	170	4	42.50	3/50	—	3	—
Peach W.	1	2	0	10	10	5.00	0	46	4	11.50	4/46	—	1	—
Pearson L. I.	2	4	0	24	18	6.00	0					—	—	—
Pink H. S.	3	5	0	24	11	4.80	0	33	0	—		—	—	—
Platts J. T. B. D.	90	167	6	2064	115	12.82	1	3433	183	18.76	6/39	6	52	—
Pope A. V.	211	312	46	4928	103	18.53	1	12144	542	22.41	7/84	21	96	—
Pope G. H.	169	265	33	6606	207*	28.47	8	11240	567	19.82	8/38	32	126	—
Pope H.	10	16	3	81	24*	6.23	0	599	15	39.93	3/80	—	3	—
Porter G.	36	55	15	378	93	9.45	0	2760	129	21.40	7/49	7	24	—
Pratt R.	5	10	1	73	17*	8.11	0					—	3	—
Prince W.	1	1	1	2	2*	—	0	38	0	—		—	—	—

Name	M	Inns	NO	Batting Runs	HS	Avge	100s	Bowling Runs	Wkts	Avge	Best	5wI	Ct	St
Purdy H. F.	16	30	4	170	21	6.54	0	661	26	25.42	6/84	1	5	—
Purdy J. H.	9	13	4	39	10	4.33	0	310	9	34.44	3/53	—	4	—
Radford H. W.	3	6	2	23	14	5.75	0	86	4	21.50	2/18	—	—	—
Ratcliffe G.	5	10	0	145	64	14.50	0	8	0	—	—	—	—	—
Ratcliffe G.	1	2	1	8	5*	8.00	0	10	1	10.00	1/10	—	2	—
Reader-Blackton W.	8	15	1	107	31*	7.64	0	81	5	16.20	3/40	—	6	—
Regan C.	5	10	0	90	22	9.00	0						1	—
Revill A. C.	321	537	42	13334	156*	26.94	15	1843	45	40.96	3/12	—	327	—
Revill T.	11	20	4	231	65*	14.44	0						6	—
Rhodes A. E. G.	267	413	33	7195	127	18.93	4	18084	642	28.17	8/162	29	82	—
Rhodes H. J.	288	357	123	2197	48	9.39	0	18785	993	18.91	7/38	42	73	—
Richardson A. W.	159	239	30	3982	90	19.05	0	34	0	—	—	—	58	—
Richardson B. H.	27	36	11	279	29	11.16	0	1003	33	30.39	4/39	—	14	—
Richardson G. W.	62	94	13	1206	91	14.89	0	3712	134	27.70	8/54	5	11	—
Richardson J.	11	21	4	117	18	6.88	0	517	32	16.15	7/76	1	9	—
Richardson S.	14	25	0	202	25	8.08	0	43	1	43.00	1/43	—	8	1
Richardson T. H.	3	5	0	34	11	6.80	0						4	—
Rickman R. B.	65	118	8	1262	68	11.47	0	1967	62	31.73	5/80	1	7	—
Rigley W.	57	106	0	1312	69	12.38	0	30	3	10.00	2/10	—	20	—
Rimmer J.	3	3	2	1	1*	1.00	0	264	5	52.80	2/71	—	—	—
Roberts B.	116	185	19	5016	184	30.21	7	1722	41	42.00	4/77	—	84	1
Root C. F.	57	94	10	927	55	11.04	0	1935	63	30.71	6/42	2	42	—
Rose A.	1	1	0	0	0	0	0						—	—
Rowe L. G.	17	30	1	1059	94	36.52	0	84	1	84.00	1/22	—	15	—
Rudd C. F. B. P.	4	5	1	14	9	3.50	0	249	5	49.80	3/27	—	1	—
Rumsey F. E.	1	1	1	2	2*	—	0	97	2	48.50	1/34	—	—	—
Russell P. E.	170	210	46	2020	72	12.31	0	10351	339	30.53	7/46	5	124	—
Ryder R. T.	1	1	0	10	10	10.00	0						1	—
Sale R.	23	43	2	570	69	13.90	0	273	5	54.60	2/25	—	3	—
Sale R.	24	39	3	835	146	23.19	1	4	1	4.00	—	—	8	—
Selby T. G.	1	2	0	3	2	1.50	0	7	0	—	—	—	—	—
Severn A.	13	24	2	342	73	15.55	0						5	—
Shacklock F. J.	18	34	2	287	50	8.97	0	988	59	16.75	5/42	6	6	—
Shardlow W.	38	42	14	201	39*	7.18	0	1939	56	34.63	5/41	1	16	—
Sharma R.	49	70	15	1441	111	26.20	1	1640	33	49.69	6/80	1	44	—
Sharpe P. J.	40	69	0	2031	228	29.43	4	29	1	29.00	1/11	—	47	—
Shaw H.	14	25	7	121	22	6.72	0	158	10	15.80	5/34	1	5	—
Shearwood K. A.	1	2	0	6	4	3.00	0						0	1
Sherwin A. W.	11	21	2	152	24	8.00	0						4	—
Sherwin C. B.	1	2	0	7	7	3.50	0						—	—
Sherwin H.	1	2	2	12	9*	—	0	32	0	—	—	—	—	—
Shipton W. L.	1	2	0	4	3	2.00	0						—	—
Short J. D.	11	19	0	271	86	14.26	0	11	0	—	—	—	6	—
Shuker A.	22	40	2	601	86	15.82	0						12	—
Skinner A. F.	83	136	7	3442	102	26.88	1	250	6	41.67	2/12	—	59	—
Skinner D. A.	23	36	1	475	63	13.57	0	182	2	91.00	1/41	—	11	—
Slater A. G.	210	326	28	5933	105	19.91	1	10487	498	21.06	8/24	28	122	—

Name	M	Inns	NO	Runs	HS	Avge	100s	Runs	Wkts	Avge	Best	5wI	Ct	St
				Batting						**Bowling**				
Slater Henry	5	9	3	22	11	3.67	0	185	3	61.67	1/35	—	2	—
Slater Herbert	5	9	2	39	21	5.57	0	38	2	19.00	2/15	—	—	—
Smith A.	49	86	30	243	22	4.34	0	7	0	—	—	—	63	9
Smith D.	420	711	58	20516	225	31.42	30	706	19	37.16	5/37	1	360	5
Smith D. H. K.	112	198	14	4915	136	26.71	4	23	1	23.00	1/1	—	83	—
Smith E.	497	667	143	6884	90	13.14	0	31189	1209	25.80	9/46	51	204	—
Smith H. W.	1	2	1	34	24★	34.00	0						—	—
Smith J.	22	38	2	403	35	11.19	0	162	6	27.00	3/38	—	14	—
Smith L. S. T.	2	3	0	9	5	3.00	0						1	—
Smith R. P.	90	167	3	2424	69	14.78	0	23	0	—	—	—	64	—
Smith W.	2	4	0	13	8	3.25	0						—	—
Snape M. D.	2	3	1	0	0★	0.00	0						—	—
Southern J. D.	5	10	0	95	43	9.50	0						—	—
Sowter U.	7	11	1	128	47★	12.80	0						7	—
Sparrow G. R.	2	4	0	75	64	18.75	0						—	—
Spencer H.	1	1	0	0	0	0.00	0						—	—
Stapleton E.	1	2	0	3	2	1.50	0						—	—
Steele D. S.	64	101	18	2790	137	33.62	3	3699	148	24.99	7/53	10	56	—
Steeples A.	1	2	0	18	16	9.00	0	21	0	—	—	—	—	—
Steeples R.	3	5	0	20	16	4.00	0	214	9	23.78	4/73	—	1	—
Stephenson G. R.	9	14	0	215	64	15.36	0						14	2
Stevenson G. S.	2	4	0	10	9	2.50	0	92	1	92.00	1/79	—	1	—
Stevenson K.	47	60	19	374	33	9.12	0	2997	98	30.58	7/68	4	15	—
Stevenson M. H.	3	4	0	23	15	5.75	0						—	—
Storer H.	6	10	1	92	35	10.22	0	13	0	—	—	—	3	—
Storer H.	302	517	28	13513	232	27.63	18	7525	232	32.44	7/26	9	214	1
Storer W.	209	351	29	9887	216★	30.70	15	7209	214	33.69	5/20	4	258	26
Street H.	2	4	1	24	15★	8.00	0						1	—
Stubbings J.	4	8	3	20	10★	4.00	0	142	7	20.29	5/51	1	1	—
Stubbings W.	1	2	1	9	9★	9.00	0	80	0	—	—	—	—	—
Sugden H. E.	2	4	0	13	9	3.25	0						—	—
Sugg F. H.	33	64	2	1278	187	20.61	1	14	0	—	—	—	20	—
Sugg W.	128	217	16	3460	107	17.21	2	1560	50	31.20	4/61	—	64	—
Swallow R.	37	66	2	1296	115	20.25	1	8	0	—	—	—	12	—
Swarbrook F. W.	199	285	82	4125	90	20.32	0	12809	416	30.79	9/20	14	123	—
Swindell R. S.	23	32	11	242	38	11.52	0	1665	50	33.30	6/79	4	11	—
Sykes E.	5	10	1	105	50	11.67	0	2	0	—	—	—	—	—
Tate C. F.	4	4	1	48	21	16.00	0	112	2	56.00	2/9	—	—	—
Taylor F. H.	8	16	1	95	18	6.33	0						3	—
Taylor J. P.	7	7	2	29	11	5.80	0	487	10	48.70	4/81	—	3	—
Taylor R. W.	514	719	138	9668	100	16.64	1	69	1	69.00	1/23	—	1157	147
Taylor W. T.	4	8	1	53	11	7.57	0	56	2	28.00	1/9	—	2	—
Thompson W. H.	1	2	0	17	17	8.50	0						—	—
Thornhill F.	1	2	0	0	0	0.00	0						—	—
Tilson J.	3	5	0	26	14	5.20	0						—	—
Todd N. D.	2	4	0	6	6	1.50	0						—	—
Tomlinson D. J. W.	1	1	0	2	2	2.00	0						1	—
Tomlinson W. J. V.	26	43	3	566	43	14.15	0	982	32	30.69	5/53	1	9	—

Name	M	Inns	NO	Runs	HS	Avge	100s	Runs	Wkts	Avge	Best	5wI	Ct	St
			Batting							**Bowling**				
Topham H. G.	I	2	2	5	4*	—	0	49	I	49.00	1/49	—	—	—
Townsend A. F.	116	198	13	4313	142*	23.31	5	39	0	—	—	—	30	—
Townsend L. F.	446	713	62	17667	233	27.14	22	20380	969	21.03	8/26	42	210	—
Tunnicliffe C. J.	150	176	30	2092	91	14.32	0	10265	319	32.17	7/36	6	65	—
Turland H.	I	2	0	I	I	0.50	0						—	—
Turner A.	2	4	0	4	2	1.00	0	138	6	23.00	3/66	—	I	—
Tye J.	3	4	0	21	II	5.25	0	4	I	4.00	1/I	—	2	—
Vaulkhard P.	65	103	5	2170	264	22.14	I	36	0	—	—	—	52	4
Venkataraghavan S.	46	71	20	988	51*	19.37	0	4767	171	27.88	8/77	10	50	—
Wakefield M.	I	I	0	4	4	4.00	0	30	I	30.00	1/30	—	I	—
Walkden G. G.	7	13	0	114	33	8.76	0						2	—
Walker G. G.	70	118	24	1028	66	10.94	0	4649	187	24.86	9/68	9	24	—
Walker N. A. M.	2	3	0	22	13	7.33	0	22	I	22.00	1/12	—	—	—
Walker S. G.	I	2	0	8	7	4.00	0	6	I	6.00	1/6	—	—	—
Wallis W. A.	I	2	0	17	II	8.50	0						I	—
Wallroth C. A.	3	5	0	39	26	7.80	0						2	—
Walters J.	58	80	15	1296	90	19.94	0	1935	47	41.17	4/100	—	26	—
Walton W.	I	2	0	4	3	2.00	0						—	—
Ward A.	115	115	38	709	44	9.21	0	7504	348	21.56	7/42	14	34	—
Ward J. M.	20	35	0	536	104	15.31	I						8	—
Ward L. F.	I	2	0	0	0	0.00	0						I	—
Warner A. E.	72	101	18	1651	91	19.89	0	4390	131	33.51	5/51	I	16	—
Warren A. R.	250	439	44	5449	123	13.79	I	22563	918	24.58	8/69	71	188	—
Wass H.	I	I	0	9	9	9.00	0						—	—
Watson R. M.	6	II	3	68	25*	8.50	0						3	—
Watts A.	3	3	I	39	33*	19.50	0	118	I	118.00	1/28	—	I	—
Webster D.	I	I	0	26	26	26.00	0	28	I	28.00	1/28	—	—	—
Webster F.	I	2	0	II	10	5.50	0	65	I	65.00	1/65	—	—	—
Webster W.	I	2	0	3	3	1.50	0						—	—
Whyatt C.	I	I	0	6	6	6.00	0						2	0
Wickstead A.	14	26	3	385	68	16.74	0	2	0	—	—	—	3	—
Widdowson A.	I	I	0	I	I	1.00	0						—	—
Wild H.	32	59	7	628	68	12.08	0	129	2	64.50	1/3	—	29	—
Wilde D.	13	15	5	31	12	3.10	0	860	23	37.39	3/27	—	I	—
Wilkins C. P.	71	126	12	4060	156	35.61	9	1615	47	34.36	4/21	—	65	—
Willatt G. L.	125	199	10	5127	146	27.13	6	76	I	76.00	1/2	—	40	—
Wilmot A. A.	I	2	0	0	0	0.00	0						I	—
Wilmot W.	10	16	3	155	25*	11.92	0						II	I
Wilson G. D.	2	4	0	19	9	4.75	0	15	0	—			—	—
Wincer R. C.	23	21	8	131	26	10.08	0	1653	46	35.93	4/42	—	8	—
Wood A. J.	13	19	I	264	52	14.66	0	64	0	—	—	—	5	—
Wood A. M.	2	4	0	28	9	7.00	0						2	—
Wood B.	63	107	13	3192	153	33.95	6	1943	37	52.51	3/22	—	57	—
Wood L. J.	2	2	0	7	5	3.50	0	95	2	47.50	2/82	—	—	—
Wood S. H.	34	54	II	758	81*	17.63	0	50	0	—	—	—	12	—
Woodland A. W.	2	4	I	27	19*	9.00	0	69	0	—	—	—	I	—
Wood-Sims W.	23	42	I	461	46	11.24	0	43	I	43.00	1/16	—	12	—
Woodward K. A.	2	4	I	12	7	4.00	0						—	—
Worthington S. T.	406	648	54	17000	238*	28.62	27	17979	624	28.81	8/29	16	307	—

Name	M	Inns	NO	Batting Runs	HS	Avge	100s	Bowling Runs	Wkts	Avge	Best	5wI	Ct	St
Wright F.	1	2	0	4	4	2.00	0	37	0	—	—	—	—	—
Wright H. F.	9	16	3	298	55	22.92	0						4	—
Wright J.	6	10	1	93	53*	10.33	0	16	0	—	—	—	—	—
Wright J. G.	156	265	24	10638	190	44.14	27	193	2	96.50	1/4	—	84	—
Wright L. G.	317	577	12	14800	195	26.19	20	194	1	194.00	1/4	—	232	4
Wright W. J.	2	3	0	58	28	19.33	0						—	—
Wyatt G.	11	20	4	184	59	11.50	0	2	0	—	—	—	7	—
Yates G.	1	1	0	0	0	0	0	9	0	—	—	—	—	—
Young J. H.	28	48	9	379	42*	9.72	0	996	28	37.57	5/65	1	3	—
Young J. W.	2	2	0	0	0	0	0						—	—

Notes
F. Davidson's innings of 5 v. Yorkshire at Chesterfield in 1898 when he was 5 not out overnight and was then withdrawn from the match by his league club the following day is included as a dismissal.
W. Bestwick's innings of 2 v. Leicestershire at Chesterfield in 1899 when he was 2 not out overnight and arrived late the following morning is included as a dismissal.
* = not out.

RESULTS OF ALL INTER-COUNTY FIRST-CLASS MATCHES 1871–1988★

Year	EX	GM	GS	HA	KT	LA	LE	MX	NR	NT	SM	SY	SX	WA	WO	YO	M	W	L	D	A	Pos
1871						LW											2	1	1	–	0	–
1872						LL											2	0	2	0	0	–
1873						LL											2	0	2	0	0	–
1874					WW	DW											4	3	0	1	0	–
1875					WW	LD				LL							6	2	3	1	0	–
1876				WL	WL	LL											6	2	4	0	0	–
1877				WW	WW	WL									DL		8	5	2	1	0	–
1878				DW	LL	WL				LL					WL		10	3	6	1	0	–
1879						LL				LL					WW		6	2	4	0	0	–
1880					WL	LL						DW			LL		8	2	5	1	0	–
1881					LW	LL						WL			LD		8	2	5	1	0	–
1882						LL						WL			LL		6	1	5	0	0	–
1883						LL						WL	LW		DL		8	2	5	1	0	–
1884					LL	LL						LL	LL		LL		10	0	10	0	0	–
1885			WW			LW		LD				LL			DL		10	3	5	2	0	–
1886			L	LL	LD							LL			LL		9	0	8	1	0	–
1887						LL						LL			LL		6	0	6	0	0	–
1894					WL	WW						DL	WL		LW		10	5	4	1	0	–
1895	DL		WL		WD	DW				DD	LD	WD			LW		16	5	4	7	0	5th
1896	LD		WW		LD	DW				DL	LL	WD			DL		16	4	6	6	0	7th
1897	DL		LD		LL	DL				DD	LL	DD			LL		16	0	9	7	0	14th
1898	LL		DW		LD	WL				DD	LA	DD			LD		16	2	6	7	1	9th
1899	DW		LW		LL	DD				DL	LL	DD	DL		LL		18	2	9	7	0	15th
1900	DD		DW		LL	DL				LL	LD	DD	WD		LD		18	2	7	9	0	13th
1901	LD	DD	LL		LD	LD				DL	LL	DL	LL		LL		20	0	13	7	0	15th
1902	LW		DW			DW				LL	DL	WL	DD		DD		16	4	5	7	0	10th
1903	LD		WL		LL	WL				WL	WD	DD			LD		16	4	7	5	0	12th
1904	WW		LD		LL	LW				LD	LW	DL	WD		DL		18	5	8	5	0	10th
1905	LL		DL		LD	LL		WL	LL		LL	DL	WL		WL		20	3	14	3	0	14th
1906	LL		LL		LL	WL		LL	LL		LL	WL	LD		LL		20	2	17	1	0	16th
1907	LL		WL	LL	DL	LL		WL	LL		LL	LL	AL		LA		22	2	17	1	2	16th
1908	WL		WW	LL	DD	LD		WL	WD		LL	LL	LL		LL		22	5	13	4	0	14th
1909	LL		DL	LL	LD	LW		LL	AL		LL	DL	DW		LL		22	2	15	4	1	15th
1910	LL		LL	LL	LD	WW		LL	DD		LD	LD	DL		LL		22	2	14	6	0	15th
1911	LL		LL		LW	DD		LW	LD		LL		LL		LL		18	2	13	3	0	14th
1912	DL		LD		DL	DW			DL	DL	WD	DL	DL				18	2	7	9	0	12th
1913	DW		LW		LD	LD			LL	WL	LL	DL	WL				18	4	10	4	0	13th
1914	LL		LL		DL	WD			DL	WL	WL			LL	WW	LL	20	5	12	3	0	12th
1919					LL	LW			WL	LD	LL			LW	DL		14	3	9	2	0	9th
1920	LL				LL	LL			LL	AL	LL			LL	LL	LL	18	0	17	0	1	16th
1921	DL	WW	LL			WL		LD	WL	LL		DL	WL		LL		20	5	12	3	0	12th
1922	DL	WW	LW		LL	LD		WW	LL	DL		LD	WD		LD		22	6	10	6	0	11th
1923	DD	WD	LL		DL	DW		WL	DD	LD		DW	DD		LL		22	4	7	11	0	10th
1924	DD	LL	LD		LD	LD		DL	DL	LL	LL	DD	DL		LD		24	0	13	11	0	17th
1925	DW	WL	LL				LL	LL	DL	LD	DW	DD	WW		LL		24	5	12	7	0	14th
1926	LD	LD	DW	DD	LL	AL			WD	LD	WL	DD	WW		DD		24	5	7	11	1	11th
1927	WD	DW	DD	LW	DD	DL			WW	LD	WW		WD		DD	DD	24	8	3	13	0	5th
1928	DD	DW	DD		LD	LD		WD	WL	DD	DW		DD	LD	WW	LL	26	6	6	14	0	10th
1929	DW	DD	WW	LD	LD	LD	LL	DW	DD	WW			WL	DW	WW	DD	28	10	6	12	0	7th
1930	DD	LL	DL		WL		DD	WD	LW	DD	WL	DW	WL	DD	WL	AD	28	7	8	12	1	9th
1931	DD	WD	LL	WW	LD		DL	DD	DA	WW	DD		DD	WL	LD	WD	28	7	6	14	1	7th
1932	WD		LL	DL	LL	DW	DD	WW	WL	DD	DL		AD	WD	DD	AL	28	6	8	12	2	10th
1933	WD		WL	DD	WL	LD	WW	LW	WW	LL	WL		LL	WL	WD	DL	28	11	11	6	0	6th

Year	EX	GM	GS	HA	KT	LA	LE	MX	NR	NT	SM	SY	SX	WA	WO	YO	M	W	L	D	A	Pos
1934			DD	WL	DW	DL	WW	WL	DW	WW	WW	DL	DL	WD	DW	LD	28	12	6	10	0	3rd
1935	WW		WL	WW	WD	DW	WD		WW	WL	WW	DW	LW	WL	DL	DL	28	16	6	6	0	2nd
1936	DW		WW	DD	WL	DD	WW		DW	LD	LL	WD	WD	WW	WW	DD	28	13	4	11	0	1st
1937	LW		WL	DW	WL	DD	WW		WD	WD	WW	DD	WW	WD	WL	LL	28	14	6	8	0	3rd
1938	DL		DL	WL	DW	LW	DW		DW	WD	WL	AD	LW	WD		LL	28	11	8	8	1	5th
1939	WL	DW			WL	DL	WD	DW	WD	WD	WL	LL	DL	WD		DL	28	10	8	10	0	9th
1946	-L	WL	L-	LW	DL	LL	LL	-D	LD	DD	-D	WD	W-	DW	AL	L-	26	5	12	8	1	15th
1947	L-	WD	-L	WL	DL	LL	WL	L-	WW	WD	W-	AL	-W	DW	WW	-D	26	11	9	5	1	5th
1948	DL	W-	WW	-D	-W	DD	WW	LD	W-	WL	WW	L-	WL	LD	-D	DD	26	11	6	9	0	6th
1949	WW	-L	LL	L-	L-	WD	DW	LL	-L	DD	WW	-L	DD	DL	L-	LL	26	6	13	7	0	15th
1950	WW	DL	DL	DL	WL	DW	DL	-D	W-	LD	D-	-L	DD	DW	WL	LW	28	8	9	11	0	5th
1951	DD	LL	LD	DW	DW	LD	WD	D-	-D	WD	-W	D-	DD	LD	LD	LD	28	5	6	17	0	11th
1952	-L	LD	W-	D-	-D	DL	DW	WL	WW	WD	DD	LL	WL	WD	WW	WL	28	11	8	9	0	4th
1953	A-	DL	-D	-W	D-	WD	WL	DD	DL	WL	WW	WL	DD	DL	WD	WL	28	9	7	11	1	6th
1954	LW	LW	LW	DL	WW	WD	WD	D-	-D	DD	-W	L-	DW	DD	WL	DW	28	11	6	11	0	3rd
1955	DD	DW	WD	LW	WW	LL	DD	-D	L-	DW	W-	-L	LL	LD	WW	LL	28	9	10	9	0	8th
1956	-D	AW	D-	D-	-W	DD	WW	LW	DD	DL	WL	DD	DL	DL	DL	WD	28	7	6	14	1	12th
1957	W-	DD	-W	-D	L-	DW	WW	WW	DL	DD	LW	LD	WL	DL	DL	WL	28	10	8	10	0	4th
1958	DW	DW	WL	WL	LL	LW	LW	D-	-L	WW	-L	D-	DW	DL	DL	LD	28	9	9	10	0	5th
1959	DL	DL	LL	WD	WW	WD	DD	-W	W-	WW	D-	-D	DW	LW	WW	LD	28	12	6	10	0	7th
1960†	DW	DL	L-	WD	-L	LW	WD	D-	DL	WW	DW	-D	DD	WW	WD	LL	28	10	7	11	0	5th
1961†	LD	LD	-D	LL	D-	WL	WW	-W	DL	DW	WW	W-	DW	WD	LL	LD	28	10	9	9	0	7th
1962	WW	WW	W-	LD	-D	DD	WD	W-	WL	DD	LD	-L	DD	DD	DL	DL	28	8	6	14	0	7th
1963	-L	LD	L-	W-	-D	DD	DD	DD	LL	DL	LL	DL	DW	LL	DL	LL	28	2	14	12	0	17th
1964	L-	DD	-D	-D	L-	DW	WD	LL	DL	WD	DW	DL	DD	LW	LL	DD	28	5	9	14	0	12th
1965	LD	WW	WL	DD	LD	DL	DW	W-	DL	WW	-D	L-	DL	LL	DD	DD	28	7	9	12	0	9th
1966	DD	LL	LL	DD	LW	LW	LD	-D	DW	WW	L-	-W	D-	WW	LL	LL	28	8	12	8	0	9th
1967	W-	DW	-L	-D	D-	DD	WL	DL	DW	DD	DW	DD	DL	DL	DD	DD	28	5	5	18	0	6th
1968	-D	DW	W-	D-	-D	DL	DD	DL	DD	LL	WA	LD	DW	DD	WW	DD	28	6	5	16	1	8th
1969	D-	LD	-L	-D	W-	DW	LD	D-	DL	DD	D-	-D	-L	WD	DA	DD	24	3	5	15	1	16th
1970	-L	WL	W-	D-	-D	WD	DL	-D	DW	LD	-L	D-	W-	DW	DW	LL	24	7	7	10	0	7th
1971	LD	D-	LD	DD	DW	DL	DD	D-	-D	DD	D-	-L	-D	D-	DD	DD	24	1	4	19	0	17th
1972	L-	D-	-L	D-	-D	AD	DD	-L	D-	DD	L-	-D	W-	-D	-L	DD	20	1	5	13	1	17th
1973	-L	-W	L-	-L	D-	DD	LL	L-	-D	DD	-L	L-	-W	L-	L-	DL	20	2	10	8	0	16th
1974	-D	D-	-D	D-	-L	DD	DD	-L	L-	DD	D-	L-	W-	-D	-L	LD	20	1	6	13	0	17th
1975	L-	-W	D-	-D	L-	LL	LD	D-	-W	WD	-L	-D	-W	W-	D-	DL	20	5	7	8	0	15th
1976	-L	L-	-W	D-	-L	WD	LD	-L	L-	DD	W-	W-	L-	-D	-L	DD	20	4	7	9	0	15th
1977	DD	-D	L-	-D	L-	DD	WL	W-	DW	WD	-A	-D	-W	W-	W-	DD	22	7	3	11	1	7th
1978	DD	W-	-L	D-	-L	DW	LD	-L	DL	WL	D-	L-	-D	-D	DD	DD	22	3	7	12	0	14th
1979	LL	-D	D-	L-	DD	DD	DD	D-	LD	AD	-D	-D	-W	D-	D-	LD	22	1	6	14	1	16th
1980	DD	D-	-A	W-	-D	AD	DD	-L	LW	DL	W-	W-	D-	-D	-D	DD	22	4	3	13	2	9th
1981	DL	-W	W-	-L	W-	DD	LD	D-	LD	AL	-D	-D	-L	D-	W-	LD	22	4	7	10	1	12th
1982	DL	D-	-D	D-	-D	DD	WW	-D	WL	DD	W-	D-	D-	-D	-D	DL	22	4	3	15	0	11th
1983	L-	-W	DD	DL	D-	DD	LD	LL	D-	WW	DW	-D	-D	-W	W-	DW	24	7	5	12	0	9th
1984	DL	DD	-D	W-	LL	WD	LD	D-	-D	DW	-D	DL	W-	D-	-D	LD	24	4	6	14	0	12th
1985	-L	W-	L-	-L	-D	DL	LD	-D	LD	DL	D-	L-	WD	DW	DL	LD	24	3	9	12	0	13th
1986	L-	-W	DD	LL	W-	DD	DD	WD	D-	DD	DW	-L	-L	-D	D-	DW	24	5	5	14	0	11th
1987	DD	DW	-T	W-	DD	DW	LL	W-	-D	LD	-D	DL	W-	W-	-D	DL	24	6	5	12	1	6th
1988	DL	-D	L-	-D	D-	DD	DD	D-	WD	DL	-W	-D	-W	D-	D-	DW	22	4	3	15	0	14th

A = Abandoned match without a ball bowled, but is included in the M. total.

*The Championship placings were not put on to an official basis until 1890. Prior to that date, although the actual Champion County was recognised, the placings of the remainder were open to conjecture. Nevertheless, for a great many years Derbyshire were shown as Champions in 1874 in *Wisden* but it was never claimed by Derbyshire, and no reference to Derbyshire being the Champion County in 1874 can be found in any local newspapers. Whilst Derbyshire were restored to first-class rank for the 1894 season, it was agreed that they, together with the other newly promoted counties (Essex, Leicestershire and Warwickshire), should not compete for the Championship until 1895.

†In 1960 Derbyshire played a friendly three day match against Northamptonshire at Ilkeston, which the visitors won; in 1961 they played a friendly match against Nottinghamshire at Trent Bridge, which was drawn. Neither match is included in the above table.

T = Tied match.

RESULTS IN BENSON AND HEDGES CUP COMPETITION 1972–1988

1972 4th in North Section
1973 4th in North Section
1974 3rd in North Section
1975 3rd in North Section
1976 3rd in Group A
1977 3rd in Group B
1978 1st in Group A Q/Final: beat Middlesex; S/Final: beat Warwickshire; Final: lost to Kent
1979 2nd in Group B Q/Final: beat Glamorgan; S/Final: lost to Surrey
1980 4th in Group A
1981 3rd in Group B
1982 1st in Group A Q/Final: lost to Sussex
1983 4th in Group B
1984 3rd in Group B
1985 2nd in Group A Q/Final: lost to Essex
1986 1st in Group A Q/Final: lost to Kent
1987 3rd in Group A
1988 1st in Zone A Q/Final: beat Middlesex; S/Final: beat Glamorgan; Final: lost to Hampshire

RESULTS OF ALL SUNDAY LEAGUE MATCHES 1969–1988

Year	EX	GM	GS	HA	KT	LA	LE	MX	NR	NT	SM	SY	SX	WA	WO	YK	M	W	L	NR	T	A	Pos
1969	L	L	W	L	L	L	L	W	L	L	W	L	W	A	W	L	16	5	10	–	–	1	15th =
1970	W	W	W	W	L	L	L	W	L	W	L	W	W	W	W	W	16	11	5	–	–	–	3rd
1971	L	NR	L	L	W	L	L	W	W	W	L	W	W	L	L	W	16	7	8	1	–	–	11th
1972	L	W	W	W	L	L	W	A	W	W	L	L	L	W	A	L	16	7	7	–	–	2	9th
1973	L	W	W	A	L	L	L	W	NR	W	L	W	L	A	W	L	16	5	8	1	–	2	12th
1974	W	W	L	A	L	W	L	L	L	W	L	L	L	L	L	L	16	4	11	–	–	1	15th =
1975	L	W	L	L	L	W	L	W	W	L	W	W	A	W	L	L	16	7	8	–	–	1	9th
1976	L	W	W	L	L	W	W	L	W	L	L	L	L	L	W	W	16	7	9	–	–	–	12th
1977	L	W	W	A	L	W	L	L	W	L	L	W	L	A	L	W	16	6	8	–	–	2	9th =
1978	L	W	W	W	W	L	L	L	A	L	A	NR	W	L	L	W	16	6	7	1	–	2	8th =
1979	L	W	L	A	L	L	L	L	W	W	L	A	L	A	W	L	16	4	9	–	–	3	16th
1980	W	W	W	L	W	L	L	W	A	L	W	L	L	W	W	L	16	8	7	–	–	1	6th =
1981	L	W	W	W	W	W	W	W	W	A	L	L	L	W	W	L	16	10	5	–	–	1	4th
1982	W	L	A	L	L	W	L	W	L	L	W	L	L	W	W	L	16	6	9	–	–	1	13th
1983	A	L	W	W	NR	A	L	L	W	W	W	A	L	W	W	L	16	7	5	1	–	3	6th
1984	L	L	L	L	W	W	L	L	A	L	L	L	W	L	L	L	16	4	11	–	–	1	17th
1985	L	NR	W	W	W	L	W	L	W	W	NR	L	W	W	A	L	16	8	5	2	–	1	4th
1986	L	L	W	L	L	W	L	L	L	L	L	W	W	L	W	W	16	7	9	–	–	–	9th
1987	A	W	W	T	L	NR	W	L	L	W	L	A	W	W	W	W	16	8	4	1	1	2	4th =
1988	L	L	L	L	L	L	W	NR	W	W	W	T	W	L	L	NR	16	5	8	2	1	–	13th
																	320	132	153	9	2	24	

A = Abandoned without a ball being bowled.
NR = Some play took place but no result was achieved.

RESULTS OF ALL NATWEST TROPHY/ GILLETTE CUP MATCHES 1963–1988

1963	*1st Round*: beat Hampshire; *2nd Round*: lost to Lancashire
1964	*1st Round*: lost to Northamptonshire
1965	*1st Round*: beat Essex; *2nd Round*: lost to Middlesex
1966	*1st Round*: bye; *2nd Round*: lost to Essex
1967	*1st Round*: bye; *2nd Round*: lost to Surrey
1968	*1st Round*: bye; *2nd Round*: lost to Sussex
1969	*1st Round*: beat Somerset; *2nd Round*: beat Worcestershire; *3rd Round*: beat Glamorgan; *S/Final*: beat Sussex; *Final*: lost to Yorkshire
1970	*1st Round*: bye; *2nd Round*: lost to Middlesex
1971	*1st Round*: bye; *2nd Round*: lost to Leicestershire
1972	*1st Round*: bye; *2nd Round*: lost to Worcestershire
1973	*1st Round*: bye; *2nd Round*: lost to Sussex
1974	*1st Round*: lost to Hampshire
1975	*1st Round*: bye; *2nd Round*: beat Somerset; *Q/Final*: beat Nottinghamshire; *S/Final*: lost to Middlesex
1976	*1st Round*: beat Lincolnshire; *2nd Round*: beat Surrey; *Q/Final*: lost to Hampshire
1977	*1st Round*: bye; *2nd Round*: beat Sussex; *Q/Final*: lost to Somerset
1978	*1st Round*: beat Worcestershire; *2nd Round*: lost to Middlesex
1979	*1st Round*: bye; *2nd Round*: lost to Somerset
1980	*1st Round*: bye; *2nd Round*: lost to Hampshire
1981	*1st Round*: beat Suffolk; *2nd Round*: beat Worcestershire; *Q/Final*: beat Nottinghamshire; *S/Final*: beat Essex; *Final*: beat Northamptonshire
1982	*1st Round*: bye; *2nd Round*: lost to Hampshire
1983	*1st Round*: beat Suffolk; *2nd Round*: lost to Middlesex
1984	*1st Round*: beat Cumberland; *2nd Round*: lost to Leicestershire
1985	*1st Round*: lost to Durham
1986	*1st Round*: beat Cornwall; *2nd Round*: lost to Surrey
1987	*1st Round*: beat Cambridgeshire; *2nd Round*: beat Kent; *Q/Final*: lost to Nottinghamshire
1988	*1st Round*: beat Sussex; *2nd Round*: beat Cheshire; *Q/Final*: lost to Hampshire

GROUNDS USED BY THE COUNTY

Ground	First	Last	M	W	L	D	A
Derby	1871	1988	558	132	212	210	4
Chesterfield, Queens Park*	1898	1988	370	95	128	138	9
Ilkeston	1925	1980	90	31	19	40	0
Burton-on-Trent (53) (A)	1914	1937	13	6	4	3	0
(B)	1938	1980	38	10	9	19	0
(C)	1975	1976	2	2	0	0	0
Buxton	1923	1986	47	13	5	27	2
Glossop	1899	1910	15	2	8	4	1
Blackwell (near Alfreton)	1909	1913	7	0	2	5	0
Dore (Abbeydale Park)	1946	1947	2	1	0	1	0
Heanor	1987	1987	1	1	0	0	0
Long Eaton	1887	1887	1	0	0	1	0
Wirksworth	1874	1874	1	1	0	0	0
Total			1145	294	388	447	16

*Includes one drawn match played on the Saltergate ground in 1874.

Three grounds have been used at Burton-on-Trent: (A) The ground of the Burton-on-Trent CC., (B) The Ind Coope (later Allied Breweries) ground and (C) The Bass-Worthington ground.

Abbeydale Park, Dore was to have been the venue for a match in 1940, although already part of Yorkshire. Derbyshire used it for a home match in both 1946 and 1947. Later Yorkshire used it for home matches, and in fact Derbyshire won there in 1983.

TEAM RECORDS

HIGHEST AND LOWEST INNINGS TOTALS FOR DERBYSHIRE

Highest	Venue	Year	Opponents	Lowest	Venue	Year
552	Chesterfield	1928	Essex	31	Derby	1914
453	Swansea	1988	Glamorgan	40	Cardiff	1946
494-9	Ilkeston	1928	Gloucestershire	55	Derby	1886
645	Derby	1898	Hampshire	47	Portsmouth	1933
437	Tonbridge	1939	Kent	36	Wirksworth	1874
577	Old Trafford	1896	Lancashire	37	Chesterfield	1922
					Old Trafford	1923
509	Glossop	1906	Leicestershire	36	Chesterfield	1905
369	Ilkeston	1977	Middlesex	62	Lord's	1978
538-3*	Northampton	1933	Northamptonshire	46	Northampton	1912
570	Trent Bridge	1897	Nottinghamshire	16	Trent Bridge	1879
495-7*	Taunton	1981	Somerset	37	Bath	1919
386	Derby	1904	Surrey	42	The Oval	1887
485-8*	Derby	1937	Sussex	61	Derby	1907
561	Derby	1902	Warwickshire	39	Edgbaston	1894
513-8*	Chesterfield	1933	Worcestershire	54	Worcester	1935
491	Bradford	1949	Yorkshire	20	Sheffield	1939
336	Chesterfield	1968	Australia	45	Derby	1880
406-5*	Cambridge	1988	Cambridge Univ.	122	Burton-on-Trent	1963
366	Chesterfield	1946	India	160	Derby	1936
271	Crystal Palace	1904	London County	64	Crystal Palace	1901
383	Lord's	1900	M.C.C.	26	Lord's	1880
366	Derby	1986	New Zealand	121	Derby	1949
456	Oxford	1936	Oxford Univ.	72	Oxford	1939
333-3*	Chesterfield	1978	Pakistan and P.I.A.	162	Chesterfield	1982
305	Derby	1901	South Africa	32	Derby	1947
319	Derby	1933	West Indies	68	Chesterfield	1980

HIGHEST AND LOWEST INNINGS TOTALS AGAINST DERBYSHIRE

Highest	Venue	Year	Opponents	Lowest	Venue	Year
609-4†	Leyton	1912	Essex	58	Burton-on-Trent	1949
587-8*	Cardiff	1951	Glamorgan	49	Cardiff	1967
475-7*	Derby	1950	Gloucestershire	43	Cheltenham	1954
481	Portsmouth	1934	Hampshire	23	Burton-on-Trent	1958
615	Derby	1908	Kent	25	Wirksworth	1874
546	Old Trafford	1898	Lancashire	25	Old Trafford	1871
541-4*	Glossop	1901	Leicestershire	36	Loughborough	1965
456-9*	Derby	1949	Middlesex	29	Chesterfield	1957
439-4*	Derby	1983	Northamptonshire	42	Derby	1908
661	Derby	1901	Nottinghamshire	53	Derby	1983

* Declared.
† 9 wickets fell, one batsman absent.

Highest	Venue	Year	Opponents	Lowest	Venue	Year
508	Bath	1984	Somerset	35	Derby	1935
611-9*	Derby	1904	Surrey	60	The Oval	1935
493-9†	Brighton	1929	Sussex	45	Brighton	1880
635	Edgbaston	1900	Warwickshire	28	Derby	1937
557	Worcester	1899	Worcestershire	46	Derby	1922
662	Chesterfield	1898	Yorkshire	44	Chesterfield	1948
625	Derby	1896	Australia	123	Derby	1912
276	Ilkeston	1967	Cambridge Univ.	55	Cambridge	1968
380-9*	Chesterfield	1946	India	86	Chesterfield	1952
398	Crystal Palace	1904	London County	97	Derby	1900
488	Lord's	1905	M.C.C.	55	Lord's	1904
541-9*	Derby	1927	New Zealand	151	Derby	1958
272-8	Burton-on-Trent	1971	Oxford Univ.	47	Oxford	1939
413-7*	Chesterfield	1971	Pakistan and P.I.A.	150	Derby	1963
443	Ilkeston	1935	South Africa	113	Derby	1955
497-6*	Chesterfield	1976	West Indies	97	Buxton	1923

* Declared.
† 9 wickets fell, one batsman absent.

RECORD PARTNERSHIP AGAINST AND FOR EACH COUNTY

Essex
- 322 H. Storer and J. Bowden at Derby   1929
- 312 P. A. Perrin and C. McGahey at Leyton   1912

Glamorgan
- 192 J. E. Morris and J. G. Wright at Swansea 1988
- 224 A. Jones and R. C. Davis at Derby   1969

Gloucestershire
- 243 L. G. Wright and W. Chatterton at Bristol 1901
- 305 C. W. J. Athey and P. Bainbridge at Derby 1985

Hampshire
- 241* G. H. Pope and A. E. G. Rhodes at Portsmouth 1948
- 321 C. L. Smith and T. E. Jesty at Derby   1983

Kent
- 168 P. D. Bowler and T. J. G. O'Gorman at Chesterfield 1988
- 256 B. W. Luckhurst and G. W. Johnson at Derby   1973

Lancashire
- 321* J. G. Wright and P. N. Kirsten at Old Trafford 1980
- 265 A. Ward and J. T. Tyldesley at Derby   1901

Leicestershire
- 246 J. M. Kelly and D. B. Carr at Chesterfield 1957
- 390 B. Dudleston and J. F. Steele at Leicester 1979

Middlesex
- 209 H. Storer and D. Smith at Derby   1932
- 338 J. M. Brearley and M. W. Gatting at Derby   1981

*Unfinished partnership.

Northamptonshire
253	J. G. Wright and P. N. Kirsten at Derby	1980
279	G. Cook and D. S. Steele at Northampton	1978

Nottinghamshire
349	C. S. Elliott and J. D. Eggar at Trent Bridge	1947
345	M. Newell and D. W. Randall at Trent Bridge	1988

Somerset
291	P. N. Kirsten and D. S. Steele at Taunton	1981
290	J. C. W. McBryan and M. D. Lyon at Burton-on-Trent	1924

Surrey
198	K. J. Barnett and A. Hill at The Oval	1983
364	R. Abel and D. L. A. Jephson at The Oval	1900

Sussex
215	A. E. Alderman and L. F. Townsend at Eastbourne	1938
198	J. M. Parks and K. G. Suttle at Ilkeston	1959

Warwickshire
283	J. Chapman and A. R. Warren at Blackwell (Derbys)	1910
344	J. Devey and S. P. Kinneir at Edgbaston	1900

Worcestershire
283	J. G. Wright and B. Wood at Chesterfield	1981
309	H. K. Foster and F. L. Bowley at Derby	1901

Yorkshire
242	J. G. Wright and I. S. Anderson at Derby	1982
554	J. T. Brown and J. Tunnicliffe at Chesterfield	1891

NARROW MARGINS OF VICTORY

(a) by one wicket

Opponents	Venue	Year
Kent	Derby	1877
MCC	Lords	1896
Middlesex	Derby	1986
Sussex	Horsham	1988

(b) by five runs or less

Opponents	Venue	Year	Margin
Nottinghamshire	Chesterfield	1914	5 runs
Gloucestershire	Cheltenham	1939	1 run
Glamorgan	Cardiff	1954	5 runs
Northamptonshire	Northampton	1967	4 runs
Worcestershire	Chesterfield	1981	3 runs
Lancashire	Old Trafford	1987	3 runs

LARGE MARGINS OF VICTORY

(a) by an innings and 250 runs or more

Opponents	Venue	Year	Margin
Warwickshire	Derby	1902	Innings and 250 runs

(b) by 300 runs or more

Opponents	Venue	Year	Margin
Leicestershire	Leicester	1904	306 runs
Warwickshire	Derby	1933	317 runs
Worcestershire	Chesterfield	1939	315 runs
Glamorgan	Derby	1948	301 runs

LARGE MARGINS OF DEFEAT

(a) by an innings and 250 runs or more

Opponents	Venue	Year	Margin
MCC	Lord's	1882	Innings and 258 runs
Nottinghamshire	Derby	1885	Innings and 250 runs
Yorkshire	Chesterfield	1898	Innings and 387 runs
Yorkshire	Huddersfield	1901	Innings and 282 runs
MCC	Lord's	1905	Innings and 252 runs
Sussex	Brighton	1909	Innings and 274 runs
Lancashire	Buxton	1975	Innings and 348 runs

(b) by 300 runs or more

Opponents	Venue	Year	Margin
Nottinghamshire	Chesterfield	1904	330 runs
Kent	Derby	1910	304 runs

NARROW MARGINS OF DEFEAT

(a) by one wicket

Opponents	Venue	Year
Hampshire	Southampton	1876
Lancashire	Liverpool	1897
Yorkshire	Derby	1897
Lancashire	Old Trafford	1907
Northamptonshire	Northampton	1923
Somerset	Wells	1936*
Warwickshire	Birmingham	1949
Nottinghamshire	Ilkeston	1950
Worcestershire	Chesterfield	1964
Worcestershire	Ilkeston	1966

*In spite of their narrow defeat, Derbyshire became the County Champions on this day for the first time in their history.

(b) by five runs or less

Opponents	Venue	Year	Margin
Sussex	Brighton	1882	3 runs
Lancashire	Buxton	1947	3 runs
Sussex	Hove	1957	4 runs
Somerset	Bath	1958	4 runs
Sussex	Eastbourne	1969	5 runs
Hampshire	Portsmouth	1986	5 runs

INDIVIDUAL BATTING RECORDS

DOUBLE CENTURIES FOR DERBYSHIRE

Score	Batsman	Opponents	Venue	Year
274	G. Davidson	Lancashire	Old Trafford	1896
264	P. Vaulkhard	Nottinghamshire	Trent Bridge	1946
239*	K. J. Barnett	Leicestershire	Leicester	1988
238*	T. S. Worthington	Sussex	Derby	1937
233	L. F. Townsend	Leicestershire	Loughborough	1933
232	H. Storer	Essex	Derby	1933
229	C. A. Ollivierre	Essex	Chesterfield	1904
228	P. N. Kirsten	Somerset	Taunton	1981
228	P. J. Sharpe	Oxford University	Oxford	1976
227	A. Hamer	Nottinghamshire	Trent Bridge	1955
225	D. Smith	Hampshire	Chesterfield	1935
219	J. D. Eggar	Yorkshire	Bradford	1949
217	E. J. Barlow	Surrey	Ilkeston	1976
216*	W. Storer	Leicestershire	Chesterfield	1899
215	C. S. Elliott	Nottinghamshire	Trent Bridge	1947
213*	P. N. Kirsten	Glamorgan	Derby	1980
209	H. Storer	Essex	Derby	1929
209*	P. N. Kirsten	Northamptonshire	Derby	1980

*Not out.

Score	Batsman	Opponents	Venue	Year
207*	G. H. Pope	Hampshire	Portsmouth	1948
206*	P. N. Kirsten	Glamorgan	Chesterfield	1978
204*	P. N. Kirsten	Lancashire	Blackpool	1981
202*	P. N. Kirsten	Essex	Chesterfield	1980
202*	D. Smith	Nottinghamshire	Trent Bridge	1937
200*	T. S. Worthington	Worcestershire	Chesterfield	1933

CENTURIES FOR DERBYSHIRE IN LIMITED-OVERS MATCHES

40-overs competitions (10): Sunday League (John Player/Refuge Assurance)

Score	Batsman	Opponents	Venue	Year
120	A. Hill	Northamptonshire	Buxton	1976
101	A. J. Borrington	Somerset	Taunton	1977
102	P. N. Kirsten	Glamorgan	Swansea	1979
111	K. J. Barnett	Lancashire	Derby	1982
103	J. G. Wright	Worcestershire	Worcester	1982
108	J. G. Wright	Worcestershire	Coventry	1983
100*	K. J. Barnett	Somerset	Heanor	1983
131*	K. J. Barnett	Essex	Derby	1984
104	J. E. Morris	Gloucestershire	Gloucester	1984
101*	B. Roberts	Sussex	Hove	1987

55-overs competitions (8): Benson and Hedges Cup

Score	Batsman	Opponents	Venue	Year
111*	P. J. Sharpe	Glamorgan	Chesterfield	1976
102	J. G. Wright	Worcestershire	Chesterfield	1977
102*	A. Hill	Warwickshire	Ilkeston	1978
101	J. G. Wright	Glamorgan	Cardiff	1979
106	B. Wood	Worcestershire	Worcester	1982
107*	A. Hill	Scotland	Aberdeen	1985
115	K. J. Barnett	Gloucestershire	Derby	1987
100	B. Roberts	Northamptonshire	Derby	1987

60-overs competitions (3): NatWest Trophy/Gillette Cup

Score	Batsman	Opponents	Venue	Year
110*	P. N. Kirsten	Hampshire	Southampton	1982
153†	A. Hill	Cornwall	Derby	1986
134†	I. S. Anderson	Cornwall	Derby	1986

†Second wicket partnership of 286 by Anderson and Hill is the highest stand for *any* wicket in *any* one-day competition.

CARRYING BAT THROUGH A COMPLETED INNINGS

Batsman	Score	Total	Opponents	Venue	Year
A. E. Alderman	124*	(291)	Hampshire	Portsmouth	1934
H. Bagshaw	114*	(218)	Surrey	The Oval	1897
S. W. A. Cadman	36*	(71)	Hampshire	Derby	1912
	73*	(155)	Leicestershire	Leicester	1914

Batsman	Score	Total	Opponents	Venue	Year
C. S. Elliott	51*	(126)	Leicestershire	Ashby-de-la-Zouch	1948
A. Hamer	35*	(90)	Gloucestershire	Bristol	1950
	147*	(272)	Yorkshire	Leeds	1954†
	112*	(208)	Surrey	The Oval	1957
	57*	(105)	Gloucestershire	Bristol	1958
J. F. Harvey	23*	(67)	Surrey	The Oval	1964‡
A. Hill	48*	(127)	Kent	Maidstone	1984
C. Lee	96*	(211)	Middlesex	Chesterfield	1956
E. A. J. Maynard	28*	(55)	Lancashire	Derby	1882
A. Morton	28*	(62)	Yorkshire	Bradford	1910
	105*	(204)	Leicestershire	Derby	1920
E. Needham	58*	(111)	Surrey	Derby	1908
	107*	(195)	Essex	Leyton	1908§
L. Oliver	75*	(146)	Warwickshire	Birmingham	1912
D. Smith	140*	(265)	Hampshire	Chesterfield	1937
	57*	(112)	Kent	Ilkeston	1939
A. F. Townsend	102*	(228)	Lancashire	Manchester	1948
L. G. Wright	59*	(112)	Essex	Leyton	1899
	58*	(136)	Essex	Leyton	1903
	50*	(104)	Leicestershire	Leicester	1906
B. Wood	53*	(107)	Leicestershire	Derby	1981
J. G. Wright	141*	(259)	Nottinghamshire	Chesterfield	1982

†34 out of 55 for 3 in second innings – on field for all but 5 balls of match.
‡Two players (Hall and Morgan) absent hurt.
§104 out of 204 for 4 in the second innings of the same match.

MATCH DOUBLE—100 RUNS AND 10 WICKETS

G. M. Lee 100*; 5 for 65 and 7 for 78 v Northamptonshire at Northampton in 1927
L. F. Townsend 106*; 6 for 66 and 5 for 64 v Somerset at Weston-super-Mare 1934

CENTURIES FOR DERBYSHIRE
with centuries in all first-class cricket shown in brackets

No. of centuries	Batsman	No. of centuries	Batsman	No. of centuries	Batsman
30	D. Smith (32)	9	D. C. Morgan	4	P. D. Bowler
27	T. S. Worthington (31)		M. H. Page		J. F. Harvey
			C. P. Wilkins (18)		B. J. M. Maher
	J. G. Wright (47)	8	Dr. E. M. Ashcroft		A. E. G. Rhodes
25	K. J. Barnett		S. W. A. Cadman		D. H. K. Smith
22	L. F. Townsend		A. E. Lawton (11)		P. J. Sharpe
20	P. N. Kirsten (44)		C. Lee	3	E. J. Barlow (43)
	L. G. Wright		G. H. Pope		A. J. Borrington
19	A. Hamer		H. Bagshaw		G. Curgenven
18	H. Storer jnr	7	E. Needham		G. A. Davidson
	D. B. Carr (24)		W. Chatterton (8)		J. D. Eggar (4)
	A. Hill (19)		B. Roberts (8)		A. J. Harvey-Walker

No. of centuries	Batsman	No. of centuries	Batsman	No. of centuries	Batsman
16	G. M. Lee (24)	6	A. Morton		C. A. Ollivierre
	H. L. Johnson		L. Oliver		D. S. Steele (30)
15	A. C. Revill (16)		G. L. Willatt (13)	2	I. S. Anderson
	W. Storer		B. Wood (30)		W. Carter
13	J. E. Morris	5	I. R. Buxton		J. Chapman
12	A. E. Alderman		J. M. Hutchinson		W. P. Fowler
9	C. S. Elliott		A. F. Townsend		J. H. Hampshire (43)
	P. J. K. Gibbs (11)	4	J. B. Bolus (39)		G. Miller
	I. W. Hall		J. Bowden		W. F. Oates
	G. R. Jackson		S. H. Evershed		W. Sugg
	J. M. Kelly				

The following have each scored one century for Derbyshire:

H. Cartwright, G. O. Dawkes, L. C. Docker, J. R. Eyre, T. J. P. Eyre, T. Foster, C. Gladwin, W. W. H. Hill-Wood (3), D. G. Moir, P. G. Newman, J. Platts, A. V. Pope, R. Sale (junior) (3), R. Sharma, A. F. Skinner, A. G. Slater, F. H. Sugg (16), R. Swallow, R. W. Taylor, P. Vaulkhard, J. M. Ward, A. R. Warren.

CENTURIES IN THREE SUCCESSIVE INNINGS

Year	Batsman	Score	Opponents	Venue
1896	W. Storer	100 and 100*	Yorkshire	Derby
		142*	Leicestershire	Leicester
1905	L. G. Wright	195	Northamptonshire	Derby
		176 and 122	Warwickshire	Edgbaston
1982	P. N. Kirsten	113	Essex	Southend
		164* and 123*	Surrey	Derby

(W. Storer was the first professional cricketer to achieve this feat).

TWO SEPARATE HUNDREDS IN A MATCH

Year	Batsman	Score	Opponents	Venue
1896	W. Storer	100 and 100*	Yorkshire	Derby
1905	L. G. Wright	176 and 122	Warwickshire	Edgbaston
1907	E. Needham	107* and 104	Essex	Leyton
1929	H. Storer	119 and 100	Sussex	Derby
1938	T. S. Worthington	103 and 110*	Nottinghamshire	Ilkeston
1959	D. B. Carr	156* and 109	Kent	Canterbury
1965	I. W. Hall	101 and 101	Kent	Folkestone
1982	P. N. Kirsten	164* and 123*	Surrey	Derby

(W. Storer was the first professional cricketer to achieve this feat).

*Not out.

THREE CENTURIES IN AN INNINGS

1896 *v* Lancashire at Old Trafford: G. Davidson 274, W. Storer 116, W. Chatterton 104
1933 *v* Northamptonshire at Northampton: L. F. Townsend 142, D. Smith 129★, G. M. Lee 128
(1897 *v* Nottinghamshire at Trent Bridge: L. G. Wright 133, G. Davidson 121, E. M. Ashcroft 99,
S. H. Evershed 90. 1970 *v* Lancashire at Derby: D. H. K. Smith 136, Page 113, Wilkins 96)
★Not out.

FOUR CENTURIES IN AN INNINGS

1898 *v*. Hampshire at Derby: W. Chatterton 142, G. Davidson 108, W. Storer 100, L. G. Wright
134

SIX FIFTIES IN AN INNINGS

v Lancashire at Derby, 11 and 13 July 1914
(Chapman 88, Curgenven 86, Morton 80, Bowden 70, Oliver and Horsley 55 each)
For Lancashire Bullough did the 'hat-trick'

FAST SCORING

At Ilkeston against Nottinghamshire in 1933, T. S. Worthington scored 108 out of 117 in 70
minutes, almost snatching a victory for his side. Worthington completed his century in 60
minutes – the fastest ever for Derbyshire.

A CENTURY BEFORE LUNCH

Batsman	Score	Opponents	Venue	Date
H. Bagshaw	115	Yorkshire	Derby (2nd day)	1896
W. Sugg	102★	Worcestershire	Derby (3rd day)	1899
A. E. G. Rhodes	111★	Nottinghamshire	Ilkeston (2nd day)	1949
K. J. Barnett	103★	Somerset	Taunton (1st day)	1984
K. J. Barnett	114★	Gloucestershire	Derby (1st day)	1988

A claim that E. Needham achieved the feat *v* Leicestershire in 1910 cannot be substantiated.

OPENING STANDS OF 100 IN BOTH INNINGS OF THE SAME MATCH

Year	Batsmen	Scores	Opponents	Venue
1980	B. Wood and J. G. Wright	114 and 131	Worcestershire	Worcester
1983	I. S. Anderson and K. J. Barnett	158 and 109	Kent	Chesterfield

1,000 RUNS IN A SEASON IN DERBYSHIRE MATCHES

Batsman	Year	Runs	Av'ge	Batsman	Year	Runs	Av'ge
A. E. Alderman	1934	1293	32.32	A. E. Alderman	1938	1262	29.34
	1935	1154	24.04		1939	1275	26.56
	1936	1145	26.02	I. S. Anderson	1983	1233	37.36
	1937	1509	33.53	H. Bagshaw	1900	1055	29.30

Batsman	Year	Runs	Av'ge	Batsman	Year	Runs	Av'ge
E. J. Barlow	1976	1162	29.05	A. Hamer	1956	1341	31.92
K. J. Barnett	1983	1423	38.45		1957	1616	31.68
	1984	1734	45.63		1958	1355	27.65
	1985	1568	40.20		1959	1850	36.27
	1986	1502	37.55	J. H. Hampshire	1982	1256	41.40
	1987	1429	36.64	J. F. Harvey	1966	1112	22.24
	1988	1557	59.88		1968	1136	31.55
J. B. Bolus	1973	1167	31.54		1971	1226	32.23
	1975	1220	35.88	A. Hill	1976	1303	34.28
J. Bowden	1926	1221	30.52		1977	1014	32.70
	1928	1011	28.08		1983	1311	37.45
P. D. Bowler	1988	1725	46.62		1984	1352	32.97
I. R. Buxton	1962	1141	34.47		1986	1438	42.29
	1963	1084	21.68	G. R. Jackson	1925	1199	29.97
	1964	1219	28.34		1928	1078	29.13
	1967	1069	32.39		1929	1007	25.17
	1968	1029	24.50		1930	1177	25.04
S. W. A. Cadman	1909	1021	24.30	H. L. Johnson	1959	1480	35.23
	1911	1036	29.60		1960	1872	37.44
D. B. Carr	1955	1462	29.83		1961	1655	36.77
	1957	1324	30.09		1962	1757	34.45
	1958	1058	24.04		1964	1451	31.54
	1959	2165	48.11		1965	1026	21.37
	1960	1187	27.60	J. M. Kelly	1953	1145	29.35
	1961	1635	36.33		1954	1143	23.81
	1962	1006	23.95		1955	1110	21.76
W. Chatterton	1896	1019	40.76		1956	1033	25.82
	1901	1079	26.97		1957	1535	30.70
G. A. Davidson	1896	1033	41.32	P. N. Kirsten	1978	1133	36.54
C. S. Elliott	1947	1416	32.93		1979	1148	31.88
	1948	1338	32.39		1980	1895	63.16
	1949	1477	30.77		1981	1605	55.34
	1950	1454	28.50		1982	1941	64.70
	1951	1496	34.79	A. E. Lawton	1901	1005	23.37
	1952	1599	34.76	C. Lee	1956	1482	31.53
P. J. K. Gibbs	1968	1357	27.14		1957	1172	22.53
	1969	1001	27.05		1958	1373	28.02
	1970	1441	41.17		1959	1455	28.52
	1971	1307	31.11		1960	1304	26.61
	1972	1119	28.69		1961	1472	28.30
S. C. Goldsmith	1988	1071	30.60		1962	1503	37.57
I. W. Hall	1960	1177	24.52		1963	1202	25.04
	1962	1226	27.86	G. M. Lee	1925	1238	28.13
	1964	1167	31.54		1926	1150	28.75
	1965	1262	26.29		1928	1221	28.39
	1971	1449	33.69		1929	1242	32.68
A. Hamer	1950	1133	29.83		1931	1152	32.91
	1951	1519	31.00		1933	1078	24.50
	1952	1478	28.42	D. C. Morgan	1958	1167	24.82
	1953	1519	34.52		1959	1202	25.04
	1954	1560	33.91		1962	1517	45.96
	1955	1639	31.51		1963	1039	28.86

Batsman	Year	Runs	Av'ge	Batsman	Year	Runs	Av'ge
D. C. Morgan	1964	1616	36.72	H. Storer	1926	1235	36.32
	1966	1012	23.53		1928	1254	31.35
	1967	1110	30.83		1929	1652	36.71
	1968	1057	39.14		1930	1488	33.81
J. E. Morris	1986	1703	47.30		1931	1042	30.64
	1987	1305	35.27		1933	1109	42.65
	1988	1204	37.62	W. Storer	1896	1125	51.13
A. Morton	1914	1023	27.64		1898	1148	49.91
E. Needham	1908	1178	28.73		1899	1170	40.34
W. F. Oates	1961	1288	33.02		1900	1255	39.21
	1962	1175	26.70		1901	1170	26.59
C. A. Ollivierre	1904	1268	34.27	A. F. Townsend	1946	1188	27.63
M. H. Page	1968	1227	30.67		1947	1348	30.63
	1969	1037	39.88	L. F. Townsend	1930	1273	29.60
	1970	1344	40.72		1932	1373	29.84
	1971	1050	30.88		1933	1966	42.73
	1973	1229	40.96		1934	1156	26.27
	1975	1037	31.42		1935	1560	35.45
G. H. Pope	1937	1318	35.62		1936	1454	34.62
	1939	1457	32.37		1937	1261	28.02
	1948	1152	38.40		1938	1457	38.34
A. C. Revill	1949	1269	32.25	C. P. Wilkins	1970	1510	38.71
	1950	1643	35.71		1971	1517	35.27
	1951	1509	37.72		1972	1033	32.28
	1952	1433	29.85	G. L. Willatt	1952	1438	34.23
	1953	1268	30.92		1953	1114	26.52
	1954	1122	24.39		1954	1223	27.79
	1955	1199	24.46	B. Wood	1981	1439	46.41
A. E. G. Rhodes	1949	1156	25.68	T. S. Worthington	1928	1059	28.62
A. W. Richardson	1932	1258	29.95		1929	1031	23.43
B. Roberts	1985	1128	29.68		1932	1253	32.12
	1987	1643	43.23		1933	1243	29.59
L. G. Rowe	1974	1059	36.51		1934	1196	26.57
P. J. Sharpe	1976	1277	34.51		1935	1357	33.92
D. Smith	1931	1241	30.26		1936	1519	37.97
	1932	1551	35.25		1937	1558	38.95
	1934	1599	34.76		1938	1521	41.10
	1935	1767	42.07		1939	1045	27.50
	1936	1333	31.73	J. G. Wright	1977	1080	32.72
	1937	1914	40.72		1979	1249	39.03
	1938	1182	28.14		1980	1504	48.51
	1939	1597	31.94		1981	1257	40.54
	1946	1391	35.66		1982	1830	55.45
	1948	1076	28.31		1984	1201	60.05
	1949	1033	29.51	L. G. Wright	1899	1177	32.69
	1950	1117	33.84		1900	1040	32.50
D. H. K. Smith	1967	1337	27.28		1901	1422	32.32
	1968	1397	28.51		1904	1322	34.78
	1970	1241	28.86		1905	1716	42.90
D. S. Steele	1979	1190	39.66		1906	1043	24.83

THE WHOLE XI (INC. EXTRAS) REACHING DOUBLE FIGURES IN AN INNINGS

v Somerset at Taunton, August 1932

Worthington	70	Townsend	27	A. V. Pope	15
Richardson	60	Blaxland	26	Clarke	13
H. Elliott	56★	Smith	24	Mitchell	10
Lee	40	Copson	15	Extras	18
				Total	374

HIGHEST SCORE ON DEBUT

Score	Batsman	Inns.	Opponents	Venue	Year
155★	P. D. Bowler	1st	Cambridge Univ.	Cambridge	1988
110★	A. J. Harvey-Walker	2nd	Oxford Univ.	Burton-on-Trent	1971
94	L. G. Rowe	2nd	Sussex	Derby	1974
80	B. Roberts	2nd	Leicestershire	Derby	1984
74★	D. S. Steele	1st	Leicestershire	Derby	1979
74	J. M. Kelly	2nd	Surrey	The Oval	1950
73	M. Jean-Jacques	1st	Yorkshire	Abbeydale Park, Sheffield	1986
73	F. H. Sugg	1st	Lancashire	Old Trafford	1884
71	J. D. Eggar	1st	Glamorgan	Chesterfield	1946
70	A. J. Borrington	1st	Essex	Ilford	1971
66★	I. Gibson	1st	Nottinghamshire	Ilkeston	1957
64	G. R. Sparrow	1st	Northamptonshire	Northampton	1905
64	G. R. Stephenson	1st	Middlesex	Derby	1967
62	W. S. Eadie	2nd	Lancashire	Old Trafford	1885
58	F. A. Barrs	1st	Surrey	Derby	1900
57	E. Needham	1st	S. Africans	Derby	1901
56	R. Kenward	2nd	Essex	Leyton	1899
56	J. L. Crommelin-Brown	1st	Worcestershire	Worcester	1922
55	S. C. Goldsmith	1st	Cambridge Univ.	Cambridge	1988
53	W. Foulke	1st	Essex	Leyton	1900
51★	J. Burton	1st	Nottinghamshire	Derby	1901
51	A. J. Wood	1st	Leicestershire	Chesterfield	1911
50	E. Sykes	1st	Gloucestershire	Chesterfield	1925

(In 1986 Bowler scored 100 not out on his debut for Leicestershire *v* Hampshire at Leicester).

HIGHEST INDIVIDUAL SCORES AGAINST EACH OPPONENT

Score	Batsman	Opponents	Venue	Year
232	H.. Storer	Essex	Derby	1933
213★	P. N. Kirsten	Glamorgan	Derby	1980
169	W. Chatterton	Gloucestershire	Bristol	1901
225	D. Smith	Hampshire	Chesterfield	1935
191	G. M. Lee	Kent	Derby	1926

★Not out.

Score	Batsman	Opponents	Venue	Year
191	J. E. Morris	Kent	Derby	1986
274	G. Davidson	Lancashire	Old Trafford	1896
233	L. F. Townsend	Leicestershire	Loughborough	1933
170	H. Storer	Middlesex	Derby	1932
209★	P. N. Kirsten	Northamptonshire	Derby	1980
264	P. Vaulkhard	Nottinghamshire	Trent Bridge	1946
228	P. N. Kirsten	Somerset	Taunton	1981
217	E. J. Barlow	Surrey	Ilkeston	1976
238★	T. S. Worthington	Sussex	Derby	1937
198	J. Chapman	Warwickshire	Coventry	1909
200★	T. S. Worthington	Worcestershire	Chesterfield	1933
219	J. D. Eggar	Yorkshire	Bradford	1949
144	J. G. Wright	Australia	Derby	1981
144	P. D. Bowler	Cambridge Univ.	Burton-on-Trent	1976
127★	D. S. Steele	India	Derby	1979
149	A. E. Lawton	London County	Derby	1902
175★	W. Storer	M.C.C.	Lord's	1900
145★	A. C. Revill	New Zealand	Derby	1949
228	P. J. Sharpe	Oxford Univ.	Oxford	1976
164	J. G. Wright	Pakistan	Chesterfield	1978
93	Dr. E. M. Ashcroft	South Africa	Derby	1904
75★	A. Hill	Sri Lanka	Derby	1979
96	J. G. Wright	West Indies	Chesterfield	1980

(For England *v* All India at The Oval in 1936 T. S. Worthington made 128).

★Not out.

INDIVIDUAL BOWLING RECORDS
'HAT-TRICKS' FOR DERBYSHIRE IN FIRST-CLASS MATCHES

Bowler	Opponents	Venue	Year
J. T. B. D. Platts	Yorkshire	Derby	1880
H. Evans	Sussex	Hove	1881
J. Marlow	Kent	Derby	1884
W. Cropper	Hampshire	Southampton	1885
G. A. Davidson	Lancashire	Derby	1895
G. A. Davidson	M.C.C.	Lord's	1898
F. Davidson	Nottinghamshire	Derby	1898
J. Horsley	Australian Imperial Forces XI	Derby	1919
H. Storer	Northamptonshire	Chesterfield	1922
L. F. Townsend	Northamptonshire	Northampton	1931
W. H. Copson	Lancashire	Burton-on-Trent	1937
W. H. Copson	Warwickshire (4 in 4 balls)	Derby	1937
W. H. Copson	Oxford Univ. (4 in 5 balls)	Oxford	1939
E. J. Gothard	Middlesex	Derby	1947
G. H. Pope	Nottinghamshire	Ilkeston	1947
A. E. G. Rhodes	Gentlemen of Ireland	Buxton	1947
A. E. G. Rhodes	Essex	Colchester	1948

Bowler	Opponents	Venue	Year
A. E. G. Rhodes	Oxford University	Oxford	1950
A. E. G. Rhodes	Sussex	Derby	1951
C. Gladwin	New Zealand	Derby	1958
H. L. Jackson	Worcestershire	Kidderminster	1958
H. L. Jackson	Worcestershire	Derby	1960
H. J. Rhodes	Oxford University	Buxton	1961
'I. R. Buxton	Oxford University	Derby	1969
M. Hendrick	West Indians	Chesterfield	1980
D. S. Steele	Glamorgan	Derby	1980
O. H. Mortensen	Leicestershire	Derby	1987

HAT-TRICKS IN ONE-DAY MATCHES

Sunday League

Bowler	Opponents	Venue	Year
A. Ward	Sussex (4 in 4 balls)	Derby	1970
C. J. Tunnicliffe	Worcester	Derby	1979

NatWest Trophy/Gillette Cup

Bowler	Opponents	Venue	Year
M. Jean-Jacques	Nottinghamshire	Derby	1987

NINE OR TEN WICKETS IN AN INNINGS FOR DERBYSHIRE

Analysis	Bowler	Opponents	Venue	Year
10-40	W. Bestwick	Glamorgan	Cardiff	1921
10-64	T. B. Mitchell	Leicestershire	Leicester	1935
9-80	W. Mycroft	Lancashire	Derby	1875
9-25	W. Mycroft	Hampshire	Southampton	1876
9-42	G. A. Davidson	Gloucestershire	Derby	1886
9-27	J. J. Hulme	Yorkshire	Sheffield	1894
9-39	G. A. Davidson	Warwickshire	Derby	1895
9-68	G. G. Walker	Leicestershire	Leicester	1895
9-71	A. Morton	Nottinghamshire	Blackwell	1911
9-65	W. Bestwick	Warwickshire	Edgbaston	1921
9-119	C. Gladwin	Lancashire	Buxton	1947
9-60	H. L. Jackson	Lancashire	Old Trafford	1952
9-41	C. Gladwin	Worcestershire	Stourbridge	1952
9-46	E. Smith	Scotland	Edinburgh	1955
9-17	H. L. Jackson	Cambridge University	Cambridge	1959
9-20	F. W. Swarbrook	Sussex	Hove	1975

SEVENTEEN OR SIXTEEN WICKETS IN A MATCH

Analysis	Bowler	Opponents	Venue	Year
17-103	W. Mycroft	Hampshire	Southampton	1876
16-84	C. Gladwin	Worcestershire	Stourbridge	1952

FIFTEEN OR FOURTEEN WICKETS IN A MATCH

Analysis	Bowler	Opponents	Venue	Year
14-100	G. Porter	Hampshire	Derby	1895
15-116	G. A. Davidson	Essex	Leyton	1898
15-112	A. R. Warren	Nottinghamshire	Welbeck	1904
14-213	T. Forester	Essex	Leyton	1914
14-104	S. W. A. Cadman	Northamptonshire	Northampton	1920
14-111	W. Bestwick	Glamorgan	Cardiff	1921
14-48	A. G. Slater	Somerset	Chesterfield	1930
14-90	L. F. Townsend	Gloucestershire	Chesterfield	1933
14-159	C. Gladwin	Lancashire	Buxton	1947
14-112	E. Smith	Scotland	Edinburgh	1955

FIVE WICKETS IN AN INNINGS ON DEBUT

Bowler	Analysis	Year	Bowler	Analysis	Year
D. Gregory	6/9	1871	J. O'Connor	5/56★	1900
W. Mycroft	6/35	1873	W. J. V. Tomlinson	5/53	1920
A. H. J. Cochrane	6/51	1884	A. J. Mellor	5/52	1978
F. J. Shacklock	5/47	1884	P. J. Hacker	5/61	1982

★O'Connor also took 5 for 69 in the second innings of the same match.

100 WICKETS IN A SEASON

Bowler	Year	Wkts	Av'ge	Bowler	Year	Wkts	Av'ge
W. Bestwick	1905	104	21.98	T. B. Mitchell	1929	111	19.01
	1906	115	18.46		1930	138	18.30
	1908	103	21.79		1931	110	21.04
	1921	147	16.72		1932	121	21.17
W. H. Copson	1936	153	12.54		1933	142	19.30
	1938	101	19.75		1934	145	17.27
	1939	129	15.26		1935	168	19.54
C. Gladwin	1946	105	18.43		1936	121	21.42
	1947	104	17.88		1937	129	21.99
	1948	125	16.47		1938	131	19.61
	1949	110	20.09	A. Morton	1910	116	22.67
	1951	128	17.94		1922	100	17.24
	1952	151	18.55	W. Mycroft	1878	101	9.45
	1953	130	18.11	G. H. Pope	1947	113	17.79
	1954	131	16.60		1948	100	17.24
	1955	142	15.35	A. E. G. Rhodes	1950	128	21.88
	1956	104	19.36	H. J. Rhodes	1961	108	19.61
	1957	104	18.36		1965	119	11.04
	1958	117	15.35		1967	102	15.53
A. B. Jackson	1965	120	12.42	A. G. Slater	1931	108	16.26
H. L. Jackson	1949	103	20.99	E. Smith	1955	105	17.65
	1952	114	18.03	L. F. Townsend	1928	103	22.45
	1953	103	15.28		1929	100	20.00
	1954	125	14.80		1932	113	18.15

Bowler	Year	Wkts	Av'ge	Bowler	Year	Wkts	Av'ge
H. L. Jackson	1956	122	17.47	A. R. Warren	1904	124	20.94
	1957	138	16.03		1908	105	21.60
	1958	135	10.09				
	1959	132	16.86				
	1960	150	13.56				
	1962	105	19.16				

In 1958 H. L. Jackson took 143 wickets in all first class matches, average 10.99. This was the lowest for a bowler taking at least 100 wickets in a season since 1894 when T. Richardson (Surrey) took 196 wickets, average 10.32.

WICKET WITH FIRST BALL BOWLED

Bowler	Opponents	Venue	Year
H. G. Curgenven	Essex	Leyton	1896
W. H. Copson	Surrey	The Oval	1932
F. C. Brailsford	Sussex	Derby	1958
J. G. Wright	West Indians	Chesterfield	1980

(S. G. Walker, R. Sale (junior) and T. J. P. Eyre each took a wicket with their second deliveries).

BOWLERS UNCHANGED IN A MATCH

1894 v Yorkshire at Sheffield

	O	M	R	W	O	M	R	W
G. Davidson	29	18	33	8	18	5	21	1
J. J. Hulme	28	12	43	1	17.4	8	27	9

(Yorkshire's scores were 81 and 50. Derbyshire's 104 and 28 for 1).

1912 v Northamptonshire at Northampton

	O	M	R	W	O	M	R	W
T. Forester	17.5	7	18	7	13	5	30	1
A. Morton	17	7	37	3	13	4	28	3

(Derbyshire scored 67 and 46. Northamptonshire 56 and 58 for 4).

REMARKABLE BOWLING ANALYSES

Bowler	Opponents	Venue	Year	O	M	R	W
W. H. Copson	Warwickshire	Derby	1937	8.2	2	11	8
W. H. Copson	Oxford Univ.	Oxford	1939	6.0	2	12	5
				4.7	2	9	5
H. L. Jackson	Cambridge Univ.	Cambridge	1959	14.0	7	16	3
				17.3	9	17	9
T. B. Mitchell	Sussex	Chesterfield	1931	10.2	4	11	6
				10.2	3	19	6
G. H. Pope	Yorkshire	Chesterfield	1948	14.1	9	12	6
				17.0	11	13	4

(Six Yorkshire wickets down in second innings)

THE WHOLE XI BOWLING IN AN INNINGS

Opponents	Venue	Year
Worcestershire	Worcester	1902
Leicestershire	Ashby-de-la-Zouch	1955

BOWLING RECORDS

The table below includes bowlers who have taken 1,000 wickets

Bowler		Wkts	Runs	Av'ge
H. L. Jackson	1947–1963	1670	28589	17.11
C. Gladwin	1939–1958	1536	27147	17.67
W. Bestwick	1898–1925	1452	30881	21.26
T. B. Mitchell	1928–1939	1417	28630	20.20
D. C. Morgan	1950–1969	1216	30523	25.10
E. Smith	1951–1971	1209	31189	25.79
W. H. Copson	1932–1950	1033	19380	18.76

PROGRESSIVE WICKET PARTNERSHIP RECORDS

First wicket

Score	Batsmen	Opponents	Venue	Year
50	R. P. Smith (47) and J. Smith (27)	Kent	Tunbridge Wells	1874
61	W. Rigley (35) and W. Hickton (27)	Kent	Derby	1878
86	R. P. Smith (50) and W. Rigley (69)	Lancashire	Derby	1878
113	A Shuker (40) and L. C. Docker (80)	Sussex	Brighton	1881
160	L. G. Wright (133) and S. H. Evershed (90)	Nottinghamshire	Trent Bridge	1897
173	L. G. Wright(90) and C. A. Ollivierre (91)	Surrey	The Oval	1904
191	L. G. Wright (68) and C. A. Ollivierre (229)	Essex	Chesterfield	1904
206	W. W. H. Hill-Wood (107) and J. Bowden (114)	Somerset	Bath	1923
322	H. Storer (209) and J. Bowden (120)	Essex	Derby	1929

Second wicket

Score	Batsmen	Opponents	Venue	Year
73	J. Smith (35) and A. Hind (77)	M.C.C.	Lord's	1876
76	W. Rigley (64) and G. B. Barrington (24)	Lancashire	Old Trafford	1880
109†	A. Shuker (86) and L. C. Docker (60)	Sussex	Brighton	1882
192	S. H. Evershed (85) and H. Bagshaw (115)	Yorkshire	Derby	1896
198	L. G. Wright (170) and W. Storer (176)	Essex	Leyton	1900
210	L. G. Wright (149) and E. M. Ashcroft (73)	Sussex	Derby	1905
349	C. S. Elliott (215) and J. D. Eggar (173)	Nottinghamshire	Trent Bridge	1947

†Wisden gives 108, Sussex scorebook 109 which must take precedence.

Third wicket

Score	Batsmen	Opponents	Venue	Year
80	G. Frost (52) and R. P. Smith (43)	Hampshire	Derby	1876
99	R. P. Smith (55) and W. Rigley (65)	Sussex	Derby	1880
136	L. G. Wright (90) and W. Chatterton (70)	Warwickshire	Edgbaston	1895
208	W. Chatterton (104) and G. A. Davidson (274)	Lancashire	Old Trafford	1896
215	D. Smith (131) and G. M. Lee (147)	Essex	Leyton	1931
222	L. F. Townsend (233) and H. Elliott (94)	Leicestershire	Loughborough	1933
235	D. Smith (225) and L. F. Townsend (52)	Hampshire	Chesterfield	1935
246	J. M. Kelly (127) and D. B. Carr (141)	Leicestershire	Chesterfield	1957
291	P. N. Kirsten (228) and D. S. Steele (137)	Somerset	Taunton	1981

Fourth wicket

Score	Batsmen	Opponents	Venue	Year
85	T. Foster (40) and R. P. Smith (69)	Hampshire	Southampton	1878
118	L. C. Docker (60) and T. Foster (61)	Kent	Derby	1881
128	L. C. Docker (107) and R. P. Smith (43)	Kent	Maidstone	1881
159	W. Chatterton (113) and W. Sugg (56)	Essex	Leyton	1886
190	H. Bagshaw (127*) and S. H. Evershed (112)	Yorkshire	Derby	1895
308	G. A. Davidson (274) and W. Storer (116)	Lancashire	Old Trafford	1896
328	P. Vaulkhard (264) and D. Smith (146)	Nottinghamshire	Trent Bridge	1946

Fifth wicket

Score	Batsmen	Opponents	Venue	Year
83	W. G. Curgenven (71) and U. Sowter (39)	Kent	Derby	1875
83	L. C. Docker (58) and W. Chatterton (45)	Surrey	Derby	1884
85	F. H. Sugg (61) and W. Cropper (39)	Kent	Gravesend	1884
170	W. Chatterton (127) and W. Storer (87)	Leicestershire	Derby	1895
176	W. Chatterton (142) and G. A. Davidson (108)	Hampshire	Derby	1898
191	A. G. Slater (96) and A. Morton (90)	Hampshire	Basingstoke	1914
203	C. P. Wilkins (156) and I. R. Buxton (57*)	Lancashire	Old Trafford	1971

Sixth wicket

Score	Batsmen	Opponents	Venue	Year
86	L. C. Docker (52) and W. Cropper (36)	Surrey	Derby	1883
86	W. Cropper (51) and E. A. J. Maynard (84)	Surrey	The Oval	1883
113	F. H. Sugg (187) and W. Cropper (42)	Hampshire	Southampton	1885
163	G. A. Davidson (97) and W. Sugg (84)	Essex	Derby	1897
212	G. M. Lee (130) and T. S. Worthington (93)	Essex	Chesterfield	1932

Seventh wicket

Score	Batsmen	Opponents	Venue	Year
71	J. T. B. D. Platts (48) and T. Foster (36)	Hampshire	Southampton	1877
98	W. Chatterton (61) and W. Evershed (56)	Sussex	Brighton	1883
138	W. Storer (216*) and W. Ellis (58)	Leicestershire	Chesterfield	1899
153	J. M. Hutchinson (138) and A. G. Slater (89)	Somerset	(Burton-on-Trent)	1929
170	G. M. Lee (107) and A. V. Pope (72)	Leicestershire	Chesterfield	1933
241*	G. H. Pope (207*) and A. E. G. Rhodes (105*)	Hampshire	Portsmouth	1948

*Not out.

Eighth wicket

Score	Batsmen	Opponents	Venue	Year
95	A. H. J. Cochrane (50) and G. G. Walker (66)	Surrey	The Oval	1884
123	S. H. Evershed (80) and W. Storer (56)	Nottinghamshire	Trent Bridge	1895
134	S. W. A. Cadman (126) and J. Humphries (44)	Essex	Leyton	1904
182	W. Carter (145) and A. H. M. Jackson (75)	Leicestershire	Leicester	1922

Ninth wicket

Score	Batsmen	Opponents	Venue	Year
73	T. Foster (81) and W. Cropper (24)	Surrey	The Oval	1883
78	W. Sugg (104*) and G. G. Walker (19)	Leicestershire	Leicester	1895
81*	W. Storer (100*) and J. J. Hulme (51*)	Yorkshire	Derby	1896
93	A. E. Lawton (126) and J. J. Hulme (33*)	Warwickshire	Derby	1902
132	S. W. A. Cadman (93) and A. Morton (56)	Warwickshire	Glossop	1904
283	J. Chapman (165) and A. R. Warren (123)	Warwickshire	Blackwell	1910

(The ninth wicket stand of 283 is a World Record.)

Tenth wicket

Score	Batsmen	Opponents	Venue	Year
53	W. Chatterton (49) and T. Mycroft (24)	Surrey	The Oval	1884
56	G. Davidson (75) and J. Disney (22*)	Yorkshire	Derby	1887
69	G. G. Walker (44*) and G. Porter (34)	Leicestershire	Leicester	1895
72	W. Storer (216*) and W. Bestwick (2)	Leicestershire	Chesterfield	1899
87	T. Forester (61*) and J. Humphries (40)	Warwickshire	Edgbaston	1910
93	J. Humphries (46*) and J. Horsley (55)	Lancashire	Derby	1914
132	A. Hill (172*) and M. Jean-Jacques (73)	Yorkshire	Abbeydale Park	1986

*Not out.

WICKET-KEEPING RECORDS

MOST DISMISSALS IN AN INNINGS

No	Ct	St	Wicket-keeper	Opponents	Venue	Year
7	7	—	R. W. Taylor	Glamorgan	Derby	1966
7	7	—		Yorkshire	Chesterfield	1975
6	6	—		Sussex	Chesterfield	1963
6	6	—		Yorkshire	Abbeydale Park, Sheffield	1983
			(5 in an innings on 6 occasions)			
6	4	2	H. Elliott	Worcestershire	Worcester	1931
6	5	1		Middlesex	Derby	1932
6	4	2		Lancashire	Old Trafford	1935
			(5 in an innings on 10 occasions)			
6	6	—	T. Foster	Surrey	The Oval	1883

MOST DISMISSALS IN A MATCH

No	Ct	St	Wicket-keeper	Opponents	Venue	Year
10	10	–	R. W. Taylor	Hampshire	Chesterfield	1963
9	9	–		Yorkshire	Chesterfield	1975
			(7 in a match on 5 occasions)			
10	8	2	H. Elliott	Lancashire	Old Trafford	1935
8	5	3		Worcestershire	Worcester	1931
8	6	2		Essex	Derby	1933
			(7 in a match on 8 occasions)			
8	8	–	G. O. Dawkes	Essex	Westcliffe-on-Sea	1958
			(7 in a match on 5 occasions)			
			J. Humphries			
			(7 in a match on 5 occasions)			
			J. Disney			
			(7 in a match once—only 13 wkts fell)			

MOST DISMISSALS IN A SEASON

No	Ct	St	Wicket-keeper	Year
90	69	21	H. Elliott	1935
89	67	22	H. Elliott	1933
78	58	20	H. Elliott	1934
76	59	17	H. Elliott	1932
76	69	7	J. Humphries	1906
76	72	4	B. J. M. Maher	1987
86	79	7	R. W. Taylor	1965
83	81	2	R. W. Taylor	1963
80	77	3	R. W. Taylor	1962

MOST DISMISSALS IN A CAREER

Wicket-keeper	Ct	St	Total
R. W. Taylor	1,157	147	1304
H. Elliott*	889	294	1183
G. O. Dawkes	770	105	875

*In 1936 Elliott allowed no byes in 25 completed innings.

FIELDING RECORDS

SIX CATCHES IN A MATCH

Fielder	Opponents	Venue	Year
W. Chatterton	M.C.C.	Lord's	1895
	Nottinghamshire	Chesterfield	1900
A. G. Slater	Essex	Leyton	1914
D. C. Morgan	Glamorgan	Pontypridd	1953
	Glamorgan	Chesterfield	1960
I. W. Hall	Warwickshire	Coventry	1966
M. H. Page	Essex	Chesterfield	1967
G. Miller	Somerset	Derby	1982

FIVE CATCHES IN AN INNINGS

Fielder	Opponents	Venue	Year
C. Lee	Lancashire	Chesterfield	1960
D. C. Morgan	Glamorgan	Chesterfield	1960
P. E. Russell	Pakistan	Chesterfield	1978

MOST CATCHES IN A SEASON

Fielder	No.	Year
M. H. Page	49	1967
D. B. Carr	47	1960
D. C. Morgan	45	1958
D. B. Carr	44	1958
A. C. Revill	42	1952
D. B. Carr	42	1957
D. C. Morgan	42	1955
D. C. Morgan	42	1957
D. C. Morgan	40	1959

MOST CATCHES IN A CAREER

Fielder	For Derbyshire
D. C. Morgan	563
D. B. Carr	404
D. Smith	360
A. C. Revill	327
T. S. Worthington	307

TEST CAREER RECORDS OF DERBYSHIRE PLAYERS

Name	Country	Years	M	Inns	No	Runs	HS	Av'ge	Wkts	Av'ge	Ct	St
E. J. Barlow	South Africa	1961/62–1969-70	30	57	2	2516	201	45.74	40	34.05	35	—
K. J. Barnett	England	1988	1	2	0	66	66	33.00	—	—	1	—
R. Berry	England	1950	2	4	2	6	4*	3.00	9	25.33	2	—
J. B. Bolus	England	1963–1963/64	7	12	0	496	88	41.33	—	—	2	—
D. B. Carr	England	1951/52	2	4	0	135	76	33.75	2	70.00	—	—
W. Chatterton	England	1891/92	1	1	0	48	48	48.00	—	—	—	—
W. H. Copson	England	1939–1947	3	1	1	6	6	6.00	15	19.80	1	—
H. Elliott	England	1927/28–1933/34	4	5	1	61	37*	15.25	—	—	8	3
M. C. Frederick	West Indies	1953/54	1	2	0	30	30	15.00	—	—	1	—
C. Gladwin	England	1947–1949	8	11	5	170	51*	28.33	15	38.06	2	—
J. H. Hampshire	England	1969–1975	8	16	1	403	107	26.86	—	—	9	—
M. Hendrick	England	1974–1981	30	35	15	128	15	6.40	87	25.83	25	—
M. A. Holding	West Indies	1975/76–1986/87	60	76	10	910	73	13.78	249	23.68	22	—
J. Humphries	England	1907/08	3	6	1	44	16	8.80	—	—	7	—
H. L. Jackson	England	1949–1961	2	2	1	15	8	15.00	7	22.14	1	—
G. Miller	England	1976–1984	34	51	4	1213	98*	25.80	60	30.98	17	—
T. B. Mitchell	England	1932-33–1935	5	6	2	20	9	5.00	8	62.25	1	—
G. H. Pope	England	1947	1	1	1	8	8*	—	1	85.00	—	—
H. J. Rhodes	England	1959	2	1	1	0	0*	—	9	27.11	—	—
C. F. Root	England	1926	3	1	1	0	0*	—	8	24.25	1	—
L. G. Rowe	West Indies	1971/72–1979/80	30	49	2	2047	302	43.55	—	—	17	—
F. E. Rumsey	England	1964–1965	5	5	3	30	21*	15.00	17	27.11	—	—
P. J. Sharpe	England	1963–1969	12	21	4	786	111*	46.23	—	—	17	—
D. Smith	England	1935	2	4	0	128	57	32.00	—	—	1	—
F. R. Spofforth	Australia	1876/77–1886/87	18	29	6	217	50	9.43	94	18.41	11	—
D. S. Steele	England	1975–1976	8	16	0	673	106	42.06	2	19.50	7	—
W. Storer	England	1897/98–1899	6	11	0	215	51	19.54	2	54.00	11	—
F. H. Sugg	England	1888	2	2	0	55	31	27.50	—	—	2	—
R. W. Taylor	England	1970/1–1983/84	57	83	12	1156	97	16.28	—	—	167	7
L. F. Townsend	England	1929/30–1933/34	4	6	0	97	40	16.16	6	34.16	2	—
S. Venkataraghavan	India	1964/65–1983/84	57	76	12	748	64	11.68	156	36.11	44	—
A. Ward	England	1969–1976	5	6	1	40	21	8.00	14	32.35	3	—
A. R. Warren	England	1905	1	1	0	7	7	7.00	6	18.83	1	—
B. Wood	England	1972–1978	12	21	0	454	90	21.61	—	—	6	—
T. S. Worthington	England	1929/30–1936/37	9	11	1	321	128	29.18	8	39.50	8	—
J. G. Wright	New Zealand	1977/78–1988/89	61	109	4	3571	141	34.01	—	—	27	—

DERBYSHIRE CAPTAINS

1871–75	S. Richardson
1876–83	R. P. Smith
1884	L. C. Docker
1885–86	E. A. J. Maynard
1887	E. A. J. Maynard and W. Chatterton
1888–89	W. Chatterton
1890	F. R. Spofforth
1891–98	S. H. Evershed
1899–01	S. H. Wood
1902–03	A. E. Lawton
1904–05	A. E. Lawton and E. M. Ashcroft
1906	A. E. Lawton and L. G. Wright
1907	L. G. Wright
1908	A. E. Lawton and R. B. Rickman
1909	A. E. Lawton
1910–12	J. Chapman
1913–14	R. R. C. Baggallay
1919	R. R. C. Baggallay and J. Chapman
1920	J. Chapman and L. Oliver
1921	G. M. Buckston
1922–30	G. R. Jackson
1931–36	A. W. Richardson
1937–39	R. H. R. Buckston
1946	G. F. Hodgkinson
1947–48	E. J. Gothard
1949	D. A. Skinner
1950	P. Vaulkhard
1951–54	G. L. Willatt
1955–62	D. B. Carr
1963–64	C. Lee
1965–69	D. C. Morgan
1970–72	I. R. Buxton
1973–75	J. B. Bolus
1975–76	R. W. Taylor
1976–78	E. J. Barlow
1979	D. S. Steele
1979–81	G. Miller
1981–83	B. Wood
1983	K. J. Barnett

TESTIMONIALS AND BENEFITS IN DERBYSHIRE

Year		£
1947	D. Smith	1970
1948	A. E. Alderman	1659
1949	W. H. Copson	2500
1950	C. S. Elliott	1667
1952	A. E. G. Rhodes	2096
1953	C. Gladwin	3300
1955	A. C. Revill	1705
1956	G. O. Dawkes	2662
1957	H. L. Jackson (Benefit)	2944
1958	A. Hamer (Benefit)	2741
1959	W. T. Taylor (Members' Testimonials)	1785
1960	J. M. Kelly (Benefit)	2343
1961	D. C. Morgan	2891
1962	G. O. Dawkes and H. L. Jackson	2902
1964	C. Lee	2992
1965	H. L. Johnson	2383
1966	E. Smith	2810
1968	H. J. Rhodes	8495
1971	I. W. Hall	2840
1972	I. R. Buxton	5603
1973	R. W. Taylor	6672

Year		£
1975	M. H. Page	3500
1980	M. Hendrick	36050
1981	R. W. Taylor	54000
1985	G. Miller	35207
1986	A. Hill	48647
1988	J. G. Wright	52168

The above figures are the amounts collected and subscribed (and in the case of a Benefit, plus the gate money, including Pluvius Insurance income). In the case of a Benefit, the match and printing expenses, plus insurance premiums, have to be met by the player concerned.

UNIVERSITY BLUES WHO HAVE PLAYED FOR DERBYSHIRE

The following Oxford and Cambridge Blues have played for, or were born in Derbyshire, the dates given being those of their appearances at Lord's in the Varsity match.

OXFORD UNIVERSITY

E. L. Bateman	1854–1855	I. Gibson	1955–1958
G. F. Bell	1919	C. K. H. Hill-Wood	1928–1930
D. B. Carr	1949–1951	D. J. C. H. Hill-Wood	1928
A. H. J. Cochrane	1885, 1886, 1888	R. Sale	1910
J. D. Eggar	1938	R. Sale	1939, 1946
N. M. Ford	1928–1930	C. A. Wallroth	1872–1874
P. J. K. Gibbs	1964–1966	J. M. Ward	1970–1973

CAMBRIDGE UNIVERSITY

G. P. Brooke-Taylor	1919, 1920	M. H. Stevenson	1949–1952
G. M. Buckston	1903	E. J. Thornewill	1856
D. J. Green	1957–1959	W. J. V. Tomlinson	1923
W. W. Hill-Wood	1922	H. G. Topham	1883, 1884
W. E. G. Payton	1937	G. L. Willatt	1946, 1947

GENTLEMEN v PLAYERS AT LORD'S

For a great many years it was considered one of cricket's highest honours to be chosen to play in this fixture. The following Derbyshire cricketers have been honoured to play in these matches which no longer take place.

Gentlemen

D. B. Carr	1950, 1959, 1960
A. H. J. Cochrane	1886
G. L. Willatt	1947, 1952

Players

W. Bestwick	1919
W. Chatterton	1889, 1892, 1894, 1897
W. H. Copson	1936, 1939
G. A. Davidson	1895
C. Gladwin	1947
H. L. Jackson	1949, 1959, 1960
T. B. Mitchell	1931, 1934
W. Mycroft	1877
G. H. Pope	1939
D. Smith	1935
W. Storer	1894, 1895, 1896, 1897, 1898, 1899, 1901
L. F. Townsend	1929, 1933

C. F. Root (1926), F. J. Shacklock (1889) and F. H. Sugg (1890, 1893, 1895, 1896) all appeared for the Players in this fixture after they had left Derbyshire to play for Worcestershire, Nottinghamshire and Lancashire respectively. They were all born in Derbyshire.

CONSECUTIVE VICTORIES IN CHAMPIONSHIP MATCHES

It is not a common occurrence for a side to win three or more successive Championship matches – the weather alone often spoils the possibility of such a sequence.

Derbyshire first won three in a row in 1895 and have achieved this on 21 occasions. In 1927, 1935, 1937, 1947 and 1955 it was done twice. Four victories in succession came in 1929, 1934, 1937, 1952, 1958 and 1977 though it was first done in 1891 against Surrey, Leicestershire, Warwickshire and Essex when Derbyshire and the last three of the four named were rated as second class counties.

Five wins in succession came in 1935 and 1954, and six in 1957.

FATHERS AND SONS WHO HAVE REPRESENTED DERBYSHIRE

Father	*Son(s)*
G. Beet	G. H. C. Beet
G. H. C. Beet	G. A. Beet
W. Bestwick	R. S. Bestwick
G. M. Buckston	R. H. R. Buckston
Dr W. G. Curgenven	G. and H. G. Curgenven
J. Davidson	F. and G. A. Davidson
J. Gladwin	C. Gladwin
T. A. Higson	T. A. Higson jnr
Sir S. H. Hill-Wood	B. S. H., C. K. H., D. J. C. H. and W. W. H. Hill-Wood
S. Malthouse	W. N. Malthouse
T. F. Revill	A. C. Revill
A. E. G. Rhodes	H. J. Rhodes
A. W. Richardson	G. W. Richardson
R. Sale	R. Sale jnr
Henry Slater	A. G. and Herbert Slater
Harry Storer	Harry Storer jnr

BROTHERS WHO HAVE REPRESENTED DERBYSHIRE

J. Chatterton and W. Chatterton
B. O. Corbett and C. J. Corbett
G. Curgenven and H. G. Curgenven
F. Davidson and G. A. Davidson
F. D. Docker, L. C. Docker and R. Docker
J. T. C. Eadie and W. S. Eadie
H. Evans and T. Evans
E. Evershed, S. H. Evershed and W. Evershed
G. Frost and J. H. Frost
F. R. Heath and J. S. Heath
B. S. H. Hill-Wood, C. K. H. Hill-Wood, D. J. C. H. Hill-Wood and W. W. H. Hill-Wood
G. L. Jackson and G. R. Jackson
T. Mycroft and W. Mycroft (half-brothers)
A. V. Pope, G. H. Pope and H. Pope
A. W. Sherwin and C. B. Sherwin
A. F. Skinner and D. A. Skinner
A. G. Slater and Herbert Slater
A. Steeples and R. Steeples
Harry Storer jnr and William Storer
J. Stubbings and W. Stubbings
F. H. Sugg and W. Sugg
F. H. Taylor and W. T. Taylor
A. F. Townsend and L. F. Townsend

SELECT BIBLIOGRAPHY

H. S. Altham and E. W. Swanton: *A History of Cricket* (George Allen and Unwin Ltd, 1948)

F. S. Ashley-Cooper: *Derbyshire Cricket* (George W. May, 1924)

Philip Bailey, Philip Thorn and Peter Wynne-Thomas: *Who's Who of Cricketers* (Newnes Books in association with Association of Cricket Statisticians, 1984)

The Duchess of Devonshire: *Chatsworth* (Derbyshire Countryside Ltd, 1984)

L. Eardley Simpson: *The Rise of Derbyshire Cricket 1919–35* (G. C. Brittain and Sons Ltd, 1936)

David Frith: *The Fast Men* (Van Nostrand Reinhold Co Ltd, 1975)

John Heath: *The Illustrated History of Derbyshire* (Barracuda Books Ltd, 1982)

G. R. Langdale: *A History of the Bassetlaw and District Cricket League, 1904–78* (Bassetlaw League, 1979)

Christopher Martin-Jenkins: *Wisden Book of County Cricket* (Queen Anne Press, 1981)

Frank Peach: *Derbyshire Cricketers 1871–1981* (Association of Cricket Statisticians, 1982)

Frank Peach, Frank Dawn and Stan Tacey (editors): *Derbyshire County Cricket Year Books 1954–88* (Derbyshire CC Supporters Club 1954–1985. Derbyshire County Cricket Club 1986 on.)

W. J. Piper: *A History of Derbyshire Cricket* (Derby Daily Telegraph, 1897 and 1899)

Harold Rhodes: *The Harold Rhodes Affair* (Breedon Books, 1987)

Anton Rippon and John Grainger: *Derbyshire County Cricket Club – A Pictorial History* (Breedon Books, 1982)

Fred Root: *A Cricket Pro's Lot* (Edward Arnold and Co, 1937)

John Shawcroft: *A History of Derbyshire County Cricket Club 1870–1970* (Derbyshire CCC 1972)

John Shawcroft: *Derbyshire Bowlers* (J. H. Hall and Sons Ltd, 1986)

Bob Taylor with Patrick Murphy: *Standing Up, Standing Back* (Willow Books, Collins, 1985)

L. G. Wright: *Scraps from a Cricketer's Memory* (Derbyshire CC Supporters Club, 1980)

Peter Wynne-Thomas: *The Hamlyn A–Z of Cricket Records* (Hamlyn, 1983)

In addition, *The Cricketer International*, *Wisden Cricket Monthly* and *The Cricket Statistician* magazines, various newspaper files, particularly the *Derby Evening Telegraph* and *Derbyshire Times*, works on eighteenth-century cricket by H. T. Waghorn and G. B. Buckley, *Scores and Biographies*, *Cricket* and *Wisden Cricketers' Almanack*.

ACKNOWLEDGEMENTS

I would like to thank the president, chairman, officials and staff of Derbyshire County Cricket Club for their help and encouragement in the preparation of this book.

A number of players have, over the years, helped with anecdote and comment and the County Cricket Club has also been well served by press coverage over the past couple of decades from journalists such as Michael Carey, Neil Hallam and Gerald Mortimer. In this context I would like to thank Mr Mortimer, Sports Editor of the *Derby Evening Telegraph* for his assistance.

I am particularly grateful to Frank Peach, former editor of the *Derbyshire County Cricket Year Book*, who has researched so deeply into the Club's history and who has uncovered so much material about the first-class game in the county. As ever he has demonstrated a cheerful willingness to answer the most obscure questions and, of course, is responsible for the statistical section of this book. David Baggett has also been of great assistance in the compilation of the statistical section. All records are complete to 31 December 1988.

Thanks are also due to my wife Gill and my son Stephen for their support and encouragement.

With the exception of the photographs on pages 262 (reproduced by permission of Allsport) and 219 (courtesy of Patrick Eagar), all photographs in this book were supplied by Derbyshire County Cricket Club. The Club would like to thank the *Derby Evening Telegraph*, Raymonds News Agency, *Derbyshire Times*, George Eyre and Eric Gregory for supplying photographs, and *The Guardian* for the plan reproduced on page 166.

John Shawcroft,
Ripley, 1989

INDEX

This Index covers players and topics dealt with in the main text of the book. Biographical details of Derbyshire cricketers appear, in alphabetical order, on pages 266–276. Career records of players, in alphabetical order, are on pages 277–287.